MW01629949

# To My Dear Friend,

I'm excited to share this very special edition of my biography, 90 Seconds, with you and your family.

This book is about how my dream of saving lives became a reality, the history of United Hatzalah of Israel and the miracle of my recovery from Covid.

Every day, over 6,500 volunteers save lives by helping and treating over 2,000 people and they do it all for free thanks to your support. Through donations like yours to United Hatzalah of Israel, we can now respond to emergencies in 90 seconds on average and have helped over 6 million people.

I am sending you this special "United Hatzalah Supporter" Limited Edition book because without you this story would not be possible.

It is thanks to you that the stories in this book even exist and that I can share this story with the world. This is a personal thank you for being part of this mission and journey with me.

Our goal is to get this book into the hands of as many people as possible to inspire the next generation to love and support Israel, and to remember that regardless of your current abilities - you can dream big, and dreams do come true!

This is a very special edition for you, but please consider purchasing an additional copy for a family member, friend, or young person who will be encouraged to continue to spread our mission of saving lives.

United Hatzalah is not only made up of thousands of volunteers quickly responding to emergencies every day, but also an international network of supporters who make it possible for us to train the volunteers and provide them with the medical equipment and technology they use to save lives. This nationwide network of volunteer first responders is the fulfillment of the dream I had when I was 15 years old.

I cannot tell you how much I appreciate you making my dream a reality and please let me know your thoughts on the book.

**Thank you again for everything you do for Israel.**

Warmest,

3/29/23

# THE SHAAR PRESS

THE JUDAICA IMPRINT
FOR THOUGHTFUL PEOPLE

UNITED HATZALAH
איחוד הצלה

THE
SHAAR
PRESS

SYM

# 90 SECONDS

## THE EPIC STORY OF ELI BEER AND UNITED HATZALAH

### RABBI NACHMAN SELTZER

Published by **SHAAR PRESS**
Distributed by MESORAH PUBLICATIONS, LTD.
313 Regina Avenue / Rahway, N.J. 07065 / (718) 921-9000

Distributed in Israel by SIFRIATI / A. GITLER
POB 2351 / Bnei Brak 51122

Distributed in Europe by  LEHMANNS
Unit E, Viking Business Park, Rolling Mill Road
Jarrow, Tyne and Wear, NE32  3DP/ England

Distributed in Australia and New Zealand by GOLDS WORLD OF JUDAICA
3-13 William Street / Balaclava, Melbourne 3183 / Victoria  Australia

Distributed in South Africa by KOLLEL BOOKSHOP
Northfield Centre / 17 Northfield Avenue / Glenhazel 2192, Johannesburg, South Africa

ISBN 10: 1-4226-3307-1 / ISBN 13: 978-1-4226-3307-6
ITEM CODE: NSECH

Printed in the United States of America
Custom bound by Sefercraft, Inc. / 313 Regina Avenue / Rahway, N.J. 07065

# Table of Contents

כל המציל נפש אחת מישראל ... כאילו קיים עולם מלא
(*Talmud Sanhedrin* 37a)

"Our vision is a ninety-second response
time, anywhere in Israel."
— Eli Beer, founder of United Hatzalah

# Preface

I've known Eli Beer since the early 2000s, when we met at the annual United Hatzalah concert on Chol HaMoed Succos. Since then our paths have crossed on many occasions, but we never sat down together and had a real conversation. Then, in May 2022, I was at a wedding in Beit Shemesh when I saw that I had missed a phone call.

It was Rabbi Gedaliah Zlotowitz calling from America. It seemed that a mutual friend had introduced him to Eli Beer, and Reb Gedaliah wanted me to write the story of Eli Beer and United Hatzalah.

I'll be honest with you. I wasn't sure at first how it was going to happen. I knew how busy Eli is, and I doubted that he would be able to find the time to devote to such a major project.

It turned out that I was wrong, because when Eli wants something to happen, he throws himself completely into the project and does whatever he needs to do to make it happen. When he returned home from a visit to the States in June 2022, I met him at his office in Yerushalayim, and he let me know that he was taking the project as seriously as possible. He blocked off the next two and a half weeks for the purpose, and we met almost every day for a number of hours, providing me with the material that would comprise this book. By September 2022, the book was written.

If there is one thing I have come to learn about Eli Beer over the course of this project, it's this: when he feels that something is important, he gets it done.

To my mind, this facet of his personality sums up this entire book and his incredible accomplishments. It's because of that drive and sense of mission that there are over six thousand United Hatzalah volunteers ready to drop whatever they're doing to save a life at any moment of the day or night.

Now you have a chance to read the amazing story of his life and dreams, and hopefully, along the way, you will also internalize the idea that — with the help of Hashem — nothing stands in the way of a person's willpower.

Rabbi Nachman Seltzer
Ramat Beit Shemesh
2023

# Acknowledgments
## By Eli Beer

*I* want to begin by thanking Rabbi Nachman Seltzer for making my life come alive on the pages of this book. I couldn't have asked for a better partner with whom to tell my story.

The story of a young boy who had a dream, a young boy who didn't do well in school — yet who succeeded in fulfilling that dream, with the help of so many friends and, of course, with Hashem's help throughout.

How well I remember the journey — from that first memorable trip to New York to my first trips at Radio Shack. From a group of boys manning the illegal scanners and riding bikes to calls, all of us living and breathing the idea of saving lives.

It all began with the dream of saving one life. When I saw a man lying on the pavement after a bus bombing, I knew that one day I was going to do something.

Thank You, Hashem, for giving me the ability to fulfill my dream.

That was dream one.

And then —

I remember racing out of the basement of my father's store and saving the life of a man who had been hit by a car, stuffing my *kippah* into his artery to stop the bleeding. I remember visiting him in the hospital and the hug he gave me and how I saw the number on his arm.

And I knew that I had to save six million lives.

That was dream two — and our thousands of volunteers helped over 6,000,000 people so far…

I remember the dream of uniting every Hatzalah under one roof — and how it happened at the Bomb Shelter Summit in Hadera, where we took a vote and the yesses carried the day.

Dream three.

And finally the dream of reaching every emergency in the country with the goal of under 90 seconds. In many parts of Israel we are already there, and I am sure that this dream will also come true — quickly and in our days...

There are many, many people who deserve my thanks — far too numerous for me to name them all. But there are a number of people whom I need to mention. Michael Brown, for going above and beyond every single day. Batsheva Lovy, Aviva Wallick, and Tali Bennett for running my life in the best way possible. Thank you to Eli Pollak, Dovie Maisel, Laiser Heyman, Moshe Levi, and Batya Avidan along with my entire team on the ground in Israel, as well as Jerry Silverman and the entire international team, for enabling this incredible operation to continue and save lives on a daily basis. The chairman of our board, Mark and Erica Gerson, and our entire International Board, all of my friends and partners in United Hatzalah, who are so generous with funding, with fantastic ideas and practical advice — and with their friendship. To Aviad Tevel for the cover photo; to our in-house photographer, Yechiel Gurfein, for the photos in this book; and to our in-house graphic artist, Tzippy Fuchs, for her work. And all the donors to United Hatzalah, who help make our lifesaving mission possible.

My thanks also go to the amazing ArtScroll staff — Rabbi Gedaliah Zlotowitz, for encouraging me to write this memoir. Mrs. Miriam Zakon, Mrs. Suri Brand, and Mrs. Judi Dick for their editing, Mrs. Esther Feierstein for proofreading, Mrs. Estie Dicker for paginating, Eli Kroen for designing the incredible cover, and Miss Chanie Ziegler for enhancing the photos.

I'd like to offer a special thank you, from the bottom of my heart, to every single man and woman, all over the world, who davened for me — Eliezer Yehuda ben Chaya — while I was sick with Covid for so many months. There is no doubt that your *tefillos* and your acts of kindness on my behalf, as well as the amazing *chessed* of United Hatzalah volunteers, is what brought me back to life, so I can continue with my lifesaving mission — *ad* 120, until 120!

Thank you to United Hatzalah volunteers across Israel and abroad, and to all the volunteers of the different Hatzalah organizations who operate independently, for helping their communities.

I have been blessed with many blessings in my life. I was born to a wonderful and caring father and mother and was blessed with fantastic in-laws, great siblings and extended family, and the most amazing group of friends from around the world. And if that were not enough, I have the good fortune to work with a dedicated group of people who embody the ideals of *mesiras nefesh* as they never stop saving lives.

At the same time, there is nothing more important to me than my wife Gitty and my incredible children — Avigail and Aharon and their son Itamar, Penina and Uri and their son Gabi and daughter Halleli, Libby and Meir, Yisrael David and Adina. You are the lights of my life and I love you with all my heart. Not only are you the best family a

(L–R) Top: Meir, Libby, Gitty with baby Halleli, Eli, Penina, Avigail, baby Itamar, Aharon
Bottom: Yisrael, Adina, baby Gabi, and Uri (and Chika the dog).
Photo taken at a strawberry greenhouse, February 2023

father could ask for, you have made my dream your own and adopted it completely.

Thank you for being the greatest family a father could ask for.

I am a lucky man.

Eli Beer
United Hatzalah, Yerushalayim
2023
www.israelrescue.org
office@israelrescue.org

# PART ONE

> *When I grow up, I want to become a doctor and I want to save six million Jews.*
>
> — *Eli Beer*

# CHAPTER ONE

# The Kid From Bayit Vegan

The trajectory of Eli Beer's life was sharply altered on the day he witnessed a terror attack not five minutes from his home in the Bayit Vegan neighborhood of Yerushalayim. It was a Friday, on a summer's day in 1978, and Eli was on his way home from school, walking down Hapisga Street not far from his father's *sefarim* store. The weather was beautiful and balmy, and Eli didn't have a care in the world.

As he walked, he saw the number 12 bus come to a shuddering halt at a nearby bus stop, a sight he had seen thousands of times. But that day was different because moments after the doors of the bus opened to allow passengers to disembark, a terrorist blew himself up inside the crowded bus, killing, wounding, and maiming dozens of innocent people with a blast that literally shook the neighborhood.

Windows shattered all over Hapisga Street, and drivers lost control of their vehicles. For five-year-old Eli, the sight of a gigantic tongue of flame shooting out of the bus would join the noise of the blast and go on to maintain a near-constant presence in his memory.

"I remember hearing the sounds of screaming and yelling," Eli remembers, "but more than that I can never forget the sight of an old man lying on the pavement (he seemed old to me although it was possible that he was middle-aged) who couldn't move and was yelling at me to come and save him."

*Yeled, yeled, bo ta'azor li…* Little boy, come help me…"

At first, Eli was glued to the spot, paralyzed by the shock. Then it hit

The number 12 bus after the terrorist attack (Photo Credit: Uriel Davidson)

him: something really terrible had just happened right before his eyes, and he found he couldn't remain there any longer. At that moment, Eli Beer picked up his little legs and ran away.

He would find himself thinking about what happened for weeks, months, and even years to come, and he always wondered if anyone had managed to save the life of the man on the pavement, or if he had died before the rescue teams arrived.

That incident turned Eli's life around, because from that moment Eli began dreaming of becoming a doctor. If he had been a doctor, he would have had the tools needed to save the man's life. Never mind that he had ADHD and couldn't concentrate in the classroom. After what he had seen, there was no question in his mind that he had no choice but to enter the field of medicine, and once there, he needed to save lives.

But he didn't just want to check someone's throat or ears. He wanted to bring someone who was about to die — or already had — back to life.

It was clear to him that this was his destiny and that he needed to make it happen. The only question was how to go about it.

Eli Beer was the kind of child who had trouble sitting still, and this meant he didn't spend much time in the classroom. Because he got kicked out of class so often, Eli found himself searching for ways to alleviate the boredom. Since his school building was situated in an old, run-down building with no gate around it, he'd leave the building and search for some way to fill the time whenever a teacher threw him out of class.

The school was located at the edge of Bayit Vegan, only a short walk from Yad Vashem, Israel's official memorial to the victims of the Holocaust. Quite often, Eli would cross Herzl Boulevard and walk down the tree-lined road to Yad Vashem, visiting the place so often that he came to be very familiar with all its exhibits.

He would walk through the halls, stopping at the different exhibits, staring at the pictures of Nazis and listening to the headphones that were offered to the visitors. He came to know about the Eichmann trial and how Joseph Mengele sent countless Jews to the gas chambers. And in his mind, the young boy would tell himself that when he grew up, he was going to find a way to take revenge.

If the Nazis could kill six million Jews, the boy thought, he would save the lives of six million Jews.

Since he had a hard time achieving success in the classroom, he was constantly searching for worthwhile projects to keep him busy. "When I was twelve years old," Eli recalls, "I had what I thought was a good business idea. My father, Rabbi Gavriel Beer, owned a large *sefarim* store on Hapisga Street. That year I asked him if I could set up a table in an empty space at the front of the store and sell *esrogim* and *lulavim* in the weeks prior to Succos.

" 'Sure you can set up a table,' my father said. 'But just out of curiosity, where are you going to get the *esrogim* and *lulavim* from?'

"'I'll buy them from one of the big sellers.'"

Eli immediately started running around Yerushalayim doing his research. Eventually he found someone whom he felt he could trust and purchased a large quantity of merchandise from him. He soon discovered that he was a natural businessman who felt confident enough to negotiate and that he enjoyed making deals, in engaging in the give-and-take of a transaction.

Gabi Beer in his book store

"Since I'm paying you cash," he told the seller, "I want you to give me one additional *lulav* for every *lulav* that I buy from you."

"That's way too much," the seller replied.

"So what's your counter-offer?"

"I'll give you half a *lulav* for every *lulav*."

"Deal," and they shook on it.

Eli was twelve years old and in business. It was the first time in his life that he was successful at something. His father was happy, his older brother Moishe, who partnered with him, was happy, and he was happy. His table kept him busy for about a month and a half, and he made a lot of money.

The next year, he was not content with one table, but opened for business at four different locations around the city. Yet while the *esrog* business kept Eli occupied for a month and a half every year, he was going to have to find something else to do the rest of the year so that he wouldn't go out of his mind with boredom. Eli and school were just not a match.

While his father didn't make him feel bad about it, it was obvious that he would have been happier had his son been more successful in school. Eli would have liked to have had a closer relationship with his father, but it didn't seem to Eli like a closer connection was in the cards.

He did like to read, which was a good thing considering that his father owned a *sefarim* store, and Eli gravitated toward books on Jewish history, on the Holocaust and all stories written by Rabbi Marcus Lehmann. He couldn't get enough of books like *Just in Time*, *Akiba*, *Itamar*, *The Agunah*, *The Penknife*, and *The Royal Resident*. And yet his love for reading didn't transfer itself to the classroom, a place where he seldom experienced any type of success.

In the seventh grade, Eli became a banker, establishing a school bank for any student who needed a place to deposit his "*ajuim*" (apricot pits) for safekeeping. *Ajuim* were a famous form of currency among schoolboys and the object of many games in the school corridors, and Eli the banker offered a number of banking services for his fellow students.

Students were able to open accounts in Eli's bank. Once an account was opened, the student would be issued a "checkbook," which would allow the student to pay a debt of, say, one hundred *ajuim* with a "check" instead of having to spend the time counting them out or carrying them around. Under Eli's supervision, the other students felt that it was sufficient to have them available in their accounts.

The bank was so busy that Eli had seven employees working for him during every recess, and Eli became an *ajuim* billionaire. His mother, though, was not a fan, considering that their apartment began reeking of apricot pits.

Matters came to a head when business couldn't be concluded by the end of recess and began spilling over into classtime. Eventually the principal informed Eli that his time at the school had come to an end and he would not be welcome to return for eighth grade. Part of him was upset and hurt, but another part of him knew that he wasn't cut out to sit in the classroom from morning till night. Thankfully, his parents knew it, too, and never disparaged him for having so much trouble when it came to school. Yet Eli himself couldn't help feeling like a failure, especially when his older brothers were all golden boys and top students. That stung.

When he was thirteen years old, Eli had another business idea. While his father had a car — a bulky white Peugeot station wagon — the majority of religious families in the city didn't own their own vehicles at the time. The upshot of all this was that many children were stuck at home bored during school vacations.

Eli's idea was a simple one: he would rent buses from Egged, Israel's public transportation company, during vacation time and arrange trips for families from Yerushalayim on a daily basis. One day the bus would head up north to the Banyas; the next it would take the families kayaking down the Jordan. At times the buses would go to Masada and the Dead Sea; other days to Nachal Yehudia or Nachal Arugot. Every trip would be fun and exciting, and most trips would include a destination that would have been challenging for people to reach without their own private cars. Eli decided to charge a set price for every adult, thirty-five shekels, and a cheaper fare, twenty-five shekels, for every child. It was a win-win situation for everyone involved.

But how would he get access to Egged buses?

The last bus stop in Bayit Vegan was on Hapisga Street near his home. Many people who lived in the neighborhood hated this because the drivers would sit around gunning their diesel engines (as a means of cooling the engine) and making a lot of noise. But Eli loved having all the buses around and went out of his way to get to know many of the drivers, who became his friends. Some of the drivers would allow him to drive with them on their routes, punching people's bus cards as they boarded (today people pay with a smart card called the Rav Kav, but it was a different system back then). Sometimes the drivers would stop outside a kiosk, and Eli would run into the store, buy them a drink, and run back onto the bus.

Now he shared his idea with one of the drivers. Chaim Cohen was a *baal teshuvah* who was about thirty years older than Eli. Chaim thought it was a great idea and gave Eli some guidance, telling him who to speak to at Egged headquarters.

"Tell Rafi that you want Chaim Cohen to drive the bus for you."

So Eli, who was tall for his age and looked older than he was, went off to Egged headquarters and told the man behind the desk what he wanted to do.

"No problem," he was told. "The bus will cost you seven hundred shekels to rent. That includes enough gas for the entire day and a driver."

"I want Chaim Cohen to be my driver."

"No problem."

And so it began.

By the time he was fourteen, Eli was a major *"macher"* — a real mover and shaker.

There was one more thing for Eli to keep busy with. In the 1980s, many neighborhoods had a civilian watch called Mishmar Ezrachi patrolling their streets at night.

Eli went to the Mishmar Ezrachi office and let it be known that he wanted to volunteer. Avoiding the question of how old he was, since he was underage, he managed to obtain a permit to carry a gun. He was also provided with basic training to learn how to shoot the gun. Soon Eli was patrolling the neighborhood together with a partner — usually a seventy- or eighty-year-old man — who drove the jeep. Being part of Mishmar Ezrachi gave Eli the opportunity to keep his neighborhood safe. It also gave him the opportunity to carry a gun on the trips he arranged, since by law they needed someone with a gun permit for the passengers' protection.

Eli organized the trips for several years, making a lot of money along the way and garnering a reputation for being a savvy businessman. The funny part was that Eli wasn't doing any of this for the money. He was just bored and needed something to do to fill his time. Occasionally he tried out other yeshivahs, but somehow school and Eli were not a match.

And then, in the summer of 1988, Eli saw an ad for a course at Magen David Adom, Israel's national ambulance service, and he ran to sign up.

# CHAPTER TWO

# The Seventeen-Minute Ride

The course was designed to teach the basics to teenagers who streamed forward to volunteer for Magen David Adom. Sitting in the classroom and listening to the instructor, Eli didn't recognize himself. For the first time in his life, he was in a classroom with a teacher and wasn't spacing out. Not only was he not spacing out, but he was even taking notes and listening closely to every word the instructor was saying. Enjoying something in a classroom setting was a completely novel experience for him and he loved every second of it. This, he knew without a shadow of a doubt, was what he wanted to spend his life doing. Within a very short time, it became clear to him that he had found his calling.

The course was held at a small guest house in the Jerusalem Forest, and Eli was the first person to show up in the morning and the last to leave at night. He learned how to perform the Heimlich maneuver, how to do CPR, how to bandage a wound and administer an IV. While Eli had already done quite a number of exciting things in his short life, it was the first time he was filled with genuine and deep satisfaction on a daily basis. This was not about having a good time or making money. It was much more important than that, and in a way, he almost felt that it was too good to be true.

Eli finished the course first in his class. He had never been motivated before, but that Eli had disappeared and had been replaced with an Eli who couldn't get enough. He was motivated, he was fascinated by the material he was learning, and he was proud of the diploma attesting that he had finished the course and was certified to save people's lives. It was the first real diploma he had ever received, and he couldn't stop looking at it. More than that, for the entire time he was taking the course, there was a little thought hovering at the back of his mind, a thought that had never quite disappeared, a thought that took him back to that fateful Friday afternoon when he stood at a bus stop in Bayit Vegan and heard an old man begging a five-year-old to save him.

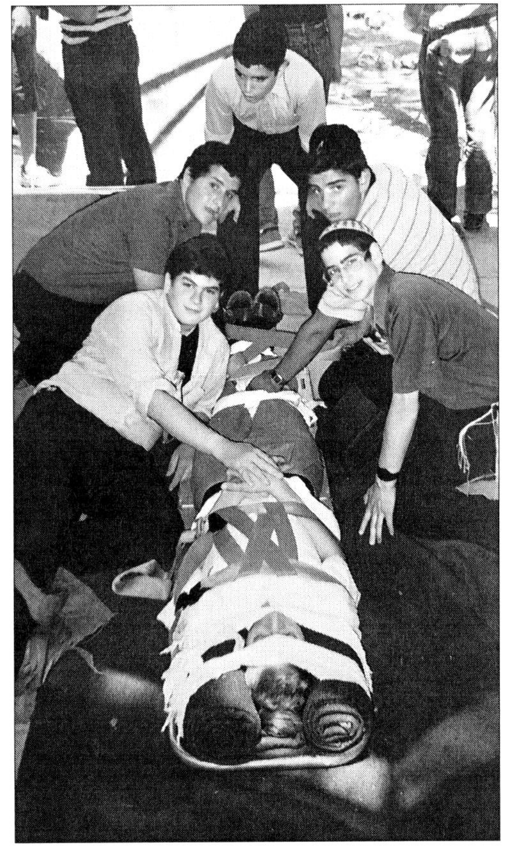
Eli as a young teen volunteering for MDA

For years his mind had taken him back to that scene any time he grew bored in class. Then his mind would wander, and he would see himself as a five-year-old and hear the sound of the explosion and see the horrendous sight of the man lying wounded on the pavement. It happened over and over again for years. He'd seen something that had traumatized him, yet instead of letting the trauma paralyze him, he had channeled it in a different direction.

He vowed to make sure that if he was ever in the same situation again, he would know what to do. He would finally be able to make a difference.

Diploma in hand, Eli Beer headed to Magen David Adom headquarters in the Romema neighborhood of Yerushalayim to begin volunteering on an ambulance. He paid the fee to register, purchased the uniform he would need to wear while engaged in MDA activity, and for the first time in his life, he was given the opportunity to take a seat in the back of an ambulance. His excitement at that moment was off the charts. For Eli, riding in an ambulance on the way to save lives was literally a dream come true, and he couldn't believe that it was actually happening.

It was heady stuff.

At the time, Magen David Adom had two intensive-care ambulances, which were staffed by a paramedic and a doctor, in addition to their seven regular ambulances, which were staffed by a bunch of fifteen- and sixteen-year-old volunteers and a driver who was a trained EMT.

Eli had never treated anything in his life with the seriousness with which he treated his volunteer work at MDA.

He came to the job equipped with a notebook and pen and took copious notes, writing down every detail of what he witnessed and learned on the calls. He also began writing down the timing of the calls — the time when the emergency call came in to the dispatcher and the amount of time it took the ambulance to reach its destination.

The volunteers weren't allowed to enter the command center where the dispatchers worked. They hung out in a large room designated for them at the MDA station until they were needed. The drivers also had their own room, where they relaxed and slept as they waited to be sent out on calls. Only volunteers who developed close relationships with the drivers were allowed into their room. There was also a room for the paramedics. Everyone had their own place to relax when they weren't out on a call, and the boundaries were strictly enforced.

When a call came in, the dispatcher would give it to the ambulance that was next in line instead of sending whichever ambulance was closest to the spot at that time. Sometimes a driver would let the dispatcher know that he was closer, but in most cases the ambulances would be sent because it was their turn to take a call.

Since Eli was just starting out, he was usually assigned to one of the regular ambulances. This meant that he wasn't being sent to real emergencies — heart attacks, stroke victims, or car accidents — since in most cases the dispatcher sent the intensive-care ambulances to deal with those situations. The young volunteers were sent to take care of people who had called complaining of stomachaches or headaches or when an elderly individual was being sent home from the hospital and needed transportation and assistance.

One of the primary tasks that the volunteers handled was writing up the bills that would be sent to the patients by the ambulance company. It didn't matter if they were elderly, Holocaust survivors, or critically ill. If Magen David Adom dispatched an ambulance for a patient, a bill needed to be sent. That was the rule, and the volunteers had to obey whether they wanted to or not. There was no such thing as a free ride. If a volunteer wrote down the wrong information on a bill, MDA wouldn't be able to charge the patient and the volunteer would be rebuked by the person in charge of billing. It wasn't long before Eli came to the realization that MDA was making a lot of money on a daily basis from the volunteers who streamed forth to assist the organization.

As soon as the announcement came over the loudspeaker about a call, Eli would rush over to the ambulance next in line and wait for the driver to unlock the ambulance so they could get inside and go save lives. Sometimes the drivers weren't young, and it took them time to get from the building and into the ambulance. Even once they were inside the ambulance, it took another thirty to forty seconds for the diesel engine to turn on.

Eli would become more and more anxious, because he knew that someone had called the ambulance because they were in pain and in a potentially life-threatening situation, and here it was taking them so long just to get out of the station.

"One freezing night a call came in and I ran to the ambulance," Eli remembered. "It took the driver a particularly long time to get out of the building, because he had been sleeping when the call came in and it took him a few minutes to wake up, put on his shoes, and get himself together. We were finally in the ambulance when the driver announced that he couldn't leave because he had forgotten his cigarettes back in the drivers' room.

Eli wasn't in a position to protest — after all, he was just a guest in the ambulance — but he was going out of his mind. He jumped out of the ambulance and ran back into the building to bring the driver his cigarettes. It took a few long minutes just to get out of the station that night and another fifteen or twenty minutes to drive to the home of the person who had made the call. By the time they reached their destination, they found a woman lying there unconscious. She wasn't breathing, and they began performing CPR on her. It was the first time Eli performed CPR in his life, and the entire team was doing its best to revive her.

Because it was such a serious situation, the station had sent an intensive care ambulance to assist, but a few minutes after their arrival, they pronounced her dead.

"For me, the whole scene came as a real shock," Eli recalls. "I knew that I would never forget the sight of the woman's family members crying and how they screamed at us when we finally arrived for taking so long to get there."

In the days that followed, Eli reviewed the incident over and over in his mind.

He saw the ambulance waiting for the driver.

The ambulance parking outside the building.

The medic team running up the stairs.

The woman lying there, not breathing.

The family crying bitter tears.

The team trying to bring her back to life.

Again and again, the scene played itself out in his mind until every detail was firmly embedded in his memory.

To his way of thinking, the problem began with the amount of time it was taking them just to get into the ambulance even before leaving the station. Over the course of the next few months, he came to see that their average response time was seventeen minutes. And while seventeen minutes isn't a very long time in the overall scheme of things, in a life-and-death situation, Eli knew that seventeen minutes was way too long.

Eli went out of his way to cultivate a connection with the different drivers. On his way to the station, he would stop off at Massov, a popular shwarma restaurant near the Central Bus Station, and order double laffas stuffed with shwarma and grilled chicken for the drivers who were starting their next shift. Everyone likes getting free food, and the MDA drivers were no exception. It wasn't long before Eli had become one of the most popular volunteers with the drivers, who not only appreciated the food he brought for them but also the seriousness with which he took his work as a volunteer.

By the time he had been working as a volunteer for a year and a half, teen-aged Eli Beer had been present and active at over a thousand emergencies, usually going out to eight or nine calls during the course of a shift. Sometimes he even did a double shift. All this meant that he came to know Magen David Adom from the inside.

"I realized that we helped a lot of people," Eli says. "But despite the fact that I'd been at so many emergencies, I never managed to bring even one person back to life. I helped deliver many babies and took care of many people who weren't feeling well, but I was never part of a team that saved the life of someone having a heart attack or stroke. We were just not getting there fast enough. Seventeen minutes or fifteen minutes or even ten minutes was too long."

He also realized something else. The regular ambulances — the ambulances used to send out volunteers — were stocked with very little in the way of actual medical equipment. They didn't even carry defibrillators. This meant that even when they arrived at the home of someone who was suffering from cardiac arrest, they had to content themselves with performing CPR until a defibrillator was brought to the scene by one of the intensive care ambulances.

And then one day something happened that completely turned his life around.

A call came in from a mother whose child had choked on a hot dog. The call originated from Bayit Vegan, while the ambulance Eli was on was in Har HaTzofim.

"I remember hearing the dispatcher asking if any ambulance was available to take a serious call," Eli says. "We had just finished another call and were really hungry. When the call came in, food was on our minds. The moment the dispatcher explained that a child was choking, all thoughts of getting something to eat were forgotten and the driver began heading to Bayit Vegan."

Since there were no seatbelts for the seats at the back of the ambulance where the volunteers sat, they bounced around as the ambulance raced down streets and bumped over sidewalks. They were getting there, but the traffic was dense, and no matter what the driver did, the odds were against getting there on time to save the child's life.

It ended up taking twenty-one minutes to get there.

Way too long.

"I don't remember the name of the street," Eli says. "What I do recall was that the apartment was located on the third floor of the building and that we could hear the mother's voice from down in the street. The seven-year-old boy was completely blue and not breathing. We started doing CPR on him, and it was even more difficult than usual because the boy had been drenched from head to toe by one of the neighbors, who had poured an entire bucket of water on him, trying to wake him up. I remember how cold he felt, how blue his lips were.

"Suddenly, a doctor (he actually worked in an emergency room) came running into the apartment. He immediately assessed the situation and began assisting. The doctor lived a block from the kid's home, but he hadn't known about the emergency until he heard the sounds of the ambulance outside his home. He ran over as fast as he could, but after about forty minutes of working on the child, the doctor told us that there was nothing more we could do. What he said next would remain with me for the rest of my life: 'Get a sheet to cover him.'

"They were the most heartbreaking words you could ever hear. When the doctor told the staff to bring a sheet to cover the boy, it was the worst moment of my life. At that second, I realized that the doctor could have saved the boy's life had he only known about the emergency sooner. He lived nearby and could have gotten there in time. But he didn't know about it, so he didn't come and the seven-year-old died. The mother thought calling an ambulance was the right thing to do and that we would be there right away. She started screaming at us that we were the murderers.

"'You killed him!' she shouted. 'It took you two hours to get here!'

"It wasn't actually two hours, but there's no question that it must have seemed that way to a mother watching her child dying in front of her eyes. Every second must have been an absolute eternity.

"The worst part about what happened was the fact that saving someone from choking is a very simple procedure if you know what to do. If the doctor had known about what was happening so close to his home, he could have stabilized the situation and saved the boy's life. By the time we arrived, everything would have been fine. But in reality nothing was fine because the doctor hadn't known. And so the boy died."

# A Failed Attempt

The next time Eli got together with his friends and fellow volunteers at Magen David Adom, he told them about an idea that had been brewing in his mind. It was an idea that he would end up referring to many more times throughout his life.

"The only way we'll be able to save lives," he said, "is if we figure out a way to reach a patient within ninety seconds."

The others looked at him as if he were crazy.

"How on earth are you going to be able to get volunteers to people's homes within ninety seconds? It doesn't make sense!"

"If you have enough volunteers living in a certain neighborhood, you could reach anyone in that neighborhood within ninety seconds."

They looked at him, not sure where he was going with this.

"Let's say you have an apartment building, and there are ten volunteers living in that building. If there's an emergency call, then it goes without saying that a bunch of the volunteers will be able to get there within ninety seconds, right?"

They nodded.

"Well, it's the same thing with neighborhoods. The key is to have enough volunteers in every neighborhood. If you have that, you'll be able to reach everyone around the country in ninety seconds, and you're able to save the lives of every person when they need you most."

Though no one really took his idea seriously, Eli wasn't discouraged. Especially since he had another idea that he wanted to try.

Eli had always prided himself on the fact that he wasn't afraid to do anything. He was a person who had the chutzpah to suggest ideas others wouldn't suggest and to try things other people shied away from. After serving as a volunteer for many months in the back of an ambulance and having learned so much about how to save people's lives, he suddenly had a major breakthrough.

Israel might be able to boast of having one of the best ambulance services in the world, but if the ambulances weren't able to reach patients in the critical window of time before all was lost, it didn't matter how great a service it was. People were dying every day despite their best efforts to reach them on time. In Eli's opinion, the system was broken and needed to be rebuilt.

At that moment, Eli had one of his out-of-the-box brainstorms.

What if he were to go to the national radio station — Reshet Bet was the only major station at the time — and deliver his message to the citizens of Israel.

"Every day," he imagined himself saying, "there are numerous life-threatening health emergencies occurring all over Israel. If we could convince Magen David Adom to share emergency information with the radio, like if a baby is choking on a certain street in Tel Aviv, then anyone listening to the radio who is a medical professional would be able to drop what they are doing and run over to save a life if the person is close enough and they could get there in time."

At that time, everyone in Israel listened to the radio because there weren't as many options for entertainment as there are today. Which meant that if Reshet Bet made such an announcement, and television's Channel One did the same, all their bases would be covered and a staggering number of lives could be saved.

Eli shared this idea with his fellow volunteers at MDA. Without exception, every single one advised him not to waste his time trying to pitch the idea to the Israeli media. They would never agree to work with them.

In the end, Eli told himself that his friends were right. There was no way that the radio would interrupt a news program for such an announcement, especially since it wouldn't have been just a one-time announcement but a constant stream. Instead, he had another idea. It was simple, but he thought it might just work.

What if he went to all the volunteers at Magen David Adom and asked every one of them to carry a pager? (This was the prevalent technology at the time. A short voice message was delivered to the intended recipient.) Whenever an emergency call came in to the dispatcher at MDA, all they needed to do was send out a message to all the pagers, and whoever was in the area of the emergency would drop whatever they were doing and run.

Armed with the chutzpah that would eventually turn United Hatzalah into one of the most effective lifesaving forces in the world, Eli Beer sought to arrange a meeting with the head of Magen David Adom — a man named Chaim. Eli asked Chaim's secretary for a meeting, and she penciled him in obligingly. Chaim was a nice guy, and Eli genuinely liked and respected him. Eli was hopeful that Chaim would see things his way and agree that what he was proposing was a good idea.

But Chaim didn't see things Eli's way.

Not even a little bit.

"It's not a good idea," he told Eli bluntly.

"Why not?"

"For one, we can't give out emergency information that comes into the dispatcher. Our insurance wouldn't allow it. Besides, people can't just walk into a patient's house without an ambulance."

When Eli put forth his counterarguments, Chaim's response was, in a nutshell, to go away and stop bothering him.

"When I saw that I wasn't getting through to him," Eli recalls, "I pulled out my log book and showed Chaim the numbers I had written down detailing the details of every call I had gone on — in real time.

" 'These are the real numbers,' I said. 'These are the times from the moment a call comes into the dispatcher, not from the minute the ambulance leaves the station. I've been keeping this log for the last year and a half. This tells the real story.' "

But Eli could see that he still wasn't getting through to the boss.

"Chaim," he said, a hint of desperation coming through, "I can help you save lives! All I need is for you to allow the dispatcher to send the emergency information to the pagers that every volunteer will have.

"Give me the go-ahead, and I'll start working on recruiting more volunteers so that we have a better chance of getting to every emergency in time to save lives — even if there is traffic on the road and the ambulance is having a hard time making it there.

"I can help you save lives! I can help! Let me be your liaison with the volunteers. You have nine ambulances in Yerushalayim, but I'll be able to arrange for another thirty or forty volunteers all over the city. All I'm asking is for you to give me the go-ahead and I'll get to work!"

Chaim's reply was instantaneous and resolute.

"It's not going to happen."

There was no room for negotiation. The answer was no. In Chaim's opinion, there was no need for volunteers to be available to run to the scene of an emergency — even if they would be able to arrive there before the ambulances. Eli's idea had never been done before in Israel, and people have a hard time changing the status quo.

But even though change can take a long time to implement, that doesn't mean you don't try. Eli wasn't ready to give up.

"Chaim, I can help you save lives," he insisted.

Chaim was impatient with the kid who wouldn't leave his office.

"Are you suggesting that we're not saving lives?"

"Of course Magen David Adom is saving lives," Eli said, trying to contain his frustration. "But there are major emergencies happening all the time, and we're just not reaching the people in time. In all the time that I've been volunteering with Magen David Adom, I haven't had the chance to bring a person back to life, and that's because by the time the ambulance was able to get through traffic, it was too late."

Now Chaim was really mad. "You know what," Chaim said at last, truly angry at this upstart teen who was wasting his time, "I think you're bored. Why don't you go work in a falafel shop?"

Chaim wasn't the only angry one. Eli left the office, furious. He had a revolutionary idea and no agenda other than his burning desire to save lives. When he had walked into Chaim's office, Eli had genuinely thought the CEO was going to jump at the idea. The only thing he was asking for was the willingness to share the information needed to make the idea a reality. Now he was upset and disillusioned. After seeing a boy who had choked to death on a hot dog, part of him wanted to stop volunteering even though that had been his whole life until that point. Suddenly he didn't see any reason to volunteer if he couldn't save lives.

While he was standing in Chaim's office, many traumatic scenes had flashed through his mind. It was like a movie with the sound turned off — just scene after scene after scene.

One scene he recalled was the aftermath of the first terror attack where he served as a volunteer for MDA. It happened on Jaffa Road. He could still hear the words of the dispatcher over the radio.

"All ambulances to 40 Jaffa Road. There's a terrorist with a knife stabbing people at the bus stops."

When they arrived, they found an elderly man lying on the ground, the terrorist's knife still lodged in his back. Eli performed CPR on the man — with the knife still in his back. But he died.

Then there was the car accident on Herzl Boulevard. The car was totaled before they got there, and the driver was no longer alive.

So many traumas — but he had never managed to save anyone. It happened again and again. Eli knew that he couldn't save everyone. But too many times it was only a matter of getting there sooner.

When Eli left the office that day, he said one last thing.

"Chaim, I will do this with you or without you. But it's going to happen."

Chaim would end up becoming good friends with Eli Beer. There would come a day when Hatzalah even presented Chaim with a trauma bag for his car sporting the Hatzalah logo — a gift he gratefully accepted. That, however, was all in years to come.

# Welcome to New York

Eli returned home from his unsuccessful meeting with the head of Magen David Adom. Once in his room, he counted the money he had at his disposal. It was enough for him to buy a ticket to the United States and to begin purchasing the equipment he needed to turn his dream into a reality.

The year was 1989, and Eli was sixteen years old.

He had several cousins living in Brooklyn whose homes would be open to him. But he didn't plan on staying in the United States for long — just enough time for him to purchase some equipment and take a short vacation from months of endless ambulance shifts. It was clear to him that he needed a break.

One of the first stops he made after landing in New York was his favorite American store — a place called Radio Shack in downtown Brooklyn. There he knew he'd find the equipment he needed for a reasonable price.

As he walked down the New York street, his mind took him back in time to his first visit to the States not long before.

Before he began volunteering with MDA, Eli decided that he wanted to spend part of the summer in America. Although he had a lot of family in Brooklyn, he had never visited, and he wanted to see the country he had heard so much about.

His father, Rabbi Gavriel ("Gabi") Beer, gave his son permission to go for the summer on condition that he worked in a camp in the Catskill Mountains. This might have turned out to be the best thing for Eli except for one factor: the camp his father chose was geared toward children from chassidic-style homes and was more or less a learning camp. Even though Eli was a staff member, officially hired to work as a day camp counselor for the children bused in every day from the surrounding bungalow colonies, the staff was expected to be up and working at seven o'clock and to spend the entire morning learning. Staff who didn't show up on time had their pay docked. It didn't take Eli long to come to the conclusion that he and the camp were not a good match, and there was no way he could possibly remain there for an entire summer.

Five days into camp, Eli couldn't take it any longer, and he decided that he needed to leave, come what may. For most teenagers from Eretz Yisrael who had never been to the States, this would have proved daunting since they didn't know their way around, but Eli was determined to find a way to get to Brooklyn, where he could stay with relatives.

One morning Eli was walking from his room in the direction of the office when he noticed a truck that had come to make some deliveries and was getting ready to leave.

"Excuse me," he said to the driver, who was clearly chassidic, "where are you headed after you leave camp?"

"I'm going to Brooklyn."

"That's exactly where I need to go. Can I join you for the ride?"

The man scratched his head, thought for a second, and replied, "Sure."

"Great. Give me five minutes to get my stuff and we're out of here."

The man nodded.

Eli knew that his parents were bound to find out that he'd left camp without permission, but he also knew that they would understand why he did it after he explained his reasons. For a kid who had been requested to leave every school he'd attended, it was a miracle he had lasted five days in the learning camp.

Running into his room, he grabbed his clothing from his shelves and tossed them into his suitcase, closed the zipper, picked up his tefillin and a few other items that were lying around, and made his way back to the truck, praying the entire time that he wouldn't be spotted by a member of the head staff. His prayers were answered, and no one saw him. Throwing his gear into the back seat of the truck's cabin, he climbed into the front passenger side, closed the door, and said goodbye to the camp.

The truck rumbled its way down the scenic, twisting mountain roads until it reached the highway heading in the direction of Brooklyn. Eli took in the trees lining the road and the fresh air and wallowed in the heady feeling of freedom. Half an hour out of Brooklyn, the driver turned to him.

"Where should I drop you off?"

It was a good question. Eli had never been to Brooklyn before, but he remembered his parents mentioning the name of a cousin of theirs named Mendel Beer who lived in Boro Park.

"Take me to Boro Park. I'm going to Boro Park."

"Where in Boro Park?"

"I have a cousin named Mendel Beer. He lives in Boro Park."

Boro Park is a big place. Without an exact address, the driver took Eli to Thirteenth Avenue and let him off near a shul where a steady stream of people was coming and going.

"This is the Shomer Shabbos shul," he told Eli. "Go inside, have a piece of cake and a cup of coffee, and ask the people if anyone knows where Mendel Beer lives. I'm sure someone will be able to help you out."

Thanking the driver, Eli got out of the truck and, suitcase in hand, walked through the doors of Shomer Shabbos, where he instantly felt at home. He had been in shuls like this umpteen times, and everything was familiar to him — the *sefarim* in the bookcases lining the walls, the people swaying as they prayed, the aroma of coffee laced with the scent of old books. And, of course, the men poring over their Gemaras.

Sure, learning had always been a challenge for him, but Eli had never stopped trying. On the rare occasion he'd even made a *siyum* (a celebration upon the completion of a tractate of Talmud), and his family had attended them with pride, knowing how difficult sitting and concentrating on a page of Talmud was for him. Yet in his mind Eli never stopped dreaming of the day when he would be able to learn with ease, and he enjoyed watching others do that.

Eli followed the aroma and crossed the room where he found the makings for coffee. Taking one of the Styrofoam cups, he put in the coffee, sugar, and milk and took a sip of the steaming brew. It was just right.

Cup in hand, he approached two men engaged in conversation.

"Do you by any chance know my cousin Mendel Beer?"

"Mendel Beer the insurance man?"

"Yes."

"I'll show you where he lives."

Taking his suitcase and coffee, Eli followed the man, who led him to his cousin's home, which wasn't far. When they arrived, Eli knocked on the door. His cousin's wife Bracha opened it, and when she saw the fourteen-year-old standing on her doorstep, she asked, "Who are you?"

"I'm Eli Beer."

"Gavriel's son?"

"Yes."

"What are you doing here?"

"I came to stay with you."

"This is the first I've heard that we were hosting you."

"Well, the truth is, my father got me a job in a camp up in the Catskills, but I hated the place. I hitched a ride into Boro Park with a truck driver, and here I am."

"Okay," she said, ushering him inside the house. "Come in and sit down at the kitchen table."

She got Eli settled and went off to call his father and tell him about the runaway. Eli's father was furious, but with a business to run and a million things on his plate, there wasn't much he could do about it.

Not being in camp meant that Eli was left to fill the hours of the day on his own. His first day in Boro Park, he headed in the direction of Thirteenth Avenue, where he walked from one corner to the next, staring in wide-eyed wonder at the variety of stores and array of goods being offered for sale. He enjoyed a slice of pizza at Amnon's, and when he was finished, he left the store and sauntered along the busy avenue, taking it all in. For a kid from Bayit Vegan, Boro Park was a whole new frontier.

At some point, he encountered an Israeli teenager he knew from back home. They weren't friends but had met each other a few times in Yerushalayim.

"I'm going into Manhattan," the boy said. "Do you want to come with me?"

"Sure."

"Great, we'll go tonight."

No doubt Eli had imagined a trip to Manhattan meant visiting landmarks like the Statue of Liberty. But that's not where he was taken because the Israeli boy was a bit of a wild kid and a troublemaker, and he took Eli to a part of the city he would never have found on his own.

That night Eli Beer boarded a train to the city and, following his guide, found himself walking through some of the more derelict neighborhoods of Manhattan, which shocked him with their squalor and a host of evil-looking characters who seemed to emerge from every doorway. Eli took in the scene and hated what he was seeing.

"Why did you bring me to this place?" he demanded.

"You wanted to see Manhattan. This is Manhattan."

"If this is Manhattan, get me out of here! I've seen more than enough. I want to leave right now."

"No problem. I have a cousin who lives in Queens. We can stay there tonight, and tomorrow you can go back to Brooklyn."

The boy led Eli to the closest subway station. They descended the stairs leading beneath the city streets, and Eli felt the stairs vibrating from the power of the trains as they roared into the station. It was approaching midnight, and the platform was almost completely deserted. Looking around, Eli knew that he would remember his introduction to New York City for the rest of his life.

They waited on the dirty platform for the Queens-bound A train, getting on when it slid to a halt. There were very few people riding the train at that time of night, and Eli felt exposed and vulnerable. He was only fourteen years old and had lived a relatively sheltered life up until that point. Never in his wildest dreams had he expected to be riding the New York subway at midnight.

Their troubles, however, were just beginning.

Eli had noticed the two tough-looking African Americans who seemed to be following them down the street as they walked down the stairs to the subway and got on the train. A few minutes into the ride, there they were again, walking the length of the train in their direction. His heart sank. There was no question in his mind who the target was.

"This is bad," he whispered to the other boy.

There wasn't much time to say anything else because the enemy was already just a few feet away. His guide was a Yemenite kid with a small frame, though tough and wiry. And though Eli was tall for his age, he didn't consider himself any kind of match against the two thugs.

This was no fair fight.

Meanwhile, the few people who had been sitting in that part of the train moved away. It was obvious that no one had any intention of helping them. They were completely on their own.

"What are you guys doing?" one of the thugs asked them.

"Nothing. Just going home."

"Great, give us your money, and we'll let you go home in one piece."

Eli didn't consider himself a fighter. He could count on one hand the number of times he'd used his fists, even as a child. But he had studied karate for a while, and he'd learned a number of moves, which he'd never needed to use until that moment. More importantly, his instructor had drilled a very important lesson into his students: intimidating your opponent is half the battle.

"How do you intimidate your opponent?" Eli had asked.

The teacher was happy to demonstrate.

"One way to accomplish this is by screaming at him at the top of your lungs, while shuffling from side to side in your karate stance."

The lesson became ingrained in Eli's mind, and it helped save his life that night on the train. As the would-be muggers stepped closer to the boys, Eli went into the stance he'd spent so much time perfecting. He began yelling at the two thugs and dancing around the pole in the middle of the train, his hands up, his eyes flashing fire, while his friend stood there, frozen and helpless. All the while, the train rumbled along. It was an utter nightmare where every second felt like an eternity.

Thinking that it would be easier for them to beat up the Yemenite kid, the two thugs focused their efforts on him, punching him and demanding his money. But the boy suddenly came to life, fighting back with everything he had. Then one of their attackers took out a knife, and Eli thought that the end had come. It was all over.

At that moment, the train began slowing down as it pulled into the final station before entering the tunnel leading to Queens. The moment the doors opened, the two of them exited the train and ran for their lives down the platform and away from their attackers, who chased after them. Hearts racing wildly, they reached the transit authority booth at the end of the platform, but though they banged on the door and pleaded for assistance, no one opened up for them.

They found a payphone which, miraculously, worked, so they called the police. Seeing that the game was up, the thugs fled, leaving two extremely shaken teenagers behind.

The police arrived in record time. There were two officers. One was about six foot four. The other was an average-sized guy.

"Can you describe your attackers?" one of the officers asked.

Eli did his best.

A little while later the cops heard that two black men had been arrested at a stop not far away.

"Okay, let's go for a little ride," the tall one said.

"Where are we going?" Eli asked.

"To see if the guys who were arrested are the same guys who threatened you and tried to steal your money. Come on, we'll take you in the police car."

What a night it was turning out to be. A ride on the subway to the city. Seeing Manhattan with the lights off, as it were. Almost getting mugged and beaten on the train. Now a ride in a police car. It was like something out of a suspense novel, and Eli couldn't get over what was happening. He was also petrified of how his father was going to react when he found out about the evening's adventures.

When they arrived at their destination, the policeman told Eli to get out of the car and identify the young men.

"I'm afraid to look at them, officer," he said.

The whole night had been traumatic, and the last thing he wanted to do was look his almost muggers in the eye.

"Don't worry. We're here to protect you. These guys aren't going to do anything to you."

In the end, they weren't the same guys.

By then, it was almost five in the morning, and the police asked them where they wanted to go. The Yemenite kid gave them the address in Queens, and the police drove them there. Eli didn't even bother going to sleep. Instead he waited for the earliest permissible time to daven Shacharis, and the two of them headed to a nearby shul to pray as the sun rose above the Queens skyline.

Eli was given an *aliyah* in shul, and he recited the blessing of *hagomel*, a blessing said when a person survives a dangerous experience. It was no joke. The bruised and bloodied face of the Yemenite boy was a living testimony to just how close they had come to never seeing their homes in Israel again.

After such a night, Eli felt that he'd had enough American adventures and was more than ready to return to Bayit Vegan.

"Let's take the train back to Brooklyn," the Yemenite kid said.

Eli refused. He was too scared.

"No way. I'm not getting on another train anytime soon!"

They took a taxi back to Brooklyn. There had been enough excitement for one night.

# CHAPTER FIVE

# Two Weeks With Gabi Beer

The next morning Eli made an international call to Yerushalayim. He got his father on the line and told him the entire story. He didn't leave out any of the details. The next thing Eli knew, his father had booked a flight and flown to New York, where he spent two weeks with his son. He rented a car, and they took several trips together over the next two weeks. He took Eli through the streets of Harlem, driving quickly the entire time. When Eli asked why his father was showing him this neighborhood, which wasn't known to be the safest of areas at the time, he replied, "I want you to see where your grandmother was born."

They didn't stay in Harlem for long, and afterward they drove to the Twin Towers, which blew Eli away. He had never seen buildings like these before. Then Gabi took Eli to the Lower East Side and introduced him to the world that had been his before he made the decision to move to Israel.

Eli had a taste of a sour pickle fresh from the barrel. But more importantly, for the first time in his life, he and his father were spending large amounts of quality time together. His father had always been too busy to take him places, too busy to really sit down and talk. But unexpectedly they were together for hours at a time, and Eli was introduced to a side of his father he had never seen before.

Among other things, Gabi Beer took his son to meet some very important *rabbanim*, including Rav Dovid Feinstein, the *rosh yeshivah* of Mesivta Tifereth Jerusalem, a yeshivah in the Lower East Side that was founded by Rav Dovid's father, the renowned Rav Moshe Feinstein. He himself had been a close *talmid* of Rav Moshe Feinstein and remained closely connected with his illustrious son as well.

Gabi Beer also drove his son to Williamsburg, intent on showing Eli where he had grown up. They walked down Lee Avenue, and Gabi Beer introduced Eli to a restaurant that made the best knishes in the world. But it wasn't just about food, houses, and neighborhoods. Eli's father had spent a large part of his life involved in communal causes and had developed a close relationship with Rabbi Moshe Sherer, who had headed Agudath Israel of America for decades, and even further back with the legendary Mike Tress, working with them on many sensitive assignments in Eretz Yisrael. And now that he was in the States, his contacts at the Agudah asked him to spend some of his time fundraising for the Jews who were trapped behind the Iron Curtain in the former Soviet Union.

One afternoon Eli accompanied his father to a meeting at someone's house in Boro Park. He observed his father shmoozing up the prospective donor, and the passion he conveyed when he described how the Jews in Russia were unable to daven, wear tefillin, buy a *lulav* and *esrog*, or put up a *mezuzah* like every Jew in the States was free to do. At the end of the conversation, the man pulled out his checkbook and wrote a check for five thousand dollars.

Eli was floored.

That experience never left his mind — maybe because it was one of the times in his life when he learned that anything is possible. Five thousand dollars was a lot of money back then, and his father had just been given that amount for spending forty-five minutes with someone.

Ironically, Eli had found himself bored at the beginning of the conversation and didn't understand why his father had brought him there. But when the man wrote the check, it suddenly struck him with tremendous force because he understood what his father had been able to accomplish with just a conversation.

It was a massive life lesson — a lesson that opened his eyes.

When they left the house, donor's check in hand, Eli turned to his father.

"I have a question for you."

"Yes, Eli?"

"You're a busy person with a lot going on in your life. Why did you just take a few hours to raise money for people you never met and will probably never meet?"

"That's a good question," his father replied. "And I want to give you a good answer. You see, Eli, when I was eleven years old, I lived on the Lower East Side of Manhattan. World War II was going on, and Agudath Israel was doing their best to save as many Jews as possible from the gas chambers of Europe."

He paused and turned to look Eli in the eye.

"Eli, very few people went out of their way to help the European Jews at that time. But the youth movement of the Agudath Israel — Zeirei Agudas Yisroel — did help. And since I was part of Zeirei, I helped, too. One of the things we did was to go knocking on door after door, asking people to contribute money to fund our lifesaving activities.

"One day, I began making my rounds and decided to focus on stores instead of homes. I chose a block of stores and entered one at random, hoping that the owner would give me a chance to plead my case. I knew it was a Jewish store because there was a *mezuzah* on the door, so I felt comfortable making my request.

"'What do you want?' the storeowner barked.

"'I'm raising money to help the Jews in Europe,' I told him.

"And the man started screaming at me. 'The Jews in Europe are not my problem,' he said. 'I'm an American. I take care of my own. Let them worry about their people!'

"Eli, I couldn't help it, and I started to cry. I couldn't believe that a Jew would talk this way. Here was a man who had a home to keep him warm, a bed to sleep in, food to eat — yet he wouldn't even give a dollar to help save lives because they weren't members of his family.

"I left the store still crying, and I stood outside in the street for the next two hours, unable to stop the flow of tears. I was hurt and embarrassed that the man had screamed at me when my sole concern was saving the lives of our fellow Jews. I wanted to give up and go home. But then I decided to give it one more try. I went into the next store, where I found a whole different story. The proprietor was kind. He asked me what I wanted, and I explained why I had come. He told me that he was thankful that I had given him the opportunity to help his fellow brethren across the ocean. Then he gave me five dollars and told me to come again next week, when he would give me another five dollars.

"The way the second person treated me that day gave me the motivation to continue. I ended up raising hundreds of dollars for the Jews in Europe, even though my parents had been born in America and we didn't have any close family members living across the ocean. That didn't matter. What mattered was that I was a Jew, and other Jews needed help."

Eli stared at his father in amazement. He had never known any of this about his father, who had never spoken of his experiences as a young boy. And Eli had never thought to ask. His father was always so tired and worked so hard that they never had a chance to really talk.

Eli was fourteen years old, and the two of them had never had a meaningful conversation about Gabi Beer's childhood until his father's visit to America.

By this time it was late in the afternoon, and Eli's father started heading back to Boro Park. Soon the streetlights began turning on alongside the highway, and the last light of the day began to fade. It was as if the entire world had shrunk to the inside of their car and the intense moment being shared between father and son. Part of Eli would have been more than happy to ride next to his father forever.

"When the war was over," his father continued, "and we learned the magnitude of what had been perpetrated against the Jewish people by the Germans and other nations, I was glad that I had worked so hard and done my part.

"A few years went by, and now Israel was at war, fighting for its existence. It was clear that the Israelis needed weapons to replace everything they lost in battle."

Gabi had been learning at Torah Vodaath before going to Cleveland, where he became one of the early students of the Telzer Yeshivah. Then he had to leave yeshivah to help his mother with her business.

"My father passed away at a young age from a heart attack and my mother was on her own," he continued. "She owned a small hotel at Saratoga Springs, and people would stay at the hotel when they came to the mountains to gamble at the horse races. At first I imagined that a lot of the less religious Jewish guests frequented my mother's hotel because they liked her cooking. It was the perfect place to stay if you enjoyed a nice piece of gefilte fish or a bowl of chicken and matzah ball soup.

"But eventually I realized that many of the Jews who came to the hotel were actually affiliated with the underworld. The real reason they came to my mother's hotel was not because of her food but because they could do business there without anyone bothering them.

After working at the hotel for a while, I decided to approach them.

"'Can I ask you a question?' I said to a table of tough guys one night.

"They stopped what they were doing and looked at me. 'What do you want?' one of them asked.

"'I want to know if you would consider helping me find a way to get weapons to Israel so that the soldiers will be able to defend themselves against the Arab armies.'

"'Let's say we can find a way of getting weapons to Israel,' another mobster said, 'who is going to pay us for the weapons?'

"I reassured them that I would raise the money, just as I had during the years of the Holocaust.

"So we made a deal where I would raise the money, and they would provide the weapons. I raised thousands of dollars, and these underworld figures delivered the weapons to my mother's hotel, where they stayed hidden until we were able to load them onto ships that were sailing to Tel Aviv or Haifa."

"Weren't you putting yourself in danger?" Eli asked.

"Yes. It was completely illegal. The British tried their best to stop the weapons from entering the country. Many times ships were raided, and the weapons were discovered and confiscated. But we kept at it and sent as many weapons to Israel as we could, because it was a matter of life and death and I didn't feel like I could go about my life without a care in the world when my brothers and sisters were fighting for their lives across the sea. If I was able to help, I was going to help, and that's why I did my part."

Eli sat in the car as they made their way down the FDR Drive, stunned by what he was hearing. He was blown away at the knowledge that the man he had known his entire life as a seller and lover of *sefarim* had also been a weapons smuggler and gun runner. He knew beyond a shadow of a doubt that by telling him this story, his father had just changed his life, because he now understood that a person doesn't have the liberty of sitting back and relaxing when people need help and you're in a position to do something about it.

Suddenly he was very proud of his father.

But it was more than pride. He realized that he was more like his father than he had ever imagined. And he was determined to follow in Gabi Beer's footsteps and do what he had done during the Holocaust and in the years preceding and following the formation of the State of Israel.

Bottom line: Eli Beer knew that if and when the opportunity presented itself for him to reprise history and take a page from his father's book — he was going to do just that.

# CHAPTER SIX

# Going Undercover

f Eli's initial foray to the States had been one of great excitement and drama, his second trip was noteworthy not so much for what happened but rather for what was accomplished. While his cousins took him around, introducing him to Washington, D.C., and the Liberty Bell in Philly, the most memorable part of the trip was the time he spent in Radio Shack because it was there that his plan was first put into motion. This was the real reason he had flown to the States: to purchase the radio scanners he needed to save lives. At that time it was illegal for private people to bring this kind of electronic communications equipment into Israel, and they were also unavailable for purchase there. But in America all you needed was money and you could buy as many radios as you wanted.

At Radio Shack, Eli asked one of the salesmen to show him their selection of scanners. There was a wide variety to choose from, but there was no question in Eli's mind that he was going to purchase the best.

"I want to buy two of your best-quality radio scanners," he told the man. "How much are they?"

"Seven hundred dollars each. They pick up every frequency, and distance doesn't matter. They come with antennas. If you can, put them up on the roof of the building. They'll work better."

"Are these popular?"

"Very. Anyone who wants to hear what the police are listening to on their radios buys one of these. They're the real deal."

"How do I set it up?"

"It comes with instructions. You look like a smart kid. I don't think you'll have any problem figuring it out."

Fourteen hundred dollars lighter than when he'd walked into the store, Eli left Radio Shack with two new radio scanners, feeling both excited and nervous. Excited, because now he and his friends would be able to listen to the same frequencies that MDA was hearing. This would give them the ability to run to calls and hopefully get there in time to save lives. On the other hand, it was illegal to bring this equipment into Israel because it was only allowed to be used by the police and official ambulance companies, and Eli would get into trouble if he got caught, in addition to losing the money he'd spent on the radios, since they would be confiscated.

But it was a risk he'd just have to take.

He was on a mission to save lives, and he was prepared to do whatever it took.

As he packed the radios into his suitcase, removing them from their boxes and disassembling them as much as possible — antenna here, battery there, instruction manual folded up and stuffed in his jacket pocket — Eli still couldn't help feeling at least slightly apprehensive about the possibility of getting caught while passing through the "nothing to declare" line at customs. If he was stopped and the radios were taken away, the trip would have been for nothing.

*You are a sheliach mitzvah*, he reassured himself. *You're a person on a mission to save lives. You have nothing to worry about.*

As the plane landed at Ben Gurion, Eli couldn't enjoy the sight of Tel Aviv through the cabin window as he had the other time he'd flown because his heart was racing faster than he thought possible. Trying to act nonchalant, he disembarked with all the other passengers and descended the staircase to the tarmac. He passed through passport control and went to collect his luggage, constantly repeating to himself that he was on a mission from the One above and that everything was going to work out. When his suitcases appeared, he manhandled them onto a luggage cart, and then, steeling himself, he pushed the cart in the direction of the green line — the line for people who had nothing to declare. He didn't look at the customs agents. He didn't look at anyone. He kept his eyes on the door ahead of him and focused on his burning desire to save lives.

And then all at once he was through the doors, and the air was warm on his face and he could see a thousand people coming and going and hear the sounds of taxi drivers yelling, and it was as if the sound had been turned back on again.

He was in and his radios were in.

They were in business. It was a miracle.

The next question was where to place the radios. Eli gave the matter a lot of thought, and in the end, he decided to put one of them on a shelf in the basement of his father's bookstore in Bayit Vegan. That became Eli's first command center, and it was the most beautiful sight in the world.

"I gave the other radio to my cousin Dovie Maisel, who lived on the top floor of a building in Har Nof and who had also become a volunteer for MDA, and it passed from him to other members of our team. The idea was simple. I knew that one person wouldn't be able to sit and listen to the radio all day long. So I decided that my friends and I would have to do shifts, with different boys taking different hours of the day and night. The moment we heard of an emergency, we would let everyone know the address and name via the pagers that we had. If you wanted to join our team, you needed to buy a pager. It wasn't expensive and it did the job of getting the relevant information to everyone who needed it.

"When a call came in — let's say someone was choking at 55 Jaffa Road — the volunteer who heard the details would pick up a phone and call a number. He would hear a beep and have ten seconds to leave his message: choking victim on 55 Jaffa Road.

"That voice message would then be sent out automatically to all the beepers who were part of the group. It was only later on that the technology developed further, and the message began showing itself in writing across a tiny screen. The moment an emergency was reported, the group was off and running — and more and more, they managed to reach the victims faster than ever before. "When the MDA ambulance would come rolling up to the scene, the drivers would often discover that one of the volunteers was already there hard at work. And if they asked the volunteer what he was doing there, the volunteer would reply that he had just happened to be in the neighborhood, and wasn't that a wonderful coincidence? Then he would hand over the patient to the EMT or paramedic, satisfied that things were going according to plan."

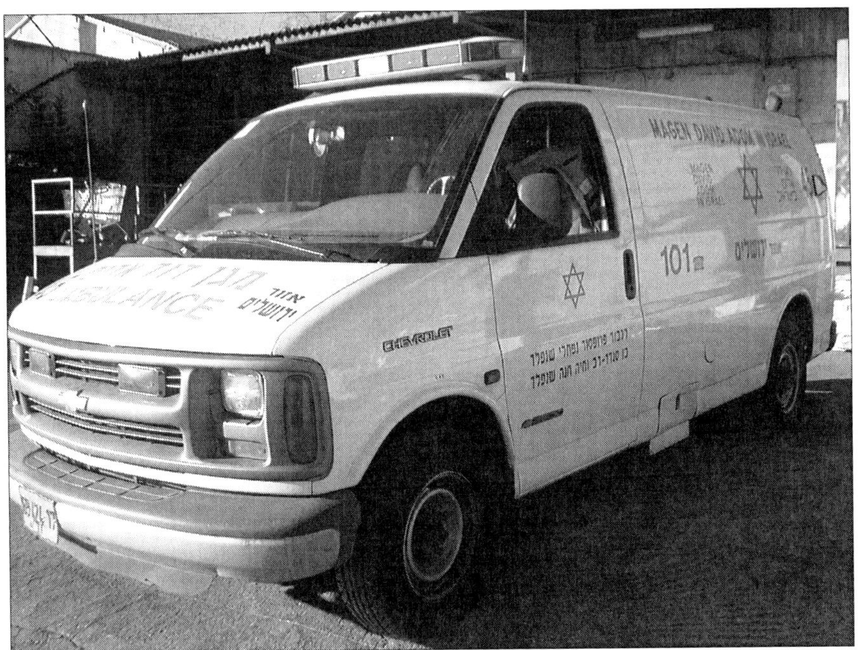
An MDA ambulance

Within weeks, the group realized that two radios weren't enough. If they really wanted to be serious about this, they needed more of them, so that they could spread them around to more members of the team. They needed more people listening because two people couldn't sit for too long at a time. So they began asking anyone they knew who was traveling to America to do them a favor and bring them back a radio. Everyone was excited about being part of something big, and their collection of radios grew by the week. Within two months they had about ten radios, and the young group of volunteers was manning them around the clock.

While this was the forerunner of Hatzalah in Israel, they operated like an undercover organization — one that didn't even have a name. In truth, what they were doing was illegal because only the police and other authorized organizations were allowed to use this kind of radio, but they were intent on saving lives and didn't feel that there was any option.

Not long after his return from the States, Eli went on a call. A seventy-year-old man had been hit by a car and was lying in front of 45 Hapisga

Street. At the time Eli was sitting in the basement of his father's store at number 50 — about fifty yards away.

Since he was down in the basement, he hadn't heard the sound of the accident. The first he knew about it was when the call came in over the radio. He heard the dispatcher at Magen David Adom sending an ambulance to 45 Hapisga for a person who had been hit by a car while crossing the street.

Eli remembers every detail of that encounter.

"I jumped out of my seat as if I had been struck by a lightning bolt!

"This was it. The reason I had traveled to America to buy the radios. Here it was. A call. And I was close enough to do something about it! I could be there in ten seconds!

"I didn't have any equipment with me (all we had was four bags of equipment total, and since I was our dispatcher right then, the bags were with the other guys), and I was scared as I ran out of the basement and up the stairs to the street. I saw a bunch of people surrounding a man who was lying on the pavement. My heart was racing even faster than the moment I went through customs.

"This was my chance to save a life. I had to get it right!"

Part of him was hoping that he would find someone there already who knew what he was doing. But when he reached the group of people, it was obvious that they were standing there helpless, and no one had even the slightest clue what to do.

He quickly assessed the situation. Blood was gushing out of the man's neck as if a faucet had been opened and couldn't be closed. "I'm an EMT," he told the crowd. "Please move out of the way!"

The people moved aside.

"Does anyone have gloves or bandages?"

No one had anything like that.

"I knew that I couldn't waste any time," Eli says. "The man was bleeding from an artery in his neck, and I needed to find something to staunch the flow of blood. Otherwise the man was going to bleed to death. Had I been wearing a long-sleeved shirt, I would have torn off one of the sleeves, but it was a warm day and I was wearing short sleeves."

Suddenly Eli had an idea. Reaching up to his head, he removed his *kippah* and folded it in half. Then he shoved it into the hole in the man's neck, trying his best to stop the blood from spurting out. He held it there with as much force as he could, and stopped the gushing flow.

"Nobody move him," Eli said. He knew that the man had been badly hit and that there was a good chance that he had a spinal injury that could kill him if he was moved in the wrong way.

Eli kept on calling out for an ambulance, even though he knew that it was already on the way. He also kept checking the man's breathing. He was happy to see that he was still breathing, and the bleeding had slowed down.

Fifteen or twenty minutes later, an ambulance showed up.

The driver jumped out of the vehicle and saw Eli crouched down next to the injured man with his *kippah* pressed to his neck.

"What are you doing here?" the driver asked.

"I happened to be passing by."

The driver shrugged. He didn't care. He was just making conversation.

The driver bandaged the wound properly. The man was then loaded into the ambulance and driven off to the hospital.

As he left the scene of the accident, Eli was sure that the man wasn't going to make it. He had been through so much trauma and had both body and head injuries. Despite his personal misgivings, everyone in the neighborhood was very appreciative of what he had done, how he had jumped right in without hesitation to save a life.

Akiva Paskesz was about fifteen years older than Eli and worked across the street at his father's bakery. "Eli, come over to the bakery," he offered.

When they were seated in the fragrant-smelling store, surrounded by mounds of cakes and cookies, Akiva gave Eli a drink and a few cookies and told him to take his time and calm down. Eli took a few swallows of cola and felt the sugary sweetness sliding down his throat, calming him down and slowing the beating of his heart.

When Akiva saw that Eli was beginning to regain his composure after the excitement and trauma that comes with sticking your *kippah* into someone else's bleeding neck, he said, "You know something? I should probably learn how to do what you just did. I should become an EMT, too."

Akiva followed through and ended up becoming a very active volunteer.

Eli's father was very proud of his son for going out there to take care of a man bleeding to death. And it wasn't only his father. It seemed like everyone in the neighborhood had something positive to say about what Eli had done. Eli himself felt good about the whole thing, as his decision to fly to America and drop fourteen hundred dollars on two radios had just been vindicated. At the same time, he wasn't sure if the man was going to make it. No one had called to tell him what happened after the ambulance took the injured man to the hospital.

Two days later, the phone rang in the Beer house.

"Is this the Beer family?"

"Yes."

"Is Eli there?"

"Speaking."

The man identified himself and said, "It was my father who was injured in the car accident two days ago."

Eli was sure that the man was about to inform him that the funeral was going to be held that day.

But no.

"I just wanted to let you know that he woke up today. During the conversation, someone mentioned that you were the one who stopped the bleeding. We wanted to thank you for saving his life. If you want to visit him, he would love to meet you."

Eli started crying. He couldn't believe it. He had actually saved someone's life! This was the moment he'd been waiting for ever since he'd seen the old man lying on the pavement when he was a little boy. At the time he was helpless to do anything about it, but now he had been given the tools to make a difference. It was an unforgettable feeling — like he was flying through a cloudless blue sky on a glorious day.

"Of course I want to visit him. Where is he?"

"He's at Hadassah Hospital."

"I'll be there."

Gabi Beer drove his son to the hospital. When they arrived, Gabi waited outside the room (he was crying with emotion and pride in his son, and Eli felt like it was the first time he'd ever given his father *nachas*…) while Eli knocked on the door and was admitted inside. The room was filled with family members. The old man, who must have been around seventy years old, was propped up in bed. His face was pale but his eyes were clear and he said, "Come here, young man, I want to give you a hug."

Eli leaned down over the hospital bed. The old man reached up and enveloped Eli in his arms, trying to convey his appreciation. And Eli felt it. It was the most incredible hug he'd ever had. For years, he had been kicked out of class, roaming the halls because he wasn't the kind of kid who was built for the classroom. He had been knocked down for his failures in school, yet now he had something to be proud of. Something immense. He was still a teenager. Still a kid. And yet he'd managed to save a life.

Then he noticed something else.

The man had a number on his arm.

Eli felt a shock, and a tremor traveled up and down his spine. Suddenly his mind was filled with memories.

Memories of walking down the hill in the direction of Yad Vashem. He could hear the sounds of the birds calling to one another, see the bright colors of the trees and flowers and smell their fragrance. And then he would enter the dimly lit halls of Israel's Holocaust museum and stare at the pictures — at the horror-filled testimonies and photos of six million people crying for salvation. He felt that in saving a man who had survived such horrors, he had come full circle.

At that moment, Eli Beer felt incredibly blessed, and he was filled with the most amazing sense of gratitude to the One above for giving him such an opportunity.

"After I saw that man lying on the floor when I was just a little boy, I had a dream. I dreamed of saving one life to make up for the life that was lost. But now, when a seventy-year-old man with a number on his arm was giving me a hug — I remembered another dream I'd had when I was a kid who just couldn't stay in school.

"As I wandered through Yad Vashem, I dreamed I would save the lives of six million people — one for every person lost in the Holocaust.

"I had saved a life — and it was easy. I hadn't had to operate on him. I hadn't had to perform surgery. All I had needed to do was get there fast enough to stop the bleeding.

"And if that was the case, then I knew that I needed to reach for the sky."

Soon after Eli arrived, a doctor walked into the room. It didn't take him long to grasp what was going on.

The doctor took Eli aside. "I want to give you some advice," he said. "The man you saved happens to take a blood-thinning medicine. The reason he takes this medication is because he has some problems with his heart. If you hadn't stopped the bleeding when you did, he would have been dead in less than three minutes. You did the right thing when you pushed against the artery. It's all about putting pressure on the wound. That's what stopped the bleeding.

"When we opened his bandages here at the hospital, we found your *kippah* stuck inside. It was sticky with blood and very hard to remove. The EMT who did the bandaging never took it out. Maybe it was too stuck to remove under such pressure. Maybe he didn't notice it in his haste to bandage him properly.

"Listen to me, kid, if you want to be a hero, don't use a *kippah* to do it. Make sure you have some real bandages handy. Use your *kippah* for your religious beliefs — but keep it far away from serious wounds."

When he left the hospital that day, Eli had tasted the sweet taste of success, and he was more determined than ever to carry on.

He had saved one life. But there were millions more to go.

# CHAPTER SEVEN

# Branching Out

After his conversation with the doctor, Eli knew that it was crucial for every volunteer to be equipped with everything he needed to do the job right. He decided that he was going to purchase a supply of essential medical equipment for every member of the team. There were fifteen guys on the team, and he was going to make sure that every one of them received his own bag with everything they needed to save lives.

So began the first Hatzalah fundraising campaign. Eli approached his father, and Gabi Beer contributed one thousand dollars toward the cause. Next he went to speak to his neighbor (and future father-in-law) Mel Heftler and asked him for a contribution as well. Mel gave a lot of money to charity, and he agreed to pay for five kits. Eli visited many other neighbors, told them what he was doing, and asked for their help. Slowly but surely, the campaign came together.

When he had sufficient money to pay for all the kits, Eli went to a store in the Geulah neighborhood that sold medical supplies wholesale and gave them a long list of things he wanted to purchase. The salesman was used to selling in bulk to hospitals and ambulance companies, but he wasn't averse to filling fifteen orders for a wide assortment of bandages, devices to take blood pressure for children and for adults, and anything else Eli could think of that would come in handy.

"I also want oxygen tanks for every kit."

"They're not going to fit. The bags are already stuffed."

"Fine, I'll take another bag for every person, just for the tank."

"So two bags per person?"

"Yes, one for the oxygen tank and one for everything else."

The cost ended up being about three thousand shekels a kit.

But it was worth it. Now they could really make a difference.

Through it all, Eli's secret group of "undercover agents" continued volunteering for Magen David Adom so they could receive the training they needed, never informing Magen David Adom that they were running their own ops at the same time. It would take Magen David Adom about a year and a half before they even realized that many of their volunteers were also building another organization and trying their hardest to respond to calls before the ambulances got there.

And for the most part, they were succeeding. By the time an ambulance arrived, there were nearly always volunteers already handling the scene.

By this point, the group of undercover radio operators was beginning to make a dent in the rescue missions taking place in Yerushalayim. Though some of the ambulance drivers were starting to understand that something was going on beneath the surface, most of them appreciated that lives were being saved — even if not necessarily by them. And if there was a call on the top floor of a building and they had to carry an overweight person down four flights of stairs, it was a bonus to find that there were people there to help you.

The MDA drivers liked the little elves who kept on showing up, materializing suddenly as if out of nowhere. And in order to make sure that they kept on liking them, Eli's group treated the drivers well, bringing over challos and cakes to their homes on Erev Shabbos and sending them *mishlo'ach manos* on Purim. The volunteers had come a long way from when they first started going out on calls, when some of the drivers would make disparaging remarks because they were religious, and would do their best to make them feel unwanted.

So the team was saving lives, but they couldn't do it openly. They knew that every life that was saved was a great cause for celebration, but they couldn't help wondering if they would be forced to hide their radios forever. Would the day ever come when they would be able to emerge from their "bunkers" and carry out their work publicly? At that point, it didn't seem very likely.

On the other hand, they had managed to smuggle radios into Israel and were already using them, and they had successfully managed to equip themselves with medical kits that they could use on calls.

It was obvious that the night was still young, and bigger and better days still lay ahead. So Eli and his team of volunteers bided their time and continued saving lives — one person at a time.

At some point, a group of older chassidic MDA volunteers from neighborhoods like Geulah and Meah Shearim noticed what Eli and his friends were doing. They liked the idea and decided to create their own group. They even gave themselves a name: Hatzalah Yerushalayim. Eventually the two groups joined together, with Eli providing the chassidic volunteers with walkie-talkies so they could be more effective.

As time passed, more and more volunteers, many of them chassidim, began joining the original core groups, and the organization started to grow in earnest. Some of the older members added structure, appointing leaders and a board, while the younger volunteers like Eli, Dovie Maisel, and Moshe Teitelbaum, another of Eli's old friends, continued going on calls.

It was only a matter of time before Hatzalah was formally launched, and by the time Eli was seventeen years old, Hatzalah had become an official organization and they ceased being an underground operation.

As they gained official status, the founders realized that they had to come up with a procedure for admitting new members who wanted to join their group. They decided that volunteers had to apply to join,

The different logos — Hatzalah Yerushalayim and Hatzalah Israel

Hatzalah Yerushalayim yellow ambucycle

and their application was reviewed by a committee. After they were approved, they were interviewed by members of the board, and only then were they allowed to take the course, after which they were required to pass a test.

Eli was still very young, and while the vision had been his in the first place, he didn't see himself as the head of an organization. While everyone knew that he was one of Hatzalah's founders, Eli wasn't interested in taking control. Though he did have a seat on the board, he wanted to continue going on calls, doing what he thought was most important. He was happy to let the older members handle operations. All he cared about was saving people.

He simply didn't see himself the way other people saw him, as a visionary and leader.

According to the bylaws of the organization, board elections would be held every two years. In the months leading up to the elections, many of the volunteers approached Eli and asked him to run for the position of chairman of the board. The rank-and-file volunteers liked his leadership style and his chutzpah, and his ability to accomplish great things, and they felt that he had what it took to take Hatzalah Yerushalayim to the next level.

"I'm only eighteen years old," he would protest. "I'm not leadership material."

Some people have a passion for politics. They love nothing more than to be the ones controlling everything that goes on. Others are doers. They like to be out in the field making things happen. Still others are dreamers, coming up with great ideas that are usually implemented by the doers. Eli himself was a blend of the consummate dreamer and the tireless doer. He had many incredible ideas and possessed the unique ability to turn those dreams into a reality. And many of the volunteers recognized those unique character traits and wanted to see him at the helm, not only out in the field, but also as the official CEO of Hatzalah Yerushalayim.

But Eli wasn't interested in administration. He was perfectly content to continue going on calls with his fellow volunteers.

While Eli's group was building Hatzalah in Yerushalayim, other groups opened their own branches of Hatzalah in cities all over the country. Hatzalah Bnei Brak, established by Mutty Barzilai, became the second biggest branch, and their members had also started purchasing radios and other equipment. Suddenly the concept of Hatzalah was a national phenomenon — as had happened years earlier in the United States — and was beginning to take root all over the country, like mushrooms after the rain. It was only natural that the members in Yerushalayim started referring to themselves as Hatzalah Yerushalayim, and that was indeed the way they became known. There were other firmly established groups, such as Hatzalah of Tzcfas and Tiveriah, founded by Nachi Klein, but the two main teams were in Yerushalayim and Bnei Brak.

Inevitably there were politics between the different groups, particularly between Yerushalayim and Bnei Brak. Members from one city didn't like it when a volunteer from a different city responded to a call in their hometown. And at some point, the Jerusalem neighborhood of Har Nof established their own branch, which they called Hachovesh. It seemed like everyone was doing their own thing, and no one was cooperating with each other.

The politics and disagreements between the different branches of Hatzalah troubled Eli. In his mind, it had always been about saving lives, and he hated that everyone was arguing instead of focusing on

Ambucycles riding outside the Old City of Jerusalem

their common goal. It pained Eli when he heard stories of volunteers from different branches being unceremoniously shown the door when they were coming to help. Every city wanted to operate with independence, and the demarcation lines were sharply defined. And even though so many of the members had begun their careers as responders for Magen David Adom, now their allegiance went first and foremost to their branch.

Eli went out of his way to unite the different units of Hatzalah in Yerushalayim, meeting with his counterparts in Meah Shearim and stressing that everyone needed to work together, even though some of them wore long jackets and had curly *peyos* and others wore small *kippot* and colored shirts. To Eli, unity and brotherhood were crucial, and he did everything in his power to increase peace among the ranks.

But the situation between Hatzalah Yerushalayim and Hatzalah Bnei Brak was only getting worse. Yerushalayim had more volunteers than it needed, while Bnei Brak had far fewer. Yerushalayim volunteers would often go to Bnei Brak to go on calls and to gain experience. The Bnei Brak members hated this and were very vocal about their feelings.

It wasn't like Eli didn't understand their perspective. "Every organization has its code, its training, and its way of doing things," Eli says.

"When their volunteers show up on a call, they know which volunteers are well trained and can be relied on and which are still green and mastering the huge amount of information an EMT needs to know. It made sense that the Bnei Brak volunteers didn't want random strangers showing up on calls when they didn't know if they could be trusted to get things right."

Along with the internal politics, there was also a backlash against Hatzalah from some who felt that religious men had no business being involved with medical emergencies in the first place. When Hatzolah was first established in the United States, its founder, Hershel Weber, faced powerful opposition from *rabbanim* who were against the volunteers responding to calls on Shabbos. It was no different in Eretz Yisrael. When a volunteer would get into his car on a Friday night to go and save a life, "*pashkevillin*" (posters) would appear after Shabbos decrying the fact that he had violated the holy day. In some neighborhoods, the local rabbis allowed the Hatzalah volunteers to go to calls on Shabbos but not to return home unless they were driven by a non-Jew. And while Rav Moshe Feinstein had already issued a halachic ruling allowing Hatzolah volunteers in the United States to return home on their own, Rav Elyashiv, the leading *posek* in Eretz Yisrael, held otherwise.

In the end, Rav Moshe Feinstein's ruling would come to be the accepted practice by the vast majority of Israeli communities, but at the beginning, the issue of going out to calls on Shabbos was steeped in dissension.

Eli realized that the organization needed to have an official rabbi, and he needed to be a rabbinical authority who would be accepted by one and all. Some of the board members turned to Rav Moshe Halberstam, who was a member of the Eidah Chareidis (Rabbinical Council of Jerusalem) and who recognized that saving lives trumped all else. For the most part, this proved to be a wise decision and calmed the storm.

Things were happening, both good and challenging, but despite the challenges, the members of Hatzalah Yerushalayim were making a difference — and saving lives.

# Two for the Price of One

&li continued going on calls and came to realize that they were sorely missing another piece of essential equipment, something that would be a real game changer. He wanted to equip each volunteer with a defibrillator, even though back then almost nobody had them. Even the standard ambulances weren't equipped with defibrillators. They could only be found on the intensive-care ambulances. But Eli was a person who dreamed big, and he dreamed of the day when every volunteer would have a defibrillator because he knew what a lifesaving device it was.

He knew that if they reached a person experiencing cardiac arrest within the first two minutes, there was a ninety percent chance that they would save the person's life with this device.

The need was real, and the need was great. The question was what to do about it.

Then Eli heard about a company in the States that was manufacturing small automatic defibrillators, unlike the defibrillators that everyone had previously been producing, which were big and bulky and mostly used for ambulances and hospitals. Eli knew that he had to start bringing some of them into Israel.

The year was 1992. Eli was nineteen years old.

"I convinced a few people to donate money. The defibrillators cost about two thousand dollars each — ten to fifteen thousand for a big one

Showing the first defibrillator to the members of Hatzalah

— and I managed to raise enough money for two mini defibrillators. I traveled to America to get them and I purchased them from a man who sold medical equipment supplies in Boro Park. Once again I had to smuggle them into the country, so I wrapped them up in some of my shirts and hoped for the best. Like radio scanners, at the time private individuals were not allowed to bring defibrillators into Israel, and if found, they would be confiscated.

"Nobody stopped me."

Once home, Eli decided to show the mini defibrillators to some people he knew who worked for the Ministry of Health. He wanted them to know the options that existed and to ask them to equip every ambulance in the country with the same kind of defibrillators that he had just smuggled in.

Eli arranged a meeting with his contact at the Ministry of Health, who happened to be the person in charge of all the ambulances in Israel. The man was shocked when he saw the device. He had never seen such a piece of equipment and was blown away by how advanced it was. It even had a monitor.

"Look," Eli said at the end of the meeting, "the technology is out there. It exists. I think you should be importing them into the country by the thousands."

Eli left the building without high hopes of change, but at least with the knowledge that he had done what he could.

The defibrillator was used on a call a month after it was brought into the country. The procedure wasn't successful. The patient was a very old man, and they were unable to save him. But a week later Eli used it again. There were a few volunteers at the call. Eli took out the defibrillator and attached it to the man. He was young — in his early forties.

"I pressed the button on the defibrillator. The first time it didn't work. I pressed it again. The second time, his heart rhythm returned and he came back to life. It was something incredible to see! An ambulance took him to the hospital and he returned home to his wife and children a few weeks later — a new man, healthy and whole."

It was more than obvious that the investment had paid off. It was also obvious that they were going to need a whole slew of them if they really wanted to make a difference. By then Eli Beer knew that he wanted to flood the entire country with defibrillators, because to his mind, it was obvious that they were the most important tool in an EMT's arsenal. But defibrillators are expensive, and he was going to have to raise the money to purchase them. Since he had to buy them in America anyway, he knew that he was going to have to start doing some serious fundraising away from home.

It was time for him to start building a network of people who could be counted on to help further the cause. The only question was where to start.

Eli visited his father's bookstore one day and spent some time helping him unpack boxes of new books that had just arrived from America. As they worked together, Eli told his father all about the new developments that were happening with his team of lifesavers.

"So you managed to use the defibrillator," his father said.

"Yes, and the man didn't suffer any brain damage. He returned home to his family healthy and whole. Hashem has given the world a gift that saves lives, plain and simple, and I need dozens of them to really make a difference."

"You know something?" Gabi Beer told his son. "Next time you visit

America, there's a person I want you to meet. A friend of mine. I think he'll want to help your cause. His name is Tzvi Gastworth. He lives in Far Rockaway. He's a really good man who loves to help people. I have a feeling that he would be more than happy to help you raise the money you need."

Not long afterward, Gabi Beer arranged for his son to meet his friend in the States. Eli found him sitting and learning with his *chavrusa* (study partner), Moshe Hirth, and he told them about the mini defibrillators and how imperative it was that they bring large quantities of them into Israel.

They loved the idea.

"Eli," they said, "how many defibrillators do you need?"

"At least a hundred."

Eli thought they were going to throw him out of the house, that they were going to think he was crazy or, at the least, *chutzpadik*.

"How much do they cost?" Tzvi asked.

"Between two thousand and twenty-five hundred dollars a piece."

They did the math.

"So you're saying that you need a hundred defibrillators times twenty-five hundred dollars. Basically we need to raise two hundred and fifty thousand dollars."

"Yes."

"It's a big ask."

"Yes, but maybe we can run a campaign to raise the money. The goal is to equip every one of our volunteers with his own defibrillator so they can get started on saving a patient's life the second they get there. Can you help me raise the money? We can go around and ask people to donate one defibrillator each."

They thought about it.

"Eli," Tzvi said, "we want to help you. If you want to run a campaign, we're right behind you. The first step we need to take is to write a letter that we'll send out to everyone we can think of. And the letter will need to be signed by a number of *rabbanim* attesting to the importance of the cause."

Eli was a little taken aback. After all, until then he had had little to do with *rabbanim*. But Tzvi and Moshe insisted that it was important. So upon his return to Israel, he headed to Meah Shearim to visit the home of the great *posek* Rav Yosef Sholom Elyashiv. He didn't realize it at the time, but he would come to develop a very close relationship with Rav Elyashiv, as well as many other of the greatest leaders of *Klal Yisrael*.

Rav Moshe Halberstam, who served as the group's first *rav* and *posek* (even before they became an official organization), accompanied Eli to meet Rav Elyashiv.

Eli also brought along a defibrillator to his meeting with Rav Elyashiv, so he could better understand the device's lifesaving potential. Rav Elyashiv asked numerous questions about what Eli was doing and what he hoped to accomplish. He wanted to understand how the mini defibrillators worked and why they were so important. Eli answered every question clearly and confidently.

"Let me give the Rav an example," he said. "When a car's battery dies, you can start the car by using the battery of another car. It's the same thing here. You can restart a person's heart by using this defibrillator. This machine is a starter for a human heart. If we can get there fast enough and have one of them with us, we can save a person's life. "

By the end of their meeting, Rav Elyashiv was convinced.

"This is a clear case of *pikuach nefesh*," he wrote in his letter, "and everyone should donate money."

Eli also visited many other *rabbanim* and Admorim. One of them was the Belzer Rebbe. Eli told the Rebbe that his great-uncle was Reb Yossele Yatchover, who had served as a *gabbai* for the Belzer Rebbe during the Holocaust and perished along with millions of other Jews.

When he heard this, the Rebbe rose from his chair.

"If you're a relative of Reb Yossele Yatchover, that's enough for me."

And the Rebbe signed as well.

As soon as the letter was ready, it was sent out to as many people as possible. The letter introduced Eli Beer and his team of volunteers to the world and described what they were trying to do. At the end of the letter was a long list of rabbinical signatures, including Rav Yosef Sholom Elyashiv, the Belzer Rebbe, Rav Chaim Kanievsky, Rav Moshe Halberstam, and Rav Aharon Leib Shteinman.

The checks came pouring in, and within a short time enough money had been raised to purchase one hundred brand-new defibrillators.

Now a new question arose.

It was one thing to smuggle one or two defibrillators into Israel, but quite another to do the same for a large quantity of expensive equipment. They were going to have to change direction. It was time to start doing things legally.

# מרנן ורבנן גדולי ישראל שליט"א
# במכתב חיזוק למען
# "איחוד הצלה"

בס"ד

כתב רבנו יונה בשערי תשובה: "וטוב ונכון מאוד להיות בכל עיר ועיר מתנדבים בעם מן המשכילים להיות נכונים ומזומנים לכל דבר הצלה בהיות איש או אשה מישראל שרויים בצער".

והנה שזכינו שקמו אנשים יקרים, העוסקים במסירות בעניין הנשגב של הצלת נפשות, בכל שעות היממה. בימי חול, שבת וימים טובים, בהתנדבות מלאה ושלא על מנת לקבל פרס, בסניפים הפרוסים בכל ארץ ישראל, והתאחדו יחדיו תחת ארגון הצלה ארצי "**איחוד הצלה**".

**ע"כ, הננו להודיע בזה בשער בת רבים, כי אף ידינו תיכון עימם. לחזקם, לעודדם ולסעדם ולקרוא בזה לאחב"י להיות להם לעזר ולאחיסמך.**

וסומכים אנו ידינו על הנהלת ארגון "איחוד הצלה" בניהולו של הרב זאב קשש הי"ו, שקיבלו על עצמם את הדרכתם והנהגתם של חברי ועד רבנים שליט"א, אשר הם גדולי תורה והוראה, אשר יפקחו וידריכו את מתנדבי "איחוד הצלה" על כל צעד ושעל, בכל עניני ההלכה, השבת, הצניעות וההנהגות הנכונות והרצויות  עבור העוסקים בהצלת חיים.

וע"ז בעה"ח בברכה להנהלה, למתנדבים, לעוזרים ומסייעים להם הן סיוע ברוח והן בגשמיות. הקב"ה ישלם שכרם וישלח ברכה והצלחה בכל מעשי ידיהם, מתוך אחווה ושלו'.

Letter signed by Rav Elyashiv and other *gedolim* in support of United Hatzalah

Eli heard about a big medical supplies company called Lifepak that could provide what they needed and arranged a meeting with one of their executives.

"For the first time," Eli recalls, "we were now in a position of relative strength. We had two hundred and fifty thousand dollars — which I wanted to leverage to the max."

Most teenagers would have felt intimidated at the idea of negotiating with a large company like Lifepak. But Eli had been running various businesses since he was twelve and was more than used to the give-and-take of a deal. Sitting down with an American businessman was not a big deal for him — not after he had cut his teeth negotiating deals with Egged drivers in a smoke-filled room just outside the Central Bus Station in Yerushalayim.

What Eli had learned was that when it comes to business, you look the other person in the eye and you ask for what you want. Lifepak wasn't interested in negotiating. They wanted twenty-five hundred dollars per defibrillator, and that was that. So Eli explored a few other possibilities. There was no reason to rush into anything — not when he could make a much better deal.

Eventually he found another company that was willing to negotiate.

"I'm looking to buy a hundred defibrillators," Eli told them.

It was a major deal and they were open to doing business.

"We'll give you a twenty percent discount," they offered.

"I don't want a twenty percent discount."

Eli's response was perplexing.

"Then what do you want?"

"For every defibrillator that I purchase from you, I want you to give me one for free."

Silence from the other end.

"Listen, Joe," Eli said to the man he was negotiating with. "Can I call you Joe?"

"Sure."

"Okay, Joe, here's the deal. I want to buy these defibrillators for a volunteer organization called Hatzalah — which means 'Rescue.' It was started by a group of young men who originally volunteered for Israel's national ambulance service. The defibrillators will be used to save lives in Israel. No one is making any money here. Everyone is working for free because they want to help people. That's why I'm doing this. I know that you're just a salesman and not the boss. But if you understand the importance of what I'm telling you, then you'll understand that I'm asking you to fight for me and help me walk away with as many defibrillators as possible. Because they won't just end up sitting in a warehouse. They will go out and save lives!"

It took a few weeks, but in the end they agreed on a "buy one, get one free," deal — which meant that Eli was going to be returning home with two hundred defibrillators, where previously they had a fraction of that. The tax issue was the next issue on the line.

From the vantage point of the Israeli government, it didn't matter to them why Eli Beer wanted to import two hundred defibrillators into the country. To the tax authority it made no difference whether he wanted to open a company selling them or to use them to save lives. The fact is, the devices were firmly in the category of a luxury item, and that meant paying an import tax — and a steep one at that.

"Shipping the devices to Israel will cost about two thousand dollars," Eli was told. "But the import tax will be in the region of eighteen percent of their total cost, and that is a lot of money."

When he returned to Israel, Eli made a visit to the tax authority headquarters to talk to them directly, but there was no one to talk to, and the visit was a complete waste of time.

Which meant that they needed to raise more money.

Eli called Tzvi Gastworth and relayed the situation. Together they decided to go back to several of the donors who had already contributed and explain that they needed another eighteen percent in order to get the defibrillators across the ocean and into Israel.

The mission was accomplished, the taxes were paid, and the defibrillators were shipped to Israel, where they were distributed to all the volunteers Eli knew, as well as to volunteers who were part of Magen David Adom. For Eli, it wasn't about his organization being better equipped than any other. It was about saving lives — and the more defibrillators placed in ambulances, the more lives could be saved on a daily basis.

# PART TWO

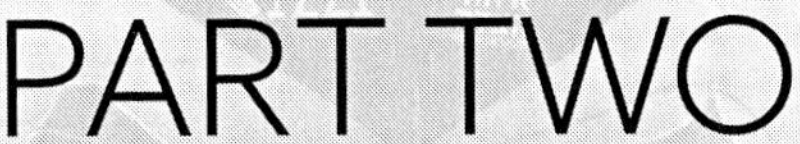

> *I decided to use Israel's greatest invention: chutzpah.*
>
> — *Eli Beer*

# CHAPTER NINE

# Motorcycles for Hatzalah

There are moments in a person's life when he has a brilliant idea. To creative people, this happens a lot. This doesn't mean that all ideas are created equal. Some can indisputably be categorized as incredible.

Eli's decision to travel to the States and smuggle radios into Israel so that the volunteers would be able to tune in to MDA frequencies was an incredible idea. His recognition that defibrillators were of the utmost importance and his subsequent decision to raise the money for them in America was another breakthrough moment.

But it was the idea he had in 1992 for using motorcycles that turned Hatzalah into an unstoppable force. Eli clearly remembers that fateful moment:

"So many times I'd see an ambulance trying to get to a call but unable to move because it was stuck in traffic.

"And then I had an idea.

"What if our volunteers stopped trying to rescue people using cars and ambulances? What if they started reaching their destinations using motorcycles instead?

"Nothing can stop a motorcycle. It can get around any truck and if traffic is backed up, the cyclist can go carefully onto the sidewalk and drive there instead — until they pass the obstruction that's keeping everyone else stuck in their places."

Eli suddenly envisioned an army of Hatzalah volunteers riding to calls on motorcycles. He knew that this was something that would change the entire concept of emergency response. Now the volunteers would have an increased chance at reaching the patient in time to save his life.

The idea might have been groundbreaking, but there was plenty of pushback. It was difficult for people to see the incredible potential of an army of motorcycling EMTs. Eli spent a lot of time trying to convince people of the benefits of using motorcycles to get to a patient.

"When it comes to saving lives," he would tell people, "it's all about timing. If you don't get there within the first three minutes, the person suffering from a stroke or a heart attack is much less likely to recover. Timing is literally the difference between life and death. You have to admit that it doesn't make sense for me to sit in traffic when I could use a motorcycle to reach my destination in a fraction of the time.

"There are also other factors that make motorcycles the ideal mode of transport. When a volunteer goes out on a call and reaches the patient's home, he still has to park. He can't just leave his car in the middle of the road because that would cause a major traffic jam. But if he's on a motorcycle, he can ride right up to a patient's front door and never has a problem with traffic or parking."

In the end, Hatzalah purchased their first motorcycle for a volunteer as a kind of trial run. This way they could see if using a motorcycle to respond to calls would prove to be as much of a breakthrough as Eli thought it would.

By 1992 Eli had become more and more convinced that using motorcycles to get to emergencies in the least amount of time was the future of the organization. He even sent out a letter to all the volunteers asking how many of them wanted a motorcycle for their own use.

"We're going to buy motorcycles and build them according to our specifications," he wrote. "Hatzalah will be the first in the world to create a motorcycle that is also an ambulance — an ambucycle."

About fifteen volunteers wanted an ambucycle. Others were skeptical. And in some neighborhoods, once again *pashkevillin* went up accusing Hatzalah of pushing the boundaries in ways that were unacceptable.

But as time passed, people began to understand that using motorcycles to save lives was a game changer in every way, and even opponents of the idea began rethinking their initial stance. Eli started getting more requests from the volunteers living in religious neighborhoods such as Geulah, Ezras Torah, and Meah Shearim, where it had been rare for a resident to ride a motorcycle, telling him that they were ready to

The first ambucycle — donated by the Reichmann family

ride the ambucycles to calls. Suddenly, the sight of a religious Jew with a beard and *peyos* on a motorcycle was reassuring — because it meant that he was utilizing yet another means to save a life.

Despite the advent of the ambucycle, most of the volunteers were still driving cars to get around in those early days. Eli used his father's car and hooked up a cherry light that he could place on the roof when he was riding to a call. Other volunteers brought in lights and sirens from the States and began using them whenever they went out on calls. The local police department wasn't amused, and the volunteers were often pulled over, their lights and sirens confiscated by the police, and given huge fines. Sometimes the police would even confiscate the volunteer's car, claiming that they were driving illegally.

But the volunteers didn't let this stop them from continuing their mission.

"At the end of the day," Eli says, "when you believe in something, you're willing to do whatever it takes to succeed, and that means using Israel's greatest invention to achieve results: chutzpah."

If something needed to be done, Eli was determined to do it, come what may. There was no choice. Not when it came to saving lives. And that was why everything was a possibility and nothing was off the table.

When Eli's friends told him that they needed to get government permits for the ambucycles, Eli responded by telling them that in Israel if you ask for permission for something, you'd be ninety years old before the permits came. Eli knew that simply applying for the permits wasn't the right way to go about it. Instead, they would do what they needed to do — and ask for forgiveness afterward if they got in trouble. (Of course, today all United Hatzalah vehicles, ambucycles included, are officially registered with the government.)

On most occasions, knowing that the ambucycles were on life-and-death calls, the police were helpful and understanding, but there were bound to be a few cops who were sticklers and made it difficult for the men to accomplish their mission.

There was one particular police officer in Yerushalayim who made it his business to spot the Hatzalah volunteers, and whenever he saw anyone driving with a Hatzalah sticker on the car, he would stop him and check to see if he had an illegal siren.

It took a little time, but the Hatzalah members came to understand that he was a rotten cop — the kind of policeman who will harass people until they pay him off. They decided that the time had come to do something about it. If until then the cop had made a point of lying in wait for passing Hatzalah members, now the volunteers turned things around and began following him and watching what he did during the course of the day. They watched his interactions with people, how he would pull over a car for a traffic infraction and accept money in lieu of giving them a ticket.

When they were sure of the facts, Eli had a conversation with the police officer. He contacted him and invited him over to the Hatzalah office and for some reason he agreed to meet. Maybe he came because he thought they were afraid of him and wanted to offer him a bribe.

"What do you want from us?" Eli demanded without preamble when they were sitting together face-to-face.

"I don't want anything," the cop blustered.

"Look, I know very well what type of operation you've been running. I know about the bribery, and I know about the shakedowns. I know that you stop cars that went through red lights and they somehow manage to drive away without getting a ticket from you.

"We know all about you. We know every intersection along your entire route. We know where you stand and stop cars. We know what you do and how you do it."

Eli could see that his words were penetrating. He could see it in the other man's eyes.

"I want you to understand something," Eli went on. "We're not interested in interfering with the things you're doing. We work for Hatzalah. We don't work for the police department. But you need to stop harassing our volunteers. Hatzalah is saving lives. We could end up saving your mother! So remember this: if you continue harassing us, we will make it our business to investigate, which is the last thing you want us to do. Do we understand one another?"

Apparently the message was clear, because the cop backed off, and they never had any trouble from him again.

One afternoon a call came into the dispatch center about a woman who was choking. A volunteer was speeding to her home in the Machaneh Yehudah neighborhood to save her life when he went through a red light and was pulled over by a cop.

"Sir," he told the officer, "I'm on the way to save a person's life!"

"What are you talking about?"

"I'm a Hatzalah member. A call came in for a woman who is choking, and I'm on the way to her house to save her life. Please let me go. You can follow me if you want, but every second that we spend here talking is crucial."

The police officer wasn't convinced and wouldn't allow the volunteer to continue. In the end, other volunteers were sent on the call, while the original volunteer was given a summons to court.

"I came with him to court that day," Eli recalls. "The situation was insane. It didn't make sense that a policeman would pull over a volunteer when he was on the way to save a person's life. I was determined to plead his case to the judge."

When the judge entered the courtroom, the prosecutor presented his case, explaining that the volunteer had driven through a red light at a very fast speed and was a menace on the road.

Things weren't looking very positive for the Hatzalah member — and then Eli Beer asked for permission to say a few words.

"Are you his lawyer?" the judge asked.

"No, Your Honor, I'm not. But I am one of the officers in command of

Hatzalah Yerushalayim, which means that this man is one of my troops, and I'm responsible for his welfare."

The judge gave Eli permission to speak.

"Your Honor, let me tell you about this man. He gets up in the middle of the night — in the dead of winter — to go out and save people's lives. He doesn't let anything get in the way of this. It doesn't matter to him if it's two in the morning or the middle of a Shabbos meal, or if he has to leave work and drop everything to save a life. All he cares about is helping people, and that's why I can't understand how a policeman can heartlessly stop a person who is clearly on his way to save a life and then give him a thousand-shekel ticket on top of that."

The courtroom was still. Everyone turned to look at the police officer to hear what he would say in self-defense.

The police officer tried to sound confident and resolute.

"This man broke the law," he said. "And he drove recklessly, endangering the lives of other drivers and pedestrians alike. I can't allow anyone to break the law in such a derelict manner, no matter who he is or what his reasons are."

After hearing both sides, the judge came to a decision.

"Since the volunteer broke the law," he said, "I have to give him a fine. So I will give him the smallest possible fine that I can give according to the law."

Everyone waited with bated breath.

"I order you to pay eighteen shekels for breaking the law and driving through a red light," the judge declared.

"Thank you, Your Honor," Eli said.

"You're welcome," the judge replied. Then he turned to the volunteer and said, "And if I were you, I would do the exact same thing if it happens again. Next case!"

It wasn't only some traffic cops who caused trouble. Some of the higher-ups in the police department had heard that there were young men belonging to an organization called Hatzalah who were making a practice of driving through red lights and had equipped themselves with lights, sirens, and all sorts of other gadgets, and they didn't like it one bit. Eli went about handling this situation in a different way.

Whenever a donor gave Hatzalah some new equipment, they would hold a ceremony in the donor's honor at Hatzalah headquarters. Eli decided to invite some of the police brass as well, because he knew this was the best way to build a relationship. As Eli had quickly surmised, good relations with the heads of the police were crucial for them to be allowed to do their work.

So Eli invited them to Hatzalah ceremonies and gave speeches praising the invaluable help and assistance they were getting from the police department. They would present the police commanders with beautiful plaques on which they had inscribed their names and rank, giving them something to display proudly in their offices. It wasn't long before the top officials in the police department had developed a positive appreciation for Hatzalah.

Rabbi Moshe Gafni

He also spent time visiting with as many Knesset members as he could, with a focus on the MKs in the religious parties. He became particularly close to a young MK named Rabbi Moshe Gafni who had been sent to the Knesset by Rav Shach. It would prove to be a very fruitful relationship. And he met with Rabbi Aryeh Deri of Shas and many other MKs, spreading the message of Hatzalah and seeking government recognition.

These efforts were to come into play in later years, when Hatzalah became a first-class ambulance service — a service that would eventually be fully recognized by the government.

# CHAPTER TEN

# A Miraculous Birth

It wasn't only a matter of getting the police and the politicians accustomed to the concept of an independent volunteer emergency service. People also needed to learn to accept Hatzalah. They were used to Magen David Adom rescue teams, which were mostly staffed by nonreligious people, and suddenly men with beards were arriving at their door. It took some getting used to.

During one call, Eli responded along with two other men. Both of them were bearded and looked extremely religious. The patient lived on Uziel Street, which was in a part of Bayit Vegan that wasn't particularly religious.

Eli knocked and the wife opened the door. Seeing the beards and the sidelocks, she said, "I didn't call the *chevrah kaddisha*." (The *chevrah kaddisha* is an organization that deals with burying the dead, and it is staffed solely by religious men.)

The volunteers explained that they weren't from the *chevrah kaddisha* but EMTs who were fully equipped to take care of her husband. And they had to do this as the seconds ticked by, knowing that every moment could mean the difference between life and death. But they couldn't enter her home and start performing CPR until she gave them permission to do so.

Finally she stepped aside and allowed them to save her husband's life.

On a different call, Eli was in the middle of performing CPR when the patient's dog, mistakenly thinking that he was attacking his master, bit him. The dog had been cooped up in a different room, and as soon as someone opened the door, it made a beeline straight for Eli and attacked. It was a big dog, and it had big teeth. Fighting off the dog, Eli and the rest of the team ran for the door, managing to escape before they were seriously hurt. One of the family members succeeded in subduing the dog, yanking it back into the next room, and only then were the volunteers able to continue doing CPR.

While he wasn't seriously wounded by the bite, Eli was traumatized and was afraid of dogs for a long time after that ordeal. An important lesson was learned that day: make sure that all dogs are locked up while treating a patient.

In those early years, especially in the very early stages of Hatzalah, there were times when Eli and his fellow volunteers went on multiple calls every day.

"One night, at two in the morning," Eli recalls, "I was on my way home from a call. As I was passing Shmuel HaNavi Street, dispatch informed me that a woman in one of the nearby buildings was about to have a baby.

"As I pulled into the parking lot and jumped out of the car, I tried getting my bearings in the darkened lot of the dingy building with about four entrances. I wasn't sure where to go. Then I heard a man screaming from across the lot, 'Come up here! Come up here!' and I knew that I was in the right place.

"The father was a big Moroccan Breslover chassid, and he kept yelling at me to run after him. I lifted my bag of medical equipment onto my shoulder and followed the man up about seven or eight flights of stairs until we reached an apartment on the top floor of the building.

"When we entered the apartment, we found the man's wife lying on the floor, about to give birth. The lighting in the apartment was very dim, but even so, I was able to see that the umbilical cord was wrapped around the baby's neck and we were dealing with a life-and-death situation. At that point, I had already delivered many babies, and I knew what to do.

"When I was finally holding the newborn baby in my arms, I saw that it was blue and I started giving it oxygen as I did my best to save its life. Meanwhile, the mother kept yelling, 'Is it a boy or a girl? Is it a boy or a girl? Is it a boy or a girl?!'

"Her shouts grew progressively louder, and I wanted to answer her, but I was really very busy trying to save her baby's life. Finally I took a quick glance at the baby and yelled back at the mother, 'It's a boy!'

"The room immediately erupted with 'mazel tovs!' as the mother and father celebrated the birth of a son at the top of their lungs. I ignored them and continued working on the child. At one point, I took another look at the baby and realized that in the heat of the action, I had made a mistake. The baby was a girl, not a boy.

*Eli*, I said to myself, *you're in big trouble here. You're in the home of a Breslover Moroccan family, and no doubt they were anxiously awaiting the birth of a son. You know the place of a baby boy in Moroccan culture… Now you're going to have to break the news that in reality they have a girl and not a boy.*

Meanwhile, the husband had gotten on the phone, and Eli could hear him calling his parents and other relatives and informing them with great joy that his wife had just given birth to a son. They were discussing the upcoming bris, and Eli only grew more nervous as he pictured the couple's reaction when they learned about their new baby daughter.

When the baby was finally settled, Eli went over to the wife. The husband was still on the phone, and the mother was holding her newborn, wrapped snugly in a soft blanket, with an exhausted smile on her face.

"I want to tell you something," Eli said to her.

"Yes?"

"You just experienced a real miracle here tonight."

"What do you mean?"

"I mean that I happened to be passing right near your building when the call came in. I was able to get here just in time."

"*Baruch Hashem!*"

"Yes," Eli confirmed. "*Baruch Hashem.* But I want to ask you a question."

"Okay."

"How many children do you have?"

"We have three children."

"Do you have boys or girls?"

"We have three boys."

A slight twinge of hope began to sprout in Eli's heart.

"You have three boys, and you wanted another one?"

"The truth is, I really wanted a girl, but G-d wanted to give us another boy."

"Let me tell you something. Not only was it a miracle that I reached you in time and the baby is completely healthy — but you had another miracle as well."

"What's that?"

"You have a baby girl."

"What are you talking about?"

"I was so busy just trying to save the baby's life that when you asked me if the baby was a boy or a girl, I made a mistake and told you that it was a boy. But I was wrong and it's really a girl."

The mother broke out in a wide smile. "I can't believe it!" she exclaimed. "I'm so excited! You can't imagine how happy I am right now!"

They called their daughter Faigele and kept in touch with Eli for years.

# Closing a Circle

$\mathcal{L}$ife hadn't been easy for Eli Beer. When he looked at his family, he saw siblings who were successful in a way he could never be. One of his sisters had married the son of Rav Gershon Edelstein, the *rosh yeshivah* (dean) of Ponevezh. One brother was a Gerrer chassid. Another a Lubavitcher chassid. One taught at Aish HaTorah. Another was a rebbi for teenage boys. Eli had always felt like the outlier, like the piece who didn't fit into the family jigsaw puzzle.

With his brothers: (L–R) Tzvi, Eli, Eliyahu, and Moishe

With his mother and brother Avrumi

Growing up, he also had not had the closest relationship with his father. It didn't help that Eli had been kicked out of school and hadn't succeeded in learning like his brothers. But after those two weeks that father and son had spent together in New York, a unique bond was forged between them, a bond that intensified and became more powerful with time, until there was no question of the pride that Gabi Beer felt for the "black sheep" of the family — a sheep who had changed the course of history by the way he lived his life. The two of them shared a passion for lifesaving, and when he watched his son in action, Eli's father was able to recognize the person he had been decades earlier — the drive, the energy, the commitment.

As Eli spent more and more time volunteering for MDA and then Hatzalah, his father asked him why he didn't set aside some of his time to start a business of his own.

"Making money is a good thing, an important thing," Eli would tell his father, "but my passion is saving lives."

In addition to managing his *sefarim* store and dabbling in real estate, Gabi Beer was one of the founders of Eretz HaChaim, a cemetery near Beit Shemesh, and when Eli formed his initial group of lifesavers, his father would jokingly say, "Eli, you're killing my business."

But it was obvious that he couldn't have been more proud of his son, and that meant the world to Eli Beer.

As Eli matured, he returned to yeshivah to learn for periods at a time. He also found that he was drawn to specific types of Jewish books. When he was growing up, one of the big sellers at his father's store was a set of *sefarim* called *Igros Moshe*, books on halachah authored by Rav Moshe Feinstein. The books contained a wide variety of fascinating questions and answers in Jewish law, and Eli enjoyed studying them and still does until this day.

Eli was now dividing his time between learning Torah in yeshivah and different business ventures, while continuing to build Hatzalah at the same time.

As his life fell into a pattern, and he had finally come into his own, Eli felt that the time had come to marry. When he met his future wife, Gitty, he knew from the first moment that she was destined to be his partner for life.

Before he became engaged, he sat down with his soon-to-be father-in-law, Mel Heftler, for a lengthy conversation about his wife's family. Eli felt very comfortable with Mel, especially since he had received *semichah* (rabbinical ordination) from Rav Moshe Feinstein and had been a close student of the rabbi, as his own father had been.

While Eli had known the Heftler family, who also lived in Bayit Vegan, his entire life, he hadn't known their background. Mel told him how he had grown up in the Bronx and how he had worked at the Pioneer Country Club in the mountains, a renowned kosher hotel owned by Leo and Gitel Gartenberg and their

Eli and Gitty Beer as *chassan* and *kallah*

partners, the Schechter family. In those days, the Pioneer was the place to be, the hotel where everyone, including Rebbes and *roshei yeshivah*, spent their vacations. It had even been the venue of the Agudah Convention.

Mel joined the Gartenberg family when he married their daughter Chavi, who had been an infant during the Holocaust and whom Leo found in a Cracow orphanage after the war.

Rabbi Yaakov (Mel) and Chavi Heftler

Leo Gartenberg was a major supporter of the Agudah's lifesaving efforts during the war. After the war, he went to Poland on rescue work. At one orphanage, filled with Jewish orphans, he was introduced to a three-year-old whom he decided to adopt and bring home with him to America.

Leo and Gitel Gartenberg

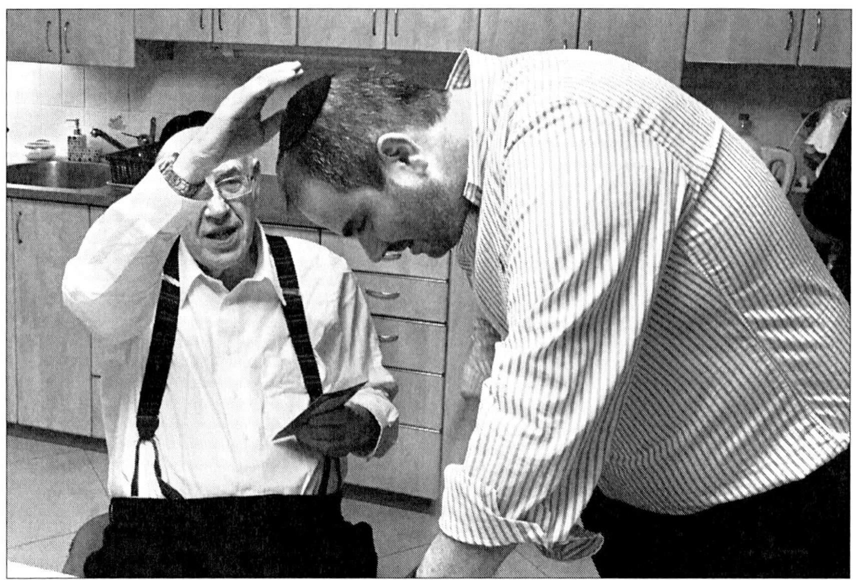

Eli receiving a *berachah* from his father-in-law Rabbi Yaakov (Mel) Heftler

"I learned what it meant to give *tzedakah* from my in-laws," Mel told Eli when he finished telling the story. Mel Heftler himself was a major *baal tzedakah* (contributor of charity), which meant that his in-laws must have been pretty good teachers, indeed.

In the early 1970s, the main building of the Pioneer Country Club burned down after an employee fell asleep with a lit cigarette in his hand, and the era of the Pioneer came to an end. Eventually the Heftler family moved to Israel, where Mel managed the Central Hotel in Yerushalayim together with Rabbi Menachem Porush. Upon their move to Eretz Yisrael, they came to know the Beer family, who ultimately became their *mechutanim*.

As the years passed and Eli's parents grew older, they decided to relocate from Bayit Vegan to Neve Yaakov in the early 2000s, close to where Eli lived with his wife, Gitty, and their children. With none of his brothers living in Yerushalayim, it made sense for his parents to move near Eli.

One Shabbos afternoon, one of their neighbors came to knock on Eli's door.

Eli opened the door.

"Your father's not feeling well."

Eli's parents, Rabbi and Mrs. Beer

Eli raced to his parents' apartment, while Gitty dashed to the car to get the medical equipment and bring it to him.

One look at his father, and Eli knew it was serious.

"Abba, I'm taking you to the hospital. You're having a heart attack."

"No, no, I'm okay. I'm just going to relax a little. I can't go on Shabbos."

"Abba, you're going now! It's *pikuach nefesh*!" (life-and-death matter).

This was a subject that Eli would come to emphasize more and more: the importance of knowing the halachos of *pikuach nefesh*, of knowing when one is permitted to desecrate Shabbos in order to save a person's life. People have the tendency to take the stringent view, as the idea of violating Shabbos is too unthinkable, but the truth is that the Torah mandates that one should go to the hospital even if there's only the slightest chance that there is a serious threat to one's health. They might think that they are treating Shabbos lightly, but in reality they are being stringent with their lives, and that's what the Torah demands.

"Abba," Eli said, "I'm telling you as your son, and also as an EMT, that you're having a heart attack right now and that you need to go to the hospital."

"Okay," Rabbi Beer relented.

And then he collapsed. Cardiac arrest. There was no pulse.

For the first time in his life, Eli Beer forgot everything he knew. At that moment, he barely remembered where he was. He stumbled around as if he were in a nightmare, the kind of nightmare where you try to make a move, but your limbs won't obey.

Gitty, however, didn't lose her bearings. She called United Hatzalah and sounded the alarm. A minute was all it took for the neighbor across the street, a Hatzalah volunteer named Rabbi Yaakov Rosenberg, to come running into the house. Rapidly assessing the situation, he said, "Eli, move aside. I'm going to begin CPR."

Another volunteer arrived a minute later. Then a third volunteer appeared: Mohammed Asli, one of Hatzalah's initial group of Arab volunteers.

They worked on Eli's father while Eli stood to the side and recited *Tehillim* with as much concentration as he could muster. Nine minutes after they started performing CPR, they shocked Gabi Beer with a defibrillator and his pulse returned.

"What happened?" he asked when he woke up, clearly disoriented.

"You went to Heaven for a short visit," one of the medics answered, "but thank G-d, you returned."

An MDA ambulance transported him to the hospital. Soon afterward, a doctor was checking his vitals with Eli hovering nearby.

"Your son saved your life," the doctor told Gabi Beer.

Tears welled up in the corners of Gabi's eyes. "All these years I used to nag you for running out on calls when you were working for me at Eretz HaChaim and in the *sefarim* store. I was trying to run a business, and you were always leaving the office and racing off on Hatzalah calls. I'm so sorry for giving you a hard time. I'm so proud of you, and you'll never hear me complaining again!"

# CHAPTER TWELVE

# The Versailles Epiphany

y the time 1995 rolled around, the founding team of Hatzalah Yerushalayim had come to the realization that something needed to change. Hatzalah was all about relying on volunteers, and it was exactly there that MDA had them in a stranglehold. What if MDA were to decide one day that Hatzalah volunteers could no longer train on the MDA ambulances? Since that was where Hatzalah volunteers received a large part of their training, this was a constant and very valid concern.

Unlike in the early days, when Hatzalah had to listen in on MDA's frequencies on radios smuggled into Israel, nowadays MDA provided them with beepers and had been doing so for years. But if MDA decided to stop allowing them access to their frequencies, Hatzalah would have no way of knowing about the calls that were coming in.

MDA also demanded veto power as to who would be allowed to become a volunteer in Hatzalah. This meant that in some areas of the country, mostly areas where the population was not religious, people who wanted to join Hatzalah were unable to do so, since MDA regarded Hatzalah as an organization for religious volunteers only.

To Eli's mind, the only way to secure their independence was by uniting Hatzalah's ranks. While he would have thought that this was something that would be as obvious to everyone else as it was to him, this wasn't the case, and the tension between the various branches of Hatzalah was only increasing. Eli held out an olive branch to the other groups on a number of occasions, but his offer was rejected again and again.

By 2001, Eli had still managed to avoid running for CEO of Hatzalah Yerushalayim, though he was serving as the acknowledged COO — chief operations officer — a position to which he was elected in 1996. Although he was the official face of the organization, all dealings with banks and government offices were delegated to other people. He wasn't one for sitting behind a desk; he was the commander in the field, the one who made sure that Hatzalah functioned as a professional unit. It was always about saving lives. That had been his focus from the beginning, and it was still his focus now.

Yet as much as he tried to keep his mind focused on the mission, he couldn't deny that he was troubled by the politics within the organization — especially around election times, when new board members were chosen — and by the tensions that existed between the Yerushalayim branch of Hatzalah and the branches in other cities. He felt like some people were forgetting the reason that Hatzalah had been established in the first place.

Then came the second intifada in the early 2000s, when Arab youths took to strapping on suicide vests and blowing themselves up on buses in what felt like a never-ending stream of mind-numbing attacks. Just as the members of Hatzalah were there during the happiest moments of people's lives, such as when they were having a baby, so too they were there during the darkest and harshest hours, during the bomb attacks when it seemed like the reign of terror was never going to end.

The terror attack at the Sbarro pizza store on the corner of King George and Jaffa Road was one of the worst attacks Eli had ever seen. As he walked between the tables trying to make sense of the horrific carnage, Eli saw his cousin Dovie Maisel performing CPR on a child who was lying on the floor. A doctor passed by, stopped in his tracks, and stared at Dovie for a few seconds.

"The kid's dead," he finally said. "Move on to someone else."

"No," Dovie replied with steel in his voice, "I'm going to save him."

Dovie continued working on him, and the boy eventually did return to life. Today he's the father of six children.

Although Magen David Adom's people were the ones transporting the victims to the hospital, it was often the Hatzalah volunteers who were the first responders after the murderous attacks. Since they were usually first on the scene, it was the Hatzalah volunteers who were tasked with performing triage, a responsibility almost beyond human endurance but something that had to be done. Triage means that the EMTs on the scene need to make split-second decisions about who they feel has a better chance of living and who is definitely going to die. The ones with a better chance are the ones that the rescue teams will usually focus their efforts on. When a bomb went off on a bus, and the Hatzalah members found forty wounded people, they needed to decide then and

The number 14 bus after a terrorist attack

there who to start working on, because they were the people with the best chance to survive. It's heart-wrenching but allows for a greater chance of saving lives.

In those days, when the second intifada was at its peak, it seemed to Eli and his team that they were doing triage at the scene of a bombing at least once a week. The number 2 bus attack was absolutely horrific. The number 18 bus — which was blown up twice — was a nightmare come to life.

The Hatzalah volunteers would drive to the site of the bombings, never knowing who they were going to find among the dead. When the number 14 bus was blown up, Dovie Maisel identified his uncle (Eli's cousin), Alan Beer, as one of the victims who perished in the blast. And he wasn't able to stop doing what he was doing just because his uncle had just been murdered. He didn't have the luxury of falling apart and mourning, because there were wounded passengers who could still be saved if he worked fast enough.

It was the same for all the volunteers. They never knew who they would see when they arrived at the scene of an attack.

One Motza'ei Shabbos, a terrorist walked into a bar mitzvah in the Beis Yisrael neighborhood of Yerushalayim and blew himself up in the middle of the room, killing numerous people and turning what was a festive celebration into a bloodbath. Eli and the other volunteers were busy for hours treating children and babies, working feverishly to save their lives.

"Years later, I met one of those kids," Eli says. "He introduced himself to me and reminded me of how I had saved his life on the same night that he'd lost his father in the bombing. I asked him about himself, and we had a conversation. He was married with kids. From the depths of despair to a fulfilling new life.

"I realized for the millionth time how gratified I was with the path I had taken in life. I was at peace with my choices and proud that I had never ignored an emergency — never said no to a person who needed help, never didn't get out of bed on a Friday night because it was freezing cold outside and I was exhausted after a grueling week. It was all worth it, and I knew that given the choice, I would have done it all again."

Even today, volunteers are shocked when they see Eli on a call. Isn't he too busy running the organization? But he wants them to understand that you never grow out of the basics. While you may have become a person who rubs shoulders with world leaders, you're never too busy to save a life.

On May 24, 2001, another tragedy struck Yerushalayim — a tragedy that was enormous in its scope and hit Israel with the force of a gigantic sledgehammer.

The Versailles Wedding Hall disaster remains one of Eli Beer's worst memories from all his years involved in rescue work.

In those days, Eli would do a shift on an ambulance with three of his close friends every Thursday night. One of them was Dave Wolf, who had made aliyah from Holland. That night a call came in from a bar mitzvah that was taking place at one of the many event halls in Talpiot. When Hatzalah arrived, they found that the grandmother of the bar mitzvah boy was suffering from chest pains. They examined her and wanted to take her to the hospital, but she refused to go, determined to remain at the *simchah*, come what may. They tried convincing her to let them take her to the hospital, because that was the right thing to do, but she wouldn't be convinced — and then she started plying them with food.

Feeling that they were given no choice in the matter, the friends sat down to partake of the delicacies. They recharged their batteries and then, after wishing the family mazel tov, began leaving the hall.

That's when they heard the sound of an explosion.

At first, Eli couldn't fathom what had just occurred. He had heard a loud boom, but it didn't sound like there was a terrorist attack. As he reached the street, he caught sight of a white cloud rising into the night sky, and for the life of him he couldn't understand what on earth he was seeing.

It turned out that the Versailles Wedding Hall had just collapsed, causing a huge dust cloud to rise into the air. As Eli and his fellow volunteers raced over to the scene, they saw a man running toward them. He was completely white from head to toe, as if he had fallen into a vat of white flour, and as he ran, he was screaming, "We need ambulances! Send ambulances! A building collapsed!"

"We have an ambulance!" Eli yelled, trying to catch the man's attention. "Where is the building?"

But the man wasn't capable of answering. He just kept on running down the street, screaming.

Eli and his group of EMTs jumped into their ambulance — it was an MDA ambulance, but they were using it with permission for their Hatzalah shift — and he got on the ambulance radio.

"Did anyone hear about any kind of emergency happening right now in Talpiot?"

"Someone was talking about a ceiling collapsing, but the call wasn't clear" was the response.

"They said something about the Versailles Wedding Hall, but we don't really know anything. Go check it out."

Eli didn't waste any time. He drove the ambulance the short distance to the wedding hall, and when he arrived there, he couldn't believe what he was seeing.

"It looked like a scene out of a horror movie," he said. "People were literally hanging from the ceiling, holding on to metal struts that were sticking out of the concrete. In the middle of the room, there were concrete pillars that hadn't collapsed, and there were still some pieces of floor and metal beams attached to the concrete. People were balancing precariously on the tiny leftover pieces of floor, or maybe they were stuck in their place — it was hard to tell — and they were screaming for help.

When Eli first approached the building, he thought that the building had been blown up by a terrorist bomb. The hall's third floor had

The Versailles Wedding Hall after the collapse

collapsed onto the second floor, which in turn had collapsed onto the first.

Eli and his fellow EMTs stood gaping at the nightmarish scene, barely able to process the sight. It didn't look real but like some kind of crazy dream.

But it was real, and it wasn't a dream.

The strangest thing about it was that besides the people who were stranded on the pillars and yelling for help, there wasn't a lot of noise, almost as if he were watching a movie with the sound turned off. Most of the four hundred and fifty people who had been in attendance at the wedding of Keren and Assaf Dror were either shocked from the trauma or had been buried in the rubble.

It was 10:45 p.m., and in Talpiot, it looked like the world was coming to an end.

It turned out that the wedding hall had been originally built with code violations, and people would end up being arrested for all sorts of violations — but that wouldn't matter to all the people whose lives would forever be altered because of the tragedy. Twenty-three people died in the collapse; three hundred and eighty people were injured, many of them seriously. The night would forever be remembered by anyone who was there, because what they witnessed was impossible to forget.

For his part, Eli would never forget the memory of the *kallah* in her white wedding dress, lying on the ground, crying.

Eli caught sight of a person's head sticking out of the rubble and understood that this was the kind of emergency that he and his friends had trained for their entire lives. People were dead and people were injured, and he needed to make sure that every single EMT got themselves over to the wedding hall so they could begin saving lives.

Eli got on the radio in the ambulance and gave the report of his life.

"Command center?"

"This is the command center. Who is this?"

It was his cousin Dovie Maisel, his right-hand man from the very start, who was manning MDA's command center that night.

"Dovie, it's Eli. Listen to me. This is an emergency. The Versailles Wedding Hall in Talpiot just collapsed. I need every single MDA ambulance that's available in Yerushalayim, Maaleh Adumim, Beit Shemesh, and everywhere else in the surrounding area.

"There are hundreds of people injured in what was either a massive terrorist attack or the collapse of the hall's floor. No one should come here with private vehicles. I repeat: This is an emergency of the highest order, and we need ambulances here as soon as is humanly possible!"

That night, Eli wasn't one of the people taking care of the patients. It was his job to be the person on the radio and liaison with the outside world — getting out the reports to all the people who needed to know what was going on. And since he was the commanding officer on the scene, it was also his job to give assignments to every new ambulance that arrived at the hall.

Ten members of Hatzalah were there within a minute — future CEO of United Hatzalah Moshe Teitelbaum among them — and Eli had to yell at him to get his car away from the scene, because they needed room for all the ambulances that were on the way.

The three EMTs who had been with Eli as he headed to the collapse were the ones who went into the rubble and performed the triage, while Eli remained on the radio, continuing to report what he saw, staying calm despite the terrible things that were happening just a few feet away from him. It was the biggest civilian disaster that had happened

Moshe Teitelbaum on the right

since the formation of the State of Israel, and it would remain that way until the Meron tragedy that occurred on April 30, 2021.

Dave Wolf found himself walking around inside the wedding hall in a daze. Then he saw a woman trapped beneath the rubble and trying to get out. She was lying on the ground, struggling. While the majority of his brain was occupied with trying to get her out from beneath the metal struts, another part of his mind noticed that she was holding a purse in her hand — a purse she had managed to retain on her person despite everything that had occurred. Since he needed to get her out, Dave eased the purse out of her hands and underneath his own arm while he worked with all his might to save her life.

Dave did his best to get her out in time, but she was firmly trapped and he was unable to save her. She ended up dying in his arms.

When it was over, Dave was left with her purse.

It was an incredibly traumatic moment for the young man from Holland who had worked so hard to save a woman's life but had been unsuccessful. When he arrived home later that Friday, he suddenly looked at himself and realized that he was still holding the lady's purse.

"Whose purse is this?" his wife asked.

"I don't know her name," he replied. "There was a lady trapped under the metal. During the craziness I put her purse on my arm because it was getting in the way. I guess I never took it off."

They decided to open it and look inside to search for the woman's information. Dave opened the purse. To his shock, he discovered many pieces of expensive jewelry inside, along with a huge amount of cash. Eventually they discovered some documents with the woman's name and address.

Dave and his wife went to pay a shivah call to the family of the purse's owner. When they returned the purse to the lady's relatives, the family couldn't believe it.

"You don't understand what happened here," one of the relatives said. "On the day of the wedding, our mother had a terrible feeling that something bad was about to happen. She knew that she had a wedding to go to that night, but she was afraid that her house was going to burn down — and she decided to take all her valuables with her to the wedding."

Needless to say, the family was incredibly thankful that Dave had come to return the purse.

The Versailles Wedding Hall catastrophe would leave an impression on Eli for the rest of his life. In the moment, he realized how important it is for the person reporting the details of everything happening at a scene to remain calm and collected (even if he is being torn apart on the inside) and to relay factual feedback so that the emergency rescue teams would know what needed to be done.

After a while, Eli handed over the job to another volunteer — Gilad Bok — and ran inside since he felt that he needed to help some victims himself, though he knew that the role he had been playing was crucial and had to be done.

Within three and a half hours, all the wounded who weren't completely trapped beneath the rubble had been removed and were on their way to the hospital. Hatzalah and Magen David Adom weren't equipped to move huge piles of rubble. For that, the army's Home Front Command had to come with their tractors and heavy equipment, and that took time since they are not on call twenty-four seven like the emergency response teams. But every single Hatzalah volunteer was there, as well as many MDA personnel, working nonstop to save as many lives as they possibly could.

It was yet another wake-up call reminding Eli of the importance of uniting all the different branches of Hatzalah. He was able to see in real time how much more effective they could be — and needed to be — if they worked together. One simply couldn't compare having volunteers from just one city available to send out on calls (no matter how many there were) with having the ability to call volunteers from all over the country as part of the same network. Eli knew that they would have to unite, that the infighting and disagreements had to stop — for the sake of the people they all wanted to help.

"I remained at the scene until just before Shabbos," Eli says. "There were a lot of people who were trapped but still alive under the rubble, and I was there to treat them when the army extracted them from underneath the beams and the concrete. I myself treated around one hundred people from Thursday night until Shabbos.

"At that moment I suddenly grasped our role in the most authentic and genuine way. We were soldiers on the battlefield of life. It was our job to deal with the worst tragedies that hit our fellow citizens and to take care of our people when they were hurt and wounded. It was our job to do the hardest things that needed to be done, and if we needed to mourn, we would have to wait until the job was over. We were soldiers, and a soldier doesn't have the liberty of mourning whenever he wants."

Eli arrived home as the sun was setting, and Shabbos was descending on the Land of Israel. Having been on the scene for almost twenty-four hours, he was drained and could barely think or talk. For the next three days, he was unable to sleep. Whenever his eyes drifted closed, all he saw were the faces of the people trapped beneath the rubble or hanging from the pillars — some deceased, others calling for help, begging for someone to come and save their lives.

His mind kept replaying the scene where he carried the *kallah* out of the wedding hall. She had fallen from the height of three floors and was seriously injured. He'd been through many traumatic moments until that night, but nothing had prepared him for what he had seen at that hall.

He didn't believe he would ever be able to fall asleep again.

Yet something had happened to him during that twenty-four-hour period. He had come to a recognition during that night of sadness, death, and loss. While giving clear and fluid guidance to thousands of people throughout the night that never seemed to end, Eli Beer came to understand something about himself.

At that moment, he grasped that he had been blessed with genuine leadership skills from the One above and that he was meant to use them for the sake of *Klal Yisrael.*

Little did he know that those skills would be put to the test in a very big way before the year was out. In the meantime, what happened at the Versailles Wedding Hall was a milestone in his decision to do whatever it took to unite all the branches of Hatzalah under one umbrella.

# The Biggest Operation Yet

There was no question in Eli's mind that for Hatzalah to become truly effective, all the branches would have to unite under one umbrella. But at the moment it seemed like that was a dream whose day would never come.

He tried opening a dialogue with the people at Hatzalah Bnei Brak many times, but it never came to anything. Eli knew that the only way they would ever be able to unify the various branches was if something big happened that would force everyone to realize that the real power lay in one unified force.

There was also something else troubling him. All the members of Hatzalah were religious men. But he knew that the organization wouldn't be able to grow and become a truly powerful lifesaving force until they also began including volunteers who weren't religious. He felt that when it came to saving lives, every person who fit their criteria should be given the opportunity to get involved. Only then would they be able to start reaching the entire population of Israel in shorter amounts of time. Sure, there were plenty of volunteers in Yerushalayim, Bnei Brak, Kiryat Sefer, Beitar, and Beit Shemesh. But if a person tried calling for Hatzalah in Herzliya or Caesarea, they wouldn't get a response, because the organization was barely active in cities that did not have a large religious population.

Change was sorely needed. The question was how to make that happen.

Eli had started off with a dream to save a life. Then he had another dream: to reach every emergency call in under ninety seconds.

That dream had grown into yet another dream: to save six million lives.

Now the dream had taken on another dimension: to unite the various branches of Hatzalah into one organization that would work together as a cohesive unit.

Lots of dreams. But how to realize them?

Then, on November 2, 2001, Rav Elazar Menachem Mann Shach, *rosh yeshivah* of Ponevezh and the *gadol hador* (leader of the generation) of Israeli Jewry, passed away, and everything changed.

The funeral was scheduled to take place on the day after the *gadol* passed away, and the police were predicting the arrival of record crowds from all over the country. The moment he heard the news, Eli Beer called together his operational team — the group of people who ran the different units of Hatzalah Yerushalayim — and addressed them with a brief speech.

"Rav Shach's *levayah* will be taking place tomorrow morning in Bnei Brak. No one is going to sleep tonight. This is going to be one of the biggest operations we've ever been involved in.

"First of all, I want every single truck and ambulance that we have to

Rav Shach's *levayah* in Bnei Brak

go out and collect as much medical equipment as we can pull together. This is going to be the biggest funeral Israel has seen in years, and we need every piece of equipment we can spare."

"Where do we get the equipment?" someone asked.

"Anywhere in the country, wherever you can find it. Next, I want you to go out and purchase at least ten truckloads of water. It's supposed to be extremely hot tomorrow, and we need to buy thousands of bottles of water so that we'll be able to distribute a bottle to anyone who needs it. Buy every bottle you can lay your hands on."

"What's our budget?" someone asked.

"Empty our bank accounts for this."

They nodded.

"What time do we need to be in Bnei Brak tomorrow morning?" another asked.

"Every single member of Hatzalah Yerushalayim must be parked and ready to begin their day in the vicinity of the Ponevezh campus at six in the morning."

It was like they were planning a war campaign under the leadership of General Eli Beer. In reality, that was exactly what it was.

As the people of Israel slumbered fitfully in preparation for the day to come, Eli and the members of Hatzalah Yerushalayim stayed up the entire night to prepare for the morrow. They cleaned out every supermarket they could find of every bottle of water on their shelves, spending thousands of shekels in the process and filling trucks and ambulances with the precious cargo.

At six in the morning, they were all there, parked outside the yeshivah and awaiting further instructions from their chief. There were twenty Hatzalah Yerushalayim vehicles on the spot and one hundred and fifty volunteers in place. Every truck and ambulance were outfitted with big signs that stated in bold lettering, "Hatzalah Yerushalayim." By seven in the morning, there were already thousands of people gathered in every street and alley leading to Ponevezh. The crowds enveloped the Hatzalah vehicles and pinned them in place. The roofs of all the trucks and ambulances had been outfitted with giant stickers emblazoned with the words "Hatzalah Yerushalayim," and they were clearly visible in the videos taken by the media crews from their helicopters above.

Eli himself was stationed in the *rosh yeshivah's* room — right beside the bed — and he was the one who decided who went in and out of the immediate area where the eulogies were delivered.

In the wake of the funeral, everyone understood that Hatzalah Yerushalayim's involvement had been a literal lifesaver. They had done a great job of keeping hundreds of thousands of people safe. People could have fainted or died from heatstroke had Hatzalah not purchased all those bottles of water to give out. Eli had been sure that they would be competing with the police and other organizations to see who could hand out more water. But in reality, they were the only ones who had prepared any water at all for the crowds. The volunteers must have given out twenty thousand bottles, using every last bottle at their disposal.

Today Reb Mutty Barzilai, former head of Hatzalah Bnei Brak, is a close friend of Eli Beer's and is on the board of United Hatzalah. But in order for that to happen, something big had to happen.

And it happened that day.

In Bnei Brak.

Because after that day — the day Hatzalah Yerushalayim showed the country what it was capable of doing — Hatzalah Bnei Brak finally decided that they were ready to start working with their rival. When Eli Beer reached out to them on the day after the funeral and asked if they could meet, they agreed.

The meeting took place at Hello Teiman, a shwarma restaurant located at the gas station right outside the city, and it was there that the two sides finally sat down together. Understandably, the leadership of Hatzalah Bnei Brak was upset at their counterparts in Yerushalayim for taking over what they felt was supposed to be their show. But for the first time they listened when Eli Beer made an impassioned argument concerning how much better it would be for everyone involved if they put aside their differences and began working together as one united organization.

It would take time (years, in fact) until that happened, but that day was a start, and Eli knew that if the first step had been taken, it was only a matter of time until the next steps followed. And when everything came together and unity reigned, he knew there would be no stopping them.

# PART THREE

*My kids refer to me as 'Abba shebashamayim' — father in heaven — because I'm always flying somewhere to raise money for United Hatzalah.*

— Eli Beer

# CHAPTER FOURTEEN

# Meeting Mark Gerson

Ask anyone who runs an organization, and they'll tell you that starting an organization is one thing, but the real challenge is financing it on a daily, weekly, monthly, and yearly basis. How do you keep it up and running? How do you convince donors from around the world that your organization is the one they need to support when there are so many worthy causes out there?

For United Hatzalah it boils down to one thing: being able to convey the fact that United Hatzalah had been founded because of a desperate need — the need to reach emergencies fast enough to make a difference.

And Eli learned how to tell the story.

Back in the early days, money started to come in from the United States, but it was nowhere near the levels needed to grow the organization and realize all of Eli's ambitions. This meant that Eli was going to have to leave Israel and do some traveling.

In the summer of 2002, Eli flew to America to meet with a potential donor. Eli had been introduced to Daniel Schwartz by a mutual friend. Daniel lived in New York City and worked for a well-known hedge fund called York Capital on Park Avenue. He was a successful businessman, but at the same time he was a quiet and humble person, humble about himself and his achievements, and he encouraged Eli to tell him all about Hatzalah.

Eli told Daniel all about Hatzalah's motorcycle unit and shared his vision for the future. He explained that at the moment the unit was still very small and underfunded.

"Sometimes we don't even have money to buy insurance for the motorcycles," he told Daniel.

"What happens then?"

"Then we have to put them aside. No choice."

Daniel made it very easy for Eli. He didn't make him work hard for the money he needed.

"You know what?" he said. "I want to donate an ambucycle in memory of my wife Debbie's father. How much does it cost?"

Later on, Eli calculated the cost of an ambucycle differently because he began figuring in insurance and maintenance, but back then he charged just for the motorcycle itself.

"Eighteen thousand dollars."

"Okay," Daniel said. "I'll give you eighteen thousand dollars, and I want you to write my father-in-law's name on the motorcycle."

Eli was overcome. No one had ever done such a thing for him before. It was hard to believe that a person he had just met was willing to give him such a large check. He almost had to pinch himself to make sure he wasn't dreaming.

"Listen," Daniel said after the deal was done, "I have a friend I think you should meet. His name is Bert Cohen. Bert is a partner in a big investment firm, and he loves Israel. I think he'll give you a donation, too."

Daniel called Bert Cohen on the spot. "No problem," Bert said. "Send him over right now."

Daniel's introduction to Bert Cohen was the start of a process that snowballed into something huge. Every time they meet, Eli likes to remind his old friend that it all began because of him and the connections he made.

This story took place before Eli really knew his way around Manhattan. For years, he did his best to stay far away from Manhattan due to the traumatic experience he'd had the first time he visited the city. The upshot of this was that he didn't know how to get to Bert's office. While he tried figuring it out, he called his wife.

"Gitty, you're not going to believe what happened."

"What happened?"

"Someone just donated eighteen thousand dollars to buy an ambu-cycle."

"Eli, that's amazing!"

"There's more. He called up a friend of his while we were meeting and asked him to meet me so that he could give us a donation, too."

Meanwhile, Eli left the underground parking lot where he'd parked his car during his meeting with Daniel and set out to meet Bert. This was a mistake since Bert's office was situated just around the corner, and he could have walked there a lot quicker. Then he made a wrong turn, and soon he didn't know where he was. The fact that he was supposed to be sitting with another donor in his office instead of idling in traffic made things a million times worse.

Finally he decided to just call Bert and tell him that he was lost.

"Mr. Cohen," Eli said when he answered the call, "this is Eli Beer. I'm supposed to be at your office right now, but I took a wrong turn and now I'm lost."

"Where are you?"

Eli looked for a street sign and told Bert Cohen where he was.

"Pull over to the side of the street and wait for me," Cohen said. "I'm leaving the office and coming to you."

Eli couldn't believe it. First Daniel Schwartz gave him eighteen thousand dollars just like that, and now Bert Cohen was actually leaving his office and coming to meet with him. It was hard to process that people were coming to him so that they could give him money.

A few minutes later, Eli saw Bert running toward the car.

"How far is your office from here?" he asked him when he reached the vehicle.

"Five blocks."

"You ran five blocks to meet me?"

Eli stared at Bert. The man was well dressed in a classy suit and tie, yet he had just run out of his corporate office for the opportunity to give *tzedakah*. Bert slipped his hand into his jacket pocket and pulled out a check.

The check was written out for five thousand dollars.

"Daniel explained what you're doing, and it sounds great," Bert said. "Keep up the wonderful work!"

Eli was happy about the five thousand, but a little disappointed that he hadn't been given the opportunity to explain about Hatzalah in depth and ask Bert to pay for a motorcycle just like his friend. It was clear to him that he was going to have to return and have another meeting with Bert Cohen, when he would hopefully have the chance to describe his vision and ask for another motorcycle. But he was very thankful that he was holding a check for five thousand dollars.

"Thank you so much for your donation," he told Bert.

"No problem," Bert replied. "And I want you to meet another friend of mine as well. Your organization is exactly the kind of cause that I can see him supporting. He's a young guy — about your age, twenty-eight, twenty-nine — and he started a business and is doing well. I think you guys are going to get along, especially since he hasn't had much to do with Israel until now and he wants to find out more."

"I'll be happy to meet him," Eli said. "What's his name?"

"Mark Gerson."

Bert promptly pulled out his phone and called Mark.

"Mark, it's Bert Cohen. Listen, there's a guy here from Israel who I want you to meet."

"What's his name?"

"Eli Beer. He's doing big things, and I have a feeling you're going to want to get involved. Can you meet him?"

"You know what?" Mark said. "Ask him if we can meet for lunch tomorrow."

Eli nodded. Lunch was good.

"Where does he want to go?" Mark asked.

Bert relayed the question.

"Anywhere is good as long as it's kosher."

"We'll go to Wolf and Lamb," Mark decided.

And that was that.

Eli left Manhattan, unable to contain his excitement. He had received a commitment for eighteen thousand dollars, and he had a check in his pocket for another five and a meeting with another prospective donor the next day. This was huge.

He drove back to Brooklyn, where friends of his had graciously offered to host him. They wanted him to stay in their house, but Eli, wanting privacy and the ability to come and go whenever he needed, opted to stay in their basement apartment. It was bitterly cold outside and raining steadily and, since the basement wasn't well insulated, pretty cold inside as well.

There was food waiting for him when he came in, but he was so tired that he just took off his shoes and lay down on the bed, intent on taking a short nap. He was drifting off to sleep when he caught a flurry of movement out of the corner of his eye. The fear of a furry intruder woke him up completely, and he sat up in bed and watched in horror as a small gray mouse raced across the basement floor and took a flying leap into his shoe.

Eli wasn't used to mice. Cats, yes. Dogs, yes. But not mice. Grabbing all his belongings, he stepped into a pair of slippers and exited the basement to take refuge in his car, leaving his shoes behind. It was a move guaranteed to make a very happy mouse.

He slept fitfully, dozing on and off until the first rays of sunlight broke through the gray clouds above, bringing the joy of morning to Brooklyn. He didn't feel rested at all, and that wasn't good considering that he had a very important meeting scheduled. But there was nothing to do about it. Groggy and disoriented, he tried to make sense of his surroundings, until the events of the previous night came back to him and he recalled the horror he had felt upon seeing the flash of gray fur diving into his shoe. Shaking his head as if to clear it from the cobwebs, Eli decided that there was one thing he needed right now more than anything else, and that was a hot shower.

Wasting no time, he pulled away from the curb and drove over to a nearby shul to find a *mikveh* (ritual bath). Then, feeling fresh and clean, it was time to pay homage to his Creator. When he was finished praying, he went looking for a shoe store. He bought a pair of shoes at Payless, purchased some pastries and coffee in a nearby bakery, and headed into Manhattan for his meeting with Mark Gerson.

Not interested in getting lost in the city again, Eli elected to take the train. No sitting in traffic, no getting lost, and no worrying about parking.

The train ride passed with surprising ease, and soon he was walking through the doors of Wolf and Lamb, an upscale, wood-paneled steakhouse, where Mark Gerson was waiting for him.

Gerson was dressed simply in a jacket, sneakers, and a baseball cap, and Eli walked over to him and asked, "Are you Mark Gerson?"

"Yes," he replied, and they shook hands.

When the waiter came by and asked what they wanted to order, Mark asked for a chicken salad, so Eli also asked for a chicken salad. Mark ordered Diet Coke, so Eli had one, too. This would become a trademark move: to find out what the donor likes to eat and have it with him.

Mark was very young but at the same time incisive and deep. He was also methodical and analytical, and he asked Eli a million questions about Hatzalah and how it worked. Eli was very impressed by Mark Gerson. He was intellectually brilliant and was clearly very focused on helping further good causes.

He was also fascinated by Israel — by the country, by the people, and by the politics. He kept asking questions, and Eli answered every one to the best of his ability. He asked the kinds of questions that Eli would want someone to ask him — the kinds of questions that would help him understand the inner workings of the organization. When Eli told Mark how babies were choking to death because help wasn't coming fast enough, Mark's eyes filled with tears.

Finally, Mark said, "I want to get involved. What do you want from me?"

"Would you agree to donate an ambucycle to Hatzalah?"

"How much is it?"

"Eighteen thousand dollars."

On the spot, Mark pulled out his checkbook and wrote a check.

"Who would you like to honor on the ambucycle?"

"No one. It's not about the honor. I just want to help the organization."

Eli then went out on a limb.

"Mark, can I ask you a question?"

"Go on."

"What would you think about becoming the chairman of our board here in the States? Would you be open to doing that?"

Eli was thinking on his feet here, going with what he felt was the right move for Hatzalah. He could see the sincerity in Mark's eyes and instinctively felt that he could trust Mark to be there for him and help the organization grow.

"Eli, I don't mind getting involved with your board," Mark replied, "but I don't think it makes sense for me to be the chairman since I'm just getting started in the business world and am not well known yet. It would make more sense for you to find someone better connected and famous than I am."

"I think you should be the one to serve as chairman," Eli insisted.

"Why is that?" Mark asked him.

"Because at the moment you're the only one on the board."

It was a joke, but at the same time it was true, and Mark appreciated the way Eli delivered the line.

"Okay," he said, "but I want you to replace me as soon as you find someone better."

Eli shook his head. "Once you're in, you're in. Once you're the chairman, that's it. I won't be looking for anyone else."

"By the way," Mark said, "how much did Bert Cohen give you yesterday?"

"Five thousand dollars."

"Wait a second. I just gave you eighteen thousand dollars, and Bert, who referred you to me, gave five?"

He immediately took out his phone and called Bert.

"Bert, I can't believe this. I just gave Eli Beer eighteen thousand dollars, and he told me you gave five thousand. What's going on here?"

"Okay, Mark," Bert replied. "Send him over to my office, and I'll give him another thirteen thousand."

It was incredible. For the first time in his life, Eli was holding fifty-four thousand dollars in his hands. He had raised a lot of money before, but that had been small donations. He had never been able to raise these large sums in the past, and the truth is, he'd never even tried. Suddenly he understood that nothing was impossible and that there were a lot of people out there with a lot of money who want to give large sums to worthy causes. Suddenly he understood that he needed to find more people who would be willing to join their board and help Hatzalah reach the sky. The people and the money were out there — it was just a question of finding the right team and convincing them to join.

Eli met with Mark Gerson the next day, and they discussed building a board in the States.

"If you could come up with some potential candidates for our board," Eli told Mark, "then I'll go and meet them."

On the spot, Mark suggested several names, and Eli took down their contact information. Mark also promised to organize a parlor meeting in his home during Eli's next trip to the States.

"Tell me when you're coming in, and I'll bring a group of my friends together at my apartment. You'll speak and we'll raise some serious money."

So it was that Mark and Eli became close friends. In fact, Eli Beer considers Mark the cofounder of the organization. At the same time, he never forgot Daniel Schwartz and Bert Cohen, because it was their generosity that taught him that his dream was attainable.

As the years passed, Eli watched as the chairman of his international board achieved great financial success. Over time, Mark Gerson began hosting beautiful Friday night dinners at his Manhattan apartment to which he would invite many friends, and would have it catered by a kosher catering company.

Eli would do his best to attend Mark's dinners whenever he was in town. After davening at a local shul, he would be the one to make Kiddush for the assembled and would deliver some sort of Torah message, usually from the *parashah* of the week. In a certain sense, Eli Beer had become something of a rabbinical figure to Mark's friends, and he ended up meeting numerous special people at Mark's home, many of whom became supporters of Hatzalah.

Mark met his wife, Erica, when she came as a guest at a Friday night meal. It was obvious from the start that the two were a match. It wasn't long before Mark and Erica were wed at a private ceremony attended mainly by family members.

Together, Mark and Erica are a great team who are constantly giving *tzedakah*, and their relationship with United Hatzalah has only intensified through the years. Today they donate five million dollars annually for many lifesaving projects and for maintaining the organization. They encourage others to donate the ambucycles and let them receive the recognition and limelight, while they are content to pay for items that most donors would rather avoid paying for, such as salaries, electricity, and other expenses.

Mark is still the chairman of the organization's international board

Mark and Erica Gerson visiting Mearas HaMachpeilah

today — all these years later. Eli is merely following Mark's directive, since Mark told him when he first agreed to accept the position that he was going to serve as chairman of the board only until Eli found someone better.

Well, that has yet to happen, and Eli is pretty sure it never will.

One Friday night in 2007, Eli attended the meal at Mark's home, as he often did when in town, and he met an Israeli named Yaron Carni.

Carni grew up in a secular home and attended a university in Herzliya. As a child, he had never kept Shabbos or had even been to shul. Yaron came to America after college and once in New York he was introduced to Mark Gerson. They became friends and business partners. Yaron also began attending Mark's Friday night meals.

When Yaron caught sight of Eli Beer and his black *yarmulke*, he went over to Mark and said, "Why on earth have you brought a *chareidi* man into your home? These *chareidim* are the worst!"

Yaron couldn't believe that a man of the world like Mark Gerson would make the mistake of associating with an Orthodox Jew, and he made no secret of his feelings.

Mark looked at Yaron and said, "What are you talking about? I don't see any difference between Eli and anyone else. Eli is a fine human being. You should go meet him! Why does it matter if he's wearing a *kippah* on his head?"

Seeing that he wasn't succeeding in getting through to his host, Yaron approached the man in the black *kippah*, and before Eli knew what was happening, the stranger from Israel was attacking him with all the arguments and clichés that some secular people use when their paths happen to cross with those of the religious public.

"I want to tell you something about going to the army," Eli told Yaron.

"What's that?"

"I built an army of my own in Israel. And most of the members of my army are religious Jews."

"What do you mean?"

"I mean that I run an army of rescue volunteers, guys who will leave their homes in the middle of their Shabbos meals and save the lives of people like you. They don't care whether you're wearing a *kippah* on your head or not. They don't care if you're rich or poor, old or young, man or woman. If someone has an emergency and their life is in danger, my guys are there. We're an army of lifesavers — so please don't bring the hatred you were fed growing up into this house!"

Carni fell silent at Eli's words. Then he said, "Okay, fine. Why don't we get to know one another?"

So they started talking. And they didn't stop for the rest of the meal.

When dinner was over, Yaron said to Eli, "I'll walk you back to where you're staying."

After saying goodbye to Mark Gerson, they left the apartment and Eli headed to the staircase. It was thirty-five flights of stairs down to the ground floor of the building, and Yaron Carni walked him down. When they exited the building, Yaron asked him where he needed to go.

"It's about twenty blocks from here."

Yaron put out his arm to hail a cab.

"No," Eli told him, "no taxis. I have to walk. It's Shabbos today, and on Shabbos we walk, so walk with me."

"Really? It's too far."

"Look, if you want to continue our conversation, then walk with me because I don't ride in cars on Shabbos."

They started walking together.

"I'm very interested in everything that you told me about your organization and I plan to look into it, to make sure that it's trustworthy. I have a legal background — I studied law — and if you're a good organization, I'm going to eat my hat."

"Go right ahead," Eli told him mildly.

"Where are you located?" Yaron asked.

"We're in Yerushalayim. Will you be coming to Israel anytime soon?"

"I'll be there next week."

"Then come by, and I'll give you a tour."

They ended up standing outside on the streets of Manhattan for a while and then sitting in the lobby of the building where Eli was staying, talking for the next four hours, and turning from would-be enemies into the best of friends.

Yaron was true to his word. When he arrived in Israel the following week, he contacted Eli and came to meet him at Hatzalah headquarters in Yerushalayim, where he spent half a day there as Eli gave him an in-depth tour of every aspect of the organization.

He was mesmerized. When the tour was over, Yaron found himself eminently satisfied by everything he had seen, and he pulled a checkbook out of his pocket and wrote a check for eighteen thousand shekels.

"This is the largest sum of charity I've ever given in my life," he told Eli. "From now on I'm supporting you. More than that, I'm about to launch a brand-new fund, and I plan on donating two percent to Hatzalah any time it makes a profit."

When they parted, Eli gave Yaron a hug in true Eli Beer fashion. And since that day, Eli and Yaron find themselves in touch usually once or twice a day.

Tammy and Ambassador David Friedman are Eli's old friends, and Eli has spent many an enjoyable Shabbos at their home in the Five Towns. David was one of his first board members and the Friedmans are great friends of United Hatzalah (a lot more on them later.)

The first time Yaron Carni kept an entire Shabbos from A to Z was at the home of David and Tammy Friedman. And as they were sitting together at the Shabbos table, and Eli saw that Yaron was really doing it — he didn't even have his phone with him — he couldn't help but remember the first time they met and how Yaron had tried to have him kicked out of Mark Gerson's home...

# CHAPTER FIFTEEN

# The Fall of a Lion

he second intifada continued unabated. During Pesach of 2002, a terrorist killed thirty people in the middle of their Pesach Seder at the Park Hotel in Netanya. The situation had spiraled out of control, and it seemed like the Israeli security forces were having little success at restoring any semblance of calm and stability to the streets of Israel.

Moshe Teitelbaum, Eli Beer, and Nir Barkat

It wasn't even a bad few months or a bad year. It was a never-ending stream of nightmarish events and almost every day seemed to bring another tragedy. Hatzalah was busier than ever.

Future mayor of Yerushalayim Nir Barkat was among those who saw the effectiveness of Eli's team up close. His introduction to Hatzalah happened on February 22, 2004, the day the number 14 bus was blown up across the street from the Liberty Bell Park in downtown Jerusalem.

"I saw the bus seconds before the explosion," Barkat remembers. "It was twenty or thirty meters away from me when it exploded. The bus appeared to expand and contract, with pieces of metal flying everywhere. I immediately understood that a bomb had exploded.

"I left my car at the gas station across the street and was the first to arrive at the scene. I remember being surrounded by total silence right after the shock of the explosion. And then, after about a minute, I could hear people crying, and the silence evaporated and was replaced by the noise of a critical emergency. I had been a company commander with the paratroopers. I had been in wars and had basic medical training so I went to see if I could help. I entered the bus and started taking people out. In the beginning, it was just me taking the injured people out of the bus.

"All of a sudden, I noticed a huge puddle of blood surrounding one of the girls I had brought out of the bus and laid on the sidewalk. The puddle was spreading more by the second. I gave her a quick examination and determined that a piece of shrapnel had pierced her artery, which was causing the blood to come gushing out of her body like a fountain. I knew that I needed to stop the blood, so I put my finger on the hole and I waited. During one of the wars, a soldier died in my hands because he had a dozen holes in his body and there was nothing I could do about it. But in this case, there was one wound, and I was able to keep the blood from spurting with my finger.

"I remember waiting for someone to come, and it wasn't long before the guys from Hatzalah arrived on the scene. They were there before anyone else, and they took over for me. When that girl arrived at Hadassah Hospital, she was down to her last drops of blood, but they managed to save her life."

These were tough years for the volunteers. It seemed like something traumatic was happening every other day, and they could barely catch their breath. They'd wake up in the morning and wonder what lay in store for them that day.

No, it wasn't an easy time to be a volunteer for Hatzalah.

September 9, 2003, was a particularly traumatic day. That morning there was a terrorist attack near the city of Holon, and many people were injured and killed. Eli was in Tel Aviv at the time, and he headed to Holon as fast as he could the moment he heard the news.

The scene was bad. What was worse was that it was a scene that kept on repeating itself. Just the previous month, a terrorist had blown himself up on the number 2 bus on Shmuel HaNavi Street, killing dozens of innocent people. Eli would never be able to forget the things he saw that night on Shmuel HaNavi Street. The bus had been blown up and was stranded at the traffic circle near the intersection. The number of dead and wounded was catastrophic.

A few months after the Shmuel HaNavi attack, New York mayor Michael Bloomberg and former mayor Ed Koch came to Israel, and an ambucycle was dedicated to Hatzalah at the scene of the bus number 2 terrorist attack in honor of Mayor Bloomberg's visit to Yerushalayim.

Dr. David Applebaum was sitting next to Eli at that event. Dr. Applebaum had made aliyah from the States and had changed the face of emergency medicine in Israel, opening the pioneering Terem urgent care network and later serving as director of the Shaare Zedek Medical Center emergency room. When Eli was younger, he did shifts at Magen David Adom with Dr. Applebaum, who was a doctor assigned to one of the intensive care ambulances. Eli looked up to the American doctor and considered him a true mentor. Dr. Applebaum taught Eli a lot, both with regard to professionalism and when it came to matters of Jewish law. Eli saw the doctor operate under pressure and watched the way he handled himself in the aftermath of terrible bomb attacks with multiple casualties and fatalities. He saw the way he would wait outside the hospital and do the triage.

During the ceremony, Dr. Applebaum turned to Eli and said, "I hope that this ambucycle never has to be used because of a terrorist attack. I hope that you just end up using it to save lives and to deliver babies…"

Eli hoped so, too.

Tragically, the attack in Holon happened just a few short weeks later.

Eli returned to Yerushalayim from the blood-soaked streets of Holon exhausted physically, mentally, and emotionally. He had a meeting that evening at the Laromme Hotel (now called the Inbal) near the Liberty Bell Park, and he rode there on his Hatzalah ambucycle. There was a lot of traffic in the capital that night, and he wasn't far from his destination when he heard a huge explosion from the direction of the German Colony.

At first, he thought he was imagining things. But it didn't take long for him to figure out that a terrorist attack had struck Yerushalayim once again.

As he drove at high speed toward Emek Refaim Street, Eli saw hordes of hysterical people running toward him and away from the scene of the attack. Moments later, he reached Café Hillel.

"It was a complete and utter nightmare. I saw people lying dead on the floor. There was blood everywhere — the sight made that much worse by the plates of ice cream and cups of coffee still sitting on the tables.

"A man was lying on the floor. I looked at him. It was obvious that he wasn't alive anymore. I saw that he had a beeper on him — the beeper used by members of Hatzalah and MDA to receive emergency calls. The beeper was beeping away."

Eli took a closer look and realized that he recognized the man lying there.

It was Dr. David Applebaum.

"I didn't know what to do or say. I didn't want to be the one to announce such terrible news. I was afraid that if I put such an idea out into the world, it might make it come true!

"I stared at my friend, at the man I loved so much, and I asked myself, 'How could such a thing happen? How can the world go on without Dr. Appelbaum, his gentle smile and his golden heart?"

While all this was going on, the medical staff was still performing CPR on a young girl, not knowing that she was Dr. Applebaum's daughter, Naava, a *kallah* who had been engaged to a boy named Chanan Sand.

Naava and Chanan were to be married the very next day.

Eli walked around the area, dazed. David Applebaum had been one of Eli's beloved mentors. He discovered that the young girl who'd been receiving CPR had died as well — and she was David Applebaum's daughter, murdered on the night before her wedding.

Eli was broken beyond anything he had ever experienced.

Normally Eli would have poured out his heart to his wife. But Gitty was in labor just then with their fourth child, who would be born two days later. It was a boy, and Eli wanted to name the baby Dovid Yaakov after Dr. Applebaum.

Gitty liked the idea very much, but her father's name was Yaakov Yechiel Michel, and he was still living. She was also concerned about calling the baby after someone who had passed away so tragically.

Eli promptly called Tzvi Sand, the *chassan*'s father, and asked him what he thought of the idea.

"I will speak to Mrs. Applebaum, and I'll call you back."

Tzvi called Eli back a short while later and told him that the family said they would be honored to have the baby named after Dr. Applebaum.

One hurdle cleared, Eli went to see Rav Mordechai Eliyahu and laid out all the concerns for the chief rabbi of Israel.

"Instead of calling him Dovid Yaakov," the *rav* suggested, "call him Yisrael David. Change one of the names and change the order."

And so it came to be that Yisrael David Beer was brought into the

Sruly Beer's *upsherin* at the Kosel with Eli and his two grandfathers

Yisrael David Beer as a young boy

covenant of Avraham Avinu a week later. As he gazed at his son lying on a pillow on the lap of his grandfather, Reb Yaakov Yechiel Michel (Mel) Heftler, Eli was overcome — by the moment, by the idea that he was naming his son after someone he had so loved and revered, and by a sense of genuine happiness because he had been blessed with a son, the next link in the chain of the generations of *Klal Yisrael*.

# CHAPTER SIXTEEN

# The First Hatzalah Video

Ron and June Daniels have been major supporters of Eli's work for many years. Like so much in his life, their relationship developed through a fascinating set of events.

It all started on Eli's first trip to Miami as a young man trying to build his fledgling organization. A neighbor of the Daniels family gave Eli their number, and he called them soon after his arrival to arrange a meeting so he could explain what he was accomplishing in Israel and ask for their help.

Eli was still young at the time, just in his thirties, and far from an expert at fundraising. But he had never allowed his personal deficiencies to get in the way of doing what he had to do. He had traveled to Miami to raise some money, and he planned on accomplishing his task with the help of G-d.

Eli called Ron Daniels and gave him a short explanation of who he was and why he had come to Miami. Then he asked if they could meet.

"You sound like a wonderful guy," Ron said, "and I'd love to meet you, but I'm very busy right now organizing a fundraiser at my home for a senator from Iowa who is a big supporter of Israel."

That was it. Eli had just gotten shot down. For most people, that would have been the end of the conversation. But Eli isn't most people, and the conversation was far from over.

Ron was about to hang up when Eli said, "Excuse me, Mr. Daniels?"

"Yes?"

"I've never met a United States senator in my life, and I would love to have that opportunity. Is there any way I could possibly join you at the event? I'll be happy to help you set up beforehand and clean up when it's over. Is that a possibility?"

That Ron said yes to Eli Beer was a life-changer for Ron… and for Hatzalah.

Eli got to the Daniels' home in time to help. He met Ron and June and was impressed with their devotion to Israel and their love for the Jewish people. Ron told Eli about their efforts on behalf of Soviet Jewry back in the seventies, when so many Jews had been trapped behind the Iron Curtain.

Eli helped them set up for the event. The party was beautiful, as was their home, which was built right on the water. During the actual event, Eli met a number of people and was introduced to the senator — the ostensible reason he was there. And so the afternoon passed, and the party was soon winding down. In another few minutes, it would be time to leave. Standing on the terrace at the back of the house and looking at the water, Eli caught sight of some fishing rods lying off to the side, and he had a brainstorm.

Ron and June Daniels

"I see you have some nice fishing rods," he said to Ron.

"That we do."

"I've never had the opportunity to go fishing."

"Is that so?"

"That's exactly so."

The stars were twinkling above them in a peaceful Miami sky. It was about ten at night — the perfect end to a perfect day.

"You want to learn how to fish?"

"Yes, sir."

On the spot, Ron asked one of his employees — he was from the Caribbean — to instruct Eli in the rudiments of the ancient art of fishing. Over the next two hours, Eli caught about twenty smaller fish, all the while engaged in an enjoyable conversation with his host. Any time he caught a fish he was overwhelmed with excitement, while his host enjoyed seeing his new friend participating in a much-loved activity for the first time.

After about an hour and a half of conversation, they started discussing Israel, and sure enough, it wasn't long before they were talking about Hatzalah and everything Eli and his friends were doing to save lives. Ron was full of questions, and Eli had all the answers — and eventually Ron offered to donate a motorcycle to Hatzalah. He also told Eli that he was invited to stay at his home and go fishing any time he found himself in Miami.

That was the beginning of a strong friendship — and as Ron likes to remind Eli every so often, "That was the most expensive event I ever made, because I let you into my house…"

Ron joined the Hatzalah board and introduced Eli to many of his friends, who also became supporters.

More than ten years later, Eli was sitting with Ron and June at a barbecue at the home of one of their friends, and during a conversation with June, he said, "You don't look good."

"I'm fine," she said.

June is a nurse, which means that she usually has a fine grasp of her state of health.

"I'm telling you that you have to go to the hospital right now because you're having a heart attack," Eli insisted.

Eli had seen the signs enough times to know that he was right.

"I'm not having a heart attack," she insisted.

"June," he said, "I am calling an ambulance right now. I've seen thousands of heart attack victims, and that's what's happening to you right now."

"Look, it's true I don't feel so well, but I just need to go lie down and relax for a bit. I'll be fine."

"June, I'm not asking you."

Eli called 911 and told the operator that a woman was having a heart attack and that she needed to send an ambulance immediately.

June was very upset and annoyed with him.

He shrugged it off.

Two fire trucks pulled up outside the house, along with an ambulance, which transported her to the hospital. There she was met by a friend — a cardiologist she had helped emigrate from Russia. The friend examined her and later let them know that her arteries had been ninety-eight percent blocked, which meant that had she gone to rest like she wanted, she would not have woken up.

So it was that Eli Beer was able to repay Ron and June for all the kindness and love they had shown him through the years.

The organization was gaining supporters and continuing to grow, but it wasn't enough. They needed to find ways to spread their message more effectively and realized that the best way to get their message out to more people was to produce a video about the organization explaining what they did. But while they understood that such a video was crucial for the organization's public relations and would bring in more donors and more volunteers, the funding for such a project was never available because there was always something more important to do with the money.

Then someone came up with the idea of discussing the project with Rabbi Uri Zohar.

Uri Zohar had been the biggest producer, director, and actor in the country before he became religious. They wanted to meet with him and get some advice. And so it was decided: they were going to go and confer with the master.

When he sat with Rabbi Zohar, Eli told him about Hatzalah and how they wanted to produce a video that would document what they were doing and why it was such a vital cause.

"Hatzalah doesn't have a video? That's a must! I will produce a drama for you."

"You're going to make the video?"

"Yes, I want to produce Hatzalah's video."

This was epic. Who would have believed that no less a superstar than Rabbi Uri Zohar had agreed to produce Hatzalah's first PR video? They were awestruck and thunderstruck all at the same time.

"Tell me some of your best stories," Reb Uri said to Eli. "We're going to choose the best story to use for the video."

Eli chose one of his favorites.

The storyline of the video was relatively simple, based on a true story that had happened not long before. It took place on an Erev Shabbos, when an exhausted mother went to lie down for a short rest, leaving her older child to babysit her two-year-old. The toddler promptly discovered a grape and popped it into her mouth. Moments later, she was choking. The five-year-old saw the baby choking and ran to wake up the mother, who called Hatzalah.

One of the volunteers who lived in the vicinity went by the name of Amit Maimon. He was getting ready for Shabbos when his wife started banging on the door. "What is it?"

"Your beeper just went off. A baby is choking a few buildings from here!"

Amit jumped out of the shower without even bothering to towel off the soap and shampoo that was still running down his face. Slipping into the most basic apparel — in this case, a pair of shorts — he dashed out of the building and ran down the street in the middle of the day intent on saving the child's life.

Amit was a *yungerman* who spent his days learning Torah, and shorts was not his or anyone's usual mode of dress in his neighborhood, but he knew that every second counted when it came to choking victims.

By the time Amit managed to get to the apartment, the two-year-old had no pulse. He began performing CPR on the toddler, and together with another volunteer who had come running in with a defibrillator, they managed to bring the heartbeat back. A short while later, the little girl was back to herself and breathing normally.

"This is going to be an amazing video," Rabbi Zohar said when Eli finished telling him the story. "The kind of video that will put Hatzalah on the map." In the actual video, Rabbi Zohar switched between footage depicting the stories they had decided to use and interviews with the family members who had been there at the time of the emergency, documentary style.

On the big day, everything was arranged. Eli met Rabbi Zohar outside the apartment where they would be filming the first story, and Rabbi Zohar emerged from a taxi holding a big bag in his hands. He proceeded to remove ten bottles of Osem ketchup from the bag, which he was planning to use for a scene that called for blood.

When the time came to set up the scene, Rabbi Zohar went around the room spilling ketchup in every direction, managing to squirt a decent-sized dollop all over Eli's shirt in the bargain.

Rabbi Uri Zohar ended up producing a very successful video for Hatzalah, which was used for fundraising purposes for years.

Rabbi Uri Zohar passed away on June 2, 2022, and in the days after his passing, his son Itamar released a short clip with a powerful message:

"My father was very careful to take full responsibility for anything he did throughout his life," he said. "If he ever did anything that he felt called for an apology, he always made sure to apologize to that person. So if my father ever did anything to anyone watching this, without having the chance to ask you for forgiveness, please forgive him and let me know about it."

Itamar sent the video out to everyone he knew — it was even on the news — and of course Eli Beer watched it, too.

After watching the video, Eli called up Rabbi Zohar's son and said, "Itamar, to tell you the truth, your father owed me an apology."

"My father owed you an apology? Why?"

"Well, you see, over twenty years ago he agreed to produce a short PR video for Hatzalah — it was our first film — and in the process of setting up a scene, he sprayed ketchup all over my favorite shirt."

Itamar burst out laughing.

"That's my one and only issue with your *tzaddik* of a father," Eli told Itamar Zohar.

Lucky is the person who needs to ask forgiveness for such things…

# CHAPTER SEVENTEEN

# A Meeting With the Founder

*I*t was a stormy night in 2005. Eli was in Manhattan, trying desperately to hail a cab to take him to JFK. As sheets of water came crashing down on him, and the streets ran like rivers, Eli stood on the pavement, arm outstretched in the universal gesture, and dreamed of being back in sunny Eretz Yisrael. Finally, a yellow cab pulled up, and the cabby's window went sliding down.

The driver was an older woman, probably in her seventies. This was a little surprising, especially when one took the weather into account. Knowing that according to the law, a taxi driver has to take a fare anywhere one wants, Eli felt bad asking her to leave the city and make the long drive to the airport in such a brutal storm and terrible traffic.

"I have to go to the airport," he told her before he got into the warm and inviting cab, "but if that's too difficult for you, I can wait for another cab."

The older lady smiled and said, "That's very thoughtful of you. The truth is, I'd rather not take such a long trip. I'm not even supposed to be out driving right now. But this is my cab, and my driver wasn't feeling well, so here I am."

"No problem," Eli said. "I'll just catch another cab."

Before she pulled away from the curb, she surprised him by asking, "Where are you flying to anyway?"

"I'm going to Israel."

"Israel? Can I give you some *tzedakah gelt* (money for charity) to take along with you?"

"Yes, of course. It would be my pleasure to take some *sheliach mitzvah* money back to Israel for you."

He was trying not to show his surprise — by the fact that the driver was a woman, that the woman was Jewish, and that she wanted to send him back home with *tzedakah* money — but he played it cool, as he always did, and took the situation in stride.

"By the way," he said, "is it okay if I give the money to Hatzalah? I'm the president."

"You're the president of United Hatzalah?" the driver exclaimed. "My cousin is Rabbi Hershel Weber, the founder of Hatzolah in America!"

"That's amazing," Eli replied. "I've always wanted to meet Rabbi Weber. He's the real revolutionary behind the incredible lifesaving organization that started in Williamsburg and has spread all around the world. It all started with him."

She took a little phone book out of her pocket and flipped through the pages.

"Here," she said at last. "I'm going to give you my cousin's number. Write it down."

Eli wrote down the number and wished her good night. Five minutes later, another cab stopped for him, and he was heading for the airport.

Through the years, Eli would come to know some of the wonderful members of Hatzolah. He became close friends with Rabbi Mechel Handler (who almost died in 9/11 and wrote a book about his experiences,) and with famed members like Shlomo Zakheim and Benish Mandel. He valued those friendships and was always happy to spend time with the members of American Hatzolah. But as of yet, he hadn't connected with the legendary American volunteer rescue service.

A few days later, Eli called Hershel Weber from Israel. He knew who Eli was, and he was happy to speak to Eli.

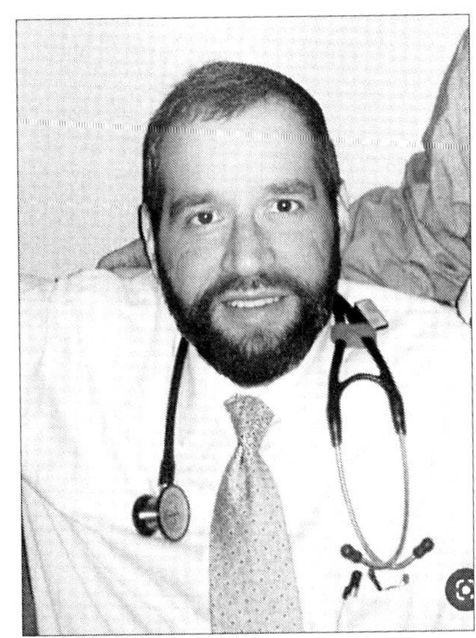
Reb Benish Mandel

"I visit Eretz Yisrael on a regular basis," he said, "and I always fly in for Lag BaOmer to join the tens of thousands who travel to Meron to mark the *yahrtzeit* of Rabbi Shimon bar Yochai. *Baruch Hashem*, I keep on seeing more and more of your volunteers."

They spoke for a while longer, and at the end of the conversation, Reb Hershel invited him to have dinner with him next time he was in the States.

Eli was planning to make a trip in the next few weeks, and they agreed to meet at the Prime Grill.

They met a few weeks later and shared a wonderful conversation.

"Why did you decide to establish Hatzolah?" Eli asked Rabbi Weber.

Hershel Weber told Eli how he had been leaving the Satmar *beis midrash* in Williamsburg one day when a man collapsed in the street right in front of him and landed on his foot.

"It took the paramedics a long time to get there," he said, "and after they arrived and examined the man, I heard one of the police officers say to the other, 'He could have been saved if we had gotten here just a few minutes earlier. What a shame!'"

It was that moment that changed everything for Reb Hershel, who drove to Boro Park and purchased an oxygen tank on that same day. So it was that Hatzolah of America was born.

Eli told Reb Hershel about some of the challenges he was facing, the politics, the opposition from Magen David Adom, and asked if he had had opposition, too.

"You want to hear about challenges? When we were just starting, we had the backing of quite a few rabbis, but there were several in particular who were opposed to the idea, each for a different reason. One of these rabbinical authorities asked me to come and see him.

"We had a short conversation, during which he told me that he was in favor of Hatzolah in general, but he didn't think we should be operating on Shabbos. He didn't think it was right for children to see their fathers running out of the house in the middle of a Shabbos meal to take a call. In his mind, this type of behavior was a denigration of Shabbos.

"The rabbi spoke for a long time, laying out his reasoning for closing down Hatzolah's operations every Shabbos."

Reb Hershel paused before continuing, "Of course, I knew that operating Hatzolah on Shabbos was the right thing to do, especially since I knew that there were other rabbis whom I could rely on. It was hard for me to disobey such a respected individual, but since people have life-and-death emergencies on Shabbos just as they do during the week, I didn't have the luxury of shutting down operations on Shabbos.

"Not long after that first meeting, another prominent rabbi in the neighborhood called me in to see him. 'I heard that you started advertising a course that teaches first aid and will also teach the Hatzolah volunteers how to deliver babies,' he said to me.

"I confirmed that it was true.

"'I don't think this is a good idea. It's not modest and should not be done.'

"I explained that I had already been called to deliver more than twenty babies since the establishment of Hatzolah, and that since I wasn't always available, other members of Hatzolah also needed to know how to handle all the basic emergency procedures, including the knowledge of how to deliver a baby. I emphasized that this was particularly needed since so many babies were born in Williamsburg.

"He didn't accept my reasoning. He just kept repeating that it was the wrong thing to do."

"What ended up happening?" Eli asked the founder of Hatzolah.

"Two fascinating developments. The first thing that happened was that the daughter of the rabbi who had told me not to open the course went into labor shortly after that conversation. She ended up having the baby at home, and I was the one who delivered it. This happened at around four thirty in the morning. Since I knew that her father usually left home very early in the morning, I waited outside the house afterward, and when he emerged, I wished him mazel tov on his new grandchild.

"When he asked me how I knew about it, I explained that I had been called to deliver the baby. He never said another word against me. After that day, he became a genuine believer in what we were doing. No further opposition from him.

"Now it was just a question of the other rabbi — the rabbi who wanted Hatzolah to be closed on Shabbos. On the Shabbos after we had that conversation, Hatzolah was called when one of the people praying in that rabbi's shul collapsed in close proximity to the rabbi himself. We arrived in record time and were able to save the man's life. By the time an ambulance arrived, he had been stabilized. That was the end of that rabbi's opposition. He had seen what Hatzolah could do and understood its importance."

"You should know," Eli told Reb Hershel, "that I had a similar story when it came to going out on Hatzalah calls on Shabbos. One of the most prominent rabbinical authorities in Yerushalayim was opposed to Hatzalah operating on Shabbos. Then one of his grandchildren fell off a high balcony on Shabbos, and Hatzalah arrived in time to save his life. After that, his attitude changed, and he understood that Hatzalah is always needed — every day of the week."

Hershel Weber and Eli Beer had undergone similar experiences, and each had held firm when faced with challenges. They understood one another. They sat and talked for hours that night, and by the end of their meeting at the Prime Grill, the two men had become firm friends.

When they parted, Eli said to his host, "I have a lot of dreams. I had a dream of saving a life, and *baruch Hashem*, I merited achieving that dream. I also have the dream of saving six million lives — one for every person lost in the Holocaust.

"I'm a dreamer. Some of my dreams are big and grand, and some are relatively small and simple. I just want you to know that I dream of the day when Hatzalah Israel and Hatzolah of America will have a wonderful and strong relationship."

Meeting a legend is usually a memorable event, and so it was for Eli Beer. His meeting with Hershel Weber was something he would never forget.

# CHAPTER EIGHTEEN

# The Turning Point

Although Hatzalah Bnei Brak joined Hatzalah Yerushalayim only in 2006, there were other branches of Hatzalah that made the decision to join forces earlier, among them Kfar Chabad and Hadera. Another branch was Hatzalah of Tzefas, run by Nachi Klein. For Eli, this was a step toward the goal of forming one cohesive organization that would eventually encompass every single branch of Hatzalah in the country.

One day Eli called a meeting of the executive members of the organization — including Eli Pollak, Moshe Teitelbaum, and Dovie Maisel.

"Here's the deal," Eli said to them. "As you know, five branches of Hatzalah have joined with us — Hadera, Netanya, Tzefas, Kfar Chabad, and Netivot. We're finally on the way to achieving the goal we've been dreaming about for so long: to bring everyone together under one organizational umbrella with one body of leadership and one vision. And since a real start has finally been made and we now have six branches, including ourselves, I propose that we change our name from Hatzalah Yerushalayim to Hatzalah Israel, with the hope that more branches will join us."

That meeting would go down in the organization's history as a pivotal moment. While Hatzalah Yerushalayim had been the largest branch of Hatzalah in the country until then, their strength and ability to have an impact increased exponentially when their one branch was combined with five others. Changing their name to Hatzalah Israel meant

Eli Pollak at the scene of an accident

that they were maneuvering away from being a local organization and transforming themselves into a national organization.

When forming the new organization, Eli paid visits to the homes of rabbinical leaders to inform them in person of the developments. He visited Rav Elyashiv and Rav Chaim Kanievsky and asked for their *berachos*, explaining that their real goal was to unite all the branches under one roof, since Eli genuinely believed that that was the best and most effective way of saving lives.

Eli with Rav Chaim Kanievsky

Several other branches joined them after that, but despite the fact that they had grown from one branch to encompass almost ten, Eli was under no illusions about the challenges of the journey that still lay ahead. There was no question in his mind that making peace between all the groups would be a difficult mission to accomplish. Causing discord between people is the easiest thing in the world, while the challenge of making shalom, making peace, can be immense. But Eli was ready to do whatever it took to achieve the goal.

Eli with Rav Elyashiv

He began visiting the members of Hatzalah Bnei Brak whenever he had a chance to persuade them to join Hatzalah Israel.

"*Chevrah*," he would say, "when we talk about combining the different branches of Hatzalah, one plus one doesn't equal two. No, one plus one equals three — the two volunteers and the life of the person they save by joining forces.

"There is no question in my mind that both of our organizations will become that much greater if we unite. The power and momentum of such a union will be stunning in its strength. When a volunteer performs CPR, he'll never succeed if he uses just one hand to do the job. He has to use two hands if he hopes to save lives — and so do we!"

Bnei Brak Hatzalah wasn't convinced.

"But why is it so important that we join together?"

"I'll tell you why it's so important. Let's say I go to visit my uncle in Bnei Brak, and let's say that while I'm there, a child starts choking in my uncle's building. True, I'm not from Bnei Brak, but I think we can all agree that I should respond to the call and save the child's life, especially since I can reach him faster than anyone else because I'm right there in the building. But I won't be able to do that because I won't know this very crucial information. Why not? Because my radio isn't tuned in to the same frequencies as Hatzalah Bnei Brak.

"The fact that every Hatzalah group has its own territory and its own bag of equipment and its own standard of training and even its own *poskim* isn't a good thing. We're dealing with life-and-death situations every day, and we have to do whatever we can to minimize the risk of death.

"And it's not just the equipment and the training. There are dozens of separate Hatzalah organizations operating at the same time, and every one of them has its own support staff, its own office, and its own fundraising team. So much money is being wasted because every branch feels that they have to do all the work for themselves. Think of how much money we could save if we were all sharing the same office and the same staff. And don't forget about the donors."

"What about the donors?"

"Think for a second how it works in America," Eli said. "Picture someone sitting in his house in Far Rockaway. He hears a knock on the door. It's someone collecting money for Hatzalah Bnei Brak. Ten minutes later there's another knock. This time someone is collecting for Hatzalah Beersheva, and then there's another for Hatzalah Tzefas and yet another for Hatzalah Tiveriah. It doesn't look good. It's not professional, and it's not productive. Everything would be dramatically improved if we were to pool our resources."

For years, Eli continued, he had been dreaming of the day he could change the name of the organization to United Hatzalah, because that would mean that they have all come together in true *achdus* (unity) to achieve the goals for which they were all dedicating their lives. Once that occurred, Eli was certain that the organization would become the kind of phenomenon that people around the world would want to emulate.

Meeting after meeting, Eli chipped away at the resistance little by little. There were times when he felt it was just never going to happen and they would always remain fragmented. Then he would remind himself that Hatzalah had started with two radios and a bunch of teenagers crashing calls that they heard by listening in on Magen David Adom's frequencies.

"We were able to get this far," he would tell himself, "and we'll continue to climb the mountain. One day it's going to happen."

Until the dream of unity was achieved, there was still a lot of work to do. Just as he wanted to make changes on a national level, Eli was beginning to understand that changes would have to be made in-house as well if he wanted to turn Hatzalah Israel into a truly professional outfit.

For years, Eli had done his best to avoid involvement in the organization's politics. He didn't want to be chairman of the board, and he devoted the lion's share of his time to supervising the volunteers as Hatzalah's commander in the field. But he was starting to realize that he would have to change his focus and start restructuring the organization from the inside out.

One of the issues they faced was how the decisions were being made to allocate funds. There were times when Eli raised money for a specific purpose, such as new medical equipment, only to find out later that the money had been spent on other things. He felt it was imperative that the volunteers be fully equipped, that it was crucial that they have a warehouse with fully stocked shelves in case of an emergency, such as a war or some other national crisis when a lot of equipment was suddenly needed. Yet, while this was his vision, there were others in the bureaucratic departments of the organization who didn't see things his way, and they had more power simply because he had always shied away from the operational side of things.

Now he was realizing more and more that he couldn't stay away any longer. Not if he wanted to see Hatzalah become a major rescue force on the national level. In his mind, he pictured Hatzalah with a local board and with an international board of wealthy businessmen who would support their vision and help them raise real money to turn their dreams into reality.

To the man in the street, he was and had always been the face of the organization. Yet he didn't possess the power to effect change, because he had never accepted the power and had left it in the hands of others — some of whom disagreed with his vision and others who had a vision of their own for where they wanted to take Hatzalah.

The Israeli version of Hatzalah had been in operation since the early nineties. It was time to start growing up.

As time passed, more branches of Hatzalah joined with Hatzalah Israel. In addition, Hatzalah began working to establish the organization in places where it had never been before. With so much going on, Magen David Adom couldn't help but start paying them more attention. MDA hadn't minded when they remained a small group of religious volunteers, essentially filling a small but important niche, but they weren't thrilled when Hatzalah started expanding so quickly into territory that had always been theirs.

Meanwhile, relations between the various branches were still complicated, and even within Hatzalah Israel itself there was dissension about the vision for the future of the organization. It came to the point where Eli was seriously considering resigning and leaving the organization altogether. Then something happened that caused all thoughts of leaving to disappear from his mind.

On July 12, 2006, the second Lebanon War erupted, and Eli Beer knew that Hatzalah Israel had a major role to play. Without wasting any time, he threw himself into the leadership role that he knew so well.

Missiles were flying into Israel from Lebanon, and the northern region of the country was under attack. In every city of the north, from Haifa to Carmiel and Tzefas, people were forced to take refuge in bomb shelters because of the steady flow of missiles that were flying their way.

On the first day of the war, Eli called his lieutenants together, determined to make plans and put them into action. It was time to gather whatever medical equipment they had in the Hatzalah Israel warehouse and go up north to assist and take care of as many people as possible.

Eli called Eli Pollak and asked him to find out how many protective vests were in stock.

"We have twenty vests."

Eli was shocked.

"What do you mean that we have twenty protective vests? I thought we have two hundred vests in stock. I'm sure I raised money for two hundred. How can it be that we have only twenty?"

"Look, I went searching for them in the warehouse, and that's what there was."

"What about trauma bags and the rest of the extra equipment?"

"Eli, I don't know how to tell you this, but the warehouse is more or less empty of equipment. Either it's all out in the field, or it was never bought in the first place."

There was no time to sit down and ascertain why the warehouse was empty. Not right then. Not with a war going on. No doubt someone on the board had thought that the money he'd allocated for protective vests and the other equipment could be better used for something else.

He didn't know how or why they had made their decision. He only knew that he had to deal with the situation as it existed, and that meant figuring out a way to get the equipment they needed — immediately.

Eli knew better than anyone how difficult it would be to raise enough money to pay for everything they needed so quickly. But he didn't see any other choice.

And so Eli Beer went into crisis mode.

In truth, Eli is at his best when he operates in that particular mode.

He went to his office. Closed the door behind him. Locked it.

Then he picked up the phone. It was time to get cracking. The first number he called was a company that sold medical supplies. He himself didn't deal directly with the local companies, but there was no time to waste and he knew that this time he needed to do it himself.

When he got through to a company representative, he identified himself and said, "I have a question for you."

"Yes?"

"How many protective vests do you currently have in stock?"

"Give me a minute to check."

The man was back on the phone a few minutes later.

"We have three hundred, but they're going fast. How many do you need?"

"I'll take them all. I also need top-quality helmets and other safety equipment so that can I send my volunteers into the war zone without getting killed."

"We sell it as a set," the man on the other end of the line informed him. "Vest and helmet."

Then they talked prices.

Eli made a quick calculation. Three hundred sets at eight hundred dollars a shot came to two hundred and forty thousand dollars. That was a lot of money.

"I need forty-eight hours to get the money together."

"No problem. We'll start packing up the equipment and prepare it to be shipped wherever you want it."

A soon as Eli hung up the phone, he called another company and ordered hundreds of specially equipped first aid kits called trauma bags, asking them for forty-eight-hour delivery as well. He also needed mattresses for the volunteers so they wouldn't have to sleep on the floor of the bomb shelters. He ordered a hundred and fifty mattresses.

They knew his name and had heard of Hatzalah. No one doubted him. Everyone he spoke with agreed to sell him whatever he needed.

He contacted five separate companies and ordered merchandise from each one. Then he made another list — this time for food — so that the volunteers would have something to eat while they did their work up north.

He went through his list, item after item, and ordered everything they needed, asking every company for a forty-eight-hour grace period. When he got off the phone and tallied up the cost of everything he had ordered, it came to a million dollars. And he had two days in which to obtain the funds.

Yes, crisis mode.

Nachi Klein called Eli from Tzefas.

"Eli, they're shooting missiles at us from Lebanon! A missile just hit a building near my house. These are big missiles, Eli. I want to go out and save people but I'm afraid to leave my house because I don't have any protective vests."

"I'm on it, Nachi. The equipment will be up north as soon as I can get it there."

Volunteers from Haifa and other cities also called. They, too, had a list of equipment that they needed. Eli reassured them that he was taking care of it, that they'd have the equipment as soon as humanly possible.

Eli promptly called a few of his closest friends, people who had been working with him for years, running into buses after bomb attacks, helping people after car accidents.

He called Yerach Toker, Zevi Kashash, Eli Pollak, and Zevi Sofer and gave them assignments. Then he called Dovie Maisel, who still had connections within Magen David Adom.

"Dovie, I need your help."

"What do you need?"

Eli Beer and Zevi Sofer

United Hatzalah volunteers at the scene of a car accident

"I need you to borrow an ambulance from MDA for us. We're going to fill it with medical equipment and drive it up north so all the volunteers will have what they need to do their jobs and save lives. Have it ready to leave in two days."

"Got it."

"And, Dovie?"

"Yes?"

"See if you can arrange to get another few trucks besides the ambulance. There's going to be a lot of equipment, and one ambulance won't be large enough to hold it all."

"I'll do my best."

When he was finished calling his closest friends, the guys who were part of his inner circle, some of whom had been with him when they first started their Hatzalah activities in Bayit Vegan, Eli took a moment to reflect on the course he'd embarked on. And he understood that by making the decision to go out on his own without consulting the executives in the organization and to do things the way he believed they should be done, he was setting the stage for the beginning of something new, something he instinctively understood was going to be huge. At that moment, Eli Beer comprehended in the deepest part of his being that he was standing poised on the cusp of a movement that would become known to the world as Ichud Hatzalah — or as they say in English — United Hatzalah.

Before he took the next step, creating a wholly new rescue organization, Eli felt that it was crucial that he receive a *berachah* from Rav Yosef Sholom Elyashiv, one of the great rabbinical authorities of the generation who had provided Eli with guidance on so many occasions.

After calling ahead to arrange a meeting, Eli drove to Rav Elyashiv's apartment in the Meah Shearim neighborhood of Yerushalayim. Rav Elyashiv was sitting and learning at the dining room table when Eli entered the room. He was told to take a seat, and for the next hour Eli told Rav Elyashiv everything that had transpired in the last day and how he felt that he needed to move in a new direction.

Rav Elyashiv spoke clearly and directly, as was his way.

"You should establish a new organization," he told his visitor. "Something brand new. At the same time, you should open the door to any volunteer who wants to join you. Don't fight for control over Hatzalah Israel. There should not be a war because of this.

"And, Eli, build your organization in an *ehrliche* (pious) way, and do not forget about halachah."

Many times, Rav Elyashiv went on to explain, people want to build an organization in what they think is a professional way — and then they forget what the halachah expects from them.

"Do your best to build your new organization in a professional way, but do not, under any circumstances, forget about the halachah. Make sure you are in close contact with rabbis to advise you and help you do things the right way."

That was it. Rav Elyashiv had just given him the guidance he needed. A minute later Eli was back in his car and driving out of Meah Shearim, his thoughts a jumbled whirl, his mind racing at a thousand miles an hour.

Eli was no longer making decisions on his own. He had asked for advice and guidance from one of the greatest and most respected Jewish rabbinic leaders of that generation.

He didn't have any money in the bank. He didn't even have a bank account to use for his new organization.

He had nothing except for a blessing from Rav Elyashiv.

And yet, somehow, that was enough.

# The Million-Dollar Campaign

rom the narrow alleyways of Meah Shearim, Eli headed to Bayit Vegan, to the office of a close friend. Shea Klein was an accountant, and Eli hoped that he would be able to help him set up a new organization literally overnight. It was imperative that he do this as soon as possible if he wanted to raise the kind of money he needed.

Ambassador David Friedman, Eli Beer, and Reb Shea Klein

Eli with Mark Gerson

Shea was in his office and listened as Eli unburdened himself and gave him a rundown of everything that had happened since the outbreak of the war.

"I need to be able to travel to the States and begin raising funds for my new organization to pay for everything I already ordered. I'll need an account set up, and I need to be able to hand out receipts. Please help me!"

"What's going to happen to the old organization?"

"Nothing. But I'm leaving it and moving on. That's what Rav Elyashiv told me to do. He said I should start again from the ground up. We'll work out the details of the breakup later."

Shea promised to do everything in his power to make it happen so that Eli's new operation could be up and running as soon as possible.

Eli also visited the office of a lawyer whom he knew in Yerushalayim and tasked him with doing the same thing — but for Israel. This way the new organization would be able to give donors receipts for their donations on both sides of the ocean.

Within hours, Shea had taken care of the paperwork.

"Eli, I need you to tell me who your board members are."

Eli didn't need a lot of time to decide who he was choosing for the chairman of the board.

"Shea, put Mark Gerson down as chairman of the board in the United States."

Mark had been a major donor since the first time they had met, and Eli knew he would be able to count on him no matter what. He gave Shea any information that he needed, and Shea hung up and went back to work.

Once the pieces were in place, Eli called a meeting of his closest friends in Israel. It was time to choose the leaders of the new enterprise, and he knew who he wanted to join him for the journey. They were the guys who had been with him at the best of times and the worst of times. The guys who had smuggled radios into the country, the guys who had been there with him doing CPR on dying people as they fought to save lives in some of the most tragic terrorist attacks ever seen. They were the ones who had started it all with him, and they were the ones he wanted at his side now that he was going out on his own. They were heroes and he needed them.

He asked Zevy Kashash to be the CEO.

Eli Pollak to be in charge of the volunteers.

Dovie Maisel was put in charge of operations.

Zevi Sofer in charge of the motorcycle unit.

Zevi Sofer — crowd control at the Kosel

Yerach Toker, Sheldon Adelson, and Eli

Yerach Toker to serve as the spokesman and computer expert.

Someone else to run logistics.

A small group of people. Each fiercely loyal to him and to one another.

It was all coming together.

There was just one thing he still needed.

Money.

Eli had never raised so much money in so short an amount of time. It was an immense challenge. He called the companies from which he'd ordered the equipment and asked them if they would be willing to accept a payment plan — the first installment after forty-eight hours and the next few installments over the next couple of months.

They all agreed. Everyone understood that there was a war happening and that they had to do their part to help the nation. Israelis had already lost their lives, and the war had only begun two days earlier. This was one situation that everyone was taking with the utmost seriousness.

Besides, it was obvious that Eli wasn't playing games and there was no question that he would do everything he promised. Within a short time, a payment plan was in place, and Eli was able to move on to the next step that he needed to do.

One of the items at the top of the list was a conversation with Mark Gerson that Eli wasn't looking forward to in the least. He was extremely embarrassed that he was even having such a conversation, because it meant having to admit that he needed to start all over again.

Yet he had no choice.

He dialed Mark's number.

"Mark, its Eli."

"How's it going?"

"To be completely honest, I have a problem and I need your help."

"Talk to me."

What followed was a relatively long conversation where Eli explained the reasons that had led him to make the decision to leave Hatzalah Israel and to begin his own organization.

"Eli, I'm a businessman," Mark said at last. "And because I've been a businessman for many years now, I understand how things work, that sometimes people discover that they have to recalibrate and maybe even start from the beginning because things aren't working out using the old methods.

"I trust you. Eli, come to America. I'll get my friends over to my house, and we'll raise some money for you."

Eli didn't tell anyone he was leaving besides the tiny group who were already committed to leadership positions in the new organization. Otherwise his exit was completely under the radar. He booked a last minute ticket, and sat through the long and miserable flight worrying whether his trip to New York was going to justify itself.

The plane landed in JFK at five in the morning. He left the airport and drove to Boro Park, where he davened Shacharis at the Shomer Shabbos shul on Thirteenth Avenue. After a quick breakfast at a nearby coffee shop, he drove to a friend of his who had agreed to be one of the first board members of the new organization. The man signed the documents Eli gave him, and Eli thanked him and left his home.

From Boro Park he drove into Manhattan, where he went to the home of another friend who had also agreed to join the board. He signed as well. Then documents in hand, Eli made his way to a local bank where he opened a new account in the name of "Friends of United Hatzalah."

"I need you to activate this account immediately," he told the banker. "I'm going to have checks coming in as soon as today, and I need to be able to deposit them."

"No problem. The account will be up and running within two hours."

United Hatzalah was now operational. They had boots on the ground, and Eli was off and running.

It was a sunny day in Manhattan, and in his mind Eli pictured the missiles flying across the Lebanese border and into cities all over the north.

He hadn't slept for close to four days other than a catnap here and there. He had been working around the clock and was basically running on pure adrenaline. His wife was worried about him, frightened that Eli was going to have a heart attack from sheer stress. If he was being honest with himself, he had to admit that she had a point.

On top of everything else, he had just one night to raise as much money as he could. His flight back to Israel was leaving at midnight. It was very little time, but he had to be back in Israel as soon as possible, and he couldn't afford to stay longer. It was time to raise some money.

The first person he met with was Daniel Schwartz, his first big donor who had been there for Eli and for Hatzalah when it counted. When they were sitting together, Eli said, "Dan, I need your help."

He didn't get into the background of what had occurred and how he was starting over. There was no time for that.

"What do you need?"

"I need to raise a million dollars. What can you do to help me get there?"

Dan thought for a few seconds.

"I'll give you seventy-five thousand dollars."

"Thank you. I want you to know that the money you're donating will be used to purchase bulletproof vests and helmets for our volunteers who are going up north to save lives."

They parted with warmth.

Eli visited four other people that morning. One of them was Bert Cohen, another of his original donors and the man who had introduced him to Mark Gerson. From there he went on to the next donor and the next. Each of them agreed to give a sizable donation. All together the five of them contributed three hundred thousand dollars. It was a wonderful start, but he still needed another seven hundred thousand.

Later that day, Eli drove to Mark Gerson's apartment for the big meeting that Mark had promised to arrange. Mark didn't disappoint him. There were sixty people there — Mark's friends all — most of them people whom Eli had never met previously.

Eli looked around him. At the beautiful room filled with wealthy people with good hearts, and his eyes swam with tears. He was also cognizant of the time. He could hear the clock ticking the seconds away to his twelve o'clock flight.

Mark spoke.

From the heart.

He spoke about Hatzalah and about his friend Eli Beer and how he had dedicated his life to saving the lives of other people.

Eli spoke.

From the heart.

He spoke about the organization and about saving lives and about reaching a victim fast enough to make a difference and about the war happening in the north of Israel at that very moment.

"My friends," he said, "right now, at this very second, there are missiles knocking down buildings in Israel. People are getting killed, and we need to protect them. That's our mission. Will you help me?"

On the spot Mark Gerson wrote a check for two hundred and fifty thousand dollars. Someone else donated one hundred and fifty thousand dollars. At the end of the event the entire amount had been raised. Seven hundred thousand dollars.

And there it was. A million dollars. Raised in one day.

By the time they were finished, the banks were closed, so Eli left the checks with Mark, telling him that someone would come and pick them up the next day. Then Eli left Mark's house and drove back to JFK. He arrived very close to the time of the flight, starving and exhausted beyond belief. As he settled into his seat on the plane, Eli was experiencing stomach pangs from sheer hunger. At the same time, he was filled with a gratified sense of happiness and contentment at having raised the money he needed to pay for the equipment they were bringing up north.

He was flying, figuratively and literally.

After enjoying the El Al meal, Eli slept for the first time in days.

# CHAPTER TWENTY

# The Bomb Shelter Summit

Dovie Maisel was waiting for Eli in Ben Gurion's arrivals area. The ambulance he had asked for was parked on the side of the road and was so crammed with equipment you would have been hard-pressed to find room for a box of matches. They got into the ambulance and left the airport for the drive up north, where they caught up with the convoy of equipment-bearing trucks waiting for them at the Magen David Adom station in Tiveriah.

When they arrived at the station, Eli went inside to say hello to the dispatcher and any EMTs and paramedics who were around.

"Who doesn't have a bulletproof vest?" he wanted to know.

Half the people didn't have a bulletproof vest, and Eli distributed them to everyone in need. The one thing he demanded was that anyone who took a vest sign a form saying that he had taken one and would return it when the war ended.

Then he let all the Hatzalah Tiveriah volunteers know that he had arrived in the city and had equipment to give them. When they streamed forth to meet him, Eli was able to give them everything they needed so that they would be able to leave the relative safety of Tiveriah and drive up north to do their lifesaving work — in the most literal sense of the word.

As Eli and Dovie drove the ambulance from city to city to distribute the equipment to every volunteer, they literally saw missiles flying in front of their eyes. At one point, an Apache helicopter blew up when the pilot didn't notice that he was flying too close to electric wires and collided with them with disastrous results.

It didn't take long for people to realize that big changes were in the offing. Suddenly volunteers were walking around with new equipment, equipment sporting a new logo that had never been seen before. Dozens of volunteers in Tzefas, Meron, and Haifa were proudly heading into battle wearing their new gear. Meanwhile, Eli and Dovie visited city after city, dispensing equipment and explaining that they were forming a new organization and that the volunteers could sign up and join them. The majority chose to do so.

Eli also decided to invite representatives from the organization he had just left to a meeting. The goal of the meeting was to bring his involvement with the organization he had built to a clear and peaceful conclusion and to begin something new — something that he hoped would include every single rescue organization in the country and represent everyone.

And so Eli called every single branch of Hatzalah in existence — those who had joined them and those who had not — and invited them to a meeting that was going to be held in a bomb shelter in the city of Hadera, right in the middle of a war.

Missiles were flying into Hadera while they were taking the opportunity to sit down and make peace between them.

As the meeting came to order, Eli rose to speak.

"I am proposing to launch a brand new organization," he began, "with a very simple goal: to unite with every single branch of Hatzalah already operating in the State of Israel. The new organization will be called 'United Hatzalah.'

"At United Hatzalah, everyone will be given equal rights around the table. A board will be formed with representatives from every single branch in the country. Everyone will have a say in creating policy, and everyone will be equally represented.

"In addition, I will also be forming an international board who will help us raise money overseas and who will provide oversight for all financial decisions. Money will be allocated to every branch based on

Meeting in the bomb shelter during the war

the number of volunteers they have, and every volunteer in every city will receive the same training and the same equipment. There will be rules and bylaws, and everything is going to be done by the book."

At this, a clamor erupted. Voices were raised and arguments made for and against. The discussion grew heated, tense, and confrontational many times throughout the endless meeting. Accusations were hurled across the table, and Eli had to defend himself over and over.

Some claimed that he was power hungry. Others focused on the fact that United Hatzalah was prepared to accept volunteers who weren't religious, loudly stressing that they were opposed to such a move.

"I can assure you," Eli said in response to the accusations, "that in United Hatzalah no power will be concentrated in the hands of one person. There will be a CEO, a CFO, a COO, and a board in America who will review all the decisions the Israeli board will make.

"Regarding your claim that we're going to change the character of the organization, I'm here to tell you that you are correct. United Hatzalah will be opening its doors to those who were never part of it before. It's not going to be only for us religious people anymore. Nonreligious people will be allowed to volunteer as well. And do you know who told me that this is okay to do?"

He paused.

Eli conferring with Rav Chaim Kanievsky

Everyone looked at him. They waited.

"I was told that we could, and should, use non-religious EMTs when I asked Rav Chaim Kanievsky." No one had anything to say about that.

"He also told me that it's a mitzvah to give every single person the opportunity to save a life."

It was quiet now in the bomb shelter.

As Eli stood there defending himself at one of the most pivotal times of his life, his mind took him back in time to the day he had gone to Rav Chaim to ask him what the right course of action was for his organization.

It had started with a phone call from an EMT from Herzliya named Niv. Niv had called Eli one day and asked to meet with him. When they were sitting together, Niv said, "I've been a volunteer with Magen David Adom for many years."

"That's great," Eli said.

"I know," Niv replied. "It gives me a chance to do wonderful things and to save lives. But I feel like I'm only able to be effective as a lifesaver when I'm out in the ambulance. The moment my shift ends and I come home, there's not much I can do to help anyone during an emergency.

"I heard about how Hatzalah volunteers have been tasked with the goal of reaching any emergency in the shortest amount of time. I heard that your goal for the organization is to be the first responders on the scene and to do it in less than ninety seconds."

"That's correct," Eli said.

"I want to join you," Niv said. "I want to be a part of that."

He was the first nonreligious Israeli who wanted to sign up, and Eli wasn't sure what to do. It was clear to him that he needed to formulate a policy on the matter of secular volunteers in what had up until then been a completely religious organization.

Eli decided to go and consult with the great rabbis of the day. He went to Rav Elyashiv, who replied that every person should have the opportunity to perform the mitzvah of saving lives.

He also consulted with Rav Chaim.

He explained to him that Hatzolah in America was comprised solely of religious Jews, yet in Israel there were also nonreligious Jews who wanted to join Hatzalah. What to do?

"Right now," he said to Rav Chaim, "it can take an ambulance twenty minutes or more to get to someone's house in Herzliya. That's way too long. A nonreligious volunteer with Magen David Adom named Niv told me that he wants to join Hatzalah."

"What's the problem?" Rav Chaim asked.

"Hatzalah was founded and built by religious Jews, and we never had a secular person in the organization before. It's just never been done."

Rav Chaim looked at Eli and said, "It's a mitzvah for them to join."

"A mitzvah?"

"Yes. It's a mitzvah for them to join and have the opportunity to save lives. It will make a big *kiddush Hashem* (sanctification of G-d's Name). And," Rav Chaim went on, "you must teach them the laws of Shabbos so that when they go out on calls there is no *chillul* Shabbos, desecration of the Holy Shabbos. But there is no problem with allowing secular people to join the organization. On the contrary, it's a wonderful thing!"

Rav Chaim's response proved to be both groundbreaking and awe-inspiring. For one thing, it would open the door for many more lives to be saved, since United Hatzalah would be able to operate in cities where the population was predominately secular. More than that, it would help to reduce the tension that existed between so many segments of the population, who were filled with preconceived notions and untruths that were fed to them by the media about the religious sectors. Being part of a group like Hatzalah and seeing how they operated would serve to prove these notions as baseless and false.

And it all came to pass. Within a short time after joining the organization, the nonreligious volunteers and those they helped were able to look at life in a completely different way and to actually become advocates for the religious segment of the population — because they had come to know the truth.

Now Eli gazed at every person in the bomb shelter.

"Right now missiles are striking buildings all over the north," he went on. "Buildings that are populated by Jews who are both religious and secular. This is an opportunity for us to make a *kiddush Hashem* on an unparalleled level, to unite all the Jewish people around a simple idea that no one can argue with — the idea of saving lives in the fastest and most effective way. Finally there is a goal toward which everyone can agree to work together — and Rav Elyashiv has instructed us to do so.

"My friends, this is our chance to join together and unite all of Hatzalah under one roof. Maybe it took a war to make it happen, so what. This is our chance! Let's not waste it!"

Eventually the time came to take a vote. Almost ninety percent of those present voted to join the new organization. The meeting had commenced at ten in the morning and now, finally, came to an end at two o'clock the next morning, sixteen hours later.

Once the vote was taken, there was no longer any question. The people had spoken, and the die was cast. The irony was that it took a war to bring about the unity that Eli had been working toward for years.

Eli ended up staying up north for the rest of the war, sleeping in a different city every night — one night in a bomb shelter in Tzefas, another night in Nahariya, the next in Haifa — doing everything he could for the volunteers, who never stopped doing their great work.

The war was an eye-opener for Eli in another way. People were calling for ambulances that were taking a very long time to arrive due to the lack of manpower. This meant that there was a lot more work for the volunteers, who stepped up and worked tirelessly for days on end.

So it came to be that another of Eli's dreams had come true.

He had dreamed of saving a life — and he'd accomplished that dream.

He dreamed of uniting all the branches of Hatzalah under one roof. Now that was happening, too.

He still had two more dreams.

He wanted to save the lives of six million people — one for every person killed in the Holocaust.

And last but not least, he wanted to reach a time when the volunteers of United Hatzalah would be able to reach any destination anywhere in the country in less than ninety seconds.

Two down, two to go.

# PART FOUR

*Nobody gets up in the morning one day
and decides to become a volunteer for an
organization like ours... Something happened
to take them out of their comfort zone and
make them say, 'I want to get the training to
become a person who can save lives.'*

— Dovie Maisel,
COO of United Hatzalah

# CHAPTER TWENTY-ONE

# The Deal

*D*ovid* was a volunteer for United Hatzalah who went out of his way to go on as many calls as he could. He truly believed in what he was doing. While his main focus was United Hatzalah, Dovid also needed to earn a livelihood to support his family, and for that he had a job in a butcher shop in Yerushalayim.

On the day prior to Pesach, Dovid left the shop with a truckload of chicken and meat that he needed to deliver to customers in time for them to prepare for Seder night. While in the middle of his route, a call came in: a woman had gone into labor, and she was close by. It turned out that the husband was driving his wife to the hospital, but the labor was progressing quickly and her husband had to pull over to the side of Highway 443 and call Hatzalah.

Dovid let the dispatcher know that he was on his way. Then he turned the truck around and drove to where the couple was waiting for help. When he arrived, he grabbed his equipment from the back seat of the truck's cab and ran to deliver the baby. It wasn't an easy birth, and Dovid had to fight to save the baby's life. Forgetting that he was in the process of doing his job, and that he had left tens of thousands of shekels worth of meat in the refrigerated truck waiting for him to continue with his deliveries, he focused all his attention on saving the baby's life. And for the next ten minutes, that's exactly what he did.

Even after the baby was born, Dovid couldn't just leave them. He waited with the couple until an ambulance arrived to take the mother and child to the hospital. Only then did return to his truck, prepared to continue on his way. The whole thing had taken a good forty-five minutes out of his day. Really happy at having just saved a life, Dovid reached over to turn the key in the ignition. Then his eye glanced down at the phone he had left in the truck when he dashed out to deliver the baby. He decided to check and see if he had missed any calls. A quick glance at the phone told him that he had indeed missed calls.

Twenty of them.

All from his boss, Chezky.*

At that moment, Dovid realized that he was in big trouble.

Chezky answered almost before the phone had had a chance to ring.

"Where are you?" he demanded. "I was looking for you, and I checked the location of the truck on the GPS. I see that you're on Highway 443. What are you doing there?"

"I had a Hatzalah call."

"Oh, that's what it was…"

"Yes."

"Turn around and please come back to the office right now."

When Dovid reached the office, Chezky clearly wasn't interested in listening to excuses or explanations. He looked Dovid in the eye and said, "You're fired. Take your stuff and get out of here. I'm sick and tired of you, and I'm sick and tired of Hatzalah! I have deliveries that I need you to do, but instead of you doing your job, I'm constantly receiving complaints from our customers because they're waiting for their meat order, and it never shows up. And why? Because you're too busy going on Hatzalah calls to do your actual job. I'm done with you. It's time for you to leave."

Dovid started begging his boss to give him another chance.

"I really need this job," he said. "If you fire me, I won't have any way to feed my family. Please don't fire me!"

But Chezky wouldn't change his mind.

"Dovid," he said, "you're out. Enough is enough."

Dovid left the butcher shop, not sure what to do. After mulling it over, he decided to call Eli Beer and tell him the entire story.

Eli answered right away.

"What's going on?"

"Eli, I have a problem."

"What kind of problem?"

"The kind where my boss fired me because I go on too many calls for Hatzalah. That kind of problem."

"I see."

"I need you to do me a favor and speak to my boss, he knows you and likes you. Maybe you'll be able to convince him to change his mind."

"I'll do my best."

Eli hadn't thought when he got up that morning that he was going to have to plead for someone's job, but that was the wonder of working at United Hatzalah: you just never knew what the day was going to bring. He got into his car and drove over to the big warehouse where the butcher shop was housed.

Eli found Chezky sitting in his office and asked him if he could take a seat and have a talk.

"Please. Sit down."

"Look," Eli said, "what you're doing is just plain wrong. He's not taking off work because he wants to go to the beach. He's missing work because he's busy saving people's lives. How can you fire a person for that?"

"Look, Eli, I'm sick and tired of this guy. All day long he's leaving work and going out on emergency calls. Why don't you hire him? I need someone who works for me, not someone who works for Hatzalah. If he went on one call every couple of days, fine, but he's out all the time. I can't run a business like this."

"I think this is a question for the local rabbi," Eli pointed out. "I don't think you should just fire him. Let's all go together to the *rav* of the neighborhood, and we'll ask him what he thinks."

It was decided. They were going to the *rav*.

The next day they were all seated before the rabbi. He looked at Eli. "Why don't you begin?"

"This man" (he pointed at Chezky) "wants to fire this man" (he pointed at Dovid) "because he keeps running out in the middle of work to go on Hatzalah calls. If Dovid were leaving work to go play soccer, or if he was coming late every day because he had a hard time getting up in the morning, I wouldn't say a word if Chezky wanted to fire him. But the reason Dovid is in trouble is because he goes out a few times a day to save people's lives, and I don't think it's right to fire a person for such a reason."

"That's all well and good," Chezky interjected, "but I'm losing a lot of money because of Dovid. My clients are up in arms, and I can't have a worker who's so unreliable."

After the rabbi had heard both sides of the case, he spoke.

"According to Jewish law," he said, "an employer is supposed to give his employee time to eat and time to daven. Maybe even a little time to rest. But it doesn't say anywhere in the *Shulchan Aruch* that a boss has to give his employee time off so that he can go and save lives. It seems pretty clear that if the boss of a Hatzalah volunteer doesn't allow him to go and engage in his work, he's not allowed to go. Of course, he can resign and do it on his own time, but he's not allowed to do it at his boss's expense."

"I'm very sorry," Eli told his volunteer, "but it doesn't look like we're going to win this case."

All of a sudden, the rabbi turned to Chezky and said, "Tell me something. Have you ever saved anyone's life?"

"No, I haven't." He added somewhat sheepishly, "I'm even afraid of the sight of blood."

Eli looked at him and said, "You're a butcher and you're afraid of blood?"

"Yes, the sight of human blood can even cause me to faint. Anyway," Chezky added, turning back to the rabbi, "the answer to your question is no, I've never saved a life."

"What if I tell you," the rabbi said to Chezky, "that we can make an agreement between you and Dovid that every time Dovid leaves work to go and save a life, part of the reward will belong to you. It will be something along the lines of a Yissachar-Zevulun business agreement."

A Yissachar-Zevulun agreement is usually done between two people, one of whom studies Torah and the other who supports the one studying and receives a portion of his reward in the World to Come.

"So fifty-fifty?"

Dovid was unhappy with the compromise.

"I'm the one running out there to save lives. I'm the one doing all the work, and I have to split the reward fifty/fifty? Why is that fair?"

The next thing Eli knew, the two of them were arguing about the percentage.

"Thirty-seventy."

"Forty-sixty."

"Thirty-five–sixty-five…"

Dovid felt that since he was the one who was doing the actual life-saving, he should receive a bigger portion of the reward. The boss felt that since he was paying Dovid to go out and save the lives, he should receive a bigger percentage of the reward.

In the end, after going around and around, they finally agreed on a fifty-fifty breakdown.

They were in the middle of writing the contract when a new problem arose.

"What about when Dovid goes out to save a life on Sunday or Shabbos?" the boss wanted to know. "He's not working on those days,

Volunteers sending a patient on a helicopter airlift

but I'm still paying him, and I want part of the reward on those days as well. I want fifty-fifty on the weekends, too."

Dovid looked at his boss as if he had completely lost his mind.

"Are you crazy? You want to get a share in my reward even on the days when I'm not supposed to come into work? This is too much!"

Now the wrangling reached such decibels that for the first time Eli feared the whole thing was going to blow up. But after a long argument that never seemed to end, they arrived at a compromise. Fifty-fifty on the normal working days and seventy-five–twenty-five on the weekends. Dovid was happy because he still had his job and would be able to continue saving lives with the blessing of his boss, and the boss was happy because he had somehow managed to join the fraternity of life-savers even though he couldn't stand the sight of blood.

Chezky was so satisfied with this new turn of events that he went out of his way to hire more members of Hatzalah, with the same terms, so that he would be able to have a share in saving even more lives.

# CHAPTER TWENTY-TWO

# Two Arabs From Abu Tur

li had witnessed a terror attack on the streets of Yerushalayim at the tender age of five. Seeing something of this sort, it might have been understandable for him to develop a hatred for Arabs and want to take revenge for all the lives that were lost on the bus that day and in so many other senseless attacks.

But Eli's thoughts didn't take him in the direction of revenge. Perhaps because he was too busy dreaming about saving lives.

One day his phone rang, and Eli found himself talking to an Arab named Morad Aliyan who, along with his friend Mohammed Asli, wanted to meet Eli.

"What's this about?"

They told him that they wanted to talk about United Hatzalah. Ironically, they could barely pronounce the word "Hatzalah" and it sounded like "Hezbollah."

At first Eli was afraid that they had called him by mistake since it sounded like they wanted to talk about a terrorist organization. But after a minute or two it became clear to him that they were coming in peace.

"We want to talk to you about saving lives," they said.

Eli was surprised. United Hatzalah was still a fairly low-key organization, and he was surprised that there were Arabs even aware of what it was doing. For the record, Eli wasn't particularly interested in sitting down with two Arabs, especially since Israel had just been engaged in a war with Lebanon where many people had died, buildings had

Morad Aliyan — all the way on the right

been destroyed by missiles, and he himself had been forced to hold a Hatzalah summit in a bomb shelter. Now he asked himself why on earth he needed what he perceived as a heap of trouble.

"We want to join your organization," Morad told him. "Please meet with us."

Eli relented, some instinct telling him to agree, and Eli had long learned to trust his intuition.

"So what brought you to decide that you wanted to meet with me?" Eli asked when they were sitting together in his office.

"It goes back to when Mohammed's father had a heart attack," Morad replied. "We live in a Jerusalem neighborhood called Abu Tur, and at the time that this happened, there were many terrorist attacks, and the tension between the Arabs and the Jews was very high. It took the ambulance about an hour until it arrived at his home — and it was accompanied by a police escort. By the time the ambulance showed up, his father had already passed away. He was fifty-five years old."

"I want to join United Hatzalah," Mohammed said, picking up the thread. "I want to be an EMT and save lives together with the Jewish

Jews and Arabs saving lives together

volunteers. I want to be able to save everyone — my family members and my Arab friends and any Jewish person who needs my help."

"Are you willing to be available to help us on Shabbat?" Eli asked them. "It's a very busy time with lots of calls."

"We're going to help you on Shabbat, and you're going to help us during Ramadan when we are fasting. We will help one another."

"I'm willing to organize the training," Eli said, "but you need to bring me twenty-five people. Do you think you can convince twenty-five Arabs to join us?"

"I can bring you fifty Arabs," Morad replied.

"Start with twenty-five and let's see how it goes. And you need to make sure that these are guys with no criminal records — that they are guys we can trust. Remember, they'll receive authorization to go wherever they want. We need to be able to trust them completely. Do you understand?"

They understood.

The first gathering of the new inductees was held at the YMCA building across the street from the King David Hotel in downtown Yerushalayim. Eli stood up and gave a passionate speech about what

United Hatzalah does and the vision of reaching a patient in less than ninety seconds.

After the speech, one of the men raised his hand.

"I have a question."

"Yes?"

"I'm excited about starting to volunteer for you. I want to volunteer every day — I want to do this around the clock. I just wanted to know how much money we will be getting paid to volunteer."

Eli looked at him.

"I don't think you understand what the word *volunteer* means," he replied. "Not only are we not going to be paying you to work for us, but you are going to be paying for the gasoline you use when you drive to a person's home to save a life."

They loved his answer. For some reason, now that they knew they were expected to volunteer for free, they were even more excited than they had been before.

At the end of the meeting, Eli let them know that if this experiment ended up working out well, he didn't see any reason why additional Arabs couldn't join, too.

The decision to allow Arabs to join United Hatzalah didn't go over quietly. On the contrary, the pushback from some quarters was more than intense. One councilman in Yerushalayim was apoplectic and opened an aggressive campaign against Eli Beer. He even reached out to some of United Hatzalah's right-wing donors to let them know what Eli was doing. The phone call from the councilman convinced one of their main donors to completely pull his support for United Hatzalah. The donor called Eli and asked him if he had gone out of his mind and informed him that they were no longer going to be making donations to United Hatzalah.

Left with no choice, Eli traveled to the States to meet with the donor. In a beautiful example of Divine Providence, the donor's Israeli grandson was also there at the time and overheard the conversation between Eli and his grandparents.

"Can I say something?" the grandson asked. "It seems clear to me that the only way that an organization like United Hatzalah can possibly reach every place in the country is by utilizing as many members of the

Arab volunteers

population as possible — even if they're not religious and even if they're Arabs. Sure, you have to do background checks and make sure that they pose no danger, but if they are well intentioned and want to save lives, having them on board changes the entire equation and makes it much easier to reach all segments of the population in under ninety seconds.

"It's not like you can ignore an Arab who is having a heart attack. They live in Yerushalayim, and you need to treat them when they call just like you have to treat anyone else. And if that's the case, let them do the same for us."

The grandson's words made an impression on his grandmother.

Then he said something else.

"While I was serving in the army, we were stationed in Shechem. I saw a child fall off a high wall and land on his head. He was knocked out and lay there, unmoving. I ran over to the kid — I was an EMT in the army — and I saved his life."

Eli saw tears in the grandmother's eyes.

At that moment, Eli knew she was back.

A few months later, he met with the councilman, and the two of them had a long conversation.

"When you allowed Arabs to join your organization, I thought you were making some sort of political move," the councilman told him, "seeking to get support from the Arab population and left wingers. I realize now that with you it's all about saving lives and nothing more."

They would become good friends.

Years later, when Eli's father went into cardiac arrest on that never-to-be-forgotten Shabbos afternoon, one of the volunteers who arrived to help was an Arab volunteer — one of the original group of twenty-five. The Arab volunteer was the one who had the defibrillator, and he was the one who actually saved Gabi Beer's life.

But let's go back to Mohammed.

Years went by and Mohammed became very active in United Hatzalah. One afternoon he was driving his Hatzalah ambucycle home when a call came in. That particular day happened to have been during Ramadan, when Muslims fast during the day and eat at night, and Mohammed had promised his wife he would be back home early to help her prepare the nightly feast. He was on his way back to East Jerusalem when he got a call that a woman was giving birth in a nearby gas station.

He had promised his wife he was going to be on time that night. On the other hand, a woman was giving birth in a gas station nearby, and he was the volunteer closest to the call.

Feeling like he had no choice, Mohammed drove to the gas station, arriving at the scene thirty seconds later. There he found the woman giving birth in a car, with her husband, a Moroccan Jew in full rabbinic garb, complete with long beard and *peyos*, hovering anxiously at her side.

Mohammed didn't even have time to get his medical equipment out of his bag because the woman was already in the process of giving birth. The mother and her baby were both in distress.

It was all too much, and the husband fainted from sheer fright while his wife was shrieking in agony.

Soon another volunteer arrived and treated the husband, while Mohammed continued trying to deliver the baby. Then a third volunteer showed up to assist with the wife while Mohammed gave oxygen to the newborn. By the time the husband was up and back to himself, he discovered that he was the proud father of a healthy baby boy.

It so happens to be that through some vagary of genetics, Mohammed looks more like an Ashkenazi Jew than an Arab. He has blond hair and blue eyes and actually looks somewhat Scandinavian. The baby's father, by now completely recovered, went running over to Mohammed and began hugging and kissing the volunteer.

"You're like the Mashiach," he exclaimed. "You saved my wife and you saved my son. You're such a *tzaddik*, such a righteous man!"

"It was my pleasure."

"Listen, I want you to come to my son's bris, and I want you to serve as the *sandak*. I want you to hold my son on your knees when he is being brought into the covenant of Avraham, Yitzchak, and Yaakov!"

It was the craziest thing Mohammed had ever heard.

"No," he said, "that's not a good idea…"

"On the contrary," the father replied, "it's a wonderful idea. You are a *tzaddik*, and I want my son's *sandak* to be a *tzaddik*. I'm not taking no for an answer!"

Mohammed realized that the Moroccan Jew had no idea that he was in fact a "cousin" and not a "brother."

"I have to tell you something," he said to the father.

"Yes?"

"First of all, I really appreciate your offer. It warms my heart. But the volunteers of United Hatzalah do not accept gifts for doing their mission, and making me *sandak* would be the biggest gift you could give. I am therefore forced to turn you down."

"Please agree to my request," the father pleaded.

"I'll tell you what," Mohammed said. "I don't usually accept anything from the people I help. But I see that you really want to give me a token of your appreciation, so maybe just send my wife a small bouquet of flowers, with a note explaining to her that I stopped on my way home to deliver your child. That will be more than enough for me."

Flowers would hopefully get the guy off his back and would appease his wife so that she wouldn't be too upset that he hadn't come home on time as promised. A win-win situation all around.

"Wow," the father marveled. "Before this, I knew you were special, but now I understand that you're not just special, but truly humble, too! Not only do I want you to be the *sandak*, but I am going to name my son after you. What is your name?"

"Trust me, a little bouquet of flowers is more than enough."

"Forget the flowers! You saved my wife. You saved my son. You're the angel who saved my son's life. Of course, I want to name him after you. Please tell me your name!"

"I'm not sure if your son will do very well in yeshivah with the name Mohammed," the Arab volunteer told the father. "You probably think that everyone in United Hatzalah is Jewish, but I'm an Arab, my name is Mohammed, and yes, I am a volunteer."

Eyes wide open, the chassid said to Mohammed, "Give me your address, and tell your wife to expect not a small bouquet of flowers but an absolutely gigantic one. You may not be serving as our *sandak*, and we won't be naming our son after you, but flowers there will be..."

# CHAPTER TWENTY-THREE

# A Quantum Leap Forward

*D*ovie Maisel, who today serves as COO of United Hatzalah, is Eli Beer's cousin, and growing up, the two of them had a lot in common. Both joined Magen David Adom, both rose in the ranks, and both of them eventually ended up working closely together in Hatzalah. There were many dreams, yet neither of them ever envisioned the success they would come to see — a rescue organization with over six thousand two hundred volunteers.

Dovie's first encounter with rescue work is almost eerily reminiscent of Eli's.

"No one gets up in the morning one day and decides to become a volunteer for an organization like ours," Dovie says. "Something has to happen, which is why I like to say that our volunteers come with six thousand two hundred stories that either happened to them, to members of their family, or to someone in their community. Something happened to take them out of their comfort zone and make them say, 'I want to get the training to become a person who can save lives.'"

For Dovie, that moment happened on an afternoon in 1983. He was in the third grade and attending a school in the Givat Shaul neighborhood of Yerushalayim. One afternoon he was waiting at the bus stop after school not far from the Central Bus Station. Suddenly a little girl came running out of the park that was behind the bus stop, and ran across the sidewalk and into the street. Seconds later, she was hit by a bus.

People were screaming at those peering out of windows of the nearby buildings to call an ambulance. It felt like forever until it arrived. The worst part of it was that the Magen David Adom station was situated just two minutes away.

At a certain point, Dovie got up and ran home. When he arrived, he didn't tell his parents about what he had seen. He didn't talk to anyone about what happened that day for many years.

The next day, all the children in the school were informed that the daughter of one of the school's teachers, Rabbi Weiss, had been killed the day before.

And Dovie had seen the whole thing with his own eyes. He told himself then and there that when he grew up, he was going to learn whatever he needed to know so that he wouldn't be helpless the next time there was an opportunity to save someone's life when no one else knew what to do.

As a third grader, there wasn't much he could do about it, but he figured that maybe one day he would become a doctor and be able to make a difference.

As he got older, Dovie found it very hard to sit all day and concentrate in a school setting.

When Dovie was fourteen, his cousin Eli Beer told him that instead of cutting school and running around the neighborhood, as Eli himself was doing, he might as well start volunteering for MDA together with him. He would learn a lot about medicine and would be able to ride around in an ambulance.

Dovie loved the idea. He was in.

From the beginning, Eli was firmly established as the visionary of Hatzalah, while Dovie gravitated toward the operational side of things, doing his best to turn Eli's ideas into facts on the ground. In 2005, the year before United Hatzalah was established, Dovie had the opportunity to attend a conference for paramedics at a hotel in Eilat.

They were all having a grand old time, when they suddenly saw an ambulance pull up outside and some local paramedics came running through the lobby. Naturally, a group of EMTs followed to see if they needed help. It turned out that a guest at the hotel had just drowned in the pool — this during a conference for paramedics.

It had taken the ambulance at least eight minutes to arrive.

Back then, Nokia had just come out with a phone called the N95, which came equipped with a GPS component, except that when you pressed the GPS button, nothing happened other than the phone showing you your coordinates.

*If a phone can have a GPS component,* Dovie said to himself, *then on some level there exists the ability to communicate with a satellite. If we can use this system to track people, we could prevent a situation where paramedics could be sitting a few hundred feet from someone who just drowned and not know about it, because all they have are beepers from Yerushalayim that are relaying them information from back home but not what is happening locally.*

Dovie understood that the moment the GPS component was figured into the equation, medics could be informed about emergencies anywhere in the country, since the dispatch center would let whichever volunteer was closest to the emergency know about it by using the GPS on their phones.

Instinctively, Dovie knew this would be a game-changer in every way. He immediately began writing notes, keeping a notebook of ideas and diagrams and possibilities.

At one point, Dovie got in touch with a company called Matrix, which was based in Herzliya. They had just opened their mobile phone division, which was using all sorts of software off of Java and other technologies. Dovie shared his ideas with them, explaining that he wanted to use a person's geographic location to be able to coordinate between a place of emergency and the nearest responder.

Two weeks later they got back to him, showing him a beautiful booklet that they had produced to illustrate the technology and explaining that the idea did indeed exist in the realm of possibility.

Now the essential question: "How much will it cost to develop?"

It turned out that it would cost a million dollars to create.

That was a lot of money.

And yet, what was the alternative?

Dovie returned to Magen David Adom, where he was still volunteering at the time, and showed the booklet to the CEO, explaining how this was the future in emergency response.

"Forget beepers and everything else you know," Dovie said. "Right now there are many volunteers in Hatzalah and thousands of people working for Magen David Adom. If we can adapt this technology for ourselves, it will revolutionize the world of dispatching emergencies for all time."

But the CEO of Magen David Adom wasn't interested. Maybe he just couldn't foresee the possibilities. Maybe the cost was too high. Maybe the idea seemed too farfetched, and they needed to channel their resources elsewhere. The bottom line was that the answer was no.

Dovie left the CEO's office and went to speak to Eli Beer instead.

He showed Eli everything he had already done and explained how the emergency responders needed to adopt this as their working model.

Eli looked at him and said, "Dovie, you're crazy."

"You're right," Dovie replied. "That's exactly why we have to do this."

"Okay," Eli said, "let's say that you're on to something. How on earth are we going to raise a million dollars?"

"The best way to do this," Dovie said, "is by sending out letters to different charity foundations. We'll explain what we're trying to do and the amount of money we need to do it. Let's see what happens."

Several months later they received a letter in the mail from the Irving and Cherna Moskowitz Foundation.

Cherna Moskowitz visiting the United Hatzalah Dispatch Center

Cherna Moskowitz

Dear Mr. Maisel,

We at the Moskowitz Foundation loved reading about your idea and the innovation you are trying to bring to the critical field of lifesaving activities in the State of Israel. We are therefore sending you a check for one million dollars to invest in the development of this technology.

Eli and Dovie read the letter in growing astonishment and almost fainted when they saw what it said. When they came back to Planet Earth, they got to work.

Had they been thinking in terms of making money, they would have patented Dovie's invention. This is exactly the type of technology that Uber and many food delivery companies use to reach their clients. Had they gotten a patent, Dovie Maisel and Eli Beer would be multimillionaires today. But they were only thinking about saving lives by leveraging the power of community and not about making money.

The technology premiered in 2007. Today every volunteer receives a special phone from United Hatzalah. There is probably no "smarter" phone in existence today, but the phone has been programmed in a way that it's able to be used only for Hatzalah business. The phone can be used as a walkie-talkie, and it comes with an advanced GPS system so that the Hatzalah command center knows where every volunteer is at any given time. And because it can't be used for anything other than saving lives, even very religious volunteers who might prefer not to use a smartphone will make an exception — because this phone can be used for only one thing: to save lives.

United Hatzalah's technology is so powerful and so well tuned that the dispatch is able to send a special message to the five volunteers closest to the scene. At the same time that the message is relayed to the closest people on hand, it's also sent to the volunteers who specialize in that particular emergency.

And so United Hatzalah took a quantum leap forward in their ability to save lives. They would never stop using the latest and best technology to further their goals.

# A Call From the Chairman

Yair Hamburger is the chairman of Harel Insurance, a mega Israeli insurance company with billions of dollars in their yearly investment fund. The company is primarily owned by Yair and his brother Gideon. For years Eli had been hoping to meet the brothers for them to get to know what United Hatzalah is all about and convince them to donate funds to the organization.

The one time they spoke it didn't go well. Eli tried explaining what United Hatzalah did, but Yair Hamburger wasn't interested.

"Look, it sounds like you're doing wonderful work, but we usually focus on organizations that serve the entire country and not just certain sectors. From what I understand, you mostly deal with the religious sector in this country…"

Eli did his best to correct Yair's mistaken impression by explaining that United Hatzalah saves the lives of every single person who calls them no matter who they are, whatever their background or outlook. He also tried explaining that United Hatzalah had volunteers from all sectors of Israeli society who worked together and were able to treat one another with genuine respect.

"I hear what you're saying, Mr. Beer. But whenever I see you on TV, you're always surrounded by religious people."

Bottom line: Yair Hamburger wouldn't agree to sit down and meet with Eli Beer.

But G-d had other plans...

One afternoon, Yair Hamburger paid a visit to a store that sold and repaired eyeglasses in Kikar HaMedinah, in the center of Tel Aviv. The name of the store was Kleiner's, and Yair entered and handed his glasses to the man behind the counter. Yitzy Kleiner, who is a religious Jew, asked Yair a few questions about what he needed and then set to work, removing the lenses and tackling the repair job.

Suddenly the man working on his glasses received a message on his phone that made him stop everything he was doing. Without a word, he set Yair's glasses down on the table, donned a motorcycle jacket that had been on a chair, shoved a helmet onto his head, and ran out of the store, without even taking the time to explain what he was doing or why he had dropped everything from one second to the next.

Kleiner only said four words, "I'll be right back!" and off he went.

Yair, who couldn't see very well without his glasses, stared out the window and was just about able to make out the man jumping onto a motorcycle that had been parked on the street. Then, siren blaring, the man from the glasses store raced off the sidewalk and into the street.

Yair's glasses were lying forlornly on the counter, its lenses still out of the frame, which meant that he had no choice but to remain where he was for the time being. And so he waited, hoping to receive an explanation when Kleiner returned.

Kleiner eventually returned from the call about half an hour later, his face red with exertion, his forehead covered in sweat.

"I'm so sorry to have left you in the middle of fixing your glasses," he apologized as he went to the sink to wash his hands, "but an emergency call came in and I had to run."

"Do you work for Magen David Adom?"

"No, I volunteer for an organization called United Hatzalah, and the call that came in was for a kid who was run over by a bus on Jabotinsky Street nearby. It was literally a matter of life and death, and I didn't even have the time to explain to you why I had to drop everything and run."

"I don't understand," Yair said. "You work in an eyeglasses shop, and you're also a member of United Hatzalah?"

"Yes, I volunteer for the organization."

"How does that work exactly?"

Then, suddenly, something clicked in his brain. "Wait a second," Yair said. "Is this Hatzalah thing connected to Eli Beer?"

"Yes, he's the founder."

"Here's my card," Hamburger told Kleiner. "Give it to him and tell him to call me right away. I want to talk to him."

Kleiner glanced at the card, and his eyes widened when he saw the words written on it: "Yair Hamburger, Chairman, Harel Insurance."

Yitzy didn't waste any time. He promptly called Eli.

"How's everything?"

"*Baruch Hashem.* You?"

"Wonderful."

Eli liked Yitzy, who was actually the head of their Petach Tikvah branch. Now he waited to hear why he was calling. Kleiner didn't tell Eli how he had met Hamburger. He just relayed the message.

"I just met this guy, Yair Hamburger, and he asked me to let you know that he wants you to call him."

Eli was a little puzzled that Yair wanted to speak to him — after all, the last time they'd spoken, he'd brushed him off, but if Yair had had a change of heart, that was fine with Eli. When they disconnected, Eli promptly called Yair.

"Eli, thank you for calling me."

"My pleasure."

"Eli, I'd like for the two of us to meet as soon as possible. When can we make that happen? Where are you right now?"

"I'm in Yerushalayim."

"Can you come down to Ramat Gan? We'll meet at the Harel headquarters."

"I can be there in forty-five minutes."

Eli jumped into his car and drove to Ramat Gan, his heart pounding with excitement the entire drive. When he arrived at the Harel skyscraper, he turned into the underground parking lot. A guard stopped him.

"Where to, sir?"

"I have a meeting with Yair Hamburger."

The gates swung open, and Eli parked the car in the first available spot. Then he took the elevator to the top floor of the building. A secretary was waiting for him.

After offering coffee, the secretary showed him to a conference room to wait. As Eli sat at the polished table sipping his coffee, he studied the vast array of plaques displayed on the walls — plaques that had been given to the Hamburger family for a range of charitable activities. Eli was impressed. It was obvious that these were people who took their charity-giving seriously.

Soon Yair entered the room.

"I just want to tell you that I am proud to meet you," Yair said without preamble.

"Why? What happened since the last time we spoke?"

Yair told Eli about the encounter he'd had when getting his glasses repaired.

"I saw what you were talking about with my own eyes. I used to think you only helped religious people. But I can't say that anymore. I saw how a religious person dropped everything he was doing to save a child who didn't come from a religious home."

Yair paused, and it was clear that he had something important on his mind.

"I like what I saw and I want to help you develop United Hatzalah. But on one condition: I'm prepared to donate one and a half million

Eli, Yair Hamburger, and Eli Pollak

shekels to your organization if you're willing to allow me to partner with you and help you widen your reach."

"What do you mean?"

"Look, Eli, I live in Kfar Shmaryahu in the city of Herzliya. I want Hatzalah volunteers in my neighborhood, in Kfar Shmaryahu. I want my money to translate into growth. I want to see United Hatzalah developing and becoming home to more and more volunteers — from all parts of the country.

"More than that, I have three thousand employees. I want to offer every one of them the opportunity to become a volunteer at United Hatzalah, and I want them to drop everything they are doing when a call comes in while they're in the middle of work. I want the concept of what you do at United Hatzalah to become part of the culture of Harel Insurance."

Eli extended his hand. "You have a deal," he said, and the two of them shook hands. "I will work with you to open a branch of United Hatzalah right here in your company."

Yair wasn't joking around. In the first year after Eli met with him, the Hamburger family dedicated one hundred ambucycles to United Hatzalah, driven to the ceremony by volunteers. On every motorcycle

Ambucycle dedication for Harel Insurance

Ambucycle dedication ceremony outside the Harel building in Ramat Gan

was written, "United Hatzalah partners with Harel Insurance," along with the company's logo, bringing home the fact that they were the first company in Israel to treat United Hatzalah as true partners in every sense of the word.

The relationship that began between them that day has never wavered. The Hamburgers have donated significantly every single year since they first met, and every Chanukah, United Hatzalah celebrates an "*Al HaNissim*" party at the company headquarters. They light the Chanukah candles and invite volunteers from the company to join them.

There are over one hundred volunteers within the company who leave work to go on emergency calls on a regular basis, and the number is constantly increasing. Yair's own secretary has even started volunteering for the Ten Kavod project, which United Hatzalah initiated for elderly people around the country, where younger people spend time with older people at their homes and make sure they have everything they need and are healthy and well.

So it was that Yair Hamburger came to see what United Hatzalah is about and what it does at a moment when he wasn't even wearing his glasses.

Oh, the irony of life.

# CHAPTER TWENTY-FIVE

# Making Mistakes

There are quite a few rules when it comes to fundraising, and by now Eli Beer knows them all. The reason he knows them so well is because he learned them the hard way. There were times along the way when he made mistakes and had to ask for forgiveness. But no matter what happened between him and any of the donors, he never gave up on any relationship.

If you happen to cross paths with Eli and ask him for advice, you'll find that he's generous with his answers, because he's been there and figures that you might as well benefit from the knowledge he's gained through experience.

"Let's say you meet a wealthy person," he says, "and he's interested in your organization and the things you're doing. Here's a piece of advice: Don't ask that donor to introduce you to his friends or family. One of the reasons donors get annoyed and stop contributing to a particular cause is if they feel they are treated like a ladder and that you want to use them to get to someone else. When that happens, you've lost them. If they want to introduce you to their relatives and friends, they need to do so on their own and not because you asked them to."

When it comes to donors, Eli puts a priority on relationships. "The donors are not donors," he says, "but partners and friends."

It should never just be about coming to them once a year for money, he says. There are times when Eli might visit a donor seven times before asking them for money. Because it's not about money — it's about friendship.

"If they need me, they know that I'm there for them — just like they are there for me. At the end of the day, we're all partners in saving lives, and it's something we are passionate about. But the relationship needs to come from the right place."

The year 2007 brought more new friends and partners into the United Hatzalah family. Eli was introduced to David Bernstein and his wife, Jean. Shortly thereafter the couple decided to sponsor an ambucycle.

Eli thanked them profusely. Then he asked them his standard question when people donate an ambucycle.

"What name should we put on it?"

They weren't sure. In the end, he left their home without an answer. Eli dropped David a line from time to time asking him if they had made a decision about the name yet, and then, during one conversation, David asked Eli if he knew his business partner.

"Who is your partner?"

"His name is Jay Schottenstein."

"I never met him personally," Eli said, "but his name and reputation as the patron of the ArtScroll Talmud precede him."

"Well, then, maybe one day I'll introduce you to him."

For some reason, Eli hung up the phone that day with the assumption that Jay and David were not only partners in business, but had also partnered in funding the ambucycle that David had donated. Which was why, when it was time to put the new motorcycle on the road, and still not having been told by David what name to write on it, Eli asked his staff to write on it, "Donated by David and Jean Bernstein and Jay and Jeanie Schottenstein."

It was one of fifty ambucycles that United Hatzalah purchased that year.

In an interesting twist of Divine Providence, the Bernstein/Schottenstein motorcycle ended up outside the Great Synagogue in Yerushalayim one day when the volunteer who drove it happened to park it right outside the world-famous house of prayer.

That same day — it was during Chol HaMoed Succos — Jay and Jeanie Schottenstein were walking through the streets of Yerushalayim,

Jay and Jeanie Schottenstein with the motorcycle that had their name on it

enjoying the sights and sounds of the Holy City, when they suddenly noticed a motorcycle that was parked nearby. Something about it caught their eye, and they walked over to examine it a little closer. To their surprise, they saw that it had been donated by their friends David and Jean — and by themselves!

Whereas most people would have known whether they had donated a motorcycle to an organization, the Schottenstein family gives such a vast sum to charity that they simply thought that they didn't realize that United Hatzalah was among their beneficiaries.

In another fascinating twist of fate, Eli Beer ran into Jay and Jeanie later that afternoon at their hotel. Chol HaMoed Succos is always a busy time for Eli since United Hatzalah holds an annual concert during that time of year, and he visits the various Yerushalayim hotels, shmoozing with the guests and convincing people to purchase tickets for the show.

Eli was in the middle of a conversation with another group of guests when they walked in.

"That's Jay Schottenstein," a man told him.

Soon enough, they were deep in conversation.

"I wanted to tell you how much I appreciate everything that you're

Eli Beer and Bob Book

doing for the Jewish people," Eli told the couple.

"Thank you," they replied. "By the way, we just saw the ambucycle with our name on it. It was parked outside the Great Synagogue."

Eli and the Schottensteins spent some time getting to know one another, and during the course of the conversation, they introduced him to another couple who was there with them at the hotel — Bob and Amy Book. Bob and Amy are best friends with Jay and Jeanie Schottenstein, and Jay insisted that he and his wife meet Eli and hear his story.

After they had spoken for a few minutes, Eli said, "You know, the best way for you to really understand what United Hatzalah is trying to accomplish is if you come and visit our headquarters and take a tour."

Bob gave Eli his card, but Jay and Jeanie were the ones who came, and they were fascinated by everything they learned about United Hatzalah. By the time the tour was over, the two of them were ready to sign up and help Eli in whatever way they could.

And so through seeing an ambucycle that they didn't actually donate, Jay and Jeanie ended up becoming deeply involved with United Hatzalah, eventually joining the international board and becoming close friends with Eli Beer along the way.

While Jay and Jeanie had become true friends of Hatzalah, Eli still had yet to connect with Bob Book. Bob hadn't come to headquarters, and when Eli tried calling him in the States, Book's assistant never put him through. This went on for three months. Many people might have given up after three months of failure. Not Eli. If anything, he had become more determined to meet the elusive Bob Book.

One year later, they met again.

Jay and Jeanie Schottenstein

Eli couldn't help feeling an acute sense of déjà vu as Jay Schottenstein began telling Bob how much he loved United Hatzalah and how they had already donated a few ambucycles to the organization.

"That's right," Bob said. "I never came to see your headquarters. I remember giving you my card. Why didn't you ever call me?"

"I did call you. I left a bunch of messages, but you never got back to me."

On the spot, Bob called his assistant. "Listen," he said, "whenever Eli Beer calls me, put him through."

Then, turning to Eli, he said, "This time we're coming to see your operation."

And Bob and Amy did. And they loved what they saw.

"Eli," he said, "I want to donate one hundred bags of medical equipment for your volunteers."

Eli Beer and Bob Book became very close. And since it was a real relationship, sometimes people make mistakes and things go wrong. Bob had grown up on the Lower East Side and built himself up from nothing. He is the nicest guy in the world, but he's also a tough businessman who expects a lot from the people around him — and sometimes Eli didn't measure up. Eli was still a relatively young man, in his thirties, and there were times when he treated their special relationship with a little too much familiarity, constantly talking about Hatzalah and hardly showing any interest in anything else, almost as if Bob was a relative of his who had to love him no matter what he did.

One day Bob reached the end of his rope, and he made it clear to Eli that the friendship was over and he wanted nothing more to do with him. Needless to say, Eli felt terrible, especially since he honestly respected Bob Book as a person and felt like he had let him down.

They didn't speak for a long time.

Eli tried to shake it off at first, but the fact that they weren't in contact any longer really troubled him since Bob had been like an older brother to him, and now a cherished connection was no more. Bob had always given Eli good advice, the kind of advice that Eli instinctively understood would be a good idea to follow. It was Bob who explained to Eli that he didn't have to talk about Hatzalah every time he had a conversation with a donor.

"Learn how to talk about other things," he used to say. "Otherwise you're going to annoy people. If you want people to want to be around you, then be an interesting person, not someone with a one-track mind who only knows how to talk about one thing."

Eli had made it a practice of going to Bob for advice before big events because Bob always had good ideas on how to capture a crowd. He even went to him for personal advice. Bob had been a real mentor to him, and he was truly saddened by the way things had turned out. He decided that he was going to make it up to him.

One day Eli was visiting Florida, and he decided to call Bob and ask if he could come over to see him.

"It's Eli," he said when Bob answered. "I'm in Florida. Can I come over and see you?"

Bob asked, "Where are you?" to which Eli answered, "I'm right outside your door."

They ended up getting together. It was a tough meeting but fruitful. Bob told Eli to his face how he had to get his act together and learn not to annoy people who cared about him, especially since they were going out of their way to help him.

Bob Book

"Look," Bob told his younger friend. "I get it. You're passionate about what you do and the organization you created, and that's exactly the way it should be. At the same time, you need to stop talking so much and to start listening more. If your donors are your friends, then treat them the way you treat a friend. Be empathetic. Be kind. Be there for them. And stop focusing on yourself so much!"

Bob looked at Eli and saw that Eli was really listening to what he was saying.

Then Bob gave him a smile.

"Eli, don't worry so much about United Hatzalah. You have a good thing going. People like you and trust you. They want to help. So keep on doing your thing, but calm down. You'll see, it will be okay.

"And, Eli," he continued, "I'm talking about the way you live as well. You can't go through life thinking about what you do twenty-four seven, no matter how important it is. Sometimes you need to take a break and decompress. Trust me, it will only make you better at what you do."

By the time they said goodbye, both of them knew that the friendship was much stronger than it had been before they had gotten into a disagreement. It was an important lesson for Eli and taught him that sometimes a conflict can lead to something even greater in the long run.

# CHAPTER TWENTY-SIX

# The Happiest Man in the World

During the course of his fundraising forays, Eli Beer has crossed paths with many fascinating individuals. One such person is Leonardo Farkas, a philanthropist from Chile. From the trademark curly blond hair cascading down to his shoulders to his penchant for handing out hundred-dollar bills to every person he meets at the Kosel, Farkas is a real personality. Despite his vast wealth, he has never lost touch with his roots. Growing up as a child in Chile, Leonardo's father told him stories of his escape from Europe before it was too late. The knowledge that his father had to run for his life from the home where he was born never left him.

A talented musician, Leonardo Farkas began his professional career playing piano at the Concord Hotel in the Catskill Mountains, where he serenaded his audience with South American music. People loved listening to him sing and play, and on a good day they gave him tips. Usually the tips were nothing much to write home about, but once in a while someone would give him one hundred dollars. He still remembers his feelings of gratitude at receiving those tips.

Over the years Leonardo became extremely wealthy through his ownership of mines and other business ventures, but the more money he made, the more he gave away. When a horrific mining accident occurred in Chile, Leonardo gave ten thousand dollars to the family of each one of the workers who had died — and it wasn't even his mine.

When he was young, before he became wealthy, Leonardo remembers watching people vie for *shishi*, the *aliyah* for the sixth portion of the weekly Torah reading. He remembers how they were willing to spend money to receive that *aliyah* and filed that piece of information away in his mind. Years later, he began frequenting a different shul every Shabbos and would always purchase *shishi*, donating a large sum of money to the shul.

Eli first met Leonardo in 2008, and after Eli had gotten to know Leonardo to some degree, he decided to ask the billionaire if he would be willing to sponsor all United Hatzalah activities in the city of Haifa.

"How much does it cost?" Farkas wanted to know.

"Fifty thousand dollars."

"I'll tell you what," Farkas said. "I'll give you a hundred thousand dollars and sponsor two cities: fifty for Haifa and another fifty for Tzefas."

Eli was blown away. It wasn't often that a donor gave him double the amount he'd asked for. It was yet another example of the type of person Leonardo is: a man who gives charity without being asked for it.

Then Eli made a mistake.

Yes, even after Bob Book had rebuked him and he had promised himself that he would never mess up again, he made a rookie error, the kind of mistake that should never have occurred.

Eli was so overcome when Leonardo had offered to sponsor two cities that he sent him an email about a week later, explaining that Tzefas was in need of a new ambucycle and asking whether he would be willing to sponsor that as well in addition to the hundred thousand dollars he'd already given.

It was too much.

While Eli is famous for using chutzpah and getting away with it, this wasn't chutzpah, it was stupidity — and Leonardo Farkas was decidedly not amused.

His response was emphatic:

"Never contact me again!" he wrote. "I've already sent the hundred thousand, which I had promised, and with that, our relationship has come to an end!"

For the next three days, Eli Beer couldn't sleep. Unlike the mistakes he'd made with Bob Book, which had stemmed from a lack of self-awareness, there was no excusing the mistake he had made with

Leonardo Farkas. It was a wrong move on every level, and there was no way to justify what he had done.

Eli felt like he'd just caused real damage to United Hatzalah because Leonardo had been so generous and had told Eli that he planned on contributing generously on an annual basis.

*How could you make such a stupid mistake?* he asked himself over and over.

Eventually Eli began drafting an apology. He must have written one hundred drafts, trying to find the exact words that expressed the level of remorse he felt for having treated such a good person with such disrespect. He wrote and erased, wrote and erased, trying to get it right. Then one day he just sat down and wrote another email — every word emanating from the deepest recesses of his heart:

> Dear Leonardo,
>
> I have learned so much from the mistake that I made. I will never make the same mistake again — not with you and not with anyone else. It was a terrible mistake. I'm so passionate about United Hatzalah, I think about it all day. It's my dream, my life, and when I know that there's a need, I ask right away and I don't think twice. And this can sometimes be a problem.
>
> I promise you that the lesson you taught me will remain with me forever, and I will make sure to be more careful in the future. I am asking you for forgiveness and begging you not to punish the organization because of my mistake. Please continue supporting Haifa and Tzefas — and I will never make the same mistake again. I have learned a lesson for life.
>
> Eli Beer

When Eli pressed the Send button, his heart was pounding. Was the email too little and too late? But there was nothing more for him to do. He had done the best he could to make amends, and the rest was up to the One above.

Leonardo Farkas replied to Eli's email two hours later:

> Dear Eli,
>
> I forgive you, and I'm sending you the ambucycle that you asked for.
>
> Leonardo

After that, they became best friends. The next time Leonardo visited Israel, Eli gave him a tour of United Hatzalah headquarters. He loved

Leonardo Farkas with Eli outside United Hatzalah HQ

everything about the organization. Eli also took him to the Kosel and watched the love for Hashem and the Jewish people that poured forth from the Chilean Jew.

They became such close friends that Leonardo asked Eli to accompany him on a very unique trip — a journey back into his past.

The destination was Ukraine and Romania.

"I did some research," Leonardo explained, "and I managed to find the location of the village where my father was born. I also found out the name of the family who helped my father escape from Europe before the war. The man himself is no longer alive, but his son still lives in the same village, and I want to visit him and give him a token of appreciation for what his father did."

Eli wasn't the only one who came along for the ride. A large group of rabbis was invited to join Leonardo for what promised to be an epic and historic moment. They flew to Ukraine in Leonardo's private plane and were driven by limo to the graves of a number of famous rabbinical figures of the past, among them the tomb of Rabbi Nachman of Breslov in Uman.

Eventually they made their way to the home of the benefactor's son, who lived in a little village near Satu Mare on the Ukrainian-Hungarian border. As they drove down the street of the little village, they passed a series of tiny houses, simple and austere. Each was bordered by a garden, and in some cases cars of uncertain vintage were parked nearby. As they approached the home of the man they were coming to see, Leonardo handed Eli a bag and asked him to hold on to it.

"What's inside?"

Eli almost fainted when he heard the answer.

It was a quarter of a million euros — enough money for the man to live calmly and peacefully for the rest of his life.

The man they had come to see lived in what was essentially a corrugated shack set a little ways back from the road. There was a goat tethered to a tree in front of the house, and a bunch of chickens were running around, pecking at the ground. An aged Russian-made Lada was parked just outside, a throwback to the days when Romania was part of the USSR.

When their vehicles came to a stop in front of the man's house, he rushed outside to greet them, ushering the entire party into his home, where he had set up a buffet in their honor.

A typical Eastern European village

Visiting the village to give away 250,000 euros

Obviously, they couldn't eat any of the cooked food, but the gesture was heartwarming, and they were at least able to eat some homegrown fruits and vegetables that were set out as well. There was a piano in the living room, and Leonardo played in honor of the occasion.

At some point in the conversation, they turned to the purpose of their visit.

"Tell me something," Leonardo said to the Romanian gentleman. "How much money do you make a month?"

"I earn three hundred euros."

"And your wife, does she work?"

"Yes."

"What does she earn?"

"Two hundred and fifty euros every month."

"Do you have children?"

"I have a daughter."

"And what does she do?"

"My daughter is currently studying in university."

Leonardo paused.

"Tell me something," he said to the son of the man who saved

Eli in the village

his father's life. "Is there anything you would want to do if you had the money? Maybe renovate your house or buy a new house? Maybe purchase a new car? I want to do something for you."

Eli was standing right there as they spoke. He could feel the two hundred and fifty thousand euros through the thin material of the bag he was holding.

"I don't need anything," the man replied. "I have everything I could possibly need."

He opened the window and pointed at the Russian Lada parked outside. "I have a car. It works well. It even has air conditioning."

"What about your house?"

"My house? Look at my beautiful house. I don't need anything. My house is perfect. I'm a lucky man."

"What about your daughter? Maybe she needs money to pay for her university?"

"No, I saved money for years to pay for that. It's all taken care of."

It was an incredible scene. Leonardo Farkas — a truly wealthy man — had traveled all that way to visit the son of a man who had saved his father because he wanted to reward him with two hundred and fifty thousand euros, and the man was refusing to accept any part of the gift.

"You don't need anything?" Leonardo asked him.

"No, I'm happy with what I have. I don't need or want anything more."

Eli was incredulous. He was looking around at the old man's old house, at his old car, and he knew that he had never imagined such a situation in his wildest dreams — where a person would turn down such a gift because he felt that he already had everything in the world. It was impossible to fathom.

Leonardo was begging him.

"Please let me give you the money."

"No, I don't want it. I'm happy that you came to visit me, and I want us to remain friends. But I don't want your money."

"Okay, I get it," Leonardo told the man. "You don't want the money. Is there anything you would want me to use the money for? Anything we can do to help your village?"

The man considered his words.

"You can donate the money to the local elementary school," he said at last. "Their building is very old, and it would be nice if it would be renovated and turned into something special for the children."

Leonardo Farkas, Mark Gerson, Ambassador David Friedman, and Eli

With that, the visit came to an end and the group took leave of the man in the shack with the Lada parked a few yards from his front door.

Leonardo ended up doing exactly as the man requested. In addition, he found the cemetery where his grandfather was buried and paid for it to be renovated as well. He also hired a caretaker to make sure it remained in good condition.

Later that day, Eli Beer sat down and wrote a letter to his children.

Dear kids,

Today I met the richest man in the world. You're probably thinking that I met Bill Gates or someone like that. But I'm actually talking about an old Romanian man who turned down 250,000 euros because he has everything in the world that he wants and needs. Meeting him really brought home the words of *Pirkei Avos*: "Who is rich? He who is satisfied with his lot."

Most rich people in the world will never be truly wealthy because they will always want more than what they have. But not this man. He wanted nothing more and was truly satisfied with everything he'd been given from Above.

Like I said — a truly wealthy man.

Abba

# PART FIVE

*I can travel up to two hundred days a year. I wake up in the morning and I'm not sure if I'm in Chicago, L.A., or Sao Paulo.*

— Eli Beer

# CHAPTER TWENTY-SEVEN

# What a Volunteer Has to Know

*A*new organization, a new beginning, and new alliances. Somehow they were standing poised on the cusp of a new reality. Peace had been achieved between the different branches and cities, and Eli wanted a blessing from a great rabbi to cement it all into place.

And so he opted to pay a call to Maran Rav Ovadia Yosef, one of the most renowned rabbinical figures in the country who had served in

Meeting with Rav Ovadia

Five Hatzalah members at the Kosel

the position of chief rabbi of Israel. The rabbi's son, Rav Dovid Yosef, accompanied Eli into his father's office and provided the introduction, explaining who he was and why he had come to see the *rav*.

As was his wont, Rav Ovadia gave Eli an affectionate slap on the cheek before questioning him at length on the way the organization was set up and how they dealt with all the halachic queries that arose.

Eli answered the *rav* question by question. He explained that Rav Moshe Halberstam had served as the organization's rabbi in its early

Rav Ovadia giving Eli an affectionate slap

Eli with Rav Nissim Karelitz

years, and after he passed away, Rav Nissim Karelitz took an active and decisive role in the development of United Hatzalah. Though Eli made sure to keep Rav Elyashiv abreast of the big picture, Rav Nissim Karelitz was the rabbinical authority who was consulted on every small detail. At the same time, Eli was also a frequent visitor to the home of Rav Chaim Kanievsky, sharing the challenges that United Hatzalah was undergoing and seeking advice and guidance, which was extremely forthcoming.

After the establishment of United Hatzalah, Rav Elyashiv, Rav Nissim Karelitz, and Rav Chaim helped Eli select four rabbinical authorities who would be in charge of answering all halachic questions that arose within the organization. Rav Shaya Karelitz would serve as the halachic secretary, coordinating between the different rabbinical authorities. Today the majority of halachic questions that arise are directed to him.

Rav Ovadia heard his reply. Then came a zinger.

"Does United Hatzalah have any Sefardic rabbis on their halachic board?"

Eli admitted that they did not. But he promised to change that. Shortly afterward, a young and dynamic Sefardic rabbi was chosen to serve as another address for the questions that arose.

Adhering to halachah plays an enormous role in the operation of United Hatzalah, and much effort is made to ensure that it remains a central focus. It isn't just about seeking answers to questions that arise, but also making sure the volunteers know which questions to ask and how. On Rav Elyashiv's directive, the organization allocates a yearly

Eli with Rav Nissim Karelitz

budget for every volunteer to take a special course where they learn all the relevant halachos they need to know. They are taught the laws of Shabbos, for example, and how they intersect with saving lives. It's complex material, and every volunteer has to be familiar with the details.

"We ended up establishing an entire department specifically geared to provide training for every volunteer," Eli says, "regardless of how they classify themselves from a religious perspective. No matter who

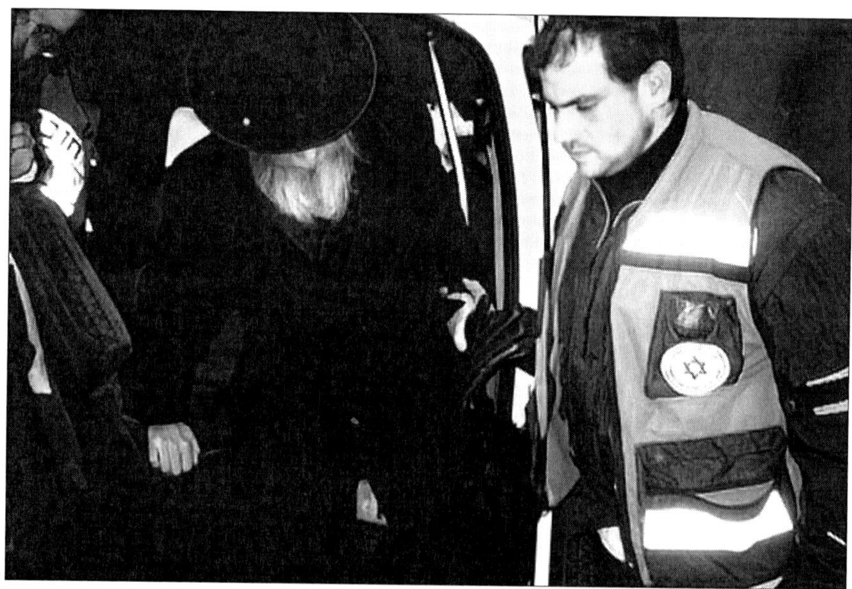

With Rav Don Segal

With Rav Dovid Feinstein

they are, they attend the course and they learn the halachos. There's a curriculum, complete with tests, which everyone has to take if they want to join the organization."

There is another aspect to this that has to be taken into account. In many cases, religious volunteers are traumatized after the first time they go on a call on Shabbos. And often the trauma comes from an unexpected direction. There are times when a volunteer will go out for a call on Shabbos, and when he reaches the patient, he realizes that the caller made a mistake and the patient had not truly been in danger in the first place. Suddenly the volunteer can't stop thinking that he desecrated Shabbos for no reason. That's very traumatic for someone who has kept Shabbos his entire life. He might even become depressed because of what he did.

Eli and his team came to the conclusion that such a volunteer needs to be treated by expert psychologists who are able to help him heal. At the same time, he needs to be well versed in the laws of Shabbos so that he understands exactly what is permissible and what is not.

Today each volunteer is given a *sefer* with all the relevant halachos. It was written by Rabbi Naftali Halpern, who invested ten years in researching the topic of medicine in halachah. He eventually penned a halachic manual containing all the guidelines. And even after they have passed their tests, the volunteers are obligated to attend a refresher course once a year. This is designed to keep their minds and memories sharp.

It's not just the Jewish volunteers who go through halachic training. Even the Arab volunteers go through a certain amount of training so that they're familiar with the basics of the laws of Shabbos.

"Otherwise we're looking at a recipe for disaster," Eli explains. "But because they have been schooled with regard to Jewish law, they understand why no one is answering them if they say something nonessential on the radio on a Shabbos afternoon. They understand why silence is maintained on Shabbos unless it is directly related to an emergency."

On the other side of the coin, having non-Jewish volunteers on the team also means becoming familiar with the laws of the religions that govern the lives of millions of people living in Israel. Interestingly enough, no one has ever had a problem with this — not the volunteers who aren't Jewish nor the volunteers who identify themselves as secular Jews. Everyone respects the guidelines and operates accordingly, ensuring that United Hatzalah remains above the politics and disagreements that fray the edges of so many other groups in Israel.

Aside from the mandatory halachah course, the volunteers have the option of attending a Talmud class that is given at Hatzalah headquarters. There are many young men who have a difficult time sitting and learning in yeshivah, much like Eli himself when he was young, and some of these boys end up volunteering for United Hatzalah. So Eli had an idea. He decided to organize a special learning session, a Talmud class, just for these boys at Hatzalah. The class is given by a rabbi who is also a volunteer with United Hatzalah and has a wonderful way with the boys. They love his style and appreciate the opportunity to get reacquainted with Gemara learning.

Eli loves dropping in and taking part in the *shiur*. It reminds him of how people deserve another chance and the potential one can uncover in every person. And as he looks around at the faces riveted to the rabbi's words, Eli sees himself thirty years earlier. And he smiles.

There are additional criteria required by United Hatzalah volunteers, other than the knowledge they need to respond to emergencies. Every volunteer has to submit police documentation proving that he has always been a law-abiding citizen. There was no way Eli would allow volunteers with criminal records into the organization, not when they would be entering the homes of people caught in the throes of an emergency. No, he needed to know that he could trust every volunteer implicitly.

But he didn't content himself with that. Even after the police documentation is submitted, phone calls are made to the references provided — to their boss, friends, and relatives. It's somewhat similar to the procedure used by religious families when they research a prospective spouse for their children. Due diligence.

Another aspect they need to take into consideration is whether the prospective candidate is the type of person who has the ability to make themselves available to go on calls and whether he will actually do so. Let's say the volunteer works as a teacher. Many schools don't want their teachers running in and out of the classroom and leaving the children in the middle of a lesson. Other schools consider such a sight the best kind of *chinuch* (education) and encourage their teachers to join Hatzalah. It depends on the individual school.

If the volunteer works for a demanding boss, there is a good chance he will run into trouble if he leaves too often on calls. Even if he's self-employed and can come and go as he pleases, it's vital to know whether he has the right kind of personality — because no one wants to spend the time and money it takes to train a volunteer only to discover that he possesses a lazy nature and isn't interested in going on more than one or two calls a week.

Eli also wanted every volunteer to know how to take blood and to administer EKGs — to become proficient in areas they simply don't have enough practice in. He came up with the idea of sending the volunteers to train in the emergency rooms of some of the local hospitals. This was good for everyone involved — for the hospitals because they're usually short-staffed, and for United Hatzalah, because it gave volunteers the opportunity to train in real time.

The first hospital that agreed to take part in the program was

Rambam Hospital in Haifa. Today United Hatzalah is running this program in twenty-seven hospitals all around the country. Several years after it was launched, Eli was visiting someone in Los Angeles and the secretary recounted how one of the female volunteers saved her daughter's life while she was waiting in the emergency room.

"My daughter didn't feel well," the secretary said, "and she was taken to Hadassah Hospital. She had terrible stomach pains, but there were so many people there that night that it was taking the doctors a very long time to get to her. Meanwhile, she was suffering terribly. Suddenly a female volunteer from United Hatzalah approached her and began asking her questions as she tried to determine what was wrong.

"It didn't take long for the volunteer to figure out that my daughter had appendicitis. She immediately went to speak with one of the top doctors, who rushed over, examined her, and sent her for X-rays. This was followed by an emergency appendectomy. The volunteer remained at her side the entire time. I just had to thank you for creating such an incredible organization, where people go above and beyond just because they care."

Eli was touched by the story. He was also curious to know the name of the volunteer in question. On the spot, he called his office in Yerushalayim. Giving them the date, he asked his secretary to please tell him the name of the volunteer who had been at Hadassah Hospital that night.

"It was your wife, Gitty," they replied.

Eli promptly called his wife and introduced her to the mother of the girl she had saved.

Knowing how important it was for the volunteers to receive an injection of *chizuk* (encouragement) from time to time, Eli decided to arrange a special event at a Petach Tikvah wedding hall called Heichalei Shlomo. The volunteers were invited to the event, where they were addressed by Rav Aharon Leib Shteinman and many other illustrious rabbinical figures. At that time there were fifteen hundred volunteers, and they packed the hall with good cheer and a rousing rendition of *"Yamim al Yemei Melech"* (a song traditionally sung to honor Torah scholars when they enter a room) as the rabbis arrived at the hall. The fact that so many respected personages had publicly come to give

Dealing with a situation

support to United Hatzalah gave the volunteers a tremendous boost and injected them with the feeling that their work was holy and worthy of the *mesiras nefesh* (self-sacrifice) it demanded of them.

It hadn't been that long ago since many had been opposed to United Hatzalah introducing the idea of riding motorcycles to the *chareidi* community. Many publicly protested their carrying a radio on Shabbos and leaving their Shabbos table to go out on calls.

Yet here was Rav Shteinman, one of the most revered leaders of the generation, addressing them at their event and encouraging them to continue their vital work. And who was he talking to? To a group consisting of all types and stripes. Everyone was represented in that group of volunteers. Litvaks and chassidim, Breslovers and Chabadniks, Vizhnitz and Satmar, Sefardim and Ashkenazim, *chareidim* and *dati leumi.* There was also a group of secular volunteers, wearing *kippot* on their heads as a sign of respect. Many of them joined the minyan for Maariv as well.

For this particular group, seeing a rabbi like Rav Shteinman speak was especially powerful since they had never encountered a *chareidi* rabbi before, and he made a huge impression, mesmerizing them with his words and presence. Every single one of the secular volunteers sought out Eli Beer after the event to tell him how impressed they had been by the rabbis who spoke and by the message they had stressed, reiterating the importance of the mitzvah of *pikuach nefesh*, of saving lives, and how happy they were making G-d with their activities.

Eli cried a lot that night. But they were happy tears — tears of joy, of satisfaction and *nachas*, at all that had been accomplished, and tears of hope for all they might achieve in the future.

Niv, United Hatzalah's first nonreligious volunteer, approached Eli later that day.

"Did I ever tell you where I grew up?"

"No, you didn't."

"I was raised on a kibbutz. My grandmother was a Holocaust survivor who lost her entire family in the camps, and she hated anything to do with religion. She hated religion so much that she would prepare a festive meal for the entire kibbutz every Yom Kippur. Not only did she prepare and serve this meal," Niv continued, "but she went out of her way to show her hatred of religion and Hashem by serving pork chops to the entire gathering! This was my life.

"Today I came to this event, and for the first time in my life I saw a great rabbi — a rabbi with a beard, who is without question an incredible Torah scholar — and this rabbi is talking about the greatness of the mitzvah of saving lives, how we are epitomizing the concept of '*v'ahavta l'rei'acha kamocha*,' of loving your friend as yourself.

"You know, Eli," he went on, "all my life I grew up thinking that rabbis were the bad guys, people who were doing their best to keep us in the Middle Ages. That's the way it had always been portrayed to me by the media, and I swallowed everything I was fed. But then I came here today, and I saw a room filled with fifteen hundred volunteers who are part of an army — not the IDF, but an army that saves lives and protects everyone who needs their help — religious and nonreligious and even non-Jews — and they are being praised for doing so by the greatest rabbis, and I realized that all of my preconceived notions had just flown out the window.

"Eli," Niv concluded, "what I saw here today has changed my life. I will never be the same person again. And I can tell you that the next time I hear someone bashing the religious, I will be the first person to jump up and tell him that he shouldn't talk when he really doesn't know what he's talking about."

It was obvious that Hatzalah had come a very long way in the general consensus of the religious public. The atmosphere at the gathering helped reinforce the knowledge that they were loved and appreciated for everything they were doing for others — whether their friends, neighbors, or total strangers.

By the end of the event, every one of the fifteen hundred volunteers felt incredibly good about themselves and ready to continue waking up in the middle of the night to go save lives.

People join United Hatzalah because they want to make a difference and save lives. It's not for everyone, and not everyone is accepted. But when the fit is right, a volunteer will have immense joy and satisfaction at being able to help  people and save their lives. It's beyond money, honor. or prestige. It's the knowledge that you are a person who with *siyatta diShmaya* saves other people's lives. And that's a feeling like no other in the world.

# CHAPTER TWENTY-EIGHT

# United Hatzalah Gets a Number

Now that the pieces of the puzzle were falling into place, now that all the branches were finally working together and the ambucycle unit was expanding by leaps and bounds, Eli invested much of his time into making sure that the volunteers received the best training possible. A big segment of that training took place on Magen David Adom ambulances, since United Hatzalah didn't have many ambulances of its own. Hatzalah relied on its volunteers receiving the kind of hands-on training that only an ambulance is equipped to give.

This is where things began getting complicated.

For years, there had been a certain divide between MDA and United Hatzalah. The Hatzalah volunteers often arrived at the scene faster than the MDA ambulances and were there to perform the initial lifesaving procedures on the patients. Then the Magen David Adom ambulances would arrive and take over to perform any complicated procedures and transport the patient to the hospital if needed.

The system worked well. The United Hatzalah volunteers learned a great deal from the experienced EMTs, paramedics, and doctors employed by Magen David Adom, and they also learned how to drive an ambulance — a skill that would be very useful if they ever decided to develop their own fleet.

But as United Hatzalah's profile became more well known throughout the country, Magen David Adom started to feel threatened. Then came the big United Hatzalah event in which fifteen hundred volunteers participated and which was written up in all the newspapers, and MDA could no longer ignore the reality: they had what they perceived as serious competition.

So it was that one fine day Eli received a notice from MDA informing him that the United Hatzalah volunteers would no longer be able to train on the MDA ambulances. From MDA's perspective, the relationship was over and the United Hatzalah volunteers had become persona non grata.

Magen David Adom had been around from before the establishment of the State of Israel. They were accustomed to having a monopoly, to not having any competition. As long as United Hatzalah had been a relatively small, low-key organization, they had been willing to work together. No more.

One issue was that United Hatzalah didn't charge for its services and depended on donations for funding, while MDA did charge a fee. This meant that people were starting to turn to United Hatzalah, knowing that using MDA would mean a bill in the mail.

Billing someone for a trip in the ambulance had troubled Eli and his fellow Hatzalah volunteers from the beginning. Eli remembers his days on the MDA ambulance: "Sometimes I would write a bill for a person and one look around their apartment told me that not only did they not have money to pay the bill, they didn't even have money to pay for food." Yet while there had always been disagreements between the two organizations, they had somehow found a way to make things work.

Not anymore.

United Hatzalah had become a threat, and MDA decided to sever the relationship and let everyone know that they would no longer tolerate a United Hatzalah logo on any uniform that volunteered for them. In essence, they were giving the message that it was time for United Hatzalah to go independent for real — "and don't expect us to help you anymore."

Faced with the new reality, Eli went to meet with the CEO of Magen David Adom, a man by the name of Eliyahu, to see whether there was any chance of working things out. The previous CEO, Avi Zohar, had a healthy respect for United Hatzalah, referring to the motorcycle rescue workers as "our elite forces." Eliyahu had a different approach, and it was doubtful that Eli would be able to bridge the gap that had opened between them. But he had to try.

On his part, Eli felt that it was crucial for United Hatzalah to continue working with Magen David Adom. He had no interest in competing with Israel's first ambulance service. His only interest was in filling the gap between the time a person called for help and the time it took for an ambulance to arrive. That was his sole concern. Nothing else mattered.

Now he just had to convince Eliyahu to see things his way. And he knew it wouldn't be easy.

He was right.

Eli met Eliyahu and a few of his executive staff at the CEO's office in the MDA building in Tel Aviv, on Yigal Alon Boulevard. He knew every one of them since they had all started out volunteering for MDA, many of them around the same time as he, and they knew him, too. No one in the room was a stranger to the others.

Once they were sitting across from one another, they chatted for a few minutes and then Eli brought the conversation around to the matter at hand.

"Look," he began, "I see no benefit in the two of us working separately. The fact is that United Hatzalah brings something to the table that MDA lacks, and vice versa. Only good things will come from our continuing to have a working relationship. It's true that we used to be smaller and now we have grown, but I don't see why anything has to change between us because of that."

"My job as the CEO of Magen David Adom," Eliyahu intoned, "is to do what is best for my organization, and that includes dealing with competition."

"But we're not your competition," Eli protested. "We're just the first responders, which is not your main focus. We're doing something you're not doing and which you have no plans to start doing."

(Today MDA actually does have a fleet of motorcycles, which enables them to also serve as first responders, but that wouldn't happen for years to come.)

"There's only competition when two companies are doing the same thing. That's not the case here."

"Eli," said the CEO of Magen David Adom, "I have nothing against you personally, but your organization is without question potential competition for Magen David Adom.

"We are done working together. From now on, we are not going to share information with United Hatzalah, and you will not know where to go for the calls. We are going to invest whatever money it takes to secure radios so that no one else will be able to listen in on our frequencies."

Eli couldn't believe what he was hearing, and he started to cry. He literally started to cry.

"How can you prevent a baby from being saved just because a volunteer is wearing a different logo on his uniform? I don't even care about the logo. We can wear both the logo of MDA and the logo of United Hatzalah. That's the way it was in the beginning anyway."

"That's not good enough," Eliyahu replied. "The people who are calling us are calling for emergency help from us and not from anyone else. From now on, when they call us, that's what they'll be getting: Magen David Adom. The people they called."

"The only reason people are calling you," Eli said, "is because you have an emergency number: 101 — the same number you've had for decades. Believe me, no mother cares which medical responder is coming to save her child, as long as someone gets there in time to save his life. If there were another number, plenty of people would call it, too."

But Eli's words fell on deaf ears.

"It's either us or nothing," the CEO of MDA said. "No working together and no compromises."

So began the start of a new challenge for United Hatzalah. They couldn't save lives if they didn't know where the emergency was located. They could have all the motorcycles in the world and a million volunteers, but if they didn't know the address of the person who needed help, they were like someone who's all dressed up with nowhere to go.

Eli left Eliyahu's office very upset and not sure of his next move. Was it all going to come to an ignominious end after so much hard work? Were they finally being forced to come to a screeching halt after helping so many people?

It was clear that they needed advice, and Eli decided to turn to a person who had long been a gift in the advice-giving department. He left Tel Aviv and headed to Bnei Brak, a short distance away geographically but separated in reality by a gulf wider than an ocean. Once in Bnei Brak, he drove in the direction of the office of a man who had been sent by Rav Shach to the Knesset to lead a party called Degel HaTorah. The man's name was Rabbi Moshe Gafni, and he and Eli Beer were long-time friends. Now, in his hour of confusion, Eli turned to Rabbi Moshe Gafni to help him come up with a plan.

Rabbi Gafni welcomed Eli into his office and told him to take a seat. Eli informed him of the meeting and recounted everything that had happened.

"They will no longer allow us to train our volunteers on their ambulances, nor will we be able to share their radio frequencies, so we won't have access to emergency information. The second they do this, we won't know where to go when a person calls 101. It's clear that Eliyahu has decided to play hardball, and he wants to shut us down."

"If they decide to stop sharing information," Gafni said, "there's a simple solution."

"What's that?"

"You need to get your own number for people to call."

"Our own number?"

"Yes, your own four-digit emergency number. Your own official government number. Think about it. If they no longer want to share their frequencies with you, you're going to have to get your own frequency."

"How do we get a number?"

"I'll help you get a number from the government. A short number. A number that will be easy for people to remember. The moment you have a number, you'll run an advertising campaign to let people know about it. And that's it — you'll be in business, with or without MDA. If you think about it, this development might be the best thing that could have ever happened to you. It will push you to become completely independent from Magen David Adom."

"You really believe that you can convince the government to authorize a number for us?"

"Yes, I do. And I plan on doing something else."

"What's that?"

"I'll work on convincing the government to recognize United Hatzalah as the second emergency response service right after Magen David Adom."

The smile was starting to return to Eli's face.

"Another thing," Gafni said.

"Yes?"

"We need to create a coalition of Knesset members who support United Hatzalah and the incredible work it does."

Gafni was true to his word and went on to put together a group comprised of MKs who were impressed by United Hatzalah and were willing to support the organization publicly. One of those Knesset members was Yitzchak Herzog — later to be elected president of Israel.

After the group was created, they decided to hold a special assembly at the Knesset to officially introduce United Hatzalah to the nation. It was to be a day where the government would show honor to a group that had given of itself selflessly for over a decade. At the same time, it would accomplish another important goal: it would show one and all that United Hatzalah was here to stay.

Rabbi Moshe Gafni came through, and United Hatzalah was awarded a number by the government of Israel. The number was 1221 — simple, catchy, and easy to remember. The moment the number was theirs, a campaign was launched informing the public that there was another operation in town — one that had proven itself extremely effective at saving lives and was even free. They distributed magnets to put on the fridge that read, "In case of an emergency, call 1221." And many of the religious radio stations informed their listeners of the new development.

Within a very short time, people began calling the number for United Hatzalah, and for the first time they had to open their own command-and-dispatch center, in a building across the road from Center One on Yirmiyahu Street, not far from Magen David Adom's headquarters in Yerushalayim. They had been ejected from MDA, yet with the help of Hashem, they had been able to pick themselves up and acquire brand-new headquarters for the first time. And the people appreciated them. How could they not? When a call for help came in, United Hatzalah responded — all free of charge.

Magen David Adom had been right. Their fear of United Hatzalah had materialized. Ironically, had they only kept them close, United Hatzalah would not have expanded the way it did.

Today, after years of ongoing negotiations, Magen David Adom does inform United Hatzalah about every call that comes in, and United Hatzalah does the same for MDA. And while there is still room to grow, there is no question that they've come a very long way. The dream is to work together, side by side.

# CHAPTER TWENTY-NINE

# Just Count to Ten

*H*eshy Jacobs was the chairman of Hatzolah in New York, and he and Eli eventually became close friends.

One day in 2006, Heshy called Eli from the States, obviously upset.

"I heard that you're starting to accept nonreligious people into your ranks."

Eli confirmed that it was true.

"How can you do such a thing?"

"Heshy," Eli said, "you run Hatzolah in New York. You deal with the unique challenges that arise in Boro Park and Flatbush. There are many problems in your neck of the woods, and I'm not denying that at all, but the kinds of issues that you face and the kinds of issues that we are confronted with in Israel have nothing in common."

"What do you mean?"

"I mean terrorist attacks, for example. You don't have buses blowing up in front of your eyes with forty people killed in the space of five seconds. But we do, and there are times when that kind of scenario keeps repeating itself. We have bus bombings. We have drive-by shootings and rock attacks. And these are tragedies that are taking place all over the country — not just in Geulah or Bnei Brak. Because we're dealing with so many life-and-death situations on so many fronts, we don't have the luxury of turning away willing and competent manpower."

Besides, it was Rav Chaim Kanievsky himself who told Eli how important it is to give every person — religious or secular — the ability to perform the mitzvah of saving lives. Not only that, Rav Elyashiv was in favor of United Hatzalah accepting non-Jews because they could drive Jewish volunteers home on Shabbos.

"Heshy, you know me," Eli went on. "I'm not the most yeshivish guy in the world. Far from it. I'm not a *rav*, and I never had *semichah* (religious ordination), but I have carte blanche to see Rav Chaim whenever I need, and I take advantage of that green light to visit him often to discuss serious halachic questions that come up all the time in the course of United Hatzalah's work. Not only do I visit him, but Rav Chaim has come to visit us at United Hatzalah twice, because he approves of United Hatzalah and what we're doing.

"So, Reb Heshy, you carry on dealing with your unique set of problems in New York, and I and my volunteers will deal with our unique set of problems in Israel. And remember that I consulted with *gedolim* in Eretz Yisrael, and they agreed wholeheartedly that this is the right course of action."

One day, only a month later, Eli's phone rang. It was Heshy, who was visiting Eretz Yisrael.

"Eli, I just saw a motorcycle accident right in front of my eyes. You need to send some guys over right now."

Reb Heshy Jacobs with Dovie Maisel and Shlomo Zakheim

Reb Heshy Jacobs

Heshy was an EMT himself, but he didn't have any equipment with him, and he had done the right thing by calling United Hatzalah.

"Where are you?"

"I'm standing in front of the Sheraton Plaza in Yerushalayim, across the street from the Great Synagogue. Don't waste time, Eli. Get them over here as soon as possible."

Eli was looking at the computer in the command center as he spoke.

"Heshy," he said, "I want you to do something for me."

"What's that?"

"I want you to count to ten."

As they spoke, Eli was watching two United Hatzalah volunteers on ambucycles make their way to where Heshy was standing. Again Eli told Heshy to count to ten. He heard him counting on the other side of the line.

"Three, four, five, six, seven —"

He hadn't even finished counting before he interrupted himself

"About an hour later, Heshy called Eli back.

Eli," he said, "you're the greatest guy in the world and I love you. What I saw tonight — two volunteers on motorcycles arriving at a call in record time, one of them religious and the other... well, the other wasn't. I just saw a wonderful example of *achdus*. Eli, what can I say? What I just saw was a real *kiddush Hashem!*"

Eli with Elliot Weiner

That same year, Eli visited Chicago for the first time. While today United Hatzalah has offices in numerous cities all over the world, at that point he was still in the process of building the organization, and there were many places he had never visited. So it was that Eli found himself sitting and having a meeting in a kosher restaurant with a group of people who wanted to hear all about what he was doing in Israel. Elliot and Larry Weiner were there and a few others.

In the middle of the conversation, Elliot suddenly said, "We need to get Jeff Aeder here. Jeff is an amazing guy and exactly the kind of person who will really connect with what Eli is saying."

Elliot didn't waste any time. On the spot, he took out his phone and called Jeff Aeder.

Jeff Aeder

Jeff Aeder and Eli

"Jeff," he said when the other man picked up, "you have to meet us right now. We're sitting with someone named Eli Beer and I know you're going to want to meet him. You always ask me to come meet your people. Now I want you to meet one of mine."

Ten minutes later, Jeff arrived.

They were enjoying their breakfast when Eli received a phone call from Israel. It was from headquarters.

"A tractor driven by an Arab working for the city of Jerusalem just went on a rampage right outside Hatzalah headquarters and started running over cars. He even managed to turn over a bus. The guy is trying to kill as many Jews as he can."

While Eli was having French toast and omelets in a restaurant in Chicago, an Arab was once again trying to kill Jews in Yerushalayim.

A volunteer for United Hatzalah named Daniel Katzenstein was the first responder at the scene of the attack. There he saw a half-crushed car — the tractor had only managed to destroy part of it — and he heard a woman screaming from inside, "Save my son! save my son!"

The mother was trapped in the front seat of the car and unable to get out of her seat, but her main concern was her baby, who was in a car seat in the back. Ignoring the sounds of screaming and honking from other cars that were stuck, and the specter of being crushed to death by the returning tractor, Daniel set to work to save the baby. Together with a passing soldier, who saw what was going on and put his own life on the line to save a child, the two succeeded in getting the baby out of the car in the nick of time. Seconds after they had removed the baby from the vehicle, the tractor returned from flipping and attacking other cars and crushed the car completely, killing the mother but missing her son — because he had been saved through the heroic efforts of a member of United Hatzalah and a young soldier.

Three people ended up being killed that day and many were injured — all of this taking place right in the middle of that meeting.

When he heard what had happened, Jeff said to Larry and Elliot, "We have to do something!"

"What can we do?"

"I think we should donate an ambucycle in memory of every life that was lost. If they want to kill us, then we need to save people."

In the wake of that experience, Jeff Aeder became a very close friend of Eli's. But it all began when a few Jewish people with big hearts were eating together and decided that they couldn't ignore a tragedy and had to do something for *Klal Yisrael*.

And so they did.

# CHAPTER THIRTY

# The Presidential Ambush

he World Economic Forum — otherwise known as the Davos conference — is one of the most prestigious gatherings in the world. Attended annually by kings, presidents, prime ministers, and a group of the wealthiest and most influential people in the world, the five-day event in Davos, Switzerland, enables leaders of the nations to come together to discuss global issues. One participates by invitation only, and those invitations are mighty hard to come by. That's why Eli Beer never imagined in his wildest dreams that he would one day be the recipient of such an invitation. Yet Hashem runs the world, and if He wants one to rub shoulders with kings and billionaires, that's exactly what will happen.

It all started when the organizers of the conference made the decision to invite a certain number of people, each separated by religious outlook and sheer geography but sharing one important feature: they were individuals whom the organizers termed "young global leaders." These individuals were universally recognized for making a positive difference in the world. The organizers decided that a number of young global leaders would be invited to attend the conference and give a speech outlining their worldview, past accomplishments, and plans for the future. This was a way of making it clear that the organizers didn't care only about the business entrepreneur but about the social entrepreneur as well.

Queen Rania al Abdullah of Jordan headed the international committee that decides which young leaders are chosen every year. Which is why Eli Beer came to receive an invitation in 2012 from the queen inviting him to come and give a presentation about United Hatzalah at a hotel on the Jordanian side of the Dead Sea, along with nine other potential candidates.

The hotel was packed, and King Abdullah was among the guests. The actual presentation took place in a smaller room in front of a small group. The queen listened closely as Eli described United Hatzalah and their mission of saving lives — both Jew and Arab — in under ninety seconds.

"I'm impressed," the queen told him. "I think it would be wonderful if we could establish such an organization here in Jordan."

"I would be honored to assist in turning that dream into a reality," Eli replied.

By the end of the day, the list of those who were chosen was made public. Eli and Gitty Beer would be going to Davos, Switzerland, for that year's World Economic Forum.

Initially, Eli wasn't comfortable at the conference and felt like he was having trouble finding his stride. It didn't take him long to grasp that the people he were meeting had come to the conference because they wanted to meet other wealthy people like themselves. They were far less interested in learning about altruistic organizations and the people who ran them. The man who had eight hundred million dollars in the bank wanted to meet a person who had a billion, and the guy with a billion wanted to meet someone ten times richer than he. It was all about furthering their own interests.

"I knew that I had a great story to tell," Eli says, "but no one really wanted to hear it. Of course, I was there because I had been invited to give a speech, but when it came to networking with the other attendees, I wasn't feeling very successful."

In the evenings there were events where the guests mingled. In theory, it was possible to approach anyone, but as with anything in life, it had to be done in the right way.

"What do you do?" people asked Eli.

They wanted to hear that he owned a bank, had five thousand employees or a hundred million dollars in assets. Instead they heard, "I have thousands of people volunteering in my organization."

"And what kind of organization is that?"

"It's called United Hatzalah. We save thousands of lives."

"That's beautiful," they would tell him, and then look around for someone else to talk to.

"Gitty," Eli finally said to his wife, "we live in a fake world. Here you have a concentration of a huge portion of the world's wealth all in one place. These people wouldn't be able to spend all the money they have even if they live for another hundred years. And yet instead of sitting down to enjoy themselves and get to know the young global leaders who were handpicked by the queen of Jordan because they have something amazing to offer, they couldn't care less. I mean, they act like they care, but anyone with a little bit of intuition will understand that it's just a show."

"What are you saying?"

"Do you want to see these people get excited?"

Gitty gave him a look.

"No one got excited by anything you said until now."

"I know. That's my point. United Hatzalah isn't resonating with these people. But I'm going to show you what will."

Gitty looked concerned. "Do me a favor and don't do anything too crazy."

"Don't worry, I'm just going to make a point."

"Now I'm really getting nervous."

"Don't get nervous. Just enjoy the ride."

They were standing in the middle of a big hall for a session hosted by the Bank of America, and the room was packed. A minute later, somebody walked over and introduced himself. It turned out that he owned a big bank in London.

"What do you do?" he asked Eli.

"I own a falafel stand in Manhattan."

(The look on Gitty's face…)

The banker was taken aback.

"You own a falafel stand?"

There was incredulity in his voice.

"Yes, I own a falafel stand on the corner of Forty-Fifth and Madison Avenue in Manhattan."

The guy was trying to figure it out.

"I don't understand. Did you say that you own a falafel stand?"

"Exactly right. It's a nice place. Very popular. Delicious hummus."

The London bank owner couldn't wrap his mind around what he was hearing. Gitty, meanwhile, was doing her best to control her laughter.

"Still not getting it."

"What's not to get? I own a falafel stand, and that's what I do for a living."

"Yes, but how did you get invited to Davos?"

"What do you mean? I make a lot of money from my business. Last year alone I sold forty-five million dollars' worth of falafel right out of my corner stand. That's why they invited me to Davos. They call me the Falafel King."

"I can't believe it. How did you become so rich just by selling falafel? What's your secret?"

"The secret," Eli replied with a straight face, "is to never change the oil. Keep the same oil — it's a guaranteed gold mine!"

Gitty couldn't hold back her laughter anymore and excused herself from the conversation. Meanwhile, the bank executive started calling over a group of his friends to introduce them to the one and only falafel magnate at Davos. Wishing everyone a good night, Eli told them that he had to go and went to find Gitty.

"You see?" he said. "These people don't care what you do. They don't care if you sell falafel or weapons. The only thing they want to know is how much money you make. That's why they're here — for business."

It was a hard thing to accept. Here he was, surrounded by some of the wealthiest people on the planet, but their focus was on piling up even more money. The irony was precious.

But Eli is Eli and that means that he didn't give up.

He was in the men's room, washing his hands at the sink, when he happened to notice that the person standing beside him one sink over was none other than Bill Gates. Gates was alone, lathering his hands with soap.

"I didn't know what to say. What do you say to Bill Gates when you meet him in the bathroom?!"

In the few seconds he had before Bill finished washing his hands and left, Eli's mind went into high gear as he tried to choose his opening line.

"You know," he finally said, "I have an idea that can make you into a rich man."

Bill Gates, one of the wealthiest men in the world, liked his delivery and started to laugh.

"What's your idea?"

"Well, it won't actually make you financially rich but rather rich in good deeds."

Then came the usual question.

"What do you do?" he asked Eli.

Eli told him all about United Hatzalah and Gates loved it.

As he dried his hands, Gates said to Eli, "I love what you do, and I'm putting you in touch with the head of my foundation. Talk to him. We do our work in Africa, so if you can figure out a way to bring what you do to Africa, let me know."

United Hatzalah wasn't doing anything in Africa at that point, but Eli made sure to develop a relationship with the head of the foundation just in case.

It was January and freezing cold outside, and most people at the conference took advantage of the buses provided by the hotel to get to the various event halls. On one of the shuttle trips, there was a couple sitting across from Eli on the bus, and he decided to introduce himself.

"I'm Eli Beer. Who are you?"

The man told him his name.

"And what do you do?"

"I'm the prime minister of Iceland. Where are you from, Mr. Beer?"

"I'm from Israel."

"So is my wife."

"Your wife is Israeli?"

"Yes, born and bred."

There followed a fascinating conversation between two Israelis who found themselves on a bus in Switzerland. It wasn't long before the conversation turned to Israel itself, and since Eli is a right winger and the prime minister's wife a leftist, the conversation grew heated. In the end, they agreed to disagree about politics, but agreed to agree about

United Hatzalah, which turned out to be one of the world's greatest openers between strangers.

Then he was introduced to Modi — the prime minister of India — to whom Eli gave a presentation on how United Hatzalah operated. Modi and his team were fascinated and tried to figure out if it would be possible to establish something similar in their country.

Of one thing Eli was sure: that meeting was a major *kiddush Hashem.*

As the days passed, Eli met other people and was able to cut through their defenses so that they wanted to learn about what he did and about the lives the volunteers were saving, how it was making a difference to every single person living in Israel. Some of them he spoke to turned away, but many were fascinated by what he had to say and wanted to hear more.

He is still in touch with many of them today.

Eli's own speech was well attended, and there were even several oil executives from Saudi Arabia and the Arab Emirates in the audience.

That was also where he met Michael Dell. (Yes, from the Dell computer that you may very well be using right now…) Dell was very impressed by Eli's speech and approached him after he left the podium.

"I was really impressed by everything you were saying," he said. "How can I get involved and help?"

So Eli told him all about their motorcycle unit and how every single Hatzalah bike had the potential to save numerous lives.

"I like what you're telling me," Michael Dell said. "Put me down for eighteen of them."

And Eli did.

One of the businessmen whom Eli met at the conference, Asaf Magal (not his real name), was building a business in Mexico and had formed connections with quite a few high-ranking Mexican government officials. One of the officials, Enrique Peña Nieto, was serving as governor of the State of Mexico at the time, and he dreamed of becoming the next president of the country. By the time this story occurred, Peña Nieto was already well into his campaign for the presidency.

During the conference, Asaf approached Eli to ask him for a favor.

"Eli, I need a favor."

"What kind of favor?"

Eli with Enrique Peña Nieto

"Enrique Peña Nieto is a Mexican politician who is running for president of his country. He's here in Davos right now. From what I understand, you have a connection with President Shimon Peres, am I correct?"

"Yes." Eli had been the recipient of the presidential award presented by President Shimon Peres the previous year, in 2011, and they had become friends of sorts.

"Can you introduce my Mexican friend to the Israeli president?"

"Look, I want to help you," Eli said, "but I don't think I'll be able to set up a meeting between this guy and President Peres. If he had already won the election and been voted in as the Mexican president, that would be something else. But as it is, he's just another politician. Peres is way too busy to meet with every politician who wants to speak to him, especially since the current president of Mexico is also here."

"Eli," Asaf said, "I know you. You're the kind of guy who can do anything. That's why I'm asking you to find a way to make this happen — and if you succeed, I will give a generous donation to United Hatzalah."

That was it. Assaf had just used the magic words. The moment the prospective mission had been linked to a donation for United Hatzalah, Eli's brain began to whir with ideas.

He began by using the normal channels and called Peres' people who had accompanied the president to Davos.

"I have a request for a meeting with the president."

"A request from whom?"

"Enrique Peña Nieto, one of Mexico's up-and-coming politicians. He is currently running for president."

"The answer is no. This guy already tried contacting us through ten different people, and we declined each time."

"Well, then, he deserves a meeting as a reward for his persistence."

"The answer is no."

Next Eli called Bibi Netanyahu's office to see if the prime minister's people would be able to help. He received the same response.

In the end, Eli decided that the only way to make it happen was with a nice healthy dose of vitamin C: chutzpah.

Shimon Peres was scheduled to speak in one of the main auditoriums. The president's speech would be one of the most widely attended events of the conference, since Peres was extremely popular at the time and everyone wanted to hear what he had to say.

When leaving the stage, the speakers at the conference generally walked off the stage and remained in the room. But VIPs were given the option of taking a left and entering the adjacent hallway, which led them away from the auditorium and into a different part of the building.

While Peres was giving his speech, Eli spoke to the Mexican politician.

"I want to show you where to stand for your meeting with Peres. The meeting isn't taking place in an office. It's going to be a more casual meeting. You'll stand here in the hallway and wait for President Peres to pass by after his speech."

Peres finished his speech to thunderous applause. He got off the stage and began walking straight — in the direction of the main part of the hall. Meanwhile, Eli Beer was waiting for him. Seeing Eli's yarmulke-covered head, Peres' Swiss security detail ignored him, apparently assuming he was part of Peres' staff. Just before Peres reached the hallway on the left, Eli said to him, "Please follow me."

Seconds later, they were in the hallway and Eli was introducing Peres to Enrique Peña Nieto, who came forward with a big smile on his face.

Shimon Peres and the future president of Mexico

"Mr. President," Eli said, "I want to introduce you to the next president of Mexico!"

Shimon Peres stopped in his tracks and the two shook hands, before settling into a lengthy conversation. That was it. The ambush had been successful.

Eli took several pictures of the meeting so that Peña Nieto would have something to show the Jewish citizens of Mexico when he told them how much he loved Israel and asked for their support.

They ended up conversing for thirty minutes. None of the members of Peres' security detail understood that the whole thing had been pre-arranged. The meeting seemed to have happened spontaneously. It was only as the conversation drew to a close that his chief of staff finally figured out what had happened and gave Eli a piece of her mind.

But at the end of the day, the meeting proved beneficial for everyone involved. Enrique Peña Nieto did become the next president of Mexico, and because of that hallway meeting, Shimon Peres built a beautiful and productive relationship with him. It was such a good relationship that he became the first president of Israel to fly to Mexico for an official visit. Most importantly, United Hatzalah received a very hefty donation from Asaf Magal in gratitude to Eli for making the impossible happen.

When Shimon Peres passed away, Eli Beer attended the funeral. As he looked around at the visiting dignitaries, he couldn't help but notice that Enrique Peña Nieto was there as well.

Walking over to him, Eli said, "Do you remember me?"

"You look familiar…"

"Think about Davos and your hallway meeting with Shimon Peres."

The lightbulb flashed. "You're the one who made it happen!"

"Yes, I introduced you to Shimon Peres back in Davos when you couldn't get a meeting."

Standing there beside the president of Mexico, Eli's mind took him back to Davos and a meeting that ended up happening against all odds. Because you see, when it comes to United Hatzalah, there is no such thing as the impossible.

One of the perks of being chosen by Queen Rania of Jordan was the opportunity to attend a series of courses at Harvard University that was given over the space of three years. So it was that Eli Beer, the boy who didn't graduate from elementary or high school, ended up successfully completing three separate courses at Harvard University.

# CHAPTER THIRTY-ONE

# Broken Leg and All

*E*li was home on a freezing winter morning in March 2012. The weather was blustery, and it seemed that snow was imminent, a rare occurrence in Yerushalayim. From Eli's porch in the neighborhood of Ramot, low-hanging clouds obscured his panoramic view of the city.

When a call came in over his radio that a child was choking in a nearby nursery school, he dropped whatever he had been doing and

Volunteering in the snow

ran down the stairs to the street. Eli's apartment is located on the top floor of an older building that doesn't have an elevator, and he has to climb or descend sixty-five steps every time he enters or leaves the building. Since time was of the essence, he didn't have the luxury of taking the stairs one at a time. Instead he jumped a few stairs at a shot, intent on exiting the building and reaching his car as quickly as possible so he could drive over to the nursery where he could picture the child gasping for air.

As always, the goal was to reach the scene of emergency in under ninety seconds.

He was descending the final flight of stairs when he slipped, lost traction, and tumbled down to the bottom.

That was bad. What was worse was the cracking sound he heard and the accompanying pain in his right leg, which alerted him that he had probably just broken his leg in the fall. There was no question of lifting himself off the floor because the pain was too intense.

"I just injured myself running to a call," Eli announced on the walkie-talkie through gritted teeth. "If anyone is close by, please let us know that you can take the call because I'm lying on the floor in agony and can't make it."

But no one else was available. Three car accidents had occurred only a short while earlier, and all the local volunteers were already tied up and unavailable to respond, which meant that a young child was now dependent on a volunteer with a broken leg.

He didn't have a choice. He didn't have the luxury of lying on the floor until Hatzalah came to help him because a baby was choking nearby. He had to get up despite the excruciating pain it would entail.

Somehow, Eli managed to lift himself up from the ground using his left leg for support, then hopped out of the building and over to his car. He got into the car, elevating his right leg while braking with his left. He turned on his lights and sirens and somehow managed to drive the three blocks to the nursery building at high speed, focusing on the upcoming mission and doing his utmost to block out the pain.

Eli reached the nursery in a minute and a half.

Eli being loaded onto an ambulance

The rain was coming down in buckets as he parked, sirens still wailing, and he hopped out of the car on one leg while holding his United Hatzalah bag with his lifesaving equipment. The door of the nursery was open, and the teacher waved him inside, where he immediately got to work on the three-year-old. He performed CPR while pumping the child with oxygen, treating him during those crucial moments that can mean the difference between life or death or life with brain damage or other terrible ramifications from oxygen deprivation.

A minute later, two other volunteers arrived on the scene. "Take over," Eli told them. The two volunteers immediately went to work while Eli lay down on a nearby couch, the pain that he'd somehow suppressed during those adrenaline-filled moments coming back in a torrent of agony. At the same time, he knew that he had just saved a child's life.

When he heard the sound of that child crying, it was the sweetest sound in the universe.

The first ambulance to arrive at the scene transported the three-year-old to the hospital. It took a while for another ambulance to show up, since the accidents took priority, but eventually another one arrived and Eli was loaded onto a stretcher and transported to Shaare Zedek Hospital, where Dr. Michael Herman (also a volunteer for United Hatzalah) took very good care of him.

When Eli's leg was stabilized and he was no longer in pain, Dr. Herman said, "Eli, I have a surprise for you."

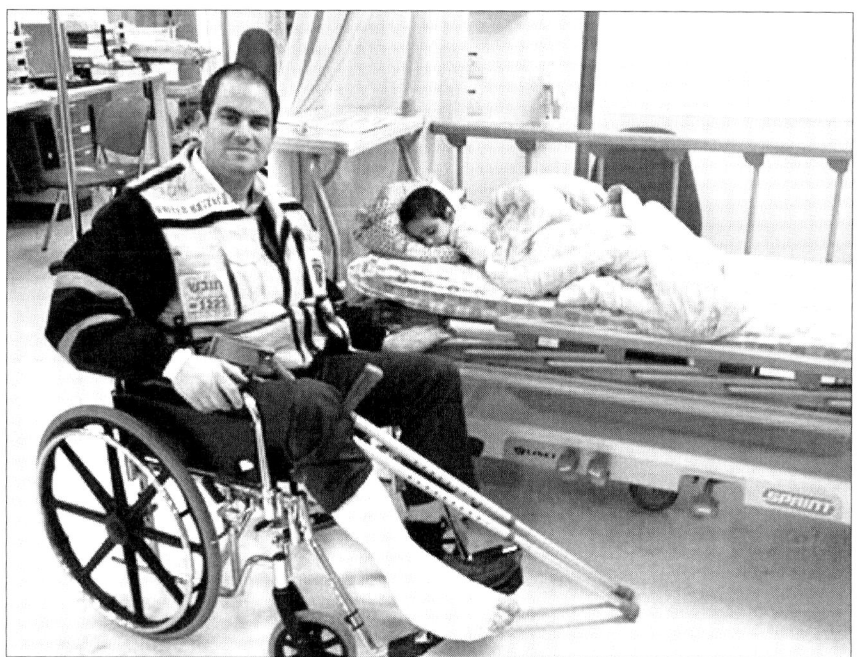

Eli visiting the sleeping child

"Great. I love surprises."

The doctor helped Eli into a wheelchair and wheeled him over to the hospital's pediatric department, where he showed Eli that the child he had saved was now sleeping peacefully in a hospital bed.

Ten years later, in 2022, Eli received an invitation to the bar mitzvah of that three-year-old child. Holding the invitation in his hand, Eli experienced a sudden rush of emotion, recalling how he'd run down the stairs and slipped, breaking his leg, and how he hadn't allowed the pain to stop him from saving a little boy's life.

# PART SIX

*I want you to continue traveling all over the world so that every Jew will have the merit of saving lives... Not everyone has the chance to fulfill the mitzvah of pikuach nefesh, of saving lives, and you're giving them that opportunity.*

— Rav Chaim Kanievsky

# CHAPTER THIRTY-TWO

# A New Building

In the year 2013, having been invited to give a TED Talk that would be viewed by people around the globe, Eli chose to focus on the importance of children and their safety. Standing in front of a huge audience, Eli delivered a speech that resonated with every person sitting in the auditorium.

"Imagine for a minute," he began, "that it's a beautiful day outside and you decide to take your little son for a walk in the city. You stop at a candy store, and you buy your smiling child something nice to enjoy. You unwrap the candy, and you hand it to him. He's so happy, you're so happy — both of you are having a wonderful time.

"All of a sudden your son stops in his tracks. You're looking at him and you see that he's turning blue in front of your eyes, and you don't know what to do. You start screaming for an ambulance, shouting for help, and meanwhile your son is choking and unable to breathe and you have no idea how to save him. Every second feels like a minute, every minute an eternity.

"Now imagine that you suddenly see a man running toward you. He's wearing an orange jacket and holding an orange bag. When he reaches your side, he bends down and performs the Heimlich maneuver on your son. The candy comes flying out of your son's mouth, and you hear the sweetest sound in the world: the sound of your son crying.

"You're looking at the man in orange and you don't know who he is or where he came from. So you ask, 'Who are you? Are you a doctor?'

"'No, I'm not a doctor,' he replies. 'I work around the corner in a shoe store, and I volunteer for United Hatzalah. My phone rang to alert me that a child was choking so I left my store and ran over here to save his life. He's okay now, and I have to get back to the store because I have customers waiting for me."

That was Eli's speech.

Simple and effective.

All the more so because it was so true.

When he finished, six thousand people started clapping and they continued for a long, long time. As always, Eli's message rang true.

By now you know that Eli Beer is totally preoccupied with turning United Hatzalah into a financially sustainable organization, and his agile entrepreneur's mind is constantly coming up with new ideas to achieve this goal. He's always open to new ideas that come his way from his donors and supporters, and such was the case with a groundbreaking idea suggested by Amy and Harlan Korenvaes from Dallas, Texas, which they dubbed "Days of Lifesaving."

Amy and Harlan lighting the menorah at a Hatzalah event

Amy was raised in the United States by a father who loved Israel, yet he made her promise on his deathbed that she would never visit the country. Simply put, he feared for her safety and didn't want her to get hurt.

After he passed away, the promise she'd made troubled Amy. Was she really beholden to keep such a promise? Eventually she decided that she couldn't abide by it and sought the advice of a rabbinical court of law who arranged for her to be *"matir neder"* — that is, for her oath to be annulled according to halachah. And so it was that Amy and Harlan traveled to Israel in 2014.

Amy and Harlan met Eli at a dinner, and at his invitation they visited United Hatzalah headquarters. During a tour of the command center, Amy asked a question.

"How many calls do your volunteers go out on every day?"

At that time, the answer was fifteen hundred calls a day.

"And how much is your budget?"

"Which element of the budget?"

"Maintenance. Keeping the lights on. Running the organization. The basic costs."

Eli gave her the number.

"Here's what I think," Amy said. "You should sell every day of support for United Hatzalah for eighteen thousand dollars. This way you'll be able to cover your expenses and pay for the oxygen, defibrillators, and equipment that needs to be replaced, in addition to the basic costs of keeping everything running smoothly, from the dispatch center to the building's maintenance staff.

"Take the cost of training a volunteer. That's a good example. How much does that cost?"

"It costs ninety-six hundred dollars to train every new volunteer," Eli said. "Then there are the expenses that come along with outfitting that volunteer so that he or she will be able to do the job properly."

"Fine," Amy said. "Let donors choose a day of the year that they will sponsor all those costs for those twenty-four hours. People will be able to pick a day — say their birthday — and you will give them a report of everything that happened that day, every emergency, every call, and every life that was saved through their financial support and generosity."

While it would have been enough had she just thought of the idea, Amy immediately announced that she was sponsoring ten days of the year in honor of different members of her family. Of course, the long-term goal was to find sponsors for all three hundred and sixty-five days of the year, whether for a *yahrtzeit*, birthday, or just to honor a friend.

Amy's idea fit with Eli's vision for United Hatzalah. It was outside the box and a little daring, and it would mean that the organization wouldn't be dependent on one donor or another.

Sustainability.

For Eli, that was the key.

Professor Alan Dershowitz, a high-profile lawyer and political commentator, as well as a former Harvard law professor, is another individual who has given unwavering support to United Hatzalah. It all started when Eli decided to ask him to join the United Hatzalah board. The next time they met at an event, Eli decided to try his luck.

"Alan," Eli said, "you're a famous lawyer. Everyone respects you, and you fight for Israel day and night. Bottom line: you love Israel, and since you grew up in Boro Park, you love Hatzalah."

"Eli," the professor replied, "I don't join any boards. People ask me to join their boards every day. I don't do it."

Eli refused to give up. It was time to employ some of his trademark chutzpah.

(L–R) Eli, Daniel Katzenstein, Professor Alan Dershowitz
and member of United Hatzalah Board, Harvey Schwartz *z"l*

Professor Alan Dershowitz riding a United Hatzalah ambucycle

"Professor Dershowitz," Eli said, "if you join our board, I promise you I'll be able to save many more lives."

The professor looked Eli in the eye.

"Do you treat all sectors and types of people with equality?"

"Yes, everyone is given the same first-class care and attention."

"Then I'm in."

They shook hands, Professor Dershowitz joined the board, and since then, he has done much vital work for the organization, whether by donating his time and giving speeches for United Hatzalah or by donating ambucycles. Most importantly, his involvement brings the kind of credibility to United Hatzalah that no money can buy. As he says, "If you want to see what Israel is all about, look at United Hatzalah." Many donors have become part of the United Hatzalah family due to Alan Dershowitz.

Wanting to show his appreciation for everything Alan Dershowitz has done for the organization, Eli decided to surprise the professor for his eightieth birthday, to do something wild and unexpected. Alan had never ridden a motorcycle, and Eli decided that after all his years of support, it was time for the famous legal light to go for a ride on a United Hatzalah ambucycle.

"I picked him up at the King David Hotel," Eli recalls, "and told him to sit behind me on the motorcycle. He was very nervous to begin with, but by the time we reached the Waldorf, he was more relaxed.

"'Eli,' he said, 'do not let me fall.'

"'Alan,' I replied, 'do you think I would risk a lawsuit from you?'

"Thankfully, we arrived at the United Hatzalah headquarters safely. I was proud to show Professor Alan Dershowitz firsthand how much his support has impacted our lifesaving organization."

As United Hatzalah grew, the need to expand arose. When Eli first established United Hatzalah, he decided to rent space for a few offices, a dispatch center, and storage space for extra equipment. There was a beautiful four-story building located on the corner of 78 Yirmiyahu Street, right at the entrance of the city, across from the Center One shopping mall and one block away from Magen David Adom headquarters. Eli set up a meeting with the owner of the building.

"How much space are you looking to rent?" the owner asked Eli.

"About one hundred meters."

At the time, it seemed like that was more than enough space.

The building's owner, Yonatan Nissim, liked United Hatzalah, and Eli was hopeful that he would give them a good deal.

He did.

"I'll give you the space for half of what I normally charge," Nissim said.

By the time they were there for a month, they already needed another fifty meters, and Yonatan Nissim rented them additional space. When the organization started using its own number in 2009, they suddenly needed room for a larger dispatch center and more classrooms for training volunteers. And more offices for staff. And a larger storage area for the oxygen tanks and defibrillators. It reached the point where they needed another floor, then another half a floor. And even though the owner was giving them an incredible deal on rent, it was still costing them a fortune. Finally, in 2015, Eli decided that the time had come to approach several members of the board and ask for contributions toward purchasing the building.

The price was seventeen million dollars for the building and another five million for the renovations needed to turn it into a real home for United Hatzalah. Eli met with Mark Silber, who agreed that it was time for them to stop spending so much money on rent. But Mark and his wife, Barbara, did more than just agree — they also gave a considerable donation toward the building fund.

Mark and Barbara Silber, Eli and his grandson Itamar

Alex Silber, the son of Mark and Barbara Silber, who had been good friends of United Hatzalah for years, came up with a great idea for a campaign for Hatzalah called "Race to Save Lives" together with a friend of his named Alex Goldberg. These two young yeshivah boys raised two hundred and fifty thousand dollars in the first year of the campaign, where people paid money in honor of their children, who participated in a five-kilometer marathon for United Hatzalah. The following year they raised a million dollars.

Eli was particularly thrilled because Mark Silber himself raced the 5K!

Another major donor to the building — and, over the years, to many vital United Hatzalah projects, both in Israel and the Ukraine — was The Helmsley Charitable Trust, under its lead trustee, Sandor Frankel.

Having made a good start toward their goal of funding the building, Eli now reached out to Harvey and Gloria Kaylie. Harvey was the founder and CEO of a company called Mini-Circuits and a pioneering developer of the microwave industry. Harvey and Gloria were also the people behind the legendary Camp Kaylie and were involved in an incredible array of charitable causes. Eli got to know them many years earlier when they still lived in Brooklyn.

When he first met Harvey Kaylie, Eli was just starting to learn how to fundraise and didn't even have a brochure to show prospective donors.

Eli visiting Harvey and Gloria Kaylie

It was Harvey who sat him down and taught him how to do his job. He had come to the meeting with Mark Gerson with a few pictures in a photo album. Mark had listened to his vision and was convinced. But Harvey Kaylie was adamant that he needed to do much, much more if he wanted to succeed.

"Eli," he said, "you need to show people visuals. People need to be able to picture what you're talking about in their mind's eye. You need to start working on your PR, and you need to make sure that a lot of people are donating money to your organization. It's not enough if just a few people are giving you big money. That won't work in the long run."

Harvey made Eli work very hard as he taught him the tricks of the trade. He wanted to know every detail of how the organization ran. It wasn't enough for Eli to tell him in words. He wanted to see the information on paper, in front of his own eyes.

Eli wanted Harvey to donate a motorcycle to United Hatzalah, but Harvey refused to give him any money until Eli returned to him with a brochure in hand.

"I don't like the fact that you're coming to me without any materials. I want to see facts, figures, and numbers. The brochure has to have great pictures, and I want to see the right kind of font for the lettering."

For Eli, who had never succeeded in school, meeting Harvey Kaylie was the most authentic type of education he could ever receive, because he was teaching him the benefit of making sure to cross the *t*'s and dot the *i*'s. Eli returned to Harvey five times with different versions of the brochure, but still Harvey wasn't satisfied and Eli was compelled to hire a different graphic designer. Eli worked really hard for months, all for one motorcycle. But it turned out to be for a lot more than that, because it was through those demands that he grew as a person, a businessman, a company president, and a visionary. It was Harvey who forced Eli to concede that the details count and that you won't succeed otherwise, since even the grandest project depends on the smallest components. Therefore, it is imperative to do things correctly from the start.

Finally, Eli returned with yet another version of the brochure, and Harvey liked everything about it, from the pictures to the captions, and the fonts of the lettering. He liked the fact that Eli had included the price of an ambucycle and the reason it was so costly.

Harvey taught Eli about PR, but he also taught him to be very careful about how much money he spent on every single item — including the brochure.

"I'm giving you an ambucycle," Harvey told him when they were done, "and I want you to come back to see me whenever you're in the States."

Then he introduced Eli to his daughter and son-in-law, Alicia and Danny Yacoby. Big lovers of Eretz Yisrael, Danny and Alicia are members of United Hatzalah's International Board, and their children are involved with United Hatzalah. In addition to their philanthropic and communal work, they also established a *hesder* yeshivah in Ramat

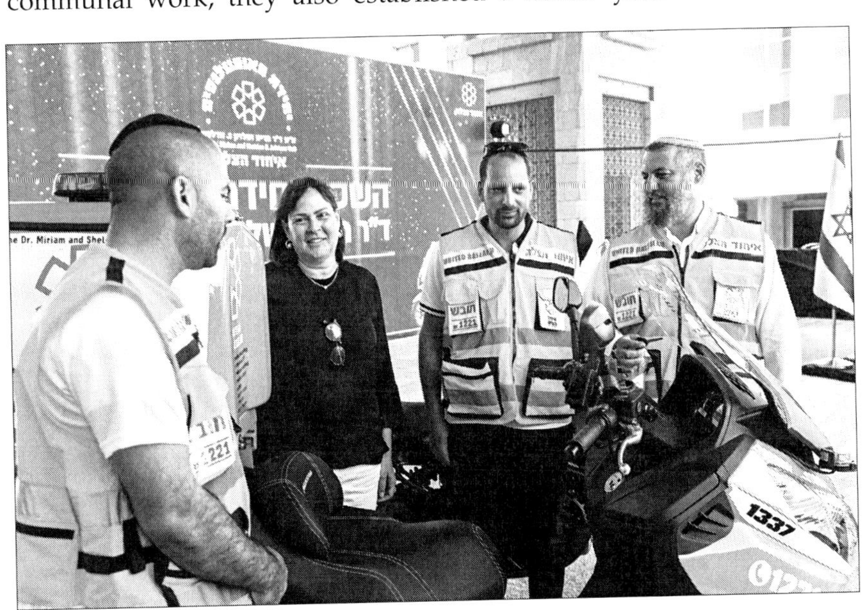

Alicia Yacoby with volunteers

HaSharon, a bastion of secular life in the center of the country, and are significant givers of charity for a wide variety of causes. It wasn't long before quite a few of the yeshivah's students began volunteering for United Hatzalah and going on calls in a part of the country that didn't yet have many volunteers.

Now it was years after that first meeting, and Eli had to turn to some of his closest friends with the biggest ask yet.

Five minutes was all it took for the Kaylies to agree to take part in the project.

Of course, Harvey was Harvey and he told Eli, "I want you to raise money from general donations that will match whatever we give."

As always, Harvey made Eli work hard for his money. And as always, he was correct — because this forced Eli to share his vision with numerous individuals who not only donated money for the building but also became close friends of the organization and of Eli himself.

Among those who contributed significantly to the project were Alberto and Vicky Saba from Mexico. As generous givers of charity,

(L–R) Alberto Saba, Shimmy Refaeli, Eli Beer, Vicky Saba and Moshe Teitelbaum

they were also extremely interested in helping with the purchase of the building. Alberto and Vicky had lost their son Moises and other family members in a fatal helicopter crash in Mexico. Moises had enjoyed an extremely close relationship with the Sefardic chief rabbi of Israel, Rav Ovadia Yosef, and had opened his home in Mexico to visiting Torah leaders, including Rav Aharon Leib Shteinman. When Moises died, the family was left reeling. Yet instead of giving up on life, they picked themselves up and redoubled their incredible generosity — now with a focus on celebrating the lives of their son and grandchildren.

For Eli, it was beautiful to see how Alberto and Vicky didn't make the decision on their own, but made sure to bring the entire family into the process because they wanted all of them to be involved in the opportunity to perform *chesed* (an act of kindness) and give *tzedakah*, which had been their family trademark for so many years. It was a classic example of *chinuch*, of educating the next generation, and Eli was moved by their generosity of mind and spirit and by the way they were going out of their way to ensure that the same character traits would continue within the Saba family for generations to come.

After an incredible amount of work, United Hatzalah was able to purchase and renovate its dream building. But that proved to be just the

The United Hatzalah building at the entrance to Yerushalayim

The United Hatzalah building at the entrance to Yerushalayim

beginning, because the municipality of Jerusalem has already given the necessary permits for the construction of an additional six floors to be added to the existing structure.

So while Eli's job is never ending — someone has to fund the next six floors — he has surrounded himself with some of the most awesome people in the world, people who appreciate what he wants to accomplish, people who believe in his vision, people who quite simply wanted to help turn his dreams into a reality.

# CHAPTER THIRTY-THREE

# A Kosel Bar Mitzvah, United Hatzalah Style

In 2014, Eli was invited by UBS, a giant in the Swiss banking industry, to address the bank's biggest investors and tell them the story of how he founded United Hatzalah. Having speakers like Eli come to address their people was the bank's way of showing that they weren't just about making money for themselves, but were also interested in giving back to society.

Eli had been sure that he was going to meet a large group of Jews at the conference, which took place at the Kempinski Hotel in St. Moritz, but he was disappointed to see that his audience was mainly comprised of non-Jewish Europeans. His old friend Yaron Carni accompanied him to the conference, but with so few Jews attending, he soon came to the realization that there wasn't going to be a minyan throughout his time in St. Moritz.

*We'll find a minyan for Friday night*, he assured himself, hoping that more Jews would emerge from the woodwork by then. On Thursday night, Eli and Yaron were walking through the lobby when they met an American couple who invited them to join them for a drink. Eli and Yaron sat down and made a *l'chaim* with the Americans, and then Eli told them a little bit about who he was and what he did for the organization that he had founded. The American, a hedge-fund manager from New York, introduced himself as George Weiss. His wife's name was Lydia. They had a nice conversation, and when they finished and signaled the waiter for a bill,  he handed it to Eli.

The bill came to about two hundred Swiss francs, a lot of money for a few drinks, but nothing outrageous for a fancy hotel in Switzerland.

"Cover the bill," George said to Eli. "You know what? If you cover the bill, I'll donate two motorcycles to your organization."

Eli didn't hesitate for a second. Handing the waiter his credit card, he turned to Mr. Weiss and said with a smile, "What time are we meeting for breakfast?"

Five minutes later, Eli heard George on the phone talking to his secretary.

"Rachel, there's an organization based out of Israel. I never heard of them before. Apparently, they save people's lives by rapidly arriving wherever they are needed by motorcycle. Send them seventy-two thousand dollars for two motorcycles." (Initially, the cost to sponsor an ambucycle was $18,000. But the organization soon realized that there were additional costs of insurance, maintenance, and equipment, and it was raised to $26,000. Today, the cost of donating an ambucycle is $36,000.)

When George was free, Eli asked him, "Tell me, what are you doing tomorrow night?"

"What, this Friday night?"

"Yes."

"Why? What do you have in mind?"

"I want to make a minyan."

"That's interesting. Matter of fact, I just met a guy here who worked as the secretary for President Jimmy Carter. Now he runs the Carter Foundation. Anyway, this guy is Jewish. I'll introduce you to him. Maybe he'll want to join the minyan."

When they met, Eli told Carter's former secretary that he wanted to organize a minyan for Friday night. The reaction was overwhelming, powerful, and shocking, because Eli couldn't help but see that the man was tearing up.

"Tomorrow night is my father's *yahrtzeit*, and I would love to say *Kaddish* for my father."

The news that there was a Jew at the hotel who needed to recite *Kaddish* for his father made Eli more motivated than ever to make the minyan happen. Instead of spending his time the night before his speech networking with people, Eli went on the prowl for the elusive ten Jews needed to make a minyan. He asked whoever he met over the next day whether he was Jewish and agreeable to taking part in a minyan.

There was one problem: there were very few Jews at the hotel. In the end, he had no choice but to continue his search the next morning.

His speech was a success. At the end of his speech, just before he stepped off the stage to grand applause, Eli said, "Ladies and gentlemen, I just want to inform you all that we will be holding a Jewish prayer ceremony this evening in honor of the Sabbath. Right now we have eight men and we need ten, so if you're Jewish and interested in joining us, please let me know."

Then he walked off the stage.

As he was leaving the room, a young man approached him.

"I heard your request for Jews for a minyan. I'm a waiter at the hotel, and I'm Jewish. I'll be happy to join you for the minyan. And by the way, I usually keep a few bottles of kosher wine with me, so if you need one for Kiddush, it will be my pleasure to supply it."

Now Eli had nine prospective members and was missing just one. It was difficult for him to believe that at a hotel that catered to hundreds of people, there wasn't even one more Jew, but no matter how long he searched, he kept coming up empty-handed.

In the end, Eli wasn't able to put together a minyan despite his best efforts. So the nine of them davened together. Some of the people in the room had never davened in their lives and were profoundly touched by the experience. They sang *Lechah Dodi* and other parts of the service, and after they were finished Eli made Kiddush on the kosher wine the waiter had provided and gave some to every member of the almost minyan. The secretary of former President Carter had a lot of appreciation for his efforts, but even so, Eli was disappointed that he hadn't managed to assemble a minyan.

The next time Eli flew into New York, he made a point of visiting George Weiss. When they were sitting together, George said, "I can't tell you how impressed I am with United Hatzalah and everything you're doing in Israel. I want to do something big for the organization. What major project is going on that I can get involved with?"

"You know what, George?" Eli replied. "I'm in the process of purchasing a building for United Hatzalah headquarters. We've been renting until now, but we need to own our space, and the time has finally come. I have a few wonderful donors who are helping me with this. The Silber family. The Kaylie family. The Saba family. All the partners involved are great people. Is this something that speaks to you?"

George was intrigued.

"Well then, George, what about if you donated the front entrance of the United Hatzalah building in Yerushalayim?"

"How much are you asking for?"

Eli gave him a price. "We'll call it the 'George and Lydia Weiss Gate of Life.'"

George looked at Eli Beer and said, "You got it."

The two grew closer, and Eli worked on convincing George and Lydia to visit Israel so he could take them on a tour of United Hatzalah and give them the opportunity to see firsthand where their money was going.

"But I visited Israel not long ago," George protested.

"Yes, but you never saw the renovated building."

George wasn't having any of it. "Eli, I'm not as young as I used to be, and it's getting harder for me to travel."

They were still in touch when Covid struck. By then George had been a major supporter of United Hatzalah for years, and their friendship had become rock solid.

Eli had recovered from Covid and was visiting New York when George called him.

"Eli, I need you to come to my office as soon as possible!"

When Eli walked into the office, he took a good look at his friend. To his surprise and concern, he saw tears welling up in George's eyes.

"Eli," he said without preamble, "my father was a Holocaust survivor. He escaped from Austria with his immediate family, but everyone else was killed by the Nazis. I grew up in a very small family — with barely anyone outside the little circle of relatives who miraculously survived. It goes without saying that I always hoped that one day I would find out more information about my family. Recently my niece discovered that we have two cousins living in Israel who are still alive. One is eighty-seven years old. The other is ninety-two. These cousins survived the war, but I learned about this only now, many years later. They married. They have children and grandchildren. Suddenly I found out that I'm part of a big family who all live in Israel.

"Eli, I want to go to Israel and meet my family."

There were many delays because of Covid-19, but eventually the momentous trip was arranged. Eli had done a lot of research into George's two cousins — Oscar and Walter Blau. They had been left at a Red Cross orphanage in Belgium and so had been saved from the Nazis. After the war, orphaned of their parents, they were sent to Israel, first to a kibbutz, then to the army. Eventually they were released from the army, married, and raised families of their own. As he learned more about this family's history, a thought occurred to Eli, and he called Dafna, the daughter of one of George's cousins, to confirm it.

"Dafna, tell me something. Did Oscar and Walter ever have a chance to celebrate their bar mitzvah?"

"To the best of my knowledge, neither of them had a bar mitzvah."

"They never had a bar mitzvah? Are you sure?"

"Never."

"Did they ever go to shul?"

"Never."

"Did either of them ever put on tefillin?"

"I don't think so."

It was ironic. George, the cousin who had grown up in America, had gone to shul and celebrated his bar mitzvah and put on tefillin. But his two cousins who had survived the Holocaust and ended up in Israel had never done any of those things.

George Weiss and his newfound cousins, Holocaust survivors Walter and Oscar Blau

And Eli Beer decided it was about time. He was going to give this family the surprise of their lives.

George invited his cousins to spend time with him at the King David Hotel where he was staying, and in the morning, after a delicious breakfast, a bus arranged by Eli pulled up outside the hotel to take the entire party to United Hatzalah headquarters, where George and Lydia were dedicating the third floor of the building (this was above and beyond everything else they had done) in honor of Walter and Oscar Blau.

On the way to the Hatzalah building, the bus made a surprise stop. It pulled up outside the Kosel, where a long line of drummers stood waiting to welcome the two "bar mitzvah" boys (eighty-seven and ninety-two, respectively), who were utterly surprised by the idea that they were about to take part in such a ceremony at their ages. The drummers pounded away at their drums, and the accompanying shofar blowers blew dozens of blasts that seemed to shake the very plaza itself. It was obvious that something big was happening, but no one in George's party knew what.

And then…

Wearing *talleisim* for the first time

Davening in tefillin for the first time in their lives

The group walked slowly across the Kosel plaza before entering the area in front of the Kosel. There they approached the wall itself, where a table was waiting for them. On the table was a *sefer Torah*.

Eli removed three brand-new *talleisim* (every tallis had the name of its new owner embroidered on it) from their bags and draped the *talleisim* over Walter, Oscar, and George while reciting the *berachah* one

The bar mitzvah boys davening at the Kosel

makes when donning a tallis. Once each of the three was wearing a tallis, Eli personally helped them put on tefillin.

It was an incredible sight to behold: a ninety-two-year-old wearing
tefillin for the first time in his life and crying with sheer emotion. Later
his children told Eli that in all their lives, they had never seen their
father cry. It was the first time he had cried since his childhood back
in the Belgium orphanage. But now he was crying — because it was a
moment that evoked all manner of emotion unlike anything else.

The three were called up to the Torah, which was read by Eli Pollak,
CEO of United Hatzalah, and (soft) candies were thrown at the "bar
mitzvah boys" to mark the occasion.

From the Kosel, the bus took everyone to the Hatzalah building,
where the third floor was dedicated in Walter and Oscar's honor. The
event was filmed by Channel 12 of Israeli TV, who showed footage of
the rare bar mitzvah celebration on the news.

"Eli," George said to his friend when the commotion had died down
and the festivities were over, "you changed my life. I never grasped the
meaning of Judaism until today. I'm going to bring my entire family
back in a few months — including all my children and grandchildren
— and we're going to celebrate my granddaughters' bas mitzvahs here
in Israel."

George was true to his word. The family returned to celebrate the bas
mitzvahs in June 2022, with a magnificent and meaningful event organized by United Hatzalah, culminating with the entire family joining
the Beer family at their home for the Friday night meal.

A chain of events that had begun at the Kempinski Hotel in
Switzerland had culminated in a truly satisfying conclusion at the
Western Wall, when three cousins — two of whom survived the war —
stood in tallis and tefillin for the first time in their lives and thanked G-d
for everything He had done for them.

It was a great day.

But then, every day is a great day at United Hatzalah.

# CHAPTER THIRTY-FOUR

# Amar'e, Povarsky, and Miles Nadal

NBA superstar Amar'e Stoudemire shocked the world when he made the decision to convert to Judaism, taking the name Yehoshofat and committing to a life of Torah and mitzvos. Amar'e was introduced to Eli Beer through a friend of Mark Gerson's while he was still playing for the New York Knicks. This was back in 2014, a few years before his conversion, when he was still a very active player for the NBA. Amar'e instantly fell in love with the idea.

"How can I help?" he wanted to know.

Eli knew what he wanted from Amar'e. "Why don't we go to the public and ask them to donate a sum of money to United Hatzalah for every basket you hit this season? This way we can turn your ball playing into something incredibly meaningful. Do it" — here Eli used a Jewish term — "*l'sheim Shamayim.* For the sake of Heaven."

Amar'e thought it was a

Amar'e

good idea, and United Hatzalah built a website specifically for the campaign, which they called "Amaresaves.com." Amar'e recorded a video of himself explaining the campaign to his fans, and since Amar'e was a popular player, the video was an instant hit and suddenly people all over were watching him talk about United Hatzalah.

"I'm Amar'e Stoudemire," he said in the announcement. "I love Israel and I love United Hatzalah. They save lives every day. Join me this upcoming season to help save lives by pledging to donate for every point I score."

Some people pledged ten cents for every point he made.

Some pledged a dollar per point.

Some pledged twenty dollars for every point.

In an interesting turn of events, it took Amar'e two hours to record the video because he couldn't figure out how to pronounce the word "Hatzalah," which was completely unfamiliar to him. He said "Chizballa." He said "Chazala," "Hazhbala," and "Hazala." They had to try again and again, because the last thing they wanted was for people to hear him on the video saying, "Donate your money to United Hizbollah."

(It's an interesting phenomenon, but in general those who are not Jewish from birth have a challenging time saying the word "Hatzalah," which literally means "rescue.")

Eventually they managed to get a take that was close enough to the real word, and they went with that. Thousands of people pledged money for every shot Amar'e made, and they raised four hundred and twenty-five thousand dollars just because of people's love for basketball and Amar'e Stoudemire.

With the vast number of events they are involved with, United Hatzalah can never afford to rest and is constantly upping the training for its volunteers.

One day Hatzalah was holding a massive simulated casualty drill. This is where United Hatzalah teaches the volunteers what to do in a situation where a bus is blown up (may this never happen again). Inside the bus, "victims" of the "bombing" were painted to look like they had been injured, and there were many ambulances, motorcycles, and even helicopters on the scene. It was a huge drill, and some of the organization's donors had chosen to attend and experience the day from a close vantage point. One of the donors was a special man named Steven B.

The drill was about to begin when Steven's eye was caught by the sight of an obviously religious volunteer sitting on the side and studying from what was clearly a Torah book while he waited for the drill to begin. A closer look and Steven realized that he was studying the *daf yomi*, the daily folio of Talmud that Jewish people all over the world study each and every day. What really interested Steven was how this man had clearly trained himself to be able to concentrate on what he was studying even in the midst of incredible tumult and commotion.

Steven asked the young man his name, and he introduced himself as Dov Povarsky (a grandson of the *rosh yeshivah* of Ponevezh).

"What are you studying?" Steven asked.

"It's a discussion about a person who gives his wife a divorce contract, which is contingent on certain conditions being fulfilled."

Steven found this fascinating because he had just visited a  museum where, for the first time in his life, he  had seen a *"get al tenai,"* a "conditional" divorce contract given from a man to his wife, used on very rare occasions during wartime,  when couples were separated from one another and didn't know if they would be reunited or even know the fate of the husband. In that case, the divorce contract could be enforced and his wife would be able to remarry.

Now here was a man learning about that very concept.

Early the next morning, Steven woke suddenly, feeling ill. He felt bad enough that he fainted. When he regained consciousness a short while later, it was already five thirty in the morning. He called 1221, the number for United Hatzalah, giving them the address of his home in Yerushalayim.

"Don't worry," the dispatcher said. "Someone will be there soon."

He had barely gotten off the phone, and someone was already knocking on his door.

The next thing he knew, Dov Povarsky was walking into his home — the same young man who had been sitting and learning the previous day in the midst of a noisy drill. After he stabilized Steven's blood pressure and made certain he did not need hospitalization, Steven asked him why he was visiting his neighborhood so early in the morning.

"I try to make a habit of davening Shacharis at the earliest time possible," he explained. "I usually go to the Kosel to daven. I was driving through your neighborhood when the call came in, so I took it, and the next thing I know we're having a reunion."

Before Dov left, Steven turned to him and said, "Rabbi Povarsky, there's a favor I want to ask of you."

"What's that?"

"Would it be possible for the two of us to study today's *daf yomi* together?"

Steven happened to own a set of Talmud that had survived the Holocaust. Dov went to the shelf and removed the tractate of *Gittin*, which they studied together, exactly one day after Steven had first seen him sitting and learning the *daf yomi* in the midst of the hustle and bustle of a major emergency drill, unfazed by all the noise and completely at peace with his inner world, no matter what was going on around him.

Things happen to Eli wherever he goes. He's just that type of guy. One week he was in New York, and he called up Rabbi Yaakov Kermaier, then *rav* of the Fifth Avenue Synagogue, and asked if he could join him for the Friday night meal.

Eli had previously spoken from the podium of the Fifth Avenue Synagogue, as he had at numerous shuls and other venues, and he was looking forward to seeing everyone again.

"We already have a scholar in residence with us this Shabbos," the rabbi said, "but you're more than welcome to join us at a special meal we are hosting at the shul this Friday night. It's a catered dinner, and I'm sure you'll enjoy it immensely. Just one thing."

"What's that?"

"We're fully booked for the meal, so please don't bring anyone with you."

At the shul that Friday night, the room was packed, the chazzan (prayer leader) was in top form, and the congregation was participating nicely. And yet Eli's eye was drawn to a man who was standing off to the side. When the time came, the man recited *Kaddish*, but since he was standing apart from everyone else, he said the *Kaddish* in a low voice. People couldn't hear him, and they were answering *amen* to the other people saying *Kaddish* instead, who were moving at a different pace.

Eli, who has a soft spot in his heart for the underdog in any situation, decided to go and stand next to the man near the back of the room, figuring that at least he would have one person answering *amen* to his *Kaddish* when he said it at the end of davening.

When the davening was over, Eli turned to the man and introduced himself.

"Eli Beer."

"Miles Nadal."

"Where are you from?"

"I'm from Toronto."

"And who are you saying *Kaddish* for?" Eli asked.

"My father."

Soon they were having a conversation, and Miles was telling him all about his parents. When Eli asked his new friend where he would be eating that night, the other man informed him that he hadn't really made any plans.

"So you're all by yourself?"

"Yes."

Miles Nadal

Eli just plain forgot that the rabbi had told him that they were all full and that he wasn't supposed to bring any more guests. When faced with Miles Nadal, who was going into a *yahrtzeit* week and didn't have anywhere warm and welcoming to be at that moment, Eli just had to invite him to join them downstairs.

"I wasn't invited," Miles protested.

"I'm inviting you," Eli told him.

Miles felt very uncomfortable. "Are you sure there will be room for me?"

"Of course there will be room for you! What's the question?"

Eli's earlier assurance to the rabbi that he wouldn't bring any guests with him entered his mind with a thud as he walked into the beautifully appointed room downstairs and headed in the direction of the head table, where the rabbi had seated him. He was accompanied by Miles, who would need to find a place at a table that was already completely full.

"Rabbi," he said, "I brought another guest."

Eli responded to the rabbi's questioning look with a heartfelt look of his own, trying to explain the situation without a word. Evidently the rabbi comprehended, because he welcomed Miles Nadal graciously and then proceeded to ask everyone to move their dishes over just a little bit to accommodate the new arrival.

Over dinner, conversation flowed, and when people asked Eli what he did, he explained all about United Hatzalah, sharing some stories of what they did and telling of the lives that had been saved by their team of dedicated volunteers. The concept of using motorcycles to get to emergencies faster came up, and everyone was very interested, especially because it was a phenomenon that was completely unique to Israel.

Suddenly Miles turned to Eli and said, "Would you mind if I dedicated two ambucycles in memory of my mother and father?"

He said it almost apologetically, as if he were asking Eli to do him a favor instead of the other way around.

"I mind, but I'll do it for you," Eli replied with a big smile.

And so he did.

Since that Shabbos, Miles Nadal has become a huge supporter of

United Hatzalah, making a major donation to the United Hatzalah headquarters and to its "Garden of Life." And, of course, he is a close personal friend of Eli Beer.

# A Quick Trip to Washington

On March 3, 2015, Israeli Prime Minister Binyamin Netanyahu addressed the United States Congress in Washington, D.C. Bibi's speech was the hottest event in town that day, and tickets were virtually impossible to obtain. And yet if you knew where to look in that vast hall, you would be able to spot the little boy from Bayit Vegan — now all grown up.

It all began when Amy Korenvaes, a generous AIPAC supporter, asked the head of AIPAC, the American Israel Public Affairs Committee, an organization that advocates for a strong US-Israel relationship, to invite Eli to come and address a crowd of seventeen thousand at the

Eli and Bibi at the Kosel

Bibi at a celebration for the conclusion of a Torah scroll

convention in Washington. For Eli, the invitation came as a pleasant surprise. He had never imagined giving a speech at that august gathering filled with people who loved Israel and whom he knew would be very interested in hearing about United Hatzalah and what it was doing for the country they so loved.

Since AIPAC is such a prestigious gathering, the organizers informed Eli that they wanted to hear him practice his speech before he gave it.

"And that's not all you have to do."

"What else?"

"You need to practice riding an ambucycle onto the stage."

Now that made Eli kind of nervous. The last thing he wanted was to misjudge the distance on the stage and end up flying off into the crowd. He practiced the drive about twenty times to make sure he knew when to brake.

Eli was scheduled to speak at AIPAC at nine in the morning. He couldn't have asked for a better slot, and he hoped that his message for United Hatzalah would come across well. It did, and many people came over to him later to tell him how impressed they were with what United Hatzalah was doing and asked what they could do to help. Hatzalah ambucycles kept in America for display purposes had been set up as an exhibition for people to view for themselves, and many of those present gave donations. As a result of that speech, United Hatzalah purchased twenty-five motorcycles for the organization.

On the night before the AIPAC speech, while attending a United Hatzalah reception in Washington, reuniting with old friends and meeting new ones, there was something niggling at him, a feeling he couldn't ignore.

And that little bothersome feeling had to do with still another major Washington D.C. event: the speech that Bibi Netanyahu was scheduled to give to Congress.

Eli was supposed to be there, too.

And that was the problem.

The fact that Eli even had a ticket to Bibi's speech wasn't something to be taken lightly. Obtaining the ticket hadn't been a simple matter at all. Everyone wanted to attend Bibi's speech, and it was gearing up to be a sold-out event. It was common knowledge that Bibi was about to take on President Obama with regard to the Iran deal — challenging Obama in his own backyard, if you will, and speaking in opposition to the president's wishes in front of both houses — and every AIPAC supporter wanted to be there in person at the historic event.

With everyone in town clamoring for the same few hundred tickets, the question now became who did Eli know who was a big enough supporter of Republican causes and would have access to a ticket.

He thought about it for a while and came up with one name: Joe Cayre (pronounced "Carey").

Joe was a Syrian Jew and a big supporter of both Israel and United Hatzalah. If anyone had access to a ticket, it would be him.

Eli picked up the phone and called Joe.

"Joe, it's Eli."

"How's everything, Eli?"

"Great. Question for you."

"Yes?"

"Were you planning on attending Bibi's speech in Congress?"

"No."

"Can you get a ticket?"

"Of course."

"Can you get *me* a ticket?"

"Let me check. Meanwhile, send me your passport just in case I'm able to get you a ticket."

Eli sent him a copy of his passport.

Joe called him back two hours later.

"Eli, I got you a ticket for the event. It's under your name."

"Where do I pick it up?"

"Every senator has a few tickets to give out. Yours is coming from Chuck Schumer, the Democratic senator from New York. Go to his office. He'll give it to you personally."

There it was. By some miracle, Eli had managed to obtain a ticket for Bibi's speech, but instead of feeling good about it, he was suddenly feeling as if he had lost a great opportunity.

In his mind, Eli heard a little voice speaking.

"You managed to get hold of a ticket to hear Bibi. And since this ticket is priceless, people will no doubt be willing to spend astronomical amounts of money to purchase it from you. Which means that you shouldn't be attending the speech at all. You should be auctioning off the ticket and using the money for United Hatzalah."

That's what the little voice said.

"Where should I do the selling?" he asked the little voice.

"Shouldn't be a problem," it replied. "Ask around among the United Hatzalah supporters at the reception, and see what people are willing to pay for the privilege of attending Bibi's speech in front of Congress."

"Fine," he said to himself. "I'll do that. I'll see if I can sell the ticket."

Then he had a thought.

"But isn't my name on the ticket?"

"Yes," he replied, "but it shouldn't be a big deal to change the name on a ticket."

So at the reception Eli started talking to people about the upcoming speech, and when he mentioned that he had one of the coveted tickets, someone told him that he was willing to make a donation to United Hatzalah if Eli was willing to give him the ticket.

"How much of a donation?" Eli asked him.

"One hundred thousand dollars."

That was a pretty good number, and Eli decided that he could and should forego the pleasure of hearing Bibi's speech if by doing so he would be bringing in another hundred grand for United Hatzalah.

"You got yourself a deal," he told the man who had made the offer.

Or, at least, that's what he thought.

Now Eli had to call Joe Cayre and ask his permission to change the name on the ticket for the guy who was willing to pay a hundred thousand dollars for the pleasure of hearing Bibi speak. From Joe's reaction, Eli realized that he had once again made a mistake with a person who cared about him. He shouldn't have even thought about using the ticket to make money for United Hatzalah, no matter how much he could have made, because Joe had gone out of his way for Eli and this wasn't the way to treat him after he had done him such a favor.

"I'm sorry," he said, "but if you wanted to do this, I wouldn't have gotten you the ticket in the first place. Throw it away or go — do whatever you want to do — but I'm not asking Schumer to change the name.

"And by the way, you should know that a thousand people called me after you did and asked me for a ticket, and I told them no because I had one ticket and I gave it to you."

Joe was angry at Eli and rightfully so.

Eli felt terrible for messing up what was essentially an incredible favor. He was extremely angry and upset at himself for not having thought this one through.

*You just never learn*, he said to himself. *If you wanted to do this, you should have asked Joe for a ticket for Hatzalah. But once you asked him for a ticket for yourself, that was that, and you should have known better than to ask him to change it.*

For much of the night, Eli walked around in a bad mood (which he did his best to hide), angry at himself and unable to have a good time. He hated messing up, especially when his mistakes had ramifications for United Hatzalah, and as much as he thought about what he could do to make it up to Joe, he couldn't seem to think of anything that would fix his error. He also hated having to inform the man who had offered the donation in exchange for the ticket that he couldn't have it, after all.

The next day, Eli went to Chuck Schumer's office at the Senate building to pick up his ticket. A man he had never seen before was waiting in the anteroom. They started talking and the man asked him why he was there.

"I'm supposed to pick up a ticket to hear the Israeli prime minister speak to Congress."

"Really?"

The man was impressed, thinking that Eli was a major player if Chuck Schumer was giving him one of the coveted tickets.

"No, it's not what you think. I run an organization called United Hatzalah, and that's how I was able to get a ticket."

"Who arranged for you to get one?"

"A friend of mine named Joe Cayre."

"I know Joe. And what's your name?"

"Eli Beer."

"Well, Eli, it's nice to meet you. I'm Leon Wagner."

They shmoozed for a while as they waited. It was quite a busy day since many of the people who had come in for the AIPAC conference were taking the opportunity to do some lobbying on the hill, and the wait took longer than it would have otherwise.

"By the way," Leon said, "I happen to be very involved with Israel. I'm actually the chairman of Shalva's board in the States."

"That's wonderful. I'm a huge fan of Shalva, and what they do for the families of disabled children, and for the kids themselves. It's a great organization."

At the end of the conversation, Eli gave Leon Wagner his card and said, "Next time you visit Israel, please come and see me at United Hatzalah."

Leon studied the card.

"I've never heard of United Hatzalah, though I did give an ambulance to Magen David Adom just last month."

"Well, then, come by and I'll give you a tour."

A short while after that, Eli was allowed entry into Chuck Schumer's office. They had a short conversation, and Eli told the senator about United Hatzalah. As the senator for New York, Senator Schumer knew about the American branch of Hatzolah, but he wasn't familiar with the Israeli version, so they spent a few minutes getting acquainted before he handed Eli the ticket and said goodbye.

In the hall where Bibi's speech was set to take place, hundreds of guests were milling around, along with passing senators and congressmen galore. He kept running into people who had been at his speech at the AIPAC and United Hatzalah events.

"You spoke well," many of them said. "Touched my heart. Here's my card. Give me a call. I want to donate money to United Hatzalah."

Eli probably ended up speaking with twenty-five people in the two hours before Bibi began speaking, all of whom wanted to donate money to his cause. Just by being there, he raised a lot more than the one hundred thousand that his donor wanted to pay for Joe Cayre's ticket, but he was still upset that he had hurt Joe's feelings after he had gone out of his way for Eli.

During the actual speech, Eli was seated two rows behind Elie Wiesel, the famed author and Holocaust historian. Bibi mentioned Elie during his speech, and the entire hall rose from their seats and gave him a standing ovation.

Bibi delivered a truly fantastic speech that day and received numerous standing ovations from many of the politicians who were present. He spoke so well that many people joked that he would have been a very good candidate for the GOP had he been American.

Eli Beer and Elie Wiesel

Bibi's message was clear to one and all: Israel couldn't afford to project weakness on any level and certainly not regarding nuclear power, and they had no intention of just standing around and doing nothing when an enemy stated clearly that they wanted to destroy the State of Israel.

Eli ended up leaving Washington satisfied with what he had accomplished at AIPAC. It had been a successful couple of days for United Hatzalah.

Months passed and then one day Eli got a phone call from one of his volunteers, a man by the name of Nadav Sela. Nadav and his father, Adam, were both volunteers and lived in the southern part of the country, in a kibbutz not far from Sdei Boker, where David Ben Gurion used to live. Nadav and Adam are tour guides in the region of Mitzpeh Rimon, driving tourists around in desert jeeps.

"Eli," Nadav said, "you're not going to believe who I'm taking around for a tour right now."

"Out with it. Who are you taking around?"

"I'm giving a tour to Leon Wagner and his family."

"Leon Wagner? Why does that name sound familiar? Remind me."

Nadav and Adam Sela

Jeep ambulance

"He said that he met you standing outside Chuck Schumer's office in Washington."

In a flash, it all came back to Eli. The ticket he'd been given by Joe Cayre. The deal he made with someone else for a hundred grand. Having to undo that deal. Hurting Cayre's feelings and listening to Bibi's grand speech.

Leon got on the phone.

"Eli, I have to tell you something. I know that you told me all about United Hatzalah when we met in Washington, but the truth is I'm so involved in so many other organizations that I didn't think about it for very long.

"Then I came here and hired Nadav as my tour guide and he started telling me how he used to volunteer for MDA, but that he joined your

Hatzalah Jeep ambulance

organization instead because you don't charge money for your services. Nadav just told me that United Hatzalah is the greatest organization in Israel, and if he says that, then I want to make a donation."

"Okay," Eli said. "I have a good idea for what you can donate: a United Hatzalah desert jeep ambulance. The kind of jeep that can be driven anywhere in rugged terrain and that can be used for rescue operations."

Leon liked the sound of it. "You got yourself a deal. I'm wiring you the money to make the purchase. Now listen, I'm coming to Yerushalayim soon, and I want to meet you."

Leon came to Yerushalayim and arrived at United Hatzalah headquarters during the time when it was undergoing renovations. There were still plenty of things Eli was able to show him, and he took Leon around and gave him an in-depth tour. When the tour was over, Leon, who was very impressed, pledged not only the jeep to the organization, but he promised to pay for the renovation of the lobby of the building Hatzalah was purchasing.

The second after Leon and Eli said goodbye outside the building, Eli dialed Joe Cayre's number.

"Joe, do you remember how upset you were when I wanted to give the ticket to someone else?"

He remembered.

"I'm calling you right now because I want to make you happy."

"What are you talking about?"

"I'll tell you what I'm talking about. I felt terrible about what I did and how I made you feel bad by trying to sell your ticket after you gave it to me with all your heart. And I know that you overlooked my ingratitude and kept on donating to United Hatzalah. You never held what I did against me. But I felt really bad about my mistake, and I want to make it up to you. So now I want to tell you what happened because of the ticket you gave me that day."

When Eli told him about Leon Wagner, Joe Cayre was thrilled with the outcome of the story. And he couldn't have been happier that he had given Eli the ticket and not one of the hundreds of others who asked for it.

There were other pleasant ramifications to that quick trip to Washington, D.C.

The keynote speaker at the Hatzalah event that took place at the same time as AIPAC was a young congressman from Florida named Ron DeSantis. Mark Gerson and he were good friends and he had invited the charismatic though relatively unknown politician to address their event. When he and Eli were introduced, DeSantis had a lot of questions for Eli about United Hatzalah and how it operated. At the end of their conversation, the congressman told Eli that he believed that America needed an organization like Hatzalah in every state. DeSantis gave a beautiful and heartfelt speech about United Hatzalah.

DeSantis became the governor of Florida, and once in office, one of the many things he did was to give permission for Hatzalah to operate in Miami. It was not part of Hatzalah, but Eli was very happy to hear that Miami now had a branch of Hatzalah — no matter who was running it!

A few years later, Eli met Ron DeSantis at Joe Cayre's home in New Jersey.

"Do you remember when I spoke at your event?" he asked Eli.

"What's the question," Eli replied.

"I never forgot about Hatzalah," DeSantis said, "and after I became the governor of Florida, I allowed them to operate up in Miami."

It was obvious that DeSantis thought he had given permission for Eli to run a branch of his operation in Florida.

"It's not my operation," he told the governor, "but they are great people and I'm thankful to you for helping them get it off the ground!"

# CHAPTER THIRTY-SIX

# A Lesson From the Rebbe

2016 was an important year for United Hatzalah — for a number of reasons, one of which was due to the entrance of a man named Michael Brown to the organization. Eli had long known that he needed to hire someone to serve as the vice president for all of United Hatzalah's activities outside of Israel. The VP would help with fundraising, and he had to be creative and able to think out-of-the-box. When Eli met Michael Brown he knew that he was the perfect candidate for the job.

And he was right.

Michael had grown up as a secular Jew in Boston. His parents were regular American Jews and there was no reason that Michael should have gone in a different direction, except for one thing — the decision to go to Israel on a Birthright trip. On that trip, Michael's life changed. His Birthright trip made him proud to be a Jew, and he resolved to live his life in a way that reflected the way he felt.

Michael proved to be an incredible asset to the organization, taking over much of the fundraising and operations work that had to be done outside of Israel.

Eli Beer and Yummy (Israel) Schachter go back a long way. Yummy, son of R' Herschel Schachter, the rosh yeshivah of Yeshiva University, has been a good friend to Eli and to United Hatzalah. As a person who has a

Yummy Schachter

hand in many endeavors, he was the one who initiated United Hatzalah's Succos concert — an event that has since become an annual tradition. The idea for the concert started back in the early 2000s when Eli was visiting New York and happened to attend the yearly YU concert. The first person he met when he walked into the hall was Yummy Schachter.

"Eli," Yummy said, "you need to start doing concerts like this for Hatzalah."

"I'll be honest with you," Eli replied. "I'm still getting my feet wet when it comes to fundraising, but between you and me, I find that my strength lies in raising money one-on-one, not by doing mass events."

"If you manage to get a thousand people in a room," Yummy shot back, "you just made a lot of money — quickly."

"Yes, but the risks are too big."

"You know what?" Yummy said. "I'm going to arrange a concert for you. I'll take on all the risks myself, and you won't have to worry about anything."

"Then by all means go right ahead…"

They shook hands, and Eli went to find his seat.

Yummy and Eli

Yummy had been serious about his concert idea, and he later met with Eli in Israel to discuss it further and to choose a venue.

"What did you have in mind?" Eli asked.

"I'm going to rent the wedding hall in the Great Synagogue of Yerushalayim for the event," Yummy told him.

"That sounds like a great idea. Bigger question — who will be performing?"

"I was thinking Shlomo and Eitan Katz."

"I like it."

And so it was.

The streets of Yerushalayim were plastered with posters advertising the concert, and seven hundred and fifty people showed up.

"Listen, Eli," Yummy said when they next met. "This is what we're going to do. There will be an intermission like at most concerts. But instead of just using it for people to walk around and buy some cookies and a drink, you're going to get up and give a speech about Hatzalah."

So it was that Eli found himself standing on the stage in the middle of a concert and talking about United Hatzalah's accomplishments and dreams for the future. The audience was having a good time. Everyone was feeling upbeat, and several individuals even donated an ambucycle, which, together with the ticket sales, meant that Hatzalah had done very nicely for itself that night.

Yummy was happy. Eli was also happy, even though he had spent his entire Chol HaMoed running around to different hotels and selling tickets. Little did he know that he would never have a quiet Succos again, because from then onward, he would always be busy selling tickets in the days prior to the show.

They did it again the next year in the same hall with a different singer. This time a thousand people showed up. It was obvious that they had hit on a formula that worked. But Eli felt that if they were going to be doing this in a serious way, they needed to change the venue and use a concert hall for the event. A little research, and Yummy decided on the Jerusalem Theater, which was a prestigious concert hall and more suitable for the kind of shows they wanted to organize.

"Yummy," Eli told his friend, "we need to start bringing in the top singers in the market."

"Agreed."

"And we're going to charge a hundred dollars a ticket instead of a hundred shekels. If I'm spending my entire Chol HaMoed selling tickets for the show, we need to make sure it's really worth it."

"Who should we bring in this year?" Yummy asked.

"I was thinking that we should start with Avraham Fried."

"I'll get back to you with his number."

Yummy was true to his word, and soon enough Eli had Avremel's number and was dialing the singer's home in Crown Heights.

"*Shalom aleichem*," Eli said. "My name is Eli Beer, and I'm calling you from Israel."

"What can I do for you?"

"Yummy Schachter and I produce a concert for United Hatzalah every Succos, and I wanted to invite you to perform for us this year."

Fried was intrigued.

"Are you going to be in the States any time soon?"

Eli was.

"Wonderful. Let me know when you're here, and let's try to meet at my home in Crown Heights."

Avraham Fried at a United Hatzalah concert

When they were finally sitting together, Eli said, "Reb Avraham, you don't know me, but I know you. I grew up listening to your music. In fact, my father owned a *sefarim* store in Bayit Vegan, and we sold hundreds of your tapes — back when that was the way people listened to music. I want you to perform in our concert. By doing this, you'll be saving many lives."

"I would love to participate in your show," Fried replied.

"But there's a catch," Eli said.

"What kind of catch?"

"I am asking you to do this show for free. I will, of course, pay for your plane ticket and any other expenses, but I want you to sing at my show for the mitzvah."

Avremel was taken aback.

"Eli," he said, "doing concerts is my *parnassah*."

Now Eli played his trump card.

"Can I show you something?"

Fried nodded.

Eli took out a copy of a book of the Lubavitcher Rebbe's letters to his chassidim.

"I want to show you one particular letter," he said to Reb Avraham. In the letter a chassid is asking the Rebbe whether he should support the newly established Hatzolah of Crown Heights.

"Look at what the Rebbe answered."

He read the words out loud. Here is a paraphrase of what he said:

"It is a very good thing to support Hatzalah. One cannot save the *neshamah*, soul, of a person unless it is possible to save his *guf*, his body."

"Reb Avraham," Eli said, "we see from the Rebbe's words that Hatzalah is a vital cause."

"You know what?" Fried said. "You've convinced me. I agree to your terms, and I'll perform at your first big show for free."

(Of course, this was a one-time deal…)

Avraham Fried was true to his word. He headlined a show that year at the Jerusalem Theater, singing alongside Ohad Moskowitz and the Shira Chadasha Boys Choir. Every ticket was sold, and the show was an outstanding success. It was an epic moment, and Eli knew that they were going to be doing this every single year for the foreseeable future.

Eli knew that people want to spend quality time with their children and grandchildren during Chol HaMoed and don't mind paying to make it happen. He began asking donors to ask their grandchildren which popular performers they wanted to see in the upcoming concert, and booked singers accordingly. The goal was to sell out the hall, and the best way of achieving that goal was by turning to the kids and asking their advice.

After they had been doing the concert for a few years, Eli decided that he was going to have a VIP section where he would charge one thousand dollars a ticket. People told him he was crazy — no one would pay that much. But Eli was sure that he would sell out the entire section.

"I knew that people loved Hatzalah and that they wanted to be at the concert," Eli says. "Buying those tickets was a good way for them to show their support in a truly authentic way while enjoying a first-class concert at the same time."

He started with thirty tickets.

They sold out immediately.

Eli and Albert Reichmann at a Hatzalah concert

He added another thirty tickets.

They were also snapped up.

In the years that followed, Eli organized concerts with the biggest superstars in Jewish music: Yaakov Shwekey, Lipa, MBD, 8th Day, Baruch Levine, Itche Meir Helfgot, Shloime Gertner, and Mordechai Shapiro, among others. He also held similar events during the year in different countries, constantly working on keeping United Hatzalah relevant and exciting to people everywhere.

During one of the years that Shwekey would be performing, he called Eli with a technical problem. It turned out that in addition to scheduling a concert for United Hatzalah, Yaakov was also performing at the annual concert in Chevron, and he was worried that he wouldn't be able to make it back to the hall fast enough. There's always heavy traffic on the way back to Yerushalayim after the Chevron concert, and Yaakov's concern was a real one.

Suddenly Eli had an idea.

"Yaakov, it's all going to work out!"

"What do you mean?"

"I mean that I'm going to have a motorcycle waiting for you when

Eli and Yaakov Shwekey

you get off the road from Chevron and are about to enter Yerushalayim. You will get on the motorcycle, and you'll be driven straight to the hall. This way you'll be able to bypass all the traffic, and you'll be at the hall in a matter of minutes."

And that's exactly what happened.

A volunteer with an ambucycle was waiting for him at the entrance to the city, and Yaakov climbed aboard his ride, dressed in suit and tie and ready for the show. He was deposited outside the entrance to the Jerusalem Theater in record time and wasn't even a few minutes late.

Eli likes to talk about taking an "entrepreneurial approach" to fundraising, always looking for out-of-the-box ideas. A fantastic example of the power of creative fundraising happened in 2022, at the United Hatzalah gala in Miami.

Andrea Bocelli is a world-famous tenor who plays many different instruments as well. He also happens to be blind. Bruce Gelb, a member of the United Hatzalah board, is Bocelli's producer. Bruce and his wife Amy, together with Yummy Shechter, worked for close to a year to arrange for Andrea and Veronica Bocelli to be honored at the Miami gala, together with Yoram and Margo Cohen.

At the gala itself, Yummy persuaded Bocelli to auction off his guitar, which was worth somewhere in the area of $20,000. He graciously agreed, and the bidding was so exciting, a participant wound up buying it — for $360,000!

And it didn't end there. Another bidder was so upset that he hadn't won the auction that Bocelli agreed on the spot to auction off a second guitar — which also went for $360,000!

Out-of-the-box thinking — and an extra $720,000 to save lives!

When Eli's son, Yisrael David, was approaching his bar mitzvah, he sat down with his father and informed him that he didn't want to have a classic bar mitzvah evening. Instead, he wanted the occasion to be devoted to a mitzvah purpose.

Eli and his wife have four daughters, and Yisrael David is their only son. Eli really wanted to do something nice to celebrate the milestone of his bar mitzvah. At the same time, he also wanted to honor his son's request.

"What if we hold a fundraiser instead of a bar mitzvah? That will turn the event into something more than just a party."

Yisrael David was okay with that.

"What should we raise money for?" Yisrael David asked his father.

"We're going to try to raise enough money to purchase an ambulance and to write a *sefer Torah* in memory of your two grandfathers and the

Yisrael David at his bar mitzvah

Writing a letter in the *sefer Torah*

*tzaddik* you were named after, Dr. David Applebaum. How do you like that idea?"

Yisrael David Beer liked it a lot.

The endeavor was an unbelievable success. People from around the world donated money toward the cause to the point where they were able to purchase two ambulances, as well as write a *sefer Torah*. For the actual event, people were invited to take part in what was termed "Bar and Mitzvah."

There were thirteen food stations at the event, each serving a different type of food. Some had meat dishes, some desserts, some salads. A nice variety of delicious and beautifully prepared delicacies. But there was a catch: in order to reach the bar, the guests had to pass by a mitzvah station first, where they were introduced to an assortment of mitzvos, a different mitzvah at every bar.

One station introduced the guests to the mitzvah of tefillin. There, representatives from a tefillin factory showed the guests how tefillin were made from start to finish. There was another presentation from a shofar factory. The guests were shown some two hundred different types of shofars. And since Succos was almost upon them, there was an *esrog* station where the guests were shown the different varieties of *esrogim*.

There was also a *bikur cholim* station, where guests chose from a beautiful assortment of candies to prepare care packages that would be brought to a hospital and given to the children there by the bar mitzvah boy and his friends. In addition to the candy, the guests also wrote notes to accompany the goody bags, wishing the patients a speedy recovery. Needless to say, the *bikur cholim* station was a huge hit.

At the Hatzalah station, everyone, even the children, were able to learn how to perform the Heimlich maneuver, giving them the ability to save the life of a choking victim with a few simple actions. People were also given a short course in CPR.

At the last station, the guests learned how to write a letter in a *sefer Torah*. There the guests were able to perform the mitzvah of writing a Torah scroll by contributing a letter. This was incredibly meaningful for people, particularly if they had never had such an opportunity before.

There was also a stage set up, and all the singers Eli knew came to perform. Avraham Fried was there. Yaakov Shwekey came. So did Yishai Lapidot and Yonatan Razel. It was a magnificent and meaningful evening filled with joy, song, good food, and mitzvos galore.

As for Yisrael David, he was thrilled that his bar mitzvah celebration had been used to teach people about Torah and mitzvos, and not only that, but two ambulances were purchased and a *sefer Torah* written in honor of his two grandfathers and Dr. Applebaum, the wonderful and selfless man after whom he was named.

Recently, at one of the Succos concerts, Eli gave his expected speech about United Hatzalah, and then, turning to Avraham Fried and Yaakov Shwekey, Eli said, "My friends, you know how important it is for us to be able to purchase more medical kits for our volunteers.

I am asking each of you, right here on the United Hatzalah stage, to donate a medical kit. You were hired to sing — but you should donate as well."

And they did.

# CHAPTER THIRTY-SEVEN

# Ambucycles on the Roof

It was Yummy Schachter who told Eli about a potential donor and philanthropist by the name of Stewart Rahr. Rahr had started from the ground up and had built his company into something huge. Recently he'd sold the company and was now dispensing charity with all his heart and soul.

"People call him 'Rah Rah,'" Yummy said, "and I told him all about United Hatzalah and everything you do. Eli, he agreed to donate twelve new ambucycles to the organization."

"That's amazing!"

"I'm telling you, this guy is big-time. I want you to do something nice for him to show your appreciation. And, Eli, think out-of-the-box. Make the kind of event for him that he'll never forget."

Yummy had spoken, and when Yummy talks, Eli listens. He gathered his team together and posed the question to them.

"I want you to think of a really original and out-of-the-box place where we can dedicate twelve ambucycles."

In the end, they decided to hold the event on the rooftop of Aish HaTorah right across from the Kosel. Eli could see it in his mind's eye. He pictured the orange motorcycles proudly arranged on the roof of the building with the Western Wall in the background, and he got excited by how beautiful he knew it would be.

Idea in place, the CEO of United Hatzalah, Eli Pollak, placed a call to Rabbi Yehuda Weinberg, the COO of Aish HaTorah, to ask him for permission to use the rooftop on the day in question.

"No problem at all" was the answer.

On the day before the event, the motorcycles were driven to the Aish building and brought through the ground-floor level and over to the elevator. The doors of the elevator slid open, and the first motorcycle was wheeled inside.

There was one problem.

It didn't fit.

Now what? How on earth were they going to get all twelve motorcycles onto the roof when the elevator wasn't big enough?

Eli Pollak has a line he likes to say: "At United Hatzalah, there is no such thing as impossible."

It was merely a question of coming up with the right idea.

And they did.

Minutes later, Eli Pollak was on the phone with one of the biggest crane companies in Israel, arranging for them to be at the Kosel for a job they had never done before: to lift twelve motorcycles onto the roof of a building across from the Kosel. Getting permission from the municipality for this undertaking was another hurdle. It took hours until all the necessary documents were filled out and the cranes were given the go-ahead.

The crane was there at five the next morning. The motorcycles were already lined up and waiting. And so it was that the motorcycles were lifted into the air and onto the roof of Aish HaTorah as the sun broke

Eli and Stewie Rahr on the roof of Aish

Ambucycle being lifted onto the roof at Aish

And higher...

Almost there...

At the ceremony

over the Western Wall. Stewart and his wife, Carol, were so moved by the event that they decided to donate another twelve motorcycles to United Hatzalah.

Thus started a beautiful relationship between Steward Rahr and Eli Beer, one that is still ongoing and strong. Stewart is so enamored by United Hatzalah and what it does that he attended a gala in New York and let it be known that he was going to donate another thirty-six motorcycles to the organization if people in the crowd matched him. That night Stewart earned a new nickname: the Ambucycle King.

On Israeli Independence Day 2016, Stewart Rahr — the "Ambucycle King" and his queen — were honored at an event in Tel Aviv where United Hatzalah welcomed another hundred brand-new motorcycles into their fleet, donated by Rah Rah and his wife. Four hundred guests streamed to the penthouse apartment that belonged to Eli's good friends, Menachem and Rutie Oren.

Rutie and Menachem are longtime friends and supporters of United Hatzalah, members of its board, who graciously open their beautiful

Eli and Menachem Oren

Gitty Beer, Rutie Oren, Menachem, and Eli
dedicating a defibrillator to United Hatzalah

penthouse home overlooking the Mediterranean Sea every year to hundreds of guests on Israel's Independence Day, in support of United Hatzalah. On this particularly memorable Independence Day, the guests stood on the rooftop, where they could see one hundred motorcycles lined up across from the beach, heading for a drive around the city. It was, without question, an unforgettable sight.

# Two Sheikhs in Dubai

In July of 2016, before the Abraham Accords were even a dream, Eli Beer and his COO, Dovie Maisel, found themselves walking the streets of Dubai dressed as Arab sheikhs. Obviously, there's a story here that needs telling, and tell it we will.

For years, Eli had the dream of one day being able to expand United Hatzalah into an international organization with branches worldwide. And while most countries in the world haven't given much thought to introducing United Hatzalah to their citizens, there are some that are thinking about it very seriously.

Dubai has invested billions in enhancing its hospital care and in the medical services that it can offer its citizens. They've been sending their people to some of the most prestigious hospitals in Boston and Cleveland, determined to model the Dubai hospitals after the best America had to offer.

Yet even after they had built some very impressive hospitals, many people weren't getting to those hospitals in time for their lives to be saved. When a person called for an ambulance in Dubai, it would arrive fifteen or twenty minutes later — if they were lucky.

It wasn't a good situation, and that's why Eli Beer was invited to Dubai to share his vision with a group of key government officials and businesspeople. How they came to contact him is a fascinating tale, one that's filled with *siyatta diShmaya*.

The government of Dubai had hired a leading American university to conduct research into innovative behavior and creativity in the field of lifesaving. It was the people at the university who came across Eli and invited him to Dubai so that he would share his story with them.

So it was that Eli Beer and his COO, Dovie Maisel, flew to Dubai for a four-day conference.

In the middle of the conference, Eli's phone rang. It was a donor calling from England.

"I heard that you're in Dubai right now. Is that true?"

"Yes."

"I don't understand. Aren't you Israeli? Isn't it dangerous for you to be in Dubai?"

"I have dual citizenship. I'm both Israeli and American. When I entered Dubai, I came in with my American passport."

"You're not afraid to walk around over there?"

"Not at all. I'm even walking around the streets with my yarmulke."

"I can't believe you're doing that. Aren't you afraid of getting attacked?"

"It's not like that at all!"

"Well, I'm willing to give United Hatzalah a five-thousand-dollar donation if you walk the streets of Dubai speaking Hebrew in public and out loud."

"I don't have time for these games," Eli told him. "You think I'm going to start running around the streets of Dubai for five thousand dollars? Do you have any idea how hot this place is right now? It's like a furnace outside!"

"Okay, then, what do you have in mind?"

Eli considered the matter.

"If you want to make a deal, here's what I'm prepared to offer. I will dress up like an Arab sheikh and walk through the streets of Dubai wearing the full Arab dress code and conversing in Hebrew."

"And what do I have to donate to United Hatzalah in exchange?"

"The cost for me doing this is one ambucycle for United Hatzalah."

Then Eli corrected himself and said, "You know what? I want two ambucycles."

"Why two?"

"Because there are going to be two Arab sheikhs walking the streets of Dubai in full Arab gear: Sheikh Eli ibn Gabriel Beer and Sheikh Dovie ibn Howie Maisel."

"And for this I have to pay seventy-two thousand dollars?"

"That's the deal."

"I'm prepared to pay your price, but I'm going to need proof in the form of a video that you carried out your end of the deal."

"Done."

Eli and Dovie spent a very enjoyable Shabbos. A few of the local Jews joined them for the minyan they organized in the hotel, and they partook of a wonderful *kiddush* after the Shabbos morning davening.

On Motza'ei Shabbos, Dovie and Eli left the hotel to make the seventy-two-thousand-dollar video. It was the month of Ramadan, when Muslims traditionally fast during the day and feast at night, and people were outside having a grand old time even though it was excruciatingly hot. It was probably somewhere in the region of 110°F. Hot enough that a person wouldn't even stick a finger out of the hotel under normal circumstances.

But these weren't normal circumstances.

Not when they had a chance to earn two brand-new motorcycles just for taking a walk down the street in a Purim costume.

Eli asked his wife to accompany them and take the video. Unfazed by the heat, she agreed, but before she could take the video, they had to go shopping for the kind of clothing that would give them the appearance of two authentic sheikhs out for a nighttime stroll in the broiling air of Dubai.

There was a *shuk* nearby, where one could find goods of every type and description for sale. A look through the stores and they entered one that seemed that it would cater to affluent sheikhs.

The Arab man behind the counter gave them an inquiring look.

"Can I help you?"

"Yes. We need two outfits."

"What are you looking?"

"The kind that a sheikh would wear. Not someone dressing up as a sheikh. What a sheikh actually wears, from robe to head covering."

"What do you need this for?"

Obviously they weren't sheikhs, and the man was curious. The last thing Eli wanted to do was tell the man where they were from or why he really wanted to walk through the streets dressed like an Emirati sheikh, so he told the owner that he wanted to buy the clothing to keep as a tangible memento of his time in Dubai.

The owner gave them a dubious look. Clearly, he was suspicious about their cover story, but he went about the store putting their order together.

"This is a *kandura*," he explained. "You put this on your body together with a *ghutrah* for your head. Both are made of cotton. You wear them to protect yourself from the desert heat and the sand that flies through the air when the wind blows."

The owner put everything into a few bags, and they paid. Although he had given them a short tutorial on the correct way to wear the garments, they weren't paying much attention since they were in a rush to leave in the face of his mistrust.

They went into a nearby hotel to change into their new gear, doing their best to make it look authentic, as if they wore this kind of clothing every day of the year. Eventually they felt ready to make their grand debut and stepped outside, looking for all the world like two world-class sheikhs from the upper-class neighborhoods of Dubai or Bahrain.

Eli and Dovie in Dubai

As they strolled through the streets, they began conversing in Hebrew. People were looking at them oddly — this was way before anyone dreamed that Dubai was going to turn into one of the most popular travel destinations for Israelis — and Eli whispered to his wife, "Gitty, take the video and let's get out of here!"

Gitty started filming them as they conducted an entire conversation in Hebrew. While they talked, Eli couldn't help thinking that someone was going to think that he and Dovie were Mossad agents, and they would probably be arrested and taken in for interrogation, and maybe worse.

The more they talked, the more people started gathering around them, and Eli was sure it was the police coming to arrest them.

"Gitty, did you get a good video?"

She nodded.

"How long is it?"

"Long enough."

"Okay, good."

Then they stopped speaking Hebrew, and Gitty stopped filming them and no one was looking at them anymore, and life went back to normal for Eli ibn Gabriel and Dovie ibn Howie, who were more than ready to return to their hotel and change back into their regular clothing.

When they returned to their hotel, Eli sent the donor the video, which clearly showed Eli and Dovie walking around in Dubai dressed as Arabs and speaking Hebrew. There was no question that they had kept their part of the bargain, and the donor in turn kept his.

It had been a harrowing few minutes, but the payoff was worth it.

The Dubai sheikh stroll wasn't the only time that Eli has done something out of the ordinary to raise money for United Hatzalah. In one case, it was Mark Gerson who presented the challenge.

Eli and Mark have only gotten closer over the years. They usually speak at least twice a week, and Mark (good friend that he is) spends a lot of time worrying about Eli's health. Mark himself goes running every day and has slimmed down to a healthier weight. He made a point of warning Eli that the amount of traveling that he was doing, along with bad eating habits, was a recipe for disaster.

Eli wholeheartedly agreed. It was obvious that he needed to lose weight. But dieting and exercise took time, and he never seemed able to get around to doing anything about it.

Then Mark came up with an idea that he thought would resonate with Eli.

"Eli," Mark said, "I have a deal to offer you."

"What kind of deal?"

"Lose fifty pounds and I'll give United Hatzalah twenty thousand dollars for every pound you lose. One million dollars for fifty pounds."

"What if I lose only thirty pounds?"

"Then you get nothing."

And so, with a million-dollar incentive, Eli embarked on a journey to lose fifty pounds. (At the time of this writing, he had lost more than half the weight.)

But this wasn't enough for Mark.

"You need to stop flying economy," he would tell Eli. "It's too stressful for someone who is traveling as much as you are."

But Eli didn't listen. He needed to raise money, not spend money.

"Eli," Mark persisted, "if you want Hatzalah to be strong, then you need to be healthy."

Eli would agree and then continue doing what he always did. Finally, after years of this, Mark had had enough. "Eli," he said, "I demand that you stop flying economy and start traveling business. You work eighteen-hour days, and the toll of the constant travel in tiny seats is something I can no longer watch."

It wasn't long before Eli received an email from Mark telling him that Mark was going to be sending additional money to United Hatzalah, with the funds specially marked to pay for Eli's traveling budget. He also made it clear that if Eli disobeyed him and continued flying coach, he would begin giving less money to the organization.

"Mark basically forced me to start flying business class," Eli says. "For years I couldn't bring myself to do that, because it seemed to me that flying business meant fewer defibrillators for United Hatzalah. Suddenly I had no choice and had to fly business.

"And that led to my meeting numerous people whom I would have never met otherwise. This is just another example of how Mark has proven to be an outstanding friend — one whose support for United Hatzalah has never wavered."

As the years passed, United Hatzalah's budget kept increasing, and Eli found himself traveling the world to raise the funds needed. But traveling the world gets tiring after a while, and sometimes a person feels like maybe he did enough — like maybe he would rather not travel quite so much anymore.

Eli was a frequent visitor to Rav Chaim Kanievsky's world-famous home on Rashbam Street in the heart of Bnei Brak. Since running an organization like United Hatzalah means that one is confronted by many halachic and hashkafic questions, with questions pertaining to Jewish law and theological issues, Eli made a point of conferring with Rav Chaim Kanievsky, who always gave him clear guidance.

Now Eli asked the *tzaddik* for a specific blessing.

"Rebbe," he said, "please bless me so that I shouldn't have to travel the world anymore to convince people to donate. Please bless me that one donor will agree to cover the entire budget. It's a lot of money, but there are plenty of wealthy people in the world who would be able to handle it."

"*Chas v'shalom*," Rav Chaim replied. "Heaven forbid. I want you to continue traveling all over the world so that every Jew will have the merit of saving lives. A lot of religious Jews fulfill the mitzvos, but not everyone has the chance to fulfill the mitzvah of *pikuach nefesh*, of saving lives, and you're giving them that opportunity."

Hatzalah Dispatch Center back in 2013

Volunteer on the way

Then Rav Chaim reached into his pocket, withdrew two hundred shekels, and handed the bill to Eli Beer, saying, "I also want the mitzvah!

Then Eli said to the leader of the generation, "It would be a great merit for us to be able to host the Rav at the United Hatzalah center. Our volunteers need *chizuk* (encouragement), and it would mean a lot if you would agree to come and speak to them."

Eli knew that just seeing Rav Chaim's face, and hearing even a few words from his holy mouth, would infuse his soldiers, his volunteers who were fighting the battle at the front lines, with the strength necessary to continue saving lives every single day.

"I'm an old man," Rav Chaim protested.

"If the Rav comes and talks to our boys, it will give them a lot of *chizuk*," Eli persisted. Knowing how to speak Rav Chaim's language, he added, "Many lives will be saved in the merit of such a visit."

At that, Rav Chaim agreed.

The next time Rav Chaim traveled to Yerushalayim was during Chol HaMoed, when he made his regular Yom Tov pilgrimage to the Kosel. This time, Rav Chaim made a stopover on the way to the Western Wall at the United Hatzalah headquarters to address the volunteers. It was a momentous event for the organization and its executive leadership

On the way to the hospital

— Eli Beer, Eli Pollak, and then-CEO Moshe Teitelbaum — who had never ceased working to ensure that the visit would actually take place.

Rav Chaim's visit to the headquarters in Yerushalayim was followed by a visit to their center in Bnei Brak a few months afterward. He spoke to the volunteers and made a point of donating more money to United Hatzalah, while making it crystal clear to one and all that he was very much in favor of what they were doing. People understood that if Rav Chaim was going out of his way to donate money to United Hatzalah, then it must be a worthwhile cause.

# PART SEVEN

> *By us in Hatzalah, there is no such thing as impossible.*
>
> — *Eli Pollak*
> *CEO of United Hatzalah*

# CHAPTER THIRTY-NINE

# The Senator's Vote

avid Friedman, the American ambassador to the State of Israel from 2017 to 2021, is one of the oldest and dearest friends of United Hatzalah and one of its earliest board members. Among other things, he and his wife Tammy have recently dedicated an ambucycle in honor of their daughter after she completed the course to become an EMT. But before we get into current events, we need to go back in time to when it all started.

Ambassador David and Mrs. Tammy Friedman visiting United Hatzalah Headquarters in Jerusalem

David Friedman had been in shul on Yom Kippur about twenty years before, during a visit to Israel, when he heard someone shouting from the ladies' section that a doctor was needed. He had no idea who needed help, but he went to see if there was anything he could do.

He was shocked to find his mother-in-law on the floor. She was conscious but didn't look well at all, and a Hatzalah volunteer was taking care of her. That was David's first encounter with the organization. He was impressed by what he had witnessed, how someone had arrived to treat his mother-in-law within minutes.

For years, David Friedman had worked as a lawyer. Donald Trump happened to be one of his clients, and when Trump announced that he was running for president of the United States, David made a point of letting him know that he wanted to serve as his administration's ambassador to Israel.

On election night, he was among those who attended the party at Trump Towers. No one had expected Trump to win, but suddenly the news was reporting that he had won the election. David went home to take a shower and returned to the city at seven thirty in the morning to meet with Donald Trump. The newly elected president had been up all night but looked completely fresh, as if he had just gotten up twenty minutes earlier from a restful night.

When he saw David walking into his office, he said, "Can you believe I won this thing?"

"Before people start showing up," David said, "one quick thing: I just want to remind you about appointing me as the ambassador to Israel."

"I still have to choose a secretary of state and a secretary of defense, but it's not a problem — just give me a little time."

Nothing happened for about three weeks, so David went back to see Trump when no one else was around.

"Yes," he said. "It's time — I can do it now."

And so it was.

(By the way: Sometime before he was elected president, businessman Donald Trump learned about United Hatzalah's work, and donated $100,000 to purchase three ambucycles!)

In order for a person to be appointed a US ambassador, he needs to be confirmed by the United States Senate Committee on Foreign Relations, which will then make a recommendation to the Senate, whereupon the Senate votes and a decision is made. There were twenty-three members on the committee — twelve Republicans and eleven Democrats. Since it doesn't matter if one wins by one vote or ten, David figured that he was going to nail the appointment since there were more Republicans than Democrats. He didn't count on one of the Republicans having to be hospitalized for back surgery. This meant that it was eleven against eleven — a political deadlock — and suddenly the question of David's recommendation was up in the air. He needed to figure out a way to break the deadlock.

This would end up being the single longest confirmation hearing for an ambassador in the history of the United States. Most confirmation hearings are routine and straightforward, but this was not the case now. David Friedman was the first ambassador to be nominated in Trump's administration — nominated even before Trump was inaugurated as president — and he was grilled by the Foreign Relations Committee for five hours straight. It was an incredibly intense experience.

They were three hours into the confirmation hearing when they took a break. The pressure was high. It was obvious that David was still at least one vote short. During the break, someone suggested that he meet with Robert Menendez, a Democratic senator from New Jersey.

"Look," Menendez said when they were face to face, "I think you're a good guy. I'd be inclined to help you, but give me something to work with."

"Okay," David told him, "ask me a question about United Hatzalah."

"Why should hearing about an organization change anyone's mind and make them think you're a good choice?"

David pulled a newspaper article about United Hatzalah out of his pocket. He had brought it with him, just in case.

"I'm one of their earliest supporters, and I'm on their board. Read the article. This should give you something to use."

When the break was over, everyone resumed their seats. Senator Menendez said, "Mr. Friedman, we've spent a few hours talking about some of your activities and your philosophies. I understand that you are also involved in an organization called United Hatzalah? Is that correct?"

"Yes, I'm one of the founding trustees."

"Are you active in the organization?"

"Yes, I'm very active in the organization, and I support it very strongly."

"Is it true, Mr. Friedman, that United Hatzalah has volunteers from all parts of Israeli society, from Orthodox Jews to secular Jews, Christians to Muslims, and that they all work together?"

"That's correct. The organization has volunteers from all walks of Israeli society, who are all treated equally, and they treat those who need emergency assistance without regard to their ethnicity, place of residence, or religion. It's a beautiful thing because it shows how cohesive Israeli society is. United Hatzalah is the most inclusive organization I'm aware of, and I'm very proud to be so heavily involved with it."

"Does United Hatzalah reflect your views with regard to an inclusive Israeli society?"

"Yes, Senator, very much so."

"Okay, thank you. I'm prepared to vote in favor."

And that was it.

Shortly after that conversation, the vote was taken and David Friedman was in the door.

"I knew that David Friedman was going to be the ambassador under Trump," Eli says. "At my son's bar mitzvah, I introduced David to Moshe Lion and I said to David, 'This is Moshe Lion, the next mayor of Yerushalayim.' Then I said to Moshe Lion, 'This is David Friedman, the next ambassador to Israel.'"

Moshe Lion said to Eli, "How do you know?"

"Trust me," Eli replied.

Eli knew that his friend was going to be the next ambassador because he had spent Shabbos with the Friedman family, and David had told him about his relationship with Donald Trump.

"Not long after Trump was elected," Eli says, "I got a phone call. It was an investigator from the FBI."

"What can I do for you?" Eli asked.

"I have some questions to ask you about Mr. David Friedman," the FBI man said.

Eli had been expecting such a phone call since David Friedman was on his board, and the FBI had to do a security check on him before David could stand before the Senate to be confirmed for the position. He spent the next hour and a half on the phone telling the man from the FBI all about United Hatzalah. He told him about their ambucycles and how David Friedman was one of the first people to donate an ambucycle to the organization.

The next thing Eli knew, David Friedman from the Five Towns had been confirmed as the next American ambassador to Israel — and United Hatzalah had a hand in making that happen.

The swearing-in ceremony for Ambassador Friedman took place at the White House, and he invited his old friend Eli Beer to attend. It was his first time at the White House. Vice President Mike Pence presided over the actual swearing-in.

"Mr. Vice President," Ambassador Friedman said before they began, "I know that you're used to using the regular formula when you swear people into office. In the normal formula, a person will say that they swear to protect and defend the Constitution of the United States. I don't swear. And because I don't swear — we don't have to get into the reasons at this time — instead I am going to affirm that I will protect and defend the Constitution of the United States."

"No problem," said Pence.

When the moment came, Tammy Friedman held the family Tanach in her hands, while her husband placed a *kippah* on his head. When they were ready, David Friedman raised his hand in the air, and the vice president said, "I... State your name."

"I, David Friedman..."

"Do solemnly swear..."

"Do solemnly affirm..."

After the vice president hastily readjusted the wording, the rest of the ceremony went according to the book.

While all this was going on, Eli's mind was in a completely different place. The Beer family was about to make their first wedding in a hall near the town of Psagot, and Eli wanted David and Tammy Friedman to attend.

When Ambassador Friedman had told his staff that he planned on going to the wedding — even before he was officially sworn into office — they had warned him that it was out of the question.

"United States ambassadors never cross the Green Line," he was told, "and Psagot is located over the Green Line."

"I'm the ambassador," he said. "You work for me, not the other way around, and there's no question of my not attending the wedding of the child of such an old friend."

Now they were at the swearing-in ceremony, and Eli was at the White House, at the new Ambassador's invitation, to watch it happen.

"David," he said afterward, "can you show me the person in charge of making decisions at the State Department for the Middle East?"

The ambassador pointed to one of the key people.

While David Friedman was talking to the vice president, Eli Beer introduced himself to the man from the State Department and started a conversation.

"You know," he said, "Ambassador Friedman is a very close friend of mine. My daughter is about to get married, and I wanted to know if there is any problem from your end with the ambassador attending the wedding?"

"No, no problem at all."

"Does it matter where it is?"

"No."

"Even if the hall is located in Judea and Samaria — over the Green Line?"

The man from the State Department wasn't happy, but he said that he would look into it and they would be in touch.

As the days passed, the State Department back in the United States made it clear that they were not in favor of the ambassador making the trip. But David Friedman let it be known that he was going to the wedding, even if it meant that he would be the first US ambassador to ever cross the Green Line.

"Look," his staff said to him. "We get it. You want to go. But keep in mind that it's going to cost the embassy at least two hundred thousand dollars for you to attend this wedding in order to comply with all the security protocols."

"I'll make you a deal," Friedman said. "Here is Eli Beer's number. Call and tell him that you're giving him a hundred thousand dollars, and I'm sure he'll agree to make the wedding inside the Green Line. That would be a win-win situation for everyone. You won't have to deal with my crossing the Green Line, and he'll get a free wedding."

"We can't do that."

"I didn't think you could. But nevertheless, I'm going to his daughter's wedding."

In the end, David Friedman attended the wedding, and it didn't cost anywhere close to the projections thrown at him. And while this was the first time an American ambassador had made such an audacious move, it was far from the last. Because Ambassador Friedman did everything in his power to challenge the status quo in the diplomatic relationship that had existed up until he came into office.

By and large, he succeeded.

Ambassador David Friedman served under President Trump for the next four years as the US ambassador to Israel. There he managed to accomplish great things — many of which had never been tried before, and others that had been attempted but failed. David Friedman came at the old problems with a fresh eye and a willingness to try solving a host of serious and complicated issues in brand-new ways. And they worked.

It was under his leadership — and with the backing of President Donald Trump — that the American Embassy was moved to Jerusalem from Tel Aviv, and it was during his term in office that the city of Jerusalem was officially recognized by Washington, D.C., as the capital of Israel. Knowing that he was working against the clock, that there was a limited amount of time in which to accomplish his many goals, Ambassador Friedman never stopped moving ahead. By the time he left office, the United States recognized Israel's sovereignty over the Golan Heights and, together with Jared Kushner and Jason Greenblatt, brokered the Abraham Accords — making peace between Israel, the United Arab Emirates, and Bahrain.

But it was all set into motion the moment David Friedman handed Senator Bob Menendez a newspaper cutout detailing the accomplishments of United Hatzalah. Because that showed the honorable senator from New Jersey that here was a man who really cared about helping people bridge the gaps that naturally exist between them. A few minutes was all it took for Senator Menendez to comprehend that any person who supported United Hatzalah was without question a man who desired nothing more than to make peace between nations who had been enemies — and turn them into friends.

# CHAPTER FORTY

# The Longest Night

When the phone rings in the middle of the night, very rarely is it good news. On that night in the year 2017, Eli answered the phone. Eli Pollak was on the other end of the line.

"What is it?" Eli asked his friend.

"Get dressed."

"Why?"

"I'm waiting for you downstairs." Eli noticed that he didn't receive an answer to his question.

He got dressed and walked down the sixty-five stairs from his apartment to the ground floor. Eli Pollak was waiting outside his building.

"Eli," he said, "I have the worst news possible. Something we've been worried was going to happen for years finally happened."

"What is it?"

Eli Pollak took a deep breath.

"A volunteer was just killed on his way to a call."

Effi Gadasi

Effi Gadasi

At that moment, the faces of thousands of volunteers flashed through Eli's mind — beloved faces of those he cared about — and he wondered who they had lost that night.

"It was Effi Gadasi," Eli Pollak finally said.

Effi. One of their most dedicated volunteers. A good EMT. A good friend.

And now he was gone.

Eli relayed how Effi had just finished a call at the Kosel and had chosen to go to yet another emergency — this one on Hillel Street in the center of town — when he was in an accident himself. It was raining, the roads were slippery, and visibility was low. The taxi that ran him over simply didn't see him there.

Losing a volunteer in such a way — while he was on his way to a call — was hard to fathom. In addition, it was what Eli had feared, that such a tragedy would signify that volunteers would no longer be able to ride motorcycles on their way to saving lives.

He thought about the time and resources they'd put into training thousands of volunteers over the years — and how part of that training was learning how to drive in the safest way possible. A volunteer couldn't even get a motorcycle unless he had his own license and had been driving for at least three years.

He thought about the fact that every volunteer had to wear a heavy jacket, gloves, and a helmet, no matter the weather or their personal feelings about it. Safety had always been a paramount concern. They had put so much effort into training volunteers to stay safe as they engaged in their lifesaving missions. And if they ever caught a volunteer breaking the rules — he was thrown out of the motorcycle unit.

Eli thought about the special microphones that had been installed inside the helmets that the drivers used (modeled along the same lines as those used by pilots) because they weren't allowed to touch their radios when they drove, and how the motorcycles were equipped with GPS to monitor their speeds and not allow them to exceed the limit that they had set for every bike.

But with all that, with all the safety measures that had been put in place, it wasn't enough. Eli was sure that they were going to have to shut down the motorcycle unit, that they would have to go back to using cars and other methods of transportation, even if it took longer to reach a call, because Effi had died and how could the world continue as if everything was normal when it would never be normal again?!

"What about Effi's family?" he asked Eli Pollak. "Do they know yet?"

"No one knows anything yet."

Unspoken was the fact that it was going to be major news in a short time, especially since it was Thursday night going into Friday morning, and the funeral would have to be held before Shabbos.

Eli Pollak left, and Eli Beer wearily ascended the sixty-five stairs back to his apartment. He made himself a cup of coffee and debated his next move.

The first thing he needed to do was wake up his wife, Gitty, and tell her what happened. When she heard the news, she burst into tears.

"Gitty, what should I do now? Shut down the motorcycle unit?"

Her reply came back at him rapid fire.

"Eli, do you think that Effi would want you to close down the unit?"

Eli pictured Effi's smiling face and thought about what Effi would have wanted. He went back to the kitchen, picked up his mug of coffee, and carried it outside to the porch. From the Beers' porch, it's possible to see almost every major neighborhood in the city, from Har Nof on the right to Ezras Torah, Romema, and Sorotzkin in the center, and Ramot and Ramat Shlomo all the way on the left. It's a magical view anytime you look at it night or day. Now he stood at the railing, cup in hand, and stared at a million lights twinkling at him from the city he loved so much.

He took a sip of coffee and stared at the streets, at the cars driving through the night. He would never know how long he stood there as a million memories raced through his mind, one after the next, poignant and bittersweet and happy and terrifying — a movie reel that summed up his life and, by extension, the lives of so many others who had signed on for the ride.

It was a night that never seemed to end. Even for Eli Beer, a person who had known many such nights, there was something different about this one.

He finished his coffee.

Morning was breaking over the hills of Jerusalem. The sky was

A partial view from Eli's porch

taking on a thousand shades of pink, blue, and purple. It was almost day. Day in a world without Effi Gadasi.

"At the end of the day, we're an army," Eli finally said out loud. "We're soldiers protecting Israel. The country has the IDF — and the country has United Hatzalah. We've had other soldiers who have died in our ranks. But this is the first soldier who died on a United Hatzalah motorcycle. Effi was the first casualty in the ambucycle unit.

"We started with fifteen volunteers, and now we have close to five thousand. We started with one motorcycle, and now we have seven hundred. We're here to protect the Jewish people, and we're here to save lives. We do not have the right to stop what we are doing — even for a second."

And as he said the words, he was filled with conviction, because he knew that it was the truth.

"We can't stop for a second," he repeated. "Not for a second. We are an army, and we will continue saving lives."

He gazed at the hills of Jerusalem and said to himself, "Eli, today is a very important day. Today is the day you will need to send a message to every member of your army. Today is the day that you need to bring home the message, to remind them that they are troops in the army, and that just as you don't stop fighting the war when a soldier dies on the battlefield, we will not and cannot afford to stop fighting the war that Hashem has sent us to fight. And while we will work to make the safety regulations more rigid than they were until now, there will be no talk of stopping our mission.

"This morning Effi Gadasi will be taken on his final journey. He will be escorted to the cemetery like a hero who lost his life under enemy fire. He was a volunteer in the motorcycle unit and was on his way to save someone when he lost his life. But he died a hero — on the way to save a life."

Eli knew that the volunteers were going to wake up that morning, and they would read the news and find out what happened. He needed to make sure that none of them decided to stop saving lives. He would need to write them a heartfelt letter so they could read it before they saw anything else.

And so Eli Beer sat down and wrote the most important letter of his life.

He read it again and again, fixing some words, crossing out others, and starting again. By the time he was satisfied with what he wrote, it was six thirty in the morning, and Eli sent it to every volunteer of United Hatzalah in the country.

Dear everyone,

It is with deep sorrow that I have to tell you about the tragedy that occurred last night in Yerushalayim. Last night we lost one of our volunteers — one of our family members. When I heard the news, I stood there in shock, wondering what to do. For a brief time, I even thought that maybe we needed to shut down our ambucycle unit.

But then I thought about it some more and realized that I was wrong, that we can't stop what we are doing — even for a second.

I'm asking every one of you to mourn for our loss. I want you to be filled with grief about losing one of our finest soldiers. At the same time, the moment you have another call, I want you to jump on your ambucycle and go save that person's life.

Don't stop what you're doing. Not even for a second.

I also want to make something very clear: What happened was an accident. Effi was not at fault. He didn't make any bad or rash decisions. The street was wet and slippery, and the taxi that was driving behind him couldn't see him when he fell off his ambucycle. Effi wasn't at fault, and neither was the taxi driver. It was an

Farewell to a brother

The funeral procession

accident. Still, I'm asking every single one of you to please be even more careful in the future.

Remember: we'll be sad about our loss, but we will never stop doing what we do best.

Eli Beer

⁂

In the days after the accident, United Hatzalah brought in a special investigator from abroad. He conducted a thorough investigation and presented his findings. As they had thought, the accident was no one's

Adelson Ambucycle Unit dedication with the Mayor of Jerusalem, Moshe Lion

fault. But he suggested that from now on, all motorcycles they purchased should be heavier and more stable with more motor power in the front of the bike. He explained that this would make the ambucycle less likely to lose control since the front wheel would keep the bike grounded.

This was also the moment Eli decided that the colors they had been using to paint their bikes were not bright enough. They needed something brighter — something that would make the United Hatzalah ambucycles impossible to miss, something that would be highly visible even at night and even in the dark. Until that point in time, they had gone with blue, red, and white, but from then on, the new color was going to be a very bright orange, and people were going to notice those bikes. And that would help to keep them safe.

For his part, Eli has started wearing orange wherever he goes.

Today the color orange has become synonymous with United Hatzalah.

On the first of July 2021, a few months after the passing of her husband Sheldon Adelson, Dr. Miriam Adelson (more about them soon!) dedicated one hundred and fifty new bright-orange ambucycles at a ceremony that was held at Jerusalem City Hall. The new Dr. Miriam and Sheldon Adelson Ambucycle Unit would be deployed around the country as soon as the event was over. When the inauguration ceremony was over, all one hundred and fifty bright-orange ambucycles toured the Old City in an unforgettable convoy of lifesaving dedication. It was a sight that few who saw it would ever be able to forget.

As the United Hatzalah ambucycles poured out of Kikar Safra and into the streets of Yerushalayim, Eli Beer knew that they had done the right thing by changing the color and, more importantly, by continuing to fight despite the loss of a wonderful young man who would forever be missed.

And he thought of Effi Gadasi — of his smile, his warmth, his caring, and his love.

# CHAPTER FORTY-ONE

# Meeting in the Sky

By its nature, travel exposes a person to many new faces, and since Eli's personality and passion for his cause make him a magnet for exciting interactions, he's never surprised by his incredible encounters.

On one of his numerous trips to the States, a New York customs officer pulled Eli over to the side of the room and asked him to open his luggage on his way into the country. A quick glance was all the man needed to ascertain that everything was in order, but as he was about to turn away, something caught his eye.

"What are those things?" he asked.

Those things were a bunch of silver-plated miniature ambucycles that Eli planned to present to a few of his donors. A simple thank you for their ongoing help and assistance.

Eli doesn't need much of an invitation to talk about United Hatzalah, and before the customs officer knew what hit him, he was being treated to an entire seminar on what the organization did and why the ambucycle had become their trademark. Needless to say, the officer had never heard of lifesaving being done in such an effective manner, and he couldn't understand why it hadn't been adopted by emergency personnel all over the States.

Before parting from the man, Eli handed him one of United Hatzalah's brochures and suggested that he read it when he had a spare minute.

"By the way," the officer said to Eli as he was starting to walk away, "I'm also Jewish."

"Really?"

"Yes. I grew up in Long Island. My parents were members of the local Reform synagogue."

"Really?"

"Yes. And you know, I never visited Israel, but after hearing what you're telling me, I suddenly have the urge to go there and see the country for myself."

"You should definitely make a visit," Eli told him.

"One last thing," the officer said.

"Yes?"

"I want to send you a donation."

"That's incredible! Thank you."

"I want to donate a hundred and eighty dollars. Is that okay?"

"That's way more than okay! That's amazing!"

The man sent it just as promised. It was the first time United Hatzalah received a donation from a US customs officer.

It was also while traveling that Eli ended up meeting a couple who would become part of his inner circle.

In 2018, Eli participated in a breakfast parlor meeting for a group of potential donors at a restaurant in Miami at eight o'clock in the morning. It was hosted by Paul Kruss and his good friend and business partner, Mo. The reason the breakfast was called for such an early hour was because Eli had an appointment the same day with another million-dollar donor in New York who told him that he would only be able to meet with him in the early afternoon. This meant that the breakfast meeting had to be over relatively early because Eli had to catch a flight and reach the donor's office — all before two.

As soon as the breakfast was over, Eli grabbed his carry-on and raced to the airport, determined to make his flight. It was close, but eventually he settled in his business-class seat, able to relax after his stressful morning.

Eli was seated in 1A, and there was a tall, nice-looking gentleman seated beside him in 1B, while the man's wife was seated across the aisle.

As a rule, Eli tends to spend his flights responding to all the emails that fill his inbox, and when those are done, he dictates messages for his secretary. While Eli didn't stop working for as much as a minute, his seatmate read a newspaper, very much at ease with the world, his calm demeanor the perfect foil for Eli's frenetic energy. Eli would have probably entered into conversation with the man at some point, but he looked like he was enjoying his paper and Eli didn't want to bother him. Besides, he really was very busy.

Toward the end of the flight — the pilot had already told everyone to put on their seatbelts — the man turned to Eli and said, "Can I ask you a question?"

"Sure."

"What are you so busy with?"

"I run a rescue organization based in Israel."

"Is that United Hatzalah?"

The question shocked Eli Beer, seeing as it came right out of left field. "Yes, it is."

"That's funny," the man said.

"Why is that?"

"Because Paul Kruss invited me to a breakfast this morning to hear the founder of United Hatzalah speak, but I wasn't able to make it."

Eli extended his hand. "Nice to meet you," he said. "My name is Eli Beer, and I'm the guy whose speech you were invited to come and hear."

"I can't believe what you're telling me," his seatmate said. "This is truly amazing! I guess we were supposed to meet after all. My name is Joel and this is my wife, Adele."

Joel shared the story with his wife, who was equally amazed, and told Eli that they had been hearing about what he did for a while now and had been waiting to meet him for quite some time.

"Tell me something, Eli," Joel said just before they disembarked.

"Yes?"

"Are you free to meet for coffee tomorrow?"

"Of course."

"Great, let's do it. By the way, where are you headed right now?"

"I'm going into the city."

"So are we. Do you want to join us in the cab?"

So it was that Eli Beer found himself riding in a cab from the airport with a very interested couple who had a lot of questions for him. Soon enough the cab dropped him off outside the office of the donor he was supposed to meet — he was even a little early — and Joel and Adele continued on to their hotel.

The meeting with the donor went well. He agreed to contribute a million dollars on two conditions — first, that the funds go toward the purchase of defibrillators, and second, that the donation remain anonymous.

Eli had several meetings that afternoon and then met with Mark Gerson in the evening. He didn't put much thought into the upcoming breakfast meeting since he didn't really know Joel and Adele and had zero expectations. But the next morning as they were sitting and having coffee together, Eli realized that Dr. and Mrs. Sandberg were two very fascinating people.

The conversation began with the Sandbergs asking him to delineate the differences between United Hatzalah and Magen David Adom — something Eli had done thousands of times and could pretty much do convincingly in his sleep.

They explained that they had been toying with the idea of donating an ambulance to a rescue service and wanted to know more information so that they would be able to make an informed decision.

"Magen David Adom is essentially an ambulance company," Eli explained. "United Hatzalah is more about the motorcycles, since our goal is to reach every emergency in ninety seconds. At the same time, we still need ambulances first — for situations where the patient must be transported and because they provide the most effective training for our volunteers — training that helps them do a better job than they would do otherwise. And since it's United Hatzalah who normally arrives at the scene of an accident or emergency first, that training is crucial.

"Of course, there's another benefit that comes with giving an ambulance to United Hatzalah."

"What's that?"

"Unlike any other ambulance company in Israel — whether Magen David Adom or any of the private ones — we don't charge the patients for our services. We don't charge for treating patients or for transporting them to the hospital. We don't charge, period. It's all about helping the people of Israel and nothing more."

After hearing Eli's explanation, Joel and Adele decided to donate an ambulance to United Hatzalah.

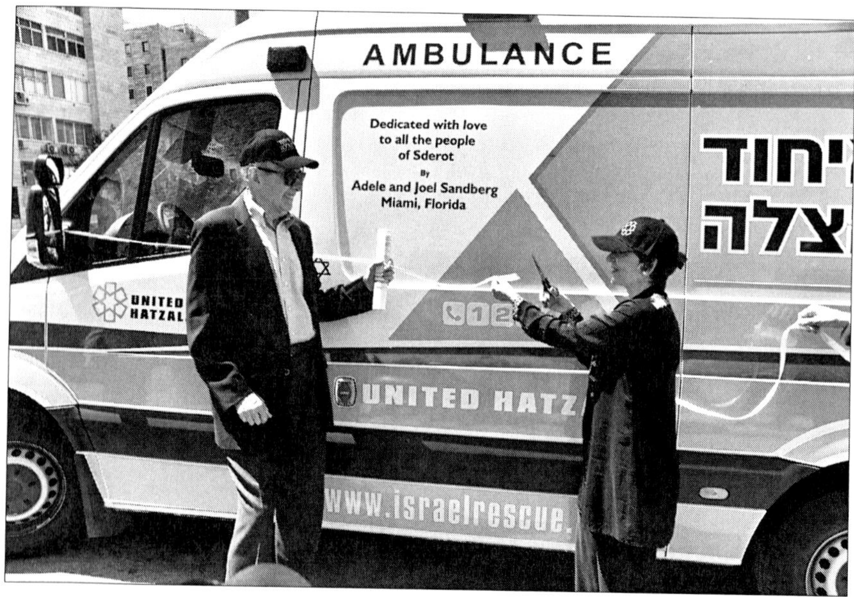


Dr. Joel and Adele Sandberg

"How much does it cost?" asked Dr. Sandberg.

"One hundred and eighty thousand dollars."

Eli couldn't believe it. Here he had come to the meeting expecting to meet some nice people and hoping that they would give a serious donation, but he had never imagined that he would be leaving with a commitment from them to pay for an ambulance.

Joel and Adele walked with him as he left the hotel, and when they reached the street, Eli said, "I want to show you a United Hatzalah ambucycle."

"You have one here in New York?"

"Yes, I keep one in the city to show people. This way they can see exactly what they are going to receive for their donation when they choose to purchase an ambucycle for United Hatzalah. Whenever I'm in the city, this motorcycle is my ride."

They loved it and took some pictures of Eli astride the orange motorcycle.

"Eli, would you mind if we posted this picture of you on Facebook?"

"No, I don't mind at all."

They parted a few minutes later with wonderful feelings all around.

A few minutes later, the phone calls began coming.

"Eli?"

"Yes?"

"How did you do it?"

"How did I do what?"

"How did you meet Sheryl Sandberg's parents?"

"Who?" Eli said.

"Sheryl Sandberg. She's the COO of Facebook."

"I've heard of Facebook, but I've never heard of Sheryl Sandberg."

While Eli understood already then that the Sandberg family was going to play a major role in the development and success of United Hatzalah, even he had no idea just how important they would come to be.

He introduced Joel and Adele to Mark Gerson, and eventually they were asked to join the executive board of United Hatzalah. They accepted the invitation, and became valued members of the team.

As Eli came to know the Sandberg family better, he discovered just what kind of people they were. He learned that Joel and Adele had made the decision to travel to the USSR back in the mid-seventies to show support for the Russian Jews trapped in the Communist regime. Russia wasn't allowing Jews to emigrate. More than that, it was illegal to practice Judaism in the Soviet Union, and Joel and Adele felt that they wanted to show solidarity with their suffering brethren. And so they applied for visas from Russia and were approved for a visit. Their youngest child was one year old at the time, but they weren't willing to postpone their trip until the children were older.

During their time in Russia, they visited many famous refuseniks, as well as numerous Russian Jews no one had ever heard of, bringing them items they needed from America and giving them much-needed *chizuk*. Eventually, Dr. and Mrs. Sandberg were arrested by the KGB in the city of Moldova and interrogated by their agents for twelve hours.

Once they'd encountered Eli, Joel and Adele viewed him and his organization as a way of continuing the vital work they had been doing in the USSR, the work of helping Jews in need.

In 2019, Joel and Adele informed Eli that they planned on visiting United Hatzalah headquarters in Yerushalayim with their daughter Sheryl, their grandchildren, and Sheryl's fiancé, Tom Bernthal. During their visit to Hatzalah on August 25, 2019, Joel and Adele dedicated an ambulance to United Hatzalah. For the Sandberg parents, this was another example of the love they felt for the organization. For their daughter Sheryl, the visit was an opportunity to become acquainted with the way United Hatzalah operates and the incredible lifesaving innovations they have developed to achieve their dream of reaching every patient in ninety seconds.

Joel and Adele had already formed a deep connection with Eli Beer and United Hatzalah, and their daughter's connection would become no less strong. The fact that Sheryl felt such a powerful connection with Hatzalah actually made a lot of sense. Sheryl had experienced real tragedy in her life, losing her first husband, Dave Goldberg, while they were on vacation in Mexico. Dave had been working out in the hotel gym when he had a heart attack and passed away, leaving Sheryl to raise their two children on her own. Had there been a branch of United Hatzalah in Mexico near their hotel, it's possible that Dave Goldberg's life could have been saved when he collapsed.

"Sheryl loved the structure of the organization," Eli said. "And it's very hard to impress Sheryl Sandberg."

Sheryl was the COO of Facebook, one of the most successful companies in the world. She was familiar with all the newest and most cutting-edge technology out there. How could a relatively small organization like United Hatzalah possibly impress a technological superstar like Sheryl Sandberg?

And yet, when Eli gave Sheryl a tour of United Hatzalah headquarters, she was blown away by the organization's use of technology. "United Hatzalah's work to respond quickly to emergencies and save lives is one of the most impressive programs I've ever seen," she commented.

Eli also introduced Sheryl to his wife, Gitty. Gitty herself is a volunteer and the founder of the Women's Division of United Hatzalah along with Noa Zohar (daughter-in-law of Rabbi Uri Zohar). She was also introduced to Sa'ana, an Arab volunteer, and to another female volunteer who happens to be a *chareidi* woman from Beitar — and the mother of eleven children.

The women's division was formed to fill a real need. From the beginning, United Hatzalah had been staffed solely by male volunteers, which meant that women in sensitive circumstances found themselves being treated by men. After discussing the issue with Rav Chaim Kanievsky and members of United Hatzalah's rabbinic board, they opened a women's division, whose primary role would be to respond to emergency calls where it was preferable for the care to be provided by a woman.

Zahava (not her real name) lives in Yerushalayim and is married to a Belzer chassid. Since women in the Belzer community don't have driving licenses, her husband is the one who drives her anytime she gets a call. Because his office is located right next to their house, he's able to drop everything he's doing whenever a call comes in and his wife has to go. He himself isn't an official volunteer, but he helps his wife save lives on a daily basis. He might not be a member, but he is definitely a facilitator.

While the female EMT's primary role is to be there for women who need them, it goes without saying that if someone in the neighborhood is experiencing an emergency and she is the closest volunteer to the scene, she will respond to those calls as well.

One day Zahava received a call that a man in his forties had just collapsed at his home, from a serious heart attack, just a few blocks from her. She and her husband raced over, and since she was the first EMT on the scene, she began stabilizing him. Moments later more volunteers arrived, and Zahava, seeing that she was no longer needed, told them to take over.

She was about to leave the apartment when she realized that while the patient was being treated, his wife was in a panic and needed some emergency therapy. Zahava was also a volunteer in United Hatzalah's psychotherapy unit, formed to help both victims and volunteers deal with trauma, and had been well trained. Taking the woman into a different room, she helped her relax and deal with her panic and shock until she regained her composure.

Meanwhile, the other volunteers had managed to bring the husband's pulse back, and he was breathing again. Once he was stable, he was transferred to the hospital and was released a few days later. Where he had been clinically dead just a few days earlier, he was now able to return home and resume his life in every sense of the word.

In June 2022, Zahava received another emergency call for the same address. This time it was for a woman giving birth. When she arrived at the apartment, she found the woman she had treated for shock not

Sheryl Sandberg with United Hatzalah female volunteers

long before lying on the floor and about to have a baby. Moments later, Zahava delivered a healthy baby boy — the son of the man whose life she had saved in that very apartment.

It was a classic United Hatzalah moment — and yet another lifesaving circle closed.

It was stories like these that so inspired Sheryl Sandberg — and she gave a speech about her admiration for United Hatzalah at a Miami gala where her parents were honored along with Dr. Ari Ciment, a renowned pulmonologist who helped hundreds of Covid-19 patients. Sheryl Sandberg delivered the keynote speech that evening and donated five million dollars in their honor to be matched by the people in the room — to go toward the United Hatzalah Women's Division. Her donation was matched on the spot by Mark Gerson. Ambassador David Friedman and his wife Tammy donated two ambucycles and many others gave generously. Close to nineteen million dollars was raised that night, surely a night to remember.

# PART EIGHT

> *Covid, you see, was an unknown. Covid was the enemy. And I had it.*
>
> — Eli Beer

# CHAPTER FORTY-TWO

# Three Bottles of Bad Wine

The first time Eli met Sheldon and Dr. Miriam Adelson was at a ceremony in 2008 celebrating the State of Israel's sixtieth birthday at Binyanei Hauma in Yerushalayim. President Shimon Peres would be presenting United Hatzalah with an award for the cutting-edge technology they were using to save lives, and Sheldon and Miriam were in the audience. Many other famous and important people were in the audience as well, including President George W. Bush and renowned legal expert Alan Dershowitz.

Sheldon grew up in Boston, the child of a poor family. One day his father gave him a charity box and told his son to put something in the box — a penny or a nickel or a dime — every single day.

"How can I give charity?" the boy asked his father. "We don't have any money to spare."

"There are people who have less than us," his father replied.

Sheldon never forgot his father's message. Sheldon would become a world-famous businessman, who owned a conglomerate of businesses, from hotels to real estate. But the love for giving charity would remain with him for the rest of his life.

Yet Sheldon didn't work alone, because he had a partner in the fullest sense of the word, a partner who helped him reach the highest levels of *tzedakah*: his wife, Miriam, a brilliant Israeli doctor who had been born and raised in Tel Aviv. As a team, the two of them were powerhouses — philanthropists of the highest order.

"I approached Sheldon after the ceremony at Binyanei Hauma and

Dr. Larry Platt, Sunny Sassoon, Michael Milken, Sheldon and Dr. Miriam Adelson,
Mark Gerson and Eli

gave him a United Hatzalah pin. 'I would be honored if you wear this,' I said to him. He nodded but I could see that I hadn't made a real impression."

Eli ran into Sheldon and Miriam several times after their initial meeting at Binyanei Hauma. He would always make a point of going over to them and asking if they remembered him. He didn't want to push too hard, so he held back. Finally, in 2019, Eli decided to ask Dr. Miriam Adelson if she would be the keynote speaker at a United Hatzalah gala in Los Angeles. But in order to do so, he needed a proper introduction by people who were already close to the Adelson family.

And so he enlisted his close friends Ambassador David Friedman and his wife, Tammy, who were more than happy to make the connection. The Friedmans invited Sheldon and Miriam to their home in Herzliya for dinner — a dinner that was primarily spent discussing United Hatzalah and what it was doing for Israel.

That dinner served as the catalyst for the connection between Eli Beer and Sheldon and Dr. Miriam Adelson.

"Dr. Adelson," Eli said when they were finally sitting down to have a conversation, "we're having a big event at the end of February 2020. You're a doctor. You know that every second counts when it comes to saving lives. Would you be willing to speak for us?"

She would. The gala was to take place in LA on February 27.

"February was one of the busiest months I had ever experienced," Eli says. "One year earlier I had been introduced to a delegation from TED India (they were affiliated with TED Talks, a platform that introduces some of the world's greatest speakers and professionals to the average individual who might not have the opportunity to hear of them otherwise). This delegation had traveled to Israel in search of innovative medical methods and wanted me to give a speech in Mumbai about United Hatzalah. They firmly believed that it would be the best thing in the world for United Hatzalah to be established in India, knowing that such an organization had the potential to prevent the deaths of millions every year.

"This was especially crucial in a country like India where the death rate is so high and people die in the streets every single day. When a car accident happens in India, the people in the accident are just pushed to the side of the road and left to die. There are simply not nearly enough ambulances to deal with the sheer volume of people in India

Eli speaking at TED India

— and because that's the case, people are abandoned without a second thought."

The first time he'd been approached by TED Talks, Eli had never heard of the organization, and when they asked him to speak in Washington, D.C., he refused, saying that he didn't have the time. When people heard that he'd turned them down, they told him he was crazy, because TED is huge and would open many doors for United Hatzalah.

TED wanted him to drive one of United Hatzalah's ambucycles onto the stage (in the same manner that he did when he spoke at AIPAC in 2015). Seeing their disappointment at his refusal and learning about their global reach, he changed his mind, delivering a speech that was watched by millions of people.

Now TED of India was asking him to come to them for an event that would take place on the twenty-third of February. But only a few days later, on the twenty-seventh, he would have to be in Los Angeles for the United Hatzalah gala. To make a busy time even more complicated, people started talking about an infectious virus called corona that had gotten loose in a Chinese laboratory and infected what seemed like the entire city of Wuhan.

Feeling like he was biting off more than he could chew, Eli called the people in India to let them know that he wouldn't be able to make it. But they were so disappointed when they heard that he reconsidered and agreed to make the forty-eight-hour journey, after all. And he decided to take his son Yisrael David along for the trip.

Eli landed in India with barely enough time to prepare for the speech he had flown halfway across the world to give. It ended up being a wonderful speech, and he enjoyed spending time with his son and meeting new people.

From Mumbai, Eli flew to LA, arriving that Tuesday. By now the news was starting to come in fast and furious, with a never-ending stream of reports about the new virus that was hitting Europe hard enough to put millions of people in the hospital. Yet while Europe was already under siege, people in LA still felt safe. The LA gala, attended by twelve hundred people, was extremely successful. Everyone who was supposed to be there was there, and they raised over eight million dollars in one night. Dr. Adelson spoke beautifully, relating her personal

(L-R) Jay Leno, Dr. Miriam Adelson, Sheldon Adelson and Eli Beer

experiences working as a doctor back in Israel.

"I was working at a Tel Aviv hospital," she told the hushed room, "when I returned home one day and a neighbor knocked on my door, telling me that her husband wasn't breathing and could I come and save him. I ran downstairs and started performing CPR. I did this by myself, for the next twenty minutes, until an ambulance arrived. That person lived for another seven years after that episode and merited witnessing the birth of many more grandchildren."

The fact that she had been able to save her neighbor's life helped connect her to United Hatzalah because she herself saw firsthand how timing makes a difference when it comes to saving lives.

Dr. Adelson ended up giving one of the greatest speeches Eli had ever heard at a United Hatzalah event.

As he sat on the stage listening to Dr. Adelson deliver a phenomenal speech, Eli had no way of knowing how much closer they were about to become — and how much he owed David and Tammy for formally introducing them. He was soon to learn for the millionth time how every single thing that G-d does in the world is part of the master plan — and that included his newfound relationship with the Adelson family.

Sheldon and Dr. Miriam Adelson ended up donating one hundred and fifty ambucycles to United Hatzalah that night, showing by personal example how much they valued all that United Hatzalah was doing all over Israel.

No one imagined that Eli's life was about to change in the most drastic way, and no one imagined that Dr. Adelson's life was about to undergo overwhelming changes as well. Not a person in the room thought for a second that the world as they knew it was about to come apart at the seams.

"Friday morning I went to AIPAC," Eli says. "There were seventeen thousand Jews there that year, and United Hatzalah had a booth downstairs. It was wonderful to see old friends and meet new supporters. They were already recommending that people wear masks, though it wasn't mandatory, and people were being encouraged to make liberal use of the sanitizers that had been placed everywhere. They also told people to stop shaking hands and to do an elbow bump if they had to make contact.

"People were talking about the pandemic, but it wasn't considered a big deal. There were still a lot of other things on people's minds, from the Iran deal to the next American election. No one had time for a world pandemic."

After three days at AIPAC, Eli flew to New York, where he had an event scheduled with the Syrian community, and then on to London, where he spent that Shabbos as a scholar in residence at a local shul. Half the shul didn't show up to davening or to the speeches. This made sense. England is a European country, and Europe was already starting the great descent into the world of Covid.

After Shabbos, Eli was supposed to fly back to Israel, but Jay and Jeanie Schottenstein were celebrating the bar mitzvah of their oldest grandson, and they were doing it in Miami, so Eli flew to Florida. In the meantime, Eli heard that Israel had instituted a two-week lockdown for anyone returning from abroad, which was another reason not to rush back home.

There was one problem: He had been away from home for over a month, and he sorely missed his wife and kids. It was a special time for the Beer family. Their daughter Libby had just gotten engaged, and their youngest daughter, Adina, had just celebrated her bas mitzvah.

"Suddenly I had an idea," Eli says. "I called up my kids and told Libby and Adina to fly to Miami so we could spend some time celebrating together. Planes were still flying, so traveling wasn't a problem."

Eli and Rabbi Lipskar

Eli's daughters jumped at the chance to fly to Miami, and so, a few days before Purim, they joined him at his hotel. He took them around to visit with some of his friends, and they had a wonderful time.

On the night of Purim, they davened at Rabbi Sholom Lipskar's shul in Bal Harbor. Eli and Rabbi Lipskar shared a big hug since they hadn't seen one another in a while.

Purim had arrived in all its glory, Eli had his daughters with him, and life was wonderful.

The next day they went to hear the Megillah reading again, then bought *mishlo'ach manos* to give to a few friends. Later on in the day, they drove to the Miami home of Uri and Elisheva Ansbacher, Eli's good friends, for what promised to be a festive and beautiful Purim *seudah*. Many other friends joined them, and Eli and his daughters enjoyed themselves immensely.

By the middle of the *seudah*, Eli wasn't feeling well. Something was weird. Uri Ansbacher has great taste in fine wines, but when he handed Eli an expensive bottle of red wine and Eli poured himself a glass and took a sip, it seemed to him that there was something wrong with the bottle.

"Uri," he said, "I know this bottle cost you a hundred and fifty dollars, but you got taken for a ride. This is totally spoiled."

Uri tasted it.

"I don't know what you're talking about. This tastes terrific!"

He handed Eli a different bottle of wine. "Here, try this one. Maybe you'll like this one better."

Eli tasted some wine from the second bottle, and it was the same thing. The wine had a very bad taste.

Above and beyond his sudden dislike of every wine he drank, Eli felt strange. He couldn't remember ever feeling this way before. His relationship with food had also become a little complicated, since some of the food tasted good, while other things didn't have much taste at all.

After the *seudah* Eli went to visit another friend who lived nearby. He also opened a bottle of wine. When he took a sip of that wine and also found it absolutely vile, Eli knew that something was very wrong. He said goodbye to his host and told his daughters that they had to leave. When they got to the car, Eli told Libby that she had to drive.

"I don't feel well," he said. "There's no way I can drive right now."

Before he began feeling sick, the plan had been to fly to Las Vegas for the Republican Jewish Convention. It was supposed to have been the biggest RJC convention ever. President Trump was scheduled to speak. Even though Eli didn't feel well, he didn't want to miss the event.

Once they arrived at the hotel, Eli called El Al.

"My kids were supposed to take the direct flight from Vegas back to Israel on Sunday," he said. "Is that flight still on?"

"Yes, sir, it is."

With Trump still planning on attending the convention and El Al still flying their planes, Eli decided he was making a big deal out of nothing. He was probably just exhausted from all the traveling and packed day of festivities. He decided to take a sleeping pill and get a good night's rest. Surely he would feel better in the morning.

But the next morning, he felt even worse. His throat hurt and his nose was stuffed. Eli called Gitty at home and described the way he was feeling.

"You probably have strep throat," she said.

So Eli called a friend and asked him for the number of a doctor. The doctor told him to come on over for a checkup. He went over with Libby and Adina, who both felt fine. Eli insisted that all three of them take strep tests. The doctor prescribed antibiotics just in case and told him to call her in a few hours for the results. He called a few hours later and was told that the test had come back negative.

He wasn't very happy with the results. If the test had been positive, at least he would have an explanation for what was wrong with him.

At that moment, he came to a decision and called El Al.

"How can I help you, sir?"

"I want to change two tickets."

"From where?"

"From Vegas to Tel Aviv. Instead, I want a flight out of Miami."

"The next flight is leaving in a few hours."

So it was that the girls packed their bags and headed to the airport, minutes after their father got off the phone. It was fortunate that El Al allowed them to switch their flight, because the airline canceled the Vegas flight only a few minutes after Eli made the call. He would have flown back, too, but he didn't feel up to it. In a million years, Eli Beer didn't dream that the world was about to shut down and that being able to fly home when he wanted could no longer be taken for granted.

No one did.

# CHAPTER FORTY-THREE

# A Five Percent Chance of Survival

*P*resident Trump let it be known the next day that he would not be attending the RJC in Vegas, that he would be staying in the White House instead due to reports about the rapidly spreading pandemic. The news of the president's decision brought an avalanche of cancellations in its wake, and it wasn't long before the entire event was canceled.

Meanwhile, Eli decided that he needed to leave the hotel and look for a more private setting. He rented the first decent-looking Airbnb he could find. It was downtown, near a hospital. He figured it wouldn't hurt to be near a hospital — just in case.

He had a few masks with him, purchased at the airport in Quatar on the way back from Mumbai for three dollars apiece. That seemed like an eternity ago. He took an Uber to the Airbnb and wore a mask in the car. No one told him to do so. It just seemed like the right move.

The Uber left him outside the apartment, and he entered and placed his luggage on the floor. The bed was made up and seemed to be calling his name. But he figured that he'd better get some medicine before he settled into bed with a cup of tea. He left the apartment and walked to the nearest pharmacy. Every shelf was empty — there had been a medicine raid — but he managed to find some Tylenol. He bought tea bags and a jar of honey, figuring that it would be soothing for his throat.

He returned to the apartment, made himself a cup of tea, and sat drinking it slowly as he looked out of the window at the beautiful view of downtown Miami. After a few minutes, he'd had enough of the view and began doing a little research about the pandemic that was already in full force all around the world. According to media reports, people were dying by the hundreds in China. There were trucks loaded with corpses in Spain, and in Italy the entire medical system seemed to have broken down. The more he read and the more he saw, the more frightened he became. And he had to acknowledge what he had been suspecting and dreading: that he had Covid.

He didn't want to be one of the first people on American soil to get this unknown illness. It was scary, it was dangerous (the doctors still didn't know what to do about it), and it was embarrassing that the head of United Hatzalah was one of the first to catch the virus in the United States.

He could already hear the conversations between people.

"Guess who has Covid?"

"Who?"

"Eli Beer."

"The head of United Hatzalah? That's ironic…"

No, he didn't want anyone knowing about this. Not if he could help it.

Danielle David is United Hatzalah's National Director of Major Gifts, based in Miami. Having spoken with Eli and hearing the symptoms he was describing, she, too, suspected that he had Covid. One of the first people she called for help was a doctor she knew, Dr. Zev Neuwirth.

"Describe his symptoms to me."

She did.

"He has Covid," Dr. Neuwirth replied. "If he's not breathing well, he should go straight to the hospital."

The problem was that Covid was brand new, and no one really knew much about it. In the beginning, Eli took a lot of Tylenol, which brought the fever down before it climbed right

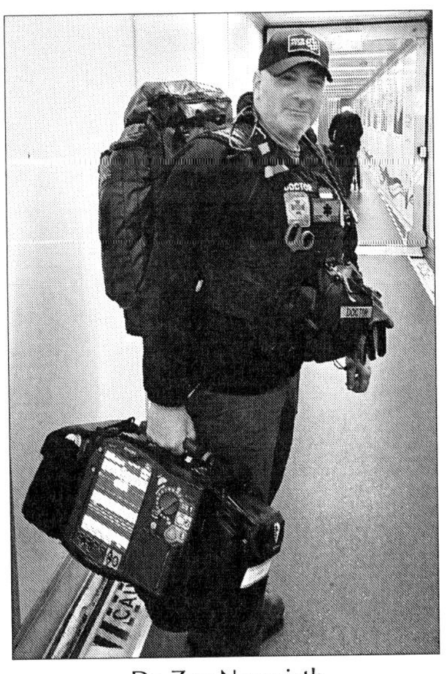

Dr. Zev Neuwirth

back up again. He took baths to cool off, but the moment he climbed back into bed he found himself feeling just as hot as he'd been before. Despite all this, he didn't want to go to the hospital.

Gitty was telling Eli to stop wasting time and go to the hospital immediately, but he only decided that he had to go when he started to have trouble breathing. That's when he knew that he was going to have to go to the hospital whether he wanted to or not.

At three in the morning that Thursday night — Eli had finally fallen asleep — the building's fire alarm began to ring and a recorded voice was heard in the apartment: "All residents should please leave their apartments immediately. This is a real fire alarm…"

Eli woke up, disoriented and terrified at the thought of being trapped on the thirty-fifth floor of a burning building. Shaking and sweating, he threw on some clothing, left the apartment, and ran down thirty-five flights of stairs to the ground floor. He only realized that he'd forgotten the key inside the apartment when he was halfway down.

Outside, about one hundred people were milling around, trying to figure out what was going on and why the alarm system had ordered them out of bed in the middle of the night for no apparent reason. By the time the doorman had let him back into the apartment (it had been a false alarm, after all), Eli had arrived at the conclusion that this was Hashem's way of letting him know that he needed to leave the apartment and go to the hospital.

He dressed, packed his clothing, tallis, and tefillin, and left for the hospital. Before he left, he took a bottle of spray sanitizer that he'd picked up in the supermarket and emptied the entire thing as he wiped down all the surfaces in the apartment, just in case he really did have Covid. After all, there was no reason to infect the next person who rented the place. Before leaving, he put on two masks and a pair of gloves. Then he stepped out of the Airbnb and took the elevator down to the ground floor.

An Uber picked him up outside the building, and he told the Nigerian driver to take him to the University of Miami Hospital.

The University of Miami Hospital was the only hospital in the area that was treating Covid patients. There were about twenty-five police cars waiting outside the hospital, alongside a smattering of the National Guard. It looked like they were preparing for a siege or something equally serious. A few big tents had been erected on the hospital grounds. When the Uber pulled up in front of the entrance, it was stopped by two members of the National Guard dressed in full regalia, holding what looked like loaded weapons.

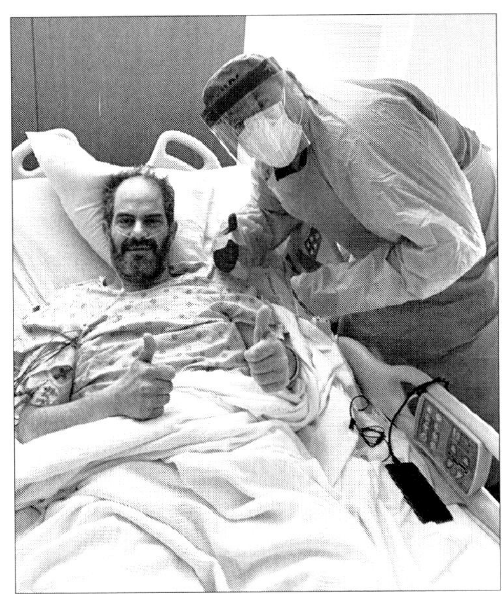
Arriving at the hospital

"You can't come in here. Please turn around."

"Why can't he come in?" the driver wanted to know.

"The hospital is only treating Covid patients."

Hearing that, Eli opened the back door of the vehicle and got out. The two officers looked at him warily.

"I think I have Covid," he said.

The soldiers stared at him for a second. Then they turned and fled.

"I never saw soldiers running so fast," Eli says. "At that moment, the fear of Covid was so great that I could have been a terrorist and they would have still run. I could have robbed a bank without a weapon. All I would have needed to do was say to the teller, 'Give me your money! I have Covid!'

"Covid, you see, was an unknown. Covid was the enemy. And I had it."

They put him in one of the tents, where he waited for an hour. Eventually a doctor arrived to check him. Like the rest of the staff, the doctor was wearing a hazmat suit and looked like he was coming from outer space.

"I think I'm going to send you for an X-ray," he told Eli.

"Don't you have a Covid test?"

"We have only a few."

"So use one."

"We're keeping them for when we have a real suspicion that the person has Covid."

"This is not enough?"

"No, it's possible that you don't have Covid."

Soon after they did the X-ray, the doctor returned.

"I examined the X-ray, and we're going to have to rush you into the ICU. There's no question that you have Covid."

Though the diagnosis was clear, they now came to Eli with a routine Covid test. It was the first time he'd seen one, and he looked at it with interest. He wasn't quite as interested once they began the test and he felt as if they were poking a stick into his brain. After they finished the first one, they did another test — just in case.

"When will you get the results?"

"In three days."

"Three days? Why so long?"

"We have to send them to special lab somewhere in the middle of Florida."

"Tell me something. How many people do you currently have in the ICU?"

"Only one. You're the second patient."

"Who is the first one?"

"Rabbi Sholom Lipskar."

The very man he'd been hugging just a day earlier on Purim.

"Can I see him?"

"Absolutely not. Both of you have your own room."

"Okay, I have one other request."

"What's that?"

"Whatever you're doing for Rabbi Lipskar, do the same for me. I'm sure that you're doing your best for such a famous rabbi. So please give me the exact same medical treatment."

The staff thought that was funny.

As for Eli, he actually meant what he said.

Very few people knew that Eli Beer had willingly admitted himself to the hospital. That Friday, Eli recorded his first hospital video.

"I am very sorry to inform you all that I have Covid. It doesn't look good. I'm begging all of you to be careful because Covid is a real thing

— and if you think it's not a real thing, you need to know that it has hit America and it has hit me. I've always been a healthy guy who never had any medical problems. But right now I'm sick with Covid, and I'm having a very hard time breathing. The doctors are trying everything they can to help me, and I'm asking everyone to please daven for me."

Eli sent out the video, and it went viral.

The doctors were pumping him with oxygen, in the hope that he would start feeling better in a day or two. But his biggest problem was that the coronavirus had caused pneumonia, which meant that he was touch and go. Eli began sending out daily updates about his condition, letting everyone know whether he was feeling better or worse. It was a constant dance of one step forward, two steps back.

For one week, the doctors tried to help him in every way they could. But by the following Thursday, they started talking about putting him on a ventilator.

Hearing this, Eli decided to call a good friend of his — Dr. Avi Rivkind at Hadassah Hospital. In addition to being one of the most respected surgeons in the world, Dr. Rivkind is the consultant for medical issues that arise at United Hatzalah.

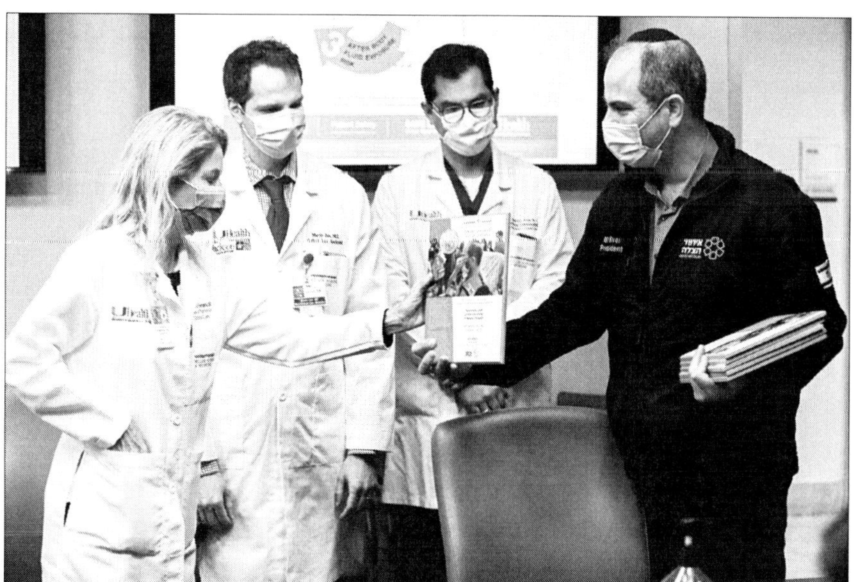

Eli and the doctors in days to come

"Eli, do not allow them to put you on a ventilator!"

He was adamant.

"But that's what they want to do," he protested.

Dr. Rivkind wouldn't relent. He was insistent that Eli should not be put on a ventilator. In the end, Eli put him on the phone with the American doctors, and a huge debate ensued.

When the conversation was over and he hung up the phone, Eli asked the local doctors why they were leaning in the direction of the ventilator.

"If we don't put you on the ventilator," one of them explained, "there is a very strong possibility that you will go into cardiac arrest. Your heart is already quite weak since you are unable to breathe properly, and it may just give out in the middle of the night."

Eli had to make a decision. Was he going on the ventilator or not? Was he going to listen to the team of American doctors or Dr. Rivkind back in Israel? It was an incredibly difficult decision to make — one with life-and-death ramifications. He asked people he knew to go in to Rav Chaim Kanievsky in Bnei Brak and ask the leader of the generation for a blessing.

The person who went in for him called him back a little later.

"What did Rav Chaim say?"

"Rav Chaim said that you will survive."

"What were his exact words?"

"'He will be okay. The world needs him.'"

Such a message from Rav Chaim made Eli smile. Still, there was no denying that he was in a precarious situation.

Because you see, at that very moment, he really couldn't breathe.

Ventilator or no ventilator — that was the question. Once again Eli asked Danielle to put him in touch with Dr. Zev Neuwirth. Dr. Neuwirth himself had a fascinating history. Originally in the jewelry business, he decided to study medicine when his wife passed away from a horrific illness, beginning his new career in the medical field at the age of forty-five.

When he was on the phone with Dr. Neuwirth, Eli said, "Zevi, I need to ask you a question."

By now Eli was on oxygen, he couldn't breathe, and he hadn't really eaten anything in a few days. He told Dr. Neuwirth about the disagreement between his doctor in Israel and his doctors in the States. He didn't know what to do.

"Let me ask you a question," he said to Eli.

"Okay."

"Do they have any available ventilators in the hospital right now?"

The question was coming on the heels of a very serious shortage of ventilators at the New York hospitals.

"Let me check."

Eli relayed Dr. Neuwirth's question to his doctor, who told him that they did have ventilators available for use.

Eli would remember Zev Neuwirth's next words for the rest of his life.

"Grab one while you still have the chance."

The words hung there, reverberating in the silence of the void — and Eli Beer suddenly grasped that Zev Neuwirth was telling him that the pandemic was about to strike American shores in a huge wave.

Zev's message was a simple one. It was possible that Eli didn't need a ventilator right at that moment. But he needed to take one anyway — just in case he needed one in another week. Because by then, there was a good chance that they would all be in use and it would be too late for Eli.

Bottom line: everyone was right. Dr. Rivkind was right that Eli was not yet at the point where he needed to go on a ventilator. The American doctors were right because they knew that he was heading in that direction. And Zev was right because he said to take one — just in case.

Later that day, the doctors informed Eli that it looked like they were going to have to put him on a ventilator the next morning. His wife and children didn't know the severity of the situation, and he knew that he was going to have to tell them the truth.

Until that point, he hadn't allowed himself to focus on the damage that the illness was causing him. Instead, he had spent his time researching Covid and trying to figure out what to do about it. He had been in constant touch with his office back in Israel and had given the order for a ten-million-shekel purchase of PPE (personal protection equipment). PPE was the name given for the clothing needed by medical workers who were constantly seeing patients with Covid. Able to breathe or not, Eli was determined that United Hatzalah would be ready for whatever was coming. Right then they had six thousand full sets, including body suits and shoes, but Eli had the feeling they were going to need more like two hundred thousand sets because their volunteers would need to change between every call. In addition, they would need a lot more equipment, such as special machines to purify the air inside the ambulances, if they were going to be able to face Covid head-on. So from his hospital bed, Eli reached out to the board for authorization — which was granted — and the purchases were made.

His meetings during those weeks were done on Zoom, the technology that had taken the world by storm, and somehow, with extraordinary *siyatta diShmaya* (Heavenly assistance), and by dint of his incredible willpower to do what needed to be done, his preparations came together, even as it seemed more and more inevitable that he himself was going to have to check out of the picture for a while. This was the ramification of going on the ventilator: he would have to be sedated. And he didn't know what kind of world he would wake up to on the other side.

On Friday morning, the doctors came to see him, informing him that his condition had deteriorated further. Meanwhile, Rabbi Lipskar was in the room next door — also not doing well, although he was showing signs of improvement. The doctors were unable to explain why one was getting better and the other was not. There was still so much that they didn't understand about Covid. It was like they were groping in the dark, trying to find a door that was impossible to discern.

"What are my chances of survival?" Eli asked one of the doctors.

"I don't like to answer those kinds of questions," the doctor replied.

"Listen, Doctor," Eli said. "I have a medical background. I know what it means to put someone on a ventilator. So do me a favor and tell me honestly what my chances are."

"Okay," the doctor said. "From what we're currently seeing in Europe, a person in your situation has a five percent chance of survival."

Some may have looked at those words and thought they were terrible. But Eli was overjoyed. To him, a five percent chance, coupled with Rav Chaim's blessing, were good enough odds. Now the question in his mind was simply this:

What was he supposed to do now?

He decided that he needed to ask all his friends and volunteers to daven for him and do *chesed* (kindness for others) as a merit for him to get better. He didn't have the strength right then to write anything, but he summoned up his last vestiges of energy to record a video in which he addressed all the people he loved and who loved him back.

"My friends," he said, "the doctors have told me that I have a five percent chance of survival… Please daven for me and don't forget: every time you do a *chesed*, think about me. And please try to do extra *chesed*. Now is a time when people need more help than ever."

Then Eli added a message that was very much on his mind.

"People usually give United Hatzalah money when I ask them to. It's very possible that I'm not going to make it through this and that I will no longer be able to ask you to give money to my organization. If I don't survive this, I'm begging you all to continue supporting United Hatzalah so that its crucial work will go on — with me or without me. Millions of people depend on our work, and I need you all to support United Hatzalah."

He sent the video out, blasting it to every corner of the world. To wherever there were people who had heard of United Hatzalah and were familiar with its lifesaving mission.

Eli called a few people personally before they put him on the ventilator. One of them was Mark Gerson.

"Mark," Eli said, "you were with me from the beginning. I'm begging you, please don't let this organization fall into poor leadership. Make sure that it continues in the way we always wanted it to go. Make sure that there are always good people running it. And make sure that all the supporters continue supporting us."

Mark was crying on the phone as Eli essentially said goodbye to him after years of the closest kind of friendship.

Eli also called Joel Sandberg.

"Joel," he said, "I trust you with my life. I met you in the sky, when we were both flying together from Miami to New York. It was literally *min haShamayim* (Heaven-sent). We have become very close friends. I don't know any doctor in the world that I trust more than you. I'm signing you in as my caretaker. Any decision that needs to be taken regarding my medical care has to go through you. Are you willing to accept this responsibility?"

"One hundred percent."

Then Eli called Bob Book and Leonardo Farkas and a few others — each for a very short conversation. He also called his closest staff, people like Dovie Maisel, Eli Pollak, Batya Avidan, Moshe Levi, Leizer Heiman, and Moshe Teitelbaum.

Then he sent a message via WhatsApp to a larger group. He also made a few more videos, just in case he didn't survive, with the intention that they be used to help the organization fundraise. He feared that United Hatzalah was still too young to stand on its feet without him at the helm.

"Hashem," Eli murmured, "if You give me my life, I will do my best to make sure that United Hatzalah will be sustainable and that this organization will never depend solely on me. Instead, it will belong to *Am Yisrael*, to the Jewish people, and it will be the responsibility of our nation as a whole. Hashem, You have shown me that You intend for us to continue. But I need to be around to cement things in place, because United Hatzalah still needs me."

In his last conversation with Michael Brown before being placed on a ventilator, he told his vice president that he wanted him to do his best to ensure that the organization should have a year and a half of surplus funds, just in case, and that he should focus on building an endowment fund for United Hatzalah.

So it was that in those final moments, Eli was busy ensuring the future of United Hatzalah.

Then he called his family.

He was crying as he spoke to Gitty and the children. He talked to Avigail — his oldest daughter. She tried to make her father laugh, tried to make the conversation a little less intense.

He spoke to Penina, married to Uri Davis and expecting his first grandchild.

"You know," he said to her, "I was really looking forward to becoming a grandfather, and I feel like I'm losing one of the greatest opportunities of my life. I'm going to do my best to stay alive because I don't want to miss it."

She was crying. Sobbing her heart out.

"Can you just do me a favor?" Eli asked.

"What?" she managed through her tears.

"Can you just tell me if the baby is a girl or a boy?"

"No, I'm not telling you. You have to wake up for that."

Now she was laughing and crying at the same time.

"Please, Penina, I'm begging you. I really want to know…"

"Abba," she said with a trace of her trademark fire and humor, "if you go to *Shamayim*, you'll definitely know if it's a girl or a boy, and if you wake up, then you'll have to wait and see, just like everyone else…"

"I tried everything to wheedle out the information," Eli says. (He even used the "I'm literally dying here" card), "but nothing worked and she wouldn't give in."

After he finished speaking to Penina, he said goodbye to his son-in-law, Uri Davis.

He said goodbye to Libby, who was a *kallah*, and asked her to daven for him and to do as much *chesed* as she possibly could.

He said goodbye to his son, Yisrael David, and told him how much he loved him and how proud he was of him.

He spoke to his youngest child, Adina, saying goodbye to his baby.

He asked all his kids to be good Jews and to live their lives as credits to *Klal Yisrael*.

"Be good Yidden," he told them, "and do *chesed*. That's the most important thing. *V'ahavta l'rei'acha kamocha* (love your friend as you love yourself). Be good to everyone you meet and help your mother — and the Jewish nation."

He was giving them his last will and testament.

Then he spoke to Gitty.

But Gitty didn't want to say goodbye.

"Eli, you're going to sleep for a few days. Then you'll get up and everything will be the same."

Eli spoke from his heart, telling his wife how proud he was of her and of everything she'd accomplished and expressing his appreciation for everything she had done for him, for standing by his side and helping him grow.

"If this is what Hashem wants," he concluded, "to take me at the age of forty-six, then so be it. I accept my lot."

When he got off the phone, Eli was at peace with himself.

He felt like he had lived a full life. He didn't have a fancy house. He didn't have a fancy car. He had spent the majority of his days traveling. But he was happy with everything he'd accomplished in the time he'd been given on earth. He felt as if he was going to his death satisfied with the way he'd lived his life and gratified that Hashem had given him the chance to succeed at the goals he'd set for himself.

Then he shut his phone.

And told the doctor that he was ready to be intubated.

"I'll see you soon," he said to the doctor after he was injected with the sedative.

Three seconds was all it took.

And then there was darkness.

# Paranoia

&li was sedated for twenty-eight days.

The hospital was bombarded with calls from people all wanting to know Eli's condition. All inquiries were directed to Avigail, Eli's oldest, who served as the family spokesman and was interviewed by media around the world. Everyone wanted to know whether they were going to see Eli return to take his place at the helm of United Hatzalah. Rumors abounded that were patently false. At one point, someone sent out word that Eli had passed away — which, of course,

Eli and Rav Yitzchak Dovid Grossman

was not true. It was Avigail's role to give the media the information they needed to know and quell the rumors.

Meanwhile, people were davening. Eli's close friend Rav Yitzchak Dovid Grossman, rabbi of Migdal HaEmek, held a special davening session for him. A mass prayer was organized, in which tens of thousands of people from all around the world participated.

Bob Book never stopped calling. Meanwhile, someone told Leonardo Farkas that buying burial plots for a person is a *segulah* for longevity. He bought two burial plots on Har HaZeisim, across the valley from the Temple Mount.

Gitty Beer would never forget the moment she learned about Leonardo's gift. She'd been busy with the kids and a million preparations for Pesach, which was fast approaching, when there was a knock on the door. She peeked through the peephole and saw two masked chassidim standing there.

"Who are you?" she asked through the door.

"*Chevrah kaddisha,*" they replied.

Her heart clenched with fear. "What do you mean, *chevrah kaddisha*? Did something happen? Did Eli die?"

"Please open the door. We have something for you."

When they were standing in the house, one of the men said, "We have graves for you and your husband on Har HaZeisim."

"Does this mean that Eli passed away? Is that what you're telling me?"

"Not at all, Mrs. Beer. Please calm down. Eli is still alive. We are here on behalf of Leonardo Farkas, who heard that purchasing graves for a person is a *segulah* for long life. That's all this is."

Meanwhile, United Hatzalah established another division, together with the Nacht Family Foundation, one solely devoted to doing acts of *chesed* for other people, so that the merits garnered by all the mitzvos, by all the good deeds, should serve as a merit for his recovery. Another dispatch center was opened where sixty people answered phone calls that had nothing to do with medical needs. The center was geared to helping people with humanitarian issues. Elderly people were encouraged to call if they needed anything — and many did, since the government had instituted a lockdown for people over the age of sixty-five. Many of the elderly were confined to their homes, isolated from their neighbors and family. Often they were unable to go shopping to obtain food or medicine and had no one they could send.

People called if they needed someone to change their lightbulb. An eighty-five-year-old woman called because her radio was broken and she was all alone and needed to listen to her favorite programs. Two chassidic volunteers who had never listened to the radio in their lives went to her home and figured out how to fix her radio. It took them two hours, but they got there in the end.

Instead of just helping people with life-and-death situations, now volunteers recruited for this task were visiting people who were all alone and needed someone to go to the store or help them with something they were unable to do themselves. It was all about the *chesed* — and it was all being done in Eli's merit. In addition, Leket Israel, an organization founded by Eli's friend Joseph Gitler, which normally gives out prepared food to thousands of elderly Holocaust survivors around the country, asked United Hatzalah if they could get involved to help make the deliveries.

On Erev Pesach, Gitty Beer still had sixty packages of food to deliver to people in Yerushalayim. Filling up an ambulance, she left her home and began making the rounds, trying to forget that her husband was currently lying in an induced coma miles away in a Miami hospital room. Gitty and Avigail visited some sixty buildings — with some of the apartments situated on the top floor — and they did it all while wearing hazmat suits over their clothing.

Meanwhile, Eli was in a deep coma and experiencing a slew of nightmares. Many of the events he had experienced in his life were traumatic and had left an impression — the terrorist attacks, the natural disasters, the bus bombings, the accidents. Now they were all coming back as he lay in a coma, completely defenseless and unable to block them out. Dream after dream came at him, and there was nothing he could do about it. Usually one would wake up when in the midst of a nightmare, but he couldn't do that while under sedation.

His final dream was about a huge earthquake that struck Europe, killing thousands. United Hatzalah was urgently needed. In the dream, he was walking down a cobblestoned European street, doing his best to run yet another operation.

Then the scene shifted, and he was watching a flood. He saw a child being sucked away by the undercurrent, and unable to watch without doing anything, he jumped into the water to save the child, but the undertow was vicious and it sucked him away, and he was being pulled inside, trapped in a whirlpool.

He kept trying to save people in his dreams — an endless collage of disasters and tsunamis and volcanoes and earthquakes and fires — and everyone was relying on him to save the people, and he wasn't succeeding.

At times he wasn't sure if he was awake or not. He tried to figure out if what he was seeing was real, but he couldn't, no matter how hard he tried.

Two weeks after Eli was sedated they brought him back, but soon realized that he had to be put back onto the ventilator. It was touch and go for a while, with the doctors doing their best to save him but not sure that they were going to be successful.

When they finally took Eli off the ventilator and woke him up, the medical staff began changing the way they were treating him. They began giving him steroids, which helped immensely because the medicine got rid of a lot of the inflammation in his lungs. It was the last day of Chol HaMoed Pesach, and he had been in a coma for twenty-eight days.

Meanwhile, a group of very influential people were hard at work to get Eli the newest medicines that scientists all over the United States were developing to treat the virus. Some of the medicines still hadn't received their FDA approval. Dr. Joel Sandberg, for instance, felt it was crucial that Eli be injected with stem cell treatment. A scientist named Dr. Josh Hare had come up with a groundbreaking treatment involving the use of stem cells, and until then the technology had mostly been used for treating heart failure, but Dr. Sandberg wanted to use it to heal Eli in a three-part complicated procedure. In addition to everything else he was doing, Joel Sandberg called the doctors for updates at least four times a day.

Meanwhile, Dr. Miriam Adelson, who called Gitty every day to see how Eli was doing, was trying to obtain other medicines that were also waiting for FDA approval.

When he finally woke up, Eli saw a group of doctors surrounding his bed and for the life of him couldn't figure out what was going on. Who were these people? Where was he?

"Where are you?" one of the doctors asked, testing to see if he was present and aware.

Eli looked around him. Memories were starting to come back to him.

"I'm in a hospital."

"Very good," they said. "Which hospital?"

"Lucerne, in Switzerland."

He said this because some of his incredibly realistic dreams had taken place in that city.

"No," they said, "you're not in Switzerland. Try again."

Eli looked around him. Looked out the window. Saw tall buildings.

"New York?"

They said, "No, you're in Miami."

"I can't be in Miami. I was just in Europe. There were two planes loaded with Hatzalah volunteers that flew out to Europe, and I was with them."

"Mr. Beer, you are mistaken. You're in Miami, Florida. You were very sick with Covid, and now you've woken up."

Eli felt as if he was going out of his mind. He was very weak and very confused, and tied to his bed because of all the tubes that were running between him and the machines that they wanted to make sure he wouldn't pull out.

"I need to speak with my wife," he told the doctors.

Gitty wasn't answering the phone. They tried for an hour and didn't get through. As a volunteer for the women's division of United Hatzalah, she had left on a call to deliver a baby only a minute before Eli called. When she was finally finished handling the call, Gitty returned to her car and saw that she had a dozen missed calls from the hospital in Miami. In a panic, she immediately called back, and when she got through to the doctors, she was told, "Mrs. Beer, your husband has woken up."

The joy was overwhelming.

"How are his lungs?"

"His lungs are clean."

The stem cell treatment had kicked in. Eli Beer was the first person in the world to receive it, and it proved itself very well.

"Eli, how are you feeling?" Gitty asked through tears of joy.

"Listen to me very carefully," he said. Then he started speaking to her in Hebrew.

"I'm talking to you in Hebrew because I don't want them to understand. I've been kidnapped!"

Gitty had been crying a second before, and now she was laughing.

"Gitty, it's true. They kidnapped me!"

"Eli, what are you talking about?!"

(Still in Hebrew.)

"Gitty, please don't laugh. This is serious!"

All this while he could barely talk, having not used his vocal cords for about a month during which he'd had a tube down his throat. There was a mirror hanging on the wall across from his bed. When he looked at his reflection, the image looking back at him looked like Saddam Hussein climbing out of the cave when the Americans caught him. His face was haggard, and he sported a long and unkempt beard. There was no question in his mind that he had been kidnapped and was being held in captivity. To make matters worse, his wife was laughing at the situation and not taking it seriously.

"Gitty, call the FBI."

"What?"

"Call the FBI!"

"Eli, what are you talking about?"

"I'm not joking, and if you don't call the FBI, I'm going to jump out of the window! Better that than to die in their hands when they realize that I'm Jewish…"

Suddenly Gitty realized that it was the medicine talking. Eli was in fact suffering from something called ICU delirium and everything that had happened to him was jumbled together with the illusions and nightmares. It was all too much for one poor brain that had just been in a coma for the majority of a month. All this was exacerbated by the normal hospital sounds he was hearing from the rooms around him. When he heard someone screaming, he was sure that the person was being tortured to death and that he was going to be next.

To make matters worse, Eli had slept through half the month of Nissan and had missed Pesach. It was his favorite Yom Tov, and he had missed the whole thing. Worse, he didn't even know it. Seeing his state of mind, Gitty understood that she couldn't tell her husband that Pesach was over.

It took Eli a few hours until he could acknowledge that he hadn't actually been kidnapped and was simply in the hospital, recovering from a serious bout of Covid. He called Gitty back and asked her if she could please make plans to come and spend Pesach with him in the States.

"Eli, how are you going to leave the hospital now?"

"Don't worry, the doctors will let me out for Yom Tov. We'll make a Seder in one of the hotels, and everything will be beautiful! We need to celebrate Pesach with all the kids…"

All the while, Gitty was thinking, *What on earth am I going to do?*

Eli called Danielle that night.

"Listen, we need to make Pesach here for my entire family. I can't travel to Israel right now, so they need to come here. I need you to book us a couple of rooms in one of the nice hotels here in Miami."

Danielle didn't bother explaining to Eli that all the hotels had been shut down and that the world as he had always known it didn't exist any longer. She also didn't tell him that Pesach had already passed and that he had missed it, because Gitty had let her know to take it slow with him and give him time to come back to himself.

"I'll take care of everything," Danielle promised him.

Eli hung up the phone, feeling slightly better about the situation and very much looking forward to spending Pesach with his family.

He called his wife a little later.

"Where are you? Are you at the airport yet?"

"We're on the way. We're taking a bus."

"A bus? What are you talking about?!"

"Not a bus. A van service."

He couldn't put his finger on it, but he couldn't help feeling like something was going on and he was out of the loop.

He decided to call Danielle back again and ask for an update.

"What's with the hotel? Did you book the rooms yet?"

"I called them, but there's a problem."

"What kind of problem?"

"They shut down part of the hotel."

"What do you mean, they shut down the hotel? What on earth are you talking about? The whole world is coming to Miami for Pesach. How could they shut down the hotel?"

"Eli, most of the hotels aren't operating anymore."

"How can that be? Just find me a hotel. I'm sure at least a few of them still have Pesach programs."

But his Florida director was sticking to her story, and no matter what he said, she wouldn't change the script.

Eli Beer just couldn't understand that while he had been asleep, most of the world had shut its doors.

That was when Eli Pollak, CEO of United Hatzalah, called his old friend.

"How are you feeling?" Pollak asked him.

"I'm feeling like I don't know what's going on. My wife keeps on telling me strange stories every time I speak to her, and Danielle just told me that all the hotels in Miami have closed down. I feel like everyone in the world has gone crazy."

"What did Gitty tell you that you're having a problem with?"

"I told her to come to America with the kids, and she isn't listening to me."

"Why do you want Gitty to come to America?"

Eli Pollak didn't know that Gitty was telling everyone to break the news of what he had been through slowly.

"I want her to come because I want to spend Pesach with her."

"Eli, Pesach is over. We already celebrated Pesach."

Eli lost it. He tried to scream but his voice was so weak from not talking for a month that he could barely get out a sound.

"You're lying to me! Pesach isn't over. Pesach didn't even start yet!"

"Eli, Pesach passed. It's over."

"But it says 'Happy Passover' on the wall in front of me. It also says don't bring *chametz* anywhere. Pesach is about to start, and I want my family here with me."

It didn't say anything on the wall. Eli was just imagining it.

"Eli, you're confused. Pesach is over. You just didn't know about it. I promise you that I'm telling the truth. You were in a coma over the entire Yom Tov."

The moment he heard those words coming from the mouth of Eli Pollak, Eli Beer hung up the phone and fell into a deep depression. He was suspicious of what Eli Pollak was telling him, his wife Gitty was telling him stories, Danielle was lying to him — he didn't trust anyone and he didn't want to talk to anyone. He felt like everyone was lying to him. Whenever a doctor came into his room to take his blood, he told them to go away. He was filled with paranoia and wondering if he had gone crazy and had been locked up in an institution.

A few hours later, Dr. Maria Carolina Delgado-Lelievre entered his room. She was wearing a hazmat suit, but he could see that she had a bright smile on her face.

"Mr. Beer," she said, "I watched your TED Talk and I know about all the incredible lifesaving work that you've been doing in Israel for so many years. Incidentally, I, too, love Israel. I even wear a Star of David necklace."

The doctor didn't look Jewish. If he had to guess, he would have said she was from South America.

"I'm a doctor and I also had the privilege of treating your friend Rabbi Lipskar, who was here at the hospital with you. He, too, had Covid, but he's doing much better now and has already returned home."

"Covid," Eli said, with a puzzled look on his face.

It turned out that he didn't even remember that he'd been sick with Covid. When he regained consciousness, no one had spoken with him about his illness or explained to him that he was still suffering from symptoms of the disease along with millions of other people around the globe.

It was Dr. Maria who realized how confused he was, and it was Dr. Maria who took the time to bring him up to date and to clear things up. He would be eternally grateful to her for taking the time to clarify his situation.

"I want to tell you everything that happened to you."

She told him the date that he arrived at the hospital and why he had been admitted. She told him that the doctors had done everything they could before finally making the decision to put him on a ventilator.

"You were on the ventilator for eighteen days before we took you off. Unfortunately, your condition grew worse, and we were forced to put you back on the ventilator."

She brought him back to reality, step by step.

"It was nothing short of a miracle. We didn't think you were going to survive. Hashem loves you!"

(She actually used the word "Hashem.")

"Everyone was praying for you. I don't think there has ever been a case in the history of the hospital where so many people kept calling to find out how a patient is doing. We couldn't handle the volume of phone calls."

Dr. Maria kept talking and explaining every detail of what had transpired over the last month — until she saw that Eli was back to himself, that she had finally managed to break through his daze.

"What about Passover?" he asked her.

"I'm sorry, but Passover is over."

For the first time, he knew that it was true.

# Time to Go Home

Eli was no longer under any delusions about what had happened to him — but he was incredibly depressed at the same time. He was depressed because of everything he had been through. He was also depressed because he had learned that millions of people were dying from the illness that had almost claimed his life. Closer to home, he discovered that three of his cousins had passed away due to Covid. In his already weakened state, every new piece of information made him feel worse.

Then he heard that a good friend from LA — Rabbi Zvi Ryzman, a *talmid chacham*, author of *sefarim*, and giver of charity — was struggling for his life, and Eli didn't know what to do with himself. Eli said a lot of *Tehillim* for Rabbi Ryzman, begging Hashem to perform a miracle and save his life. In the end, that's exactly what occurred, and Eli was absolutely thrilled when he heard, but there is no question that hearing about his cousins' death and then learning about the danger that a close friend was in made him want to take a break from the stress of his life and just remain in Miami staring at the water.

Then Eli Pollak called again, only to learn that the founder of United Hatzalah had no plans to return to Israel in the near future.

Eli had always been the man with a million ideas. Now he had no ideas. He had always been the person who achieved the impossible. Now the thought of getting out of bed was too much.

Rabbi Zvi Ryzman

Then the phone rang.

It was Eli Pollak calling from Yerushalayim. He had tried a few times, but Eli hadn't wanted to talk to him — or to anyone. But Eli Pollak was insistent, and he kept calling until his old friend picked up.

"Eli," he said, "I just wanted to let you know that we want you back here in Israel. There are no planes flying to Israel right now from America, but we're going to do whatever we can to get you back here."

Whatever Eli Pollak thought Eli Beer was going to say, it wasn't the words that emerged from his mouth.

"The truth is, Eli, I don't feel like coming back. I'm exhausted and drained, physically and emotionally, and I don't know if I can continue doing the job I've been doing for so long. Eli, I think I'm ready to retire from United Hatzalah. I'm going to hand it over to Michael Brown. He'll build a whole new team, and you, Dovie, and everyone else will continue in leadership positions. I just can't do it anymore."

"What are you talking about?"

"I almost died. I lost forty-five pounds in the past month, most of it muscle, and now I can't even walk. I can barely even lift my hands. I can't take care of myself. How can I lead the organization?"

It was unfathomable that these words were coming from the indefatigable Eli Beer.

"I'm not going back to Israel right now, and I'm not going back to the organization. I'm staying in America. I plan on making an announcement that I'm stepping down."

Eli Pollak started crying over the phone.

"You can't do this."

"I have to do this. Right now I don't feel as if I'm ever going to go back to normal. I don't think I'm ever going to be normal again."

Even as he spoke with his CEO, Eli felt vulnerable and defenseless, like a baby who can't do anything without help. Then Eli Pollak marshaled one of the greatest arguments he ever made in his life.

"Eli," he said, "you told me when we spoke for the last time, before they put you on the ventilator, to ask all the members of United Hatzalah to do extra acts of *chesed* in your merit. You know what we did? We established an entire dispatch center devoted to acts of *chesed* — and we did it all for you, so that you should have a complete recovery and return to your former self. We had twenty thousand volunteers from around the country on call, some from other organizations, all ready to take part in the initiative. They ended up going on sixty-five thousand humanitarian calls.

The United Hatzalah Dispatch Center

"Sixty-five thousand calls — and that was besides the heart attacks and the strokes and the car accidents and the babies that were born. All this was done for you. So how can you say that you aren't coming back?"

They both fell silent for a few seconds, Eli Beer because he was depressed and despondent and Eli Pollak because he had just made a heartfelt plea and given it his best shot.

Finally, Eli Beer spoke.

"Tell me one story," he said to his CEO. "One story that happened because of one of those sixty-five thousand calls. One story that will resonate with me and give me the strength to return to the organization. Something that will give me the impetus to stand on my feet again."

Eli didn't know what to expect. But the story he heard was above and beyond anything he could ever have imagined.

An elderly woman called our number shortly before Pesach (Eli Pollak recounted). The dispatcher asked her what was the reason for her call.

"I'm ninety-four years old, and I live in Bat Yam," she said. "I'm all alone and have nobody to help me."

"What's your emergency?"

"I don't have candles to light for Yom Tov. With the country on lock-down, I haven't been able to leave my home for the past few weeks and go shopping, and I wanted to know if someone could please bring me candles. It will save my life."

"I will have someone take care of this right away," the dispatcher promised. "What is your address?"

She gave the dispatcher her address, and the dispatcher immediately sent it out to the volunteers closest to where the woman lived, just as we do with every call. The first volunteer to grab the mitzvah was an Arab member of United Hatzalah, a man by the name of Ibrahim Ayuti.

Ibrahim lived in Jaffa, only a few miles from Bat Yam. He jumped onto his ambucycle and drove over to a supermarket that was still open. There he purchased a box of candles, and, seeing a bouquet of flowers, he bought that as well. He placed the two items into the box on the back of the ambucycle, next to the oxygen tank and defibrillator, then drove to the elderly woman's home in Bat Yam.

Ibrahim Ayuti

She lived on the top floor of an old, rundown building with three entrances and fifty apartments, the kind of building that was built for the Russian immigrants back in the seventies. There was no elevator, so Ibrahim climbed the rickety flights of stairs to the top floor, candles and flowers in hand.

He knocked on the door. The woman answered. She was very old. Ibrahim stood in the doorway wearing a hazmat suit and mask.

She looked at him. Saw the candles.

"You saved me," she said. "You saved my life!"

Then Ibrahim looked a little closer and saw that the woman had a number tattooed on her arm. Ibrahim's eyes welled with tears. It was obvious to him that he was helping someone special.

"I brought you flowers," he said to her.

She accepted the flowers, thanked him, and repeated what she had just said to him a minute earlier.

"You saved me."

"Do you mind if I stay with you for a little bit?" he said to her. "I see that you're all alone. I can sit with you for a little while." He was well aware that because of the lockdown, she probably wasn't getting many visitors, if any.

"Why would you want to do that?" she asked him. "Don't you have to get home to your own family? After all, it's almost Pesach."

"I'm not Jewish," he explained. "I'm Muslim, but I volunteer for United Hatzalah. I'll keep a distance from you, and I'll wear the hazmat suit and mask the entire time."

"Come in," she said, leaving the door slightly ajar.

Ibrahim took a seat on the couch, and the old woman went to light the candles that he'd brought her.

She set up fifteen candles for lighting. Then she lit them and recited the blessing. Ibrahim had never seen anything like it in his life. When she finished lighting her candles, she set up her Seder plate, arranging her matzos, *maror*, *charoses*, and the other special foods that volunteers from other organizations had brought. They had supplied her with fish and chicken, but had forgotten to bring candles.

"Would you like to sit with me during the Seder?" she asked him.

He agreed.

So Ibrahim saw a Seder for the first time in his life, as his hostess read from the Haggadah. As she ate her meal, she asked him questions about what he did for a living and how he had come to volunteer for United Hatzalah.

"I have two questions for you," he said to the old woman. "Why did you say that I was saving your life? All I did was bring you candles. And also, why do you light so many candles? I always thought Jewish women lit one or two candles, but you lit fifteen."

"Ibrahim," she said, "I grew up in a small village in Poland, and every Friday my father and brothers would head for the village shul while my mother lit the Shabbos candles and my sisters and I read from a book called *Tzenah U'Renah*.

"This was what we did every Friday night. Then it was 1939, and the Nazis came and destroyed my family. They took away my father and mother, my uncles and aunts, my brothers and sisters. I never saw any of them again. They were all killed in the concentration camps."

"What about you?"

"I was sent to a labor camp. I was strong and capable of working, and that's what I did all week long. And every Friday I would find a way to light candles in the merit of my family members. Throughout the week, if I found a piece of paper or a sliver of dry wood, I would save it for Friday afternoon and light it in their memory as night fell and Shabbos commenced. Somehow I managed to find a way to light two candles every single week.

"Eventually the war came to an end, and we were liberated. Survivors settled in different countries around the world, but I went to Israel, and that was when I promised myself that I was going to light a candle every Friday, one for every single member of my family who was murdered by the Nazis.

"I did this for decades. I never missed a week. I lit the candles even in the years when I didn't have much money. Then, about a month ago, everyone started getting sick, and suddenly I wasn't able to leave my home to go shopping. Good people brought me matzos and grape juice and even chicken and meat, but nobody thought to bring me candles. I had some candles to light, but not enough — not one for every member of my family who was killed in the war.

"I said to myself, *If I have to light a piece of paper or a sliver of wood to fill in the gap, this will be the last day of my life.* I knew that such a thing would be so traumatic that I'd have a heart attack and wouldn't survive."

She paused.

"Ibrahim," she continued, "a few years ago I wasn't feeling well and I called United Hatzalah. Two minutes later volunteers came to my house to save my life. Now, when I found myself in this predicament, I told myself that I needed to call United Hatzalah again — and then you came and saved my life."

"Eli," the CEO of United Hatzalah said to his friend when he concluded the story, "the elderly woman from Bat Yam hadn't even known that United Hatzalah had established a command center specifically for humanitarian purposes. All she knew was that she was sad enough to die if she didn't receive the candles she needed — and she got them in time to light them before Yom Tov."

It was this story that convinced Eli Beer to return home. Suddenly he felt rejuvenated, as if he'd been granted a new lease on life. When Eli Pollak finished telling him the story of the Arab volunteer who had saved the life of the elderly Holocaust survivor from Bat Yam, he didn't have to think twice. He knew that he was coming home.

Eli Beer got on the phone and called his wife.

"Gitty," he said when she answered, "I'm ready to come home."

And Gitty Beer knew that her husband was back.

# CHAPTER FORTY-SIX

# A Welcome Home, United Hatzalah Style

"Eli, Dr. Adelson has called several times," Gitty told her husband.

"About what?"

"She wants to know how you're doing and she offered the use of her private plane to fly you back home. Eli, I turned her down."

"Why?"

"I felt uncomfortable taking her up on her offer."

"Gitty, if Dr. Adelson wants to use her plane to fly me back, how can you say no to her? She loves United Hatzalah, and she loves helping people. Please call her back and accept her kind offer."

Dr. Adelson was true to her word. She flew her plane from Las Vegas to Miami and placed it at Eli's disposal. So was the stage set for Eli Beer to return home. He had come incredibly close to losing his life, yet Hashem, in His infinite mercy, had seen fit to give him another lease on life and Eli was ready to take full advantage of it. He had just come to know the Adelsons, and Dr. Miriam Adelson had turned out to be so instrumental in his recovery.

He took a moment to recall Dr. Adelson's fabulous speech at the United Hatzalah gala that had been held right before the Covid outbreak. Sadly, the gala was the last United Hatzalah event that Sheldon Adelson attended in his lifetime. He passed away in 2021. Due to Covid, attendance at his funeral was limited, with only family present.

Sheldon Adelson's grave

After the funeral, the coffin was flown to Israel, where Prime Minister Netanyahu was waiting to meet them at the airport.

Sheldon was laid to rest on the Mount of Olives, directly across the valley from the Holy of Holies. He was a giant of a man throughout his lifetime and his final resting place reflected that reality.

It might have been Dr. Miriam Adelson's plane flying him home, but it was Eli's choice to decide who was going to accompany him on the flight, and that was an old friend of his named Simcha Shain, a trained EMT who runs Paraflight, an air medical transport company.

The two of them had met years earlier in Mark Gerson's office in the city and hit it off, getting together on numerous occasions after their initial meeting. Simcha knew how much work Eli put into United Hatzalah, and it was heartwarming to see how much *siyatta diShmaya* he was receiving from Above in return.

It was a Sunday afternoon when Simcha's phone rang. Mark Gerson was on the other end of the line.

"Eli's awake, and we have to get him back home to Israel."

"Great," Simcha replied. "I'm ready to take him."

Half an hour later his phone rang again.

"Is this Simcha Shain?"

"Yes, who is this?"

"My name is Gitty Beer. I'm Eli's wife. We're on the phone with Eli Pollak, our CEO."

Simcha had never met either of them before, and he listened carefully as they explained the situation.

"Simcha, right now Eli doesn't understand what's happening with him," Eli Pollak said. "We need to ease him in slowly. We're putting you on standby, so that when he's ready to go, we'll be able to move quickly."

Suddenly Simcha said to Gitty and Eli Pollak, "I would love to continue this conversation, so let's try to talk a little later, but I have to go now, because Eli Beer is calling me on FaceTime."

It was the first time Simcha had seen Eli since he had been sedated. He had a full beard and looked absolutely awful, and Simcha felt like crying because he was looking at a living miracle.

"Simcha," Eli said, "come take me home. Come take me home."

"Eli," Simcha replied, "I'm coming."

The plans were set into motion. Simcha booked a flight from New York to Miami for the next day. Dr. Zevi Neuwirth would serve as the doctor on board. Dr. Neuwirth also arranged for an ambulance to pick up Eli from the hospital and transport him to the plane. Zalmy Cohen, a longtime member of Hatzalah Miami, would meet Simcha when he landed at the Fort Lauderdale–Hollywood International Airport, and help transport all the equipment that Simcha was bringing with him from New York — a ventilator, a cardiac monitor, as much oxygen as they could possibly use, and any medications that they would potentially need to make sure that Eli had the most comfortable and safe flight — so that he would be able to create an ICU ambulance in the sky when Eli was finally aboard the Adelsons' plane.

After Eli had regained consciousness, they had given Eli a few days of physiotherapy so that he'd be able to walk a little on his own, and shortly thereafter the Miami doctors gave their authorization for him to travel back home. When

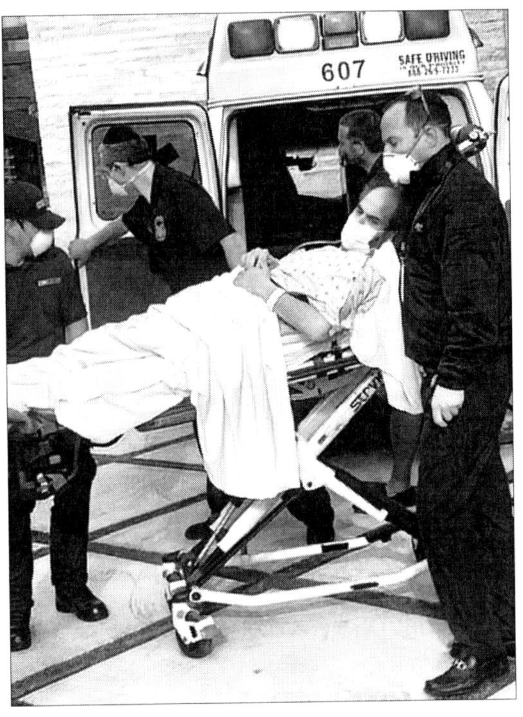

Simcha bringing Eli back to the Ansbacher home

the time came for Eli to leave the hospital, every member of the medical staff went into full celebration mode. They had all come to know and love Eli, and many of them made sure to say goodbye before he left.

When Simcha arrived at the hospital and finally saw Eli in person, it struck him that he looked like a ghost of his formerly robust self. This Eli had no clothing that fit him and his mind was not clear. Before they loaded Eli onto the ambulance, Simcha Shain informed the driver that they weren't going straight to the airport and instead gave the address of the Ansbacher home.

"Are you sure?" the driver asked dubiously, clearly not sure of the wisdom of stopping at a private home with a patient who had almost died from Covid.

"Yes, I'm sure. And just for the record, get ready for a fantastic meal."

Eli has many close friends in Miami. Tila Falic Levy, Sandra and Morris Kaplan, and Danielle David were there for him through the entire ordeal, making certain he had kosher food in the hospital, helping in any way. They were also joined by another dear friend, Asher Milstein.

Now that it was time for Eli to go home, Tila and Sandra arranged

The convoy

More of the convoy

with the Ansbachers, pulling out all the stops for a "Welcome Back and Goodbye Eli" party.

So they began driving in the direction of the Ansbacher residence, the home where Eli had tasted wine on Purim night and couldn't figure out why such high-quality wine could taste so vile. It was his first hint that he had come down with Covid. Now he was making a return visit, having almost died and miraculously come back to life.

At first Eli didn't realize what was going on, but soon enough he grasped that they were being followed by a large convoy of vehicles. The word had gotten out in Miami that Eli was on his way home, and people had come to say goodbye.

At the Ansbacher home, Uri showed Eli to one of the bedrooms, where he could freshen up and change into brand-new clothing before coming downstairs and joining in the beautiful and festive celebratory meal that had been prepared as a thank you to Hashem for saving the life of their friend.

Afterward, when Eli was brought back to the ambulance, he realized that the convoy of cars that had followed them to the Ansbacher home from the hospital was just the beginning. He now saw what appeared to be an endless line of vehicles starting to drive down the street. Hundreds of cars were part of the convoy, and as they passed the ambulance with its open doors and saw Eli, many of the people in the cars opened their windows to shout, "We love you, Eli!"

Simcha was on one side of Eli and Zalmy Cohen was on the other — all of them masked up — and the back door of the ambulance was open so that Eli had a clear view of the proceedings. The cars just didn't stop coming up the street. Imagine a beach where instead of ocean waves there are cars. People were crying and holding signs with the words "Get better!" "We love you!" and "Stay strong!"

And because people wanted Eli to know who they were, when their cars were next to him, they would slow down and call out their names and he would wave. He waved whether he recognized the name or not. It was his way of showing his gratitude to all the people who were going out of their way to show him how much he meant to them.

At that moment, he felt as if all the Jews in Miami genuinely cared about him and had davened for him and truly hoped that he would get better.

The procession lasted for forty minutes, and the entire time Simcha was in contact with the pilots who would be flying the plane that would

take them to Eretz Yisrael to make sure that they weren't going to be late
for takeoff and still had enough time to get to the airport.

Finally they arrived at the airport and boarded the plane. All the
equipment was already set up. The hope was that none of it would be
needed, but it was there, just in case. The pilots received clearance from
the tower, and they started to move down the runway. A few minutes
later they were taxiing and soaring into the sky.

The flight itself was difficult. He was still very weak, and it was hard
for Eli to lie down, and it was hard for him to sit. He couldn't seem to
find a comfortable position, no matter what he did with himself. He
spent some of the time sleeping, but for most of the flight he conversed
with Simcha, describing everything he'd been through over the last
month.

"Do you have any regrets?" Simcha asked.

"Regrets about what?"

"Well, if you hadn't been in Miami, it's very possible that you would
have never come down with Covid."

Eli looked at Simcha.

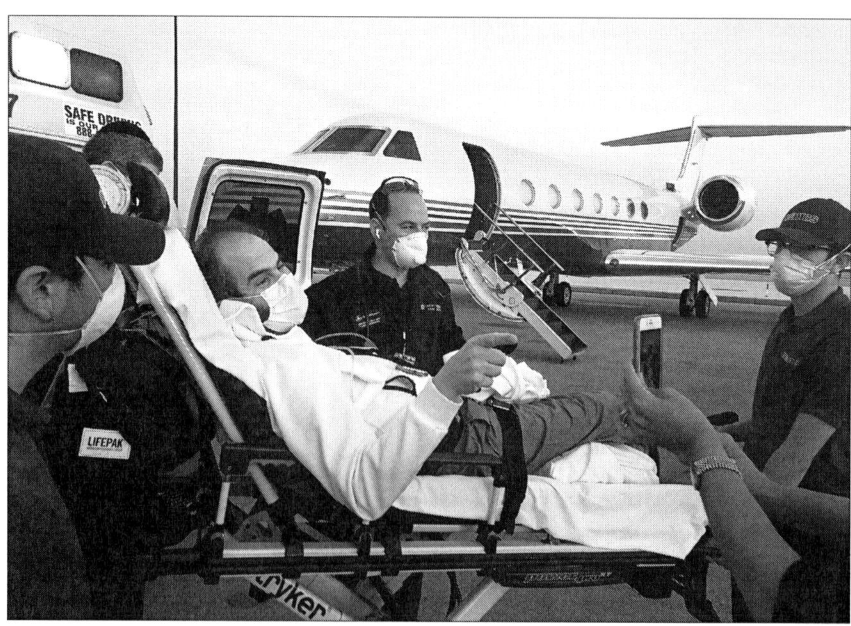

On the runway

Sharing a meal with the Dream Team — Dr. Zev and Simcha

"Simcha," he replied, "I was in America because I was collecting money for United Hatzalah. I have no regrets at all. I'm on a mission to save lives, and as long as Hashem gives me the strength to fulfill that mission, I'm going to do it."

The flight eventually ended, as everything does. When Eli emerged from the plane and stood at the top of the stairs, he recited the timeless

Eli getting off Dr. Miriam Adelson's plane

words of "*Shema Yisrael*," thanking Hashem for saving his life and bringing him home.

For a long time, his family hadn't been sure that they would ever see him alive again. The moment they were able to get to him, they ran to his side, and the hugging, kissing, and crying that followed was something you just don't see every day. It seemed as if everything that he had gone through in the past weeks had all sunk in at that moment, and he suddenly understood on the deepest level that he had come very close to never seeing his family again.

From the plane, Eli was transferred to an ambulance, which drove him to a large open area where close to one thousand United Hatzalah volunteers were waiting to welcome him back home. The doors of the ambulance were opened and Eli recited the words of the *Shema* again, reaffirming his staunch belief in the Master of the world and thanking Him for saving his life.

Looking at that crowd, Eli was filled with the kind of feeling that people would be willing to pay any amount of money in the world to receive. The sense of gratification, of *nachas*, was beyond incredible. Eli, Gitty, and Eli Pollak were all in the back of the United Hatzalah ambulance, along with Dr. Zevi Neuwirth. Then the ambulance, driven by

The setup for the welcome

A historic moment
The volunteers welcoming Eli back home

Dovie Maisel with Simcha Shain sitting next to him in the front passenger seat, started making its way down one row and up the next — past one thousand people standing at attention and telling Eli how much they loved him.

Every one of the volunteers stood beside the vehicle that had brought them there. Some had driven there in ambulances, others in their personal cars, still others on their ambucycles. It was a sea of orange, a sea of United Hatzalah jerseys and jackets, a sea of motorcycle helmets, a sea of lifesavers. (The ceremony was outdoors, United Hatzalah had received special permission to hold it, and all Covid-19 restrictions were followed.) They were all there to show their love, respect, and admiration for the boy who hadn't even graduated elementary school but had gone on to change the world, saving millions of lives in the process.

When he emerged from the ambulance and saw the United Hatzalah volunteers waiting to greet him, the selfless and wonderful members of his organization, who had come together from all over the country, Eli was overwhelmed and began to cry. Then, turning to one of the people standing nearby, Eli said, "Tell me something."

"Yes, Eli?"

"Is there a volunteer here named Ibrahim Ayuti?"

It turned out that he was there, and when he heard that Eli wanted to see him, he ran over as fast as he could.

"Ibrahim," Eli said, "I heard what you did for the Holocaust survivor who needed candles to light before Pesach. I want you to know that that story saved my life. When Eli Pollak told me that story, it gave me back the strength I needed to return home. I'm so profoundly thankful for everything you do for United Hatzalah and for the citizens of this country."

Ibrahim was beyond moved by Eli's words, and tears welled in his eyes. Eli was crying as well.

Then Eli asked him another question. Something that had been on his mind ever since Eli Pollak had told him the story.

"Ibrahim, let me ask you something. What made you decide to become a volunteer for United Hatzalah? What brought you to us?"

Ibrahim took a deep breath. Then he told Eli the story that had brought him to United Hatzalah.

"I drive a truck for a living," he related. "Seven years ago, I was driving on the highway when I was involved in a horrendous accident. My truck turned over on the road, and I was seriously injured. Gasoline began pouring out of the truck, and I was trapped in a pool of gasoline and couldn't breathe from the fumes. I feared that the whole thing was going to catch fire any second and that my life was over. I started saying my prayers, knowing that it was just a matter of time before I was consumed by the inferno that was about to erupt.

"And then suddenly I heard the sound of motorcycles rapidly approaching, and I was able to see two brightly colored motorcycles coming to a stop right beside my truck. I saw the legs of the two motorcycle drivers running toward me, and then they bent down to the ground, looking for me. One of the orange-jacketed volunteers had a long beard and sidelocks, and the other was a clean-shaven Israeli.

"Two volunteers — one secular, the other religious. Both there to save my life. The life of a person they had never met. The life of someone who wasn't even Jewish.

"A year later, when I had finally recovered, I decided that I wanted to become a volunteer myself. Since then, I've saved many people. I've saved them from car accidents, drownings, and all sorts of situations. But being able to bring those candles to the home of that Holocaust survivor was without a doubt the best and most meaningful lifesaving emergency that I have ever had the good fortune to take part in."

At that moment, Eli Beer knew beyond a shadow of a doubt that he had devoted his life to building the right organization.

# PART NINE



— *Eli Beer*

# CHAPTER FORTY-SEVEN

# A Trip to Iceland

Upon Eli's return to Israel, his good friends Menachem and Ruti Oren graciously invited him and his family to stay at their beautiful home in Tel Aviv for as long as it took him to recuperate. The apartment was on a low floor, with an elevator, and was therefore completely accessible, unlike Eli's own sixth-floor walkup apartment.

The ambulance took him straight to their home from the airport, where a physiotherapist was waiting to have a session with him.

Though Eli was happy to be back in Eretz Yisrael with his family, he was still somewhat depressed that he'd slept right through Pesach, the Yom Tov he loved so much. In the week following Pesach, Eli had an interesting conversation with his son Yisrael.

"Mommy was so busy delivering packages of food on Erev Pesach," Yisrael David told his father, "that she ended up getting home not long before Yom Tov started. Only then did she start preparing the food for our Seder. You were in a coma in Miami, Mommy was cooking for the *seudah* — and the rest of us had a huge argument."

"What kind of argument?" Eli asked.

"Avigail wanted to put a big picture of you in your seat at the head of the table," Yisrael explained. "She wanted to remind everyone that we still have a father and that we should keep on davening for you to come home safe and sound. But I was against it."

"Why?"

"I felt that it would be an *ayin hara* — as if it would be acknowledging that you weren't around anymore. It was a terrible fight. Eventually Mommy calmed everyone down and we took a vote."

"And?"

"And those in favor of the picture carried the day. But Mommy was completely exhausted from delivering food packages all day, then cooking for Yom Tov and settling the fight, that by the time we got to the eating of the *afikoman*, she didn't have the energy to do what we always did."

"You mean she wasn't able to negotiate with you for the return of the *afikoman*."

"Exactly."

For Yisrael David, this was the end of the line. For years, the highlight of his Seder was negotiating with his father for the *afikoman*. It was there that Yisrael David learned the invaluable skill of negotiating a deal, and he loved the give-and-take involved.

"Yisrael David was fantastic at the whole business of negotiation," Eli says. "He would start by asking for the world and would eventually settle for way less than he'd started with — but he was good and getting better. That year at the Seder he was all set to start negotiating with his mother for the return of the *afikoman*, but she was too tired to get into it and just agreed to whatever he asked for."

"When she just gave in to me," Yisrael said, "I couldn't hold it in any longer and I broke down in tears. If she would have at least tried to negotiate, it would have been as if you were still there — at least a little bit. But she didn't even try at all, and the lack of the *afikoman* ritual was the straw that broke the camel's back."

Eli hadn't known about any of this, and it only added to his sadness at missing Pesach with his family. At the same time, he didn't see what he could do about it.

That was when Mark Gerson called.

Mark knew Eli very well, and he could hear that his friend was feeling despondent.

"Eli, what's wrong?"

Eli told his old friend everything he had just learned about what had taken place just before Pesach and how upset his son was because he hadn't been there to negotiate a settlement over the *afikoman*.

"Eli," Mark said, "I just want to remind you of something."

"What's that?"

"Back in the time of the Beis HaMikdash, when a person wasn't able to make it to Yerushalayim for Yom Tov — if, for example, he was ritually impure — then he had the option of celebrating what is called Pesach Sheini, which took place a month later. I think your case is a perfect example of a person who should be able to celebrate Pesach Sheini."

So Eli decided that the Beer family was going to celebrate Pesach Sheini, and it was going to be an incredible experience for every member of the family.

The Beer family's Pesach Sheini Seder was a magnificent affair, held in the home of Menachem and Ruti Oren. Gitty prepared a truly delicious meal. They read the Haggadah and told the story of the Exodus from Egypt and made sure to sing every one of the songs they loved so much. They ate the thin, brittle matzah typical of Ashkenazim, and they had thick Yemenite matzah, courtesy of one of Eli's sons-in-law, who is of Yemenite descent. The evening culminated with a request from Eli

Pesach Sheini

for the return of the *afikoman* and a marathon negotiation with Yisrael David, who was in fine form that night.

"What do you want?" Eli asked his son.

"I want to go with you on a six-day hike from the Golan Heights down to Tiveriah," Yisrael promptly replied.

Eli wasn't even capable of considering such a hike, forget about actually undertaking one.

Which was just fine — since this was Yisrael's opening bid.

By the time they had come to the end of their negotiations two hours later, Yisrael had extracted a promise from his father to take him on a trip to Iceland — just the two of them — for some much-needed father-son time. When Iceland opened its borders a few months later and lifted the Covid restrictions that had been temporarily in place, Eli and Yisrael flew there for a special vacation.

"On this trip there will be no discussing of Hatzalah business," Yisrael informed his father. "This is our time."

Eli intended to keep his word about not doing any fundraising while he was out in the middle of Iceland with his son — and he actually did keep his word — until they happened to run into one of United Hatzalah's board members right there in the middle of nowhere.

It was Jeff Aeder from Chicago, who was also in Iceland with his family.

"We're going to get a motorcycle from Jeff," Eli told Yisrael.

Yisrael had nothing to say in return, clearly unable to process the fact that even in far-off Iceland, his father had managed to run into one of his generous donors.

Eli and Jeff sat down for a little shmooze. "Eli," Jeff said, "we're not discussing fundraising here. I'm on vacation and so are you. Can't you just take a break from raising money for a few days?"

Jeff was laughing as he asked the question, because he already knew the answer. True to form, Eli answered, "Absolutely not. I want you to donate a motorcycle."

Jeff turned to Yisrael and said, "You probably told your father that he wasn't allowed to do any fundraising on this trip, right?"

Yisrael nodded.

"Well, then, there it is. No motorcycle on this trip. I'm on Yisrael's side here. He wants to spend some quality time with his father without any distractions. So no business. Anyway, Eli, you don't have to *schnorr* money from me every time you see me."

And Jeff, who is a generous contributor to United Hatzalah, didn't give in — to Yisrael's satisfaction and his father's chagrin.

Of course, Eli was just a little bit disappointed that he hadn't managed to raise some money for United Hatzalah during his time in Iceland. But even he had to admit that despite his minor failure at fundraising, the rest of the trip was exceeding all expectations.

They went fly-fishing for salmon the next day. By the end of the outing, they had five beautiful kosher fish to show for their efforts, and they grilled them then and there on the portable grill they had brought with them.

They also went on a bunch of hikes, enjoying the beautiful Icelandic scenery. On their final day in Iceland, the two of them went to see one of the country's most famous tourist sites — a volcano, long dormant, that one could actually enter. An elevator built into the mountain took visitors down seven hundred feet into what feels like the center of the earth in a rapid-fire descent.

As they were walking toward the entrance of the volcano, Eli noticed a nice-looking family nearby. He didn't say anything to them, but suddenly the man approached him and said, "Are you Eli Beer?"

"Yes, I am."

"I've heard a lot about you."

The man introduced himself as Todd Richman. He told Eli that he lived in Long Island and reminded him that they had met at the AIPAC convention a few years earlier. Before they parted, the man told Eli that he wanted to make a donation to his organization. A little more chatting and Eli gave him some ideas. Then and there the man decided to donate funds for several defibrillators to United Hatzalah. So it was that Eli ended up raising money for United Hatzalah even in Iceland.

# CHAPTER FORTY-EIGHT

# Anatoly

*H*aving been out of commission for so long, Eli had hundreds of thousands of emails and other forms of communication to tackle. There were so many messages that he needed three people to help him wade through them all. One day one of his team members came across an email from someone Eli didn't know and had never met before. It seemed like a serious message, and they forwarded it to him.

"My name is Marcel Javor," the man wrote. "I live in Austria. I read in the newspapers that you are in a coma and are in grave danger. If you wake up and see this email, please call me because I would like to make a significant donation to your organization."

Eli decided to make the call.

"This is Eli Beer," he told the man who answered the phone.

"My name is Marcel," the man replied, "and I just wanted to know that you are all right. Are you happy to be alive?"

"I am very happy," Eli told him.

Marcel Javor

"In that case, you're about to become even happier."

Eli waited to hear what Marcel had in mind.

"I was praying for you while you were lying in Florida in a coma," he said. "You don't know me, but I was very sad that you, a person who has devoted his life to saving others, was in such a state himself. I said to myself, If Eli Beer survives, I am going to donate three hundred and sixty thousand dollars to United Hatzalah."

Eli was overcome. Here was a man whom he had never met in his life, but who wanted him to recover and promised Hashem that he was going to donate a truly impressive amount of money in his merit.

So began another beautiful friendship.

One day Eli said to Marcel, "Listen, I want you to become the chairman of the United Hatzalah board in Austria."

"I'm happy to be on the board," Marcel replied, "but I don't think I'm the right person to be chairman. I'm sure there are other people who are better suited than myself."

"No," Eli told him, "you have to be the one."

"Why me?"

"Because you are the only member of our Austrian board right now."

They both laughed and Marcel accepted the position, and Eli recalled how he uttered those exact same words to his dear friend Mark Gerson so many years earlier right after they met for the first time in Manhattan. As they say, "History repeats itself."

Or, as Eli likes to say, "If something worked once, there's no reason to assume it won't work again."

After Eli's recovery from Covid, the Beers' relationship with Dr. Miriam Adelson became even closer. She introduced them to a number of her friends, all of them unique and all of them incredible human beings. One of those they met was Natan Sharansky, whom Dr. Adelson had known for many years.

Natan Sharansky — born in Russia as Anatoly Borisovich Sharansky — was yet another person who loved Hatzalah's message, and he and Eli ended up becoming very close. Back when he was a kid, Eli recalled hearing stories of Jewish people chaining themselves to the gate of the Soviet Embassy in New York to gain news coverage for the plight of the three million Russian Jews trapped behind the Iron Curtain. Natan

Dr. Larry Platt and Natan Sharansky

Sharansky was one of the most famous refuseniks, and after finally being granted permission to move to Israel, he was appointed to several key positions in the Israeli government.

Not long after the Beers met him, Natan flew to Washington, D.C., where he had meetings scheduled. When he returned to Israel, he called Eli and said, "I don't feel well."

It was round three of Covid, and it seemed that Natan Sharansky was the next victim.

"I'm going to send some of my volunteers over to you," Eli told him. "They'll test you, and we'll see what you have."

The results came in fast and clear. Natan Sharansky had Covid.

"Listen," Eli told the former refusenik, "at your age and in your condition, you need to get to the hospital right away. In the meantime, I'm going to obtain for you the antibody medication, and your condition should improve."

It hadn't been easy to obtain in Israel the medication that was showing incredible results, but Eli fought like a lion to bring it in, and it was this medicine that he wanted to have administered to Sharansky.

There was one problem: Natan Sharansky wasn't cooperating.

"I'm begging you," Eli entreated Sharansky. "Let me give you the medicine you need!"

But he refused.

"Why?"

"I took a few doses of the vaccination, and I think that's enough. I'll get through this."

But it didn't turn out that way.

A few hours later Natan's wife, Avital Sharansky, called Eli in a panic. "He's getting worse," she said.

Eli called Sharansky again and tried his very best to convince Sharansky to admit himself to the hospital, where he could be given a special medication to help fight the Covid infection. Eli promised to be involved, making sure he got the best care and treatment. But he discovered just how stubborn Mr. Natan Sharansky really was. This made sense. After all, here was a man who had outlasted the KGB.

"I'll take full responsibility for you," Eli told Sharansky.

Like everyone else, Sharansky had heard terrifying things about the contagion in the hospitals. With his indomitable spirit, he was certain he could beat this disease on his own, and would actually be safer in his own home.

"I don't want to go to the hospital. It's full of sick people."

"Listen, I'm sending a United Hatzalah ambulance over to your house. My staff will take your blood. This will tell us whether there's a way to handle the illness without your having to take the medication I have in mind."

The ambulance went to Hadassah Hospital to pick up the vials they would need for the procedure. Then they went and took his blood, which was quickly transported to the hospital for testing. Soon afterward, the doctor called Eli.

"He needs to take the medication," the doctor said.

Eli was getting desperate. The doctor had just stated unequivocally that Sharansky needed to take that medicine, but Sharansky refused to go to the hospital to have it administered.

Eli picked up the phone and called his good friend Dr. Joel Sandberg to ask for his help.

"Joel, I need your help convincing Natan Sharansky to allow the doctors to administer antibody medicine that will save his life. You've known Sharansky for decades, and he trusts you. Can you help?"

Dr. Sandberg agreed.

Eli also asked Dr. Miriam Adelson to get involved. After all, she, too, was a doctor who had a close relationship with Sharansky.

Eli got Sharansky on the phone for a conference call, and he and the two doctors worked on persuading Sharansky to go to the hospital and take the medicine.

Finally, he made a concession. "The only way I am entering the hospital," he told Eli, "is if you get me in and take me out immediately after I receive the medicine. That's my condition."

Eli accepted Sharansky's condition, though he knew that the chance of that happening was extremely low. He was willing to tell the man whatever he wanted to hear if that would save his life.

Seeing Natan Sharansky in such a state was very tough for Eli. Even harder was hearing him say that he had never felt so terrible in his entire life.

"I feel like I'm dying," he said. "In the gulag I survived by playing chess in my head. But now I can't even move one pawn."

"Trust me," Eli told him. "I know this treatment. At first it makes you feel worse, but then you'll start to feel much better."

It was true. The next day Natan Sharansky felt like a new man, and Eli was able to get him discharged and bring him back home after just one day in the hospital.

The effects of Eli's experience with Covid-19 lasted for a long time — and not always in a negative way. For instance:

Eli met Lynn and Paul Leight at a speaking engagement. It wasn't long before they had become good friends, and they donated an ambucycle to United Hatzalah. While they are generous supporters of numerous causes, United Hatzalah became close to their hearts, and they identified with the organization's future goals.

"I wanted to ask them to donate one of the floors that we were about to start building on top of our Jerusalem headquarters," Eli says, "but I felt that it was too much to jump from donating an ambucycle to donating two million dollars."

Still, Eli hoped that the right opportunity would present itself at some point.

The next time Eli was in Florida, they got together for dinner. It was "Yeshivah Week," when many students are on vacation, and the restaurant was packed. But since Eli knows the owner of the establishment they were soon sitting at a table outside, surrounded by what seemed like half of Brooklyn and Lakewood.

Turning to Lynn and Paul, Eli said, "Look at this beautiful scene. Here we are, sitting in beautiful Miami, and all around us are Jews of every type and stripe."

It was true. It seemed like every kind of Jew was represented there that day.

"In my line of work," he told the couple, "I get to know Jewish people from every part of the nation."

Pointing to the tables around them, he said, "I can tell you something about every person sitting here. Just by looking at them, I can tell you what type of shul they pray in and if they are affiliated with the *litvish* (Lithuanian Jewry) community or with the chassidic community. I can even tell you which particular chassidic group they belong to. One look at them, and I know if they are Satmar, Vizhnitz, or Bobov."

There was a group of six women seated at a nearby table.

"You see that party?" Eli said. "They are all members of the Satmar chassidim."

On a whim, Paul turned to the group. Pointing at Eli, he said, "Do you know who this man is?"

They didn't.

"This is Eli Beer, the founder of United Hatzalah."

The women got very excited and started telling Eli how they had davened for him when he was in the hospital during that fateful Pesach. One of the ladies reached into her bag and pulled out her *Tehillim*. Opening it up, she showed Paul and Lynn that she had written Eli's name inside her *Tehillim* and had been praying for him to have a complete recovery.

Eli thanked every one of them for going out of their way to daven for him. Paul and Lynn then shared with the group of Satmar women that they, too, had prayed for Eli.

"So many people were praying for a perfect stranger — the founder of United Hatzalah — so that he could continue saving lives."

It was an emotional moment, made even more special by the knowledge that United Hatzalah had succeeded in living up to its name and uniting various types of Jews around one common cause.

During the course of the conversation, the ladies mentioned that they were all sisters who had come to Miami on vacation. They also mentioned that their parents were Holocaust survivors who had been through Auschwitz and miraculously escaped with their lives.

"Do you have any brothers?"

"Five. They didn't come with us."

"And how many kids do you have?" the Leights wanted to know.

The sisters began telling them how many each had. One had twelve, the next nine, the third eleven.

"All together," one of the sisters said, "our parents have about three hundred and fifty descendants when you include all the children, grandchildren, and great-grandchildren."

"Look at this family," Eli said to Paul and Lynn. "Look at how many hundreds of Jews are here today just because their parents survived the Holocaust and were saved. And saving Jews is what we do every single day."

Paul and Lynn were absolutely radiant at the idea that all the people sitting there had been praying for the same thing — and Eli knew what he needed to do.

He was about to make his move when Paul beat him to it.

"Okay, Eli," he said, "what do you want from us?"

"I would like for you to contribute to building a floor in the United Hatzalah Jerusalem headquarters. I have six floors to build, and I need help."

"How much would it cost?"

Eli named the amount. It was more than a million dollars. A very large donation and a huge jump from the price of an ambucycle.

"Eli, that's a lot of money. A lot more than what I gave you last time."

Eli nodded. He knew it was true.

When they left the restaurant, Paul said, "Eli, I'm going to think about it and I'll get back to you."

Twenty minutes after they parted, Paul called him back.

"What floor do you want us to give?"

"The fifth floor."

Eli couldn't have been more excited, and he thanked his friends over and over for their incredible dedication to the cause of saving lives.

In late 2022, Eli was passing through Miami on his way to Panama, to celebrate the 10th anniversary of the establishment of United Hatzalah in Panama, when he missed his flight. Disappointed at having missed the flight, Eli decided to use the unexpected time to meet with Paul and Lynn. During his visit to their home, Lynn handed him an envelope. There was a check inside — made out for enough funds to not only build the floor, but to furnish it with the nicest and most elegant furniture available. It was a beautiful donation, made all the more so by the way they gave it — with joy and love.

# CHAPTER FORTY-NINE

# Succos in Dubai

After his close brush with death, Eli never dreamed that Covid would still be a factor come Succos time. But it was. Israel's borders were closed and foreigners weren't allowed into the country. This meant that instead of spending Succos the way he generally did — meeting donors and selling tickets for the Hatzalah concert — Eli could look forward to spending all his time with his family.

Bibi Netanyahu had announced that there was going to be a lockdown from Rosh Hashanah until after Succos. But Miri Regev, then Minister of Transportation, let it be known that anyone who had already purchased tickets to fly abroad for Succos would be allowed to use them. The cutoff date for buying tickets was that Friday at two o'clock — which meant that Eli had two hours to decide on a destination and book tickets for the entire family. The problem was that millions of other people all over the country were doing the same.

Out of the blue, he came across an ad for hotels in Dubai. The prices were low, since very few people were flying to Dubai right then. Flights were also very cheap. Although he would have loved to fly there directly, they'd have to fly through Ethiopia since the Abraham Accords, the peace treaty between Israel and the United Arab Emirates, had not yet been signed. Most of the family would have no problem being allowed to enter Dubai since they had American passports. It was only a problem for Eli's son-in-law, Meir, who didn't have an American passport, and for his grandson, whose parents hadn't yet been able to obtain an American passport for their three-month-old as the American embassy in Israel was still on lockdown.

This was going to present a bit of a challenge. Dubai, which wasn't on lockdown, seemed like the perfect place to spend Succos, but two of their family members wouldn't be able to go since they only had Israeli passports, and Israelis were barred from entering the country.

Eli wracked his brains to consider who he knew with connections in the United Arab Emirates, and he remembered that his friend Avi Hier had a close relationship with one of the wealthiest real estate moguls in the region. His name was Mohamed Alabbar.

Among other things, Mohamed Alabbar was known for building the tallest building in Dubai, the Burj al Khalifa, as well as several malls and many of the most exclusive real estate projects in the Middle East.

Eli got Avi on the phone.

"Question?"

"Yes?"

"Would you be able to connect me with Mohamed Alabbar?"

"I can try."

Avi didn't waste any time. He promptly called Mohamed and asked if his friend Eli Beer could call him. He explained who Eli Beer was and how he had built an ambulance rescue organization in Israel that was saving many lives every day.

Mohamed told Avi that he was very interested in hearing from Eli.

"So I called him," Eli said, "and found myself speaking with the nicest man. When I told him that I wanted to bring my family to Dubai for Succos but that I had a problem with two of the passports, Mohamed said, 'Eli, don't worry about a thing. I'll have someone waiting to meet you at the airport. He'll take care of everything.'"

When the call disconnected, Eli booked the tickets, hoping for the best.

It was a four-hour flight to Ethiopia and an additional four-hour wait until their flight was announced. But they ran into trouble at the gate because they didn't have the necessary documents for two of their party, and the airline wouldn't let them board the flight since they wouldn't be able to enter Dubai upon landing. Eventually, after a lot of convincing, they were able to persuade the airline representative to allow them to board the flight, explaining that they had someone waiting for them on the other side to bring them into Dubai.

"I'll allow you onto the plane," the man said. "Just keep in mind that there is a very good chance that they will put you right back on a plane out of Dubai just as soon as you get there."

Mohamed Alabbar was true to his word. They had barely disembarked when they were approached by someone.

"Are you Mr. Beer?"

"Yes, I am."

"Mr. Alabbar sent me here to meet you and escort you out of the airport."

The man led them to the terminal, and as he opened the door leading into the building, he said, "Welcome to Dubai. Can I please have your passports?"

They handed him their passports, American for most of them, Israeli for Meir and the baby. He took the passports, approached one of the customs officials, and returned a few minutes later with all the passports stamped.

A few minutes later they were walking out of the airport.

Rabbi Levi Duchman, the Chabad rabbi in Dubai, sent over a team of his people to kasher the villa that the Beers had rented on the ocean. They also erected a succah for Eli and his family.

It ended up being an incredibly peaceful and unique holiday. There were two local shuls where they could daven, and since they hosted no guests, and there was no one for Eli to talk to, the family was able to enjoy long stretches of quality time together, reconnecting after the trauma they'd been through half a year earlier.

When Succos was over, Mohamed Alabbar asked Eli to stay for a few more days because there was something that he wanted to discuss with him. He invited Eli to his home and introduced him to his son

Eli and Mohamed

Rashid and the rest of the family. The entire Alabbar family wanted to know more about United Hatzalah. They were fascinated by the idea that unlike in Dubai, where a person might have to wait for an ambulance for half an hour, in Israel a volunteer will jump on his motorcycle and be at a patient's side in under two minutes. Mohamed wasn't just impressed by the rapid response time. He also loved the fact that strangers were willing to drop whatever they were in the middle of doing and run off to save the life of someone they had never met.

"Eli," Mohamed Alabbar said, "I want to ask you for a favor."

"Mohamed, you opened your house to me. You introduced me to your family. You helped us enter your country. Please tell me what I can do for you."

"When the time comes, I want you to help me start a branch of your organization in the Arab world."

"Mohamed, it would be an honor."

Over the next two days Eli stayed at one of Mohamed's hotels, and they shared a number of conversations about Mohamed's dream to establish United Hatzalah in the Emirates and in other countries, such as Egypt, as well.

During one of their final meetings before Eli had to leave for the airport, Eli turned to his host and said, "Mohamed, I have to ask you something that I've been wondering about for a while."

"Ask me anything you want."

"I've gotten to know you pretty well over the last few days, and it seems to be that you are a person who likes the Jewish people with a passion I have rarely encountered. I was just wondering how you came to feel that way."

"Back in my younger years, I found myself in a number of different places. I studied in a university and did a fair amount of traveling as I grew my business. During the course of my travels, I spent some time in Singapore. There I was introduced to a wonderful Jew whom I came to know and admire. The more time I spent with him and his warm and welcoming family, the more I comprehended how special they were.

"Within a very short time, I found that the mindset I'd been brought up with regarding the Jewish people had changed, and I came to the realization that Jews and Muslims need to find a way to connect with one another instead of constantly being at war. In my heart, I began to wish for the day when there would be peace between the State of Israel and the United Arab Emirates.

"These feelings were only reinforced when I visited Israel and found myself being welcomed with open arms everywhere I went."

"When was this?"

"When my friend Avi Hier made a wedding. Prime Minister Netanyahu gave me special authorization to fly in on my own plane. While in Israel, I visited the Temple Mount. As I was passing through security, a soldier stopped me and asked to see my passport. When he realized that it was an Emirati passport, he got excited. All the soldiers did. They had never met anyone from Dubai before, and they told me how impressed they were by the Emiratis, whom they considered to be top businessmen and investors who created a magnificent country in the middle of the desert. They posed with me for pictures, and once again, the truth was brought home to me. Here they were, the infamous Israeli soldiers — the people everyone likes to accuse of being so aggressive against Muslims — and yet all they were doing was making me feel welcome and showing me that they were happy I had come to visit."

For Eli Beer, it was an incredible feeling to know that a real estate magnate from Dubai could connect with the founder of an emergency response organization who had grown up in Bayit Vegan. On the surface, there was nothing connecting the two of them. And yet, unaccountably, they had become friends. And it was all because of their shared interest and love for saving lives. Such is the power of United Hatzalah.

Before they parted, Eli gave Mohamed Alabbar his own United Hatzalah vest, complete with a mini Israeli flag embroidered on it.

"This is my gift to you," he told his Emirati friend.

Mohamed loved the vest, and if you happen to visit his office at some point or other, you will see it prominently displayed in a frame on the wall, thereby cementing the relationship that exists between the two unlikely friends.

On August 13, 2020, an agreement was signed at the White House in Washington, D.C., between the State of Israel, the United Arab Emirates, and the United States of America.

It was called the Abraham Accords Peace Agreement.

Today any Israeli can fly to Dubai, no questions asked.

Pretty incredible when you think about it.

# CHAPTER FIFTY

# The Trauma of Meron

Eli wasn't in Israel on April 30, 2021, Lag BaOmer 5771. He was in Miami, fundraising for United Hatzalah as he does during a large portion of the year. Being back in the place where he had been near death the previous year brought home to him what he had been through, and he knew that he would never relate to the city in the same way as he had before.

All this meant that Eli wasn't there when *Klal Yisrael* experienced one of the worst traumas as a nation, the Meron tragedy. To lose forty-five *tzaddikim* — and there is no question that every one of the people who died that night were righteous Jews and worthy of the title — cannot help but affect every single Jew. That the tragedy occurred on Lag BaOmer, on a day that has always been considered such a happy day, was traumatic in its own right.

And while it was a terrible day for everyone on a general level, the trauma was indescribable for the members of United Hatzalah who were in the thick of the action and saw everything that transpired that night. If you watch the video of the area right outside Hatzalah's Meron stations, you will see the stream of people stuck in place — people were trapped and the crush only grew worse.

"For years," Eli says, "we had many volunteers stationed at Meron on Lag BaOmer. We had five stations on-site, and there was even a mini ER for people who needed emergency treatment. I would bring a bottle of whiskey with me up to Meron every Lag BaOmer and make a *l'chaim* with my volunteers at the end of the day, as we celebrated the fact that another year had passed and nobody died. For years I worried that something like this was going to happen, but even though I feared that a few people would die, I never dreamed of the epic tragedy that would one day occur."

"We have to be prepared," Eli would tell the volunteers, "because the crowds are too big for the police to control. Meron is a small village. More and more people have started coming every year, and while the crowds are growing in volume, the place itself stays the same size."

United Hatzalah always began preparing for the pilgrimage to Meron a month prior to Lag BaOmer, and many of the volunteers were already on-site three days before the crowds arrived. But that was just the beginning.

When people called Hatzalah to tell them that someone had fainted or had been in an accident in the vicinity of Meron, it was always very difficult for them to explain where exactly they were located. Finally, one member of United Hatzalah, Moshe Levy, thought of an idea that could solve the problem.

Well in advance of the forthcoming year's festivities, Levy made the rounds to every tree in Meron and attached a sign with a number on it, high enough on the tree so that the sign couldn't be removed and high enough so that someone in the vicinity could see it clearly. There were three thousand signs in all. Whenever anyone called, the volunteer would tell them, "Look around you. Do you see any trees?"

"Yes."

"Is there a sign with a number on it?"

"Yes."

"What number do you see?"

The moment they knew the number, tracking down the patient became a thousand times easier, because all a volunteer had to do was take a second to study the United Hatzalah map of the mountain. And just as millions of Yidden loved going to Meron, so did the thousands of United Hatzalah volunteers, who waited eagerly throughout the year for the chance to drive up north and spend a few days keeping *Klal Yisrael* safe at the *kever* of Rabbi Shimon Bar Yochai.

As the commander-in-chief of rescue operations in Meron every year, Eli would spend twenty-four hours there every year, and it was very hard for him to see what was going on. He realized that the massive crowding in such a small space was a recipe for disaster.

In the year before the tragedy, Meron was empty due to Covid. And because no one was able to go up north for Lag BaOmer in 2020, many more people than usual felt the need to go the next year. They missed visiting Rabbi Shimon and felt that they had to make the trip — to sing and dance around the bonfires and to daven at the holy graves of Rabbi Shimon and his son Rabbi Elazar.

Then came the crush in the middle of the night, and from one second to the next, the horrific news flashed across the globe, attacking people with unbearable force as everyone realized that even if they themselves hadn't lost a loved one, they knew wonderful people who had. It was such a tremendously personal tragedy, and the grief that washed over one and all the following Friday was beyond intense.

Eli would never forget the first call that came in to him from the dispatcher.

"Eli, three or four people were probably killed in Meron."

"How do you know?"

"We can see it on our cameras."

United Hatzalah had set up cameras all over Meron years before so that they would be able to direct volunteers in case of an emergency. Now the cameras provided them with footage of everything that was happening — live, in real time.

One video showed one of the United Hatzalah volunteers — a young man named Yehuda Gottlieb — being moved along by the rush of the crowd, and suddenly he was able to miraculously lift himself up and out of the crush and scale the tall wall that was fencing everyone in. He is the only one who even tried to scale the wall and succeeded, an almost miraculous feat when you consider that the wall was twelve feet tall. Once he was over the wall and on the other side, Yehuda began screaming for help, because people still didn't realize what was starting to happen.

Since virtually every person in Meron lost their phone reception during that long and endless night, people were unable to get through to loved ones. Instead, those searching for lost relatives tried calling Eli Beer, and since he was in Miami, he was able to answer his phone.

One person in particular kept calling again and again. When Eli finally answered, the man asked him to please try to find out whatever he could about his son — a young yeshivah boy from Bergenfield, New Jersey, who seemed to be missing.

"What's his name?"

"Donny Morris."

"Can you send me a picture of him, please?"

Aryeh Morris sent a picture right away.

"I'll see what I can do."

Eli immediately took action. He sent out Donny's picture to all the United Hatzalah volunteers who were in Meron and continued to update the Morris family throughout the night, as well as being in touch with the others who reached out to him.

It was a long, long night.

While all this was going on, the volunteers of United Hatzalah were growing more and more brokenhearted. It was a terribly challenging situation. They were performing CPR on dozens of people simultaneously, and they were overwhelmed by grief as they saw so many special Yidden lying dead on the ground with no chance of bringing them back to life.

Meanwhile, Eli was still in touch with Aryeh Morris — Donny's father. Donny's picture had been sent to the Hatzalah volunteers, but they hadn't managed to track him down. Then, all of a sudden, Eli's oldest daughter Avigail called him. She had seen the picture and had something important to tell her father.

Avigail was in Meron working as a volunteer for United Hatzalah in the women's section, a place where they used only female EMTs. With fifty thousand women traveling to Meron, it made sense for United Hatzalah to go out of its way to staff the women's side of the building with female volunteers.

"Abba, I heard the screams from outside. I ran out and saw thirty bodies on the floor. I had an ambulance with me to deal with any emergencies that might arise among the women, but I saw that it was needed to transport people out of Meron and over to the nearest hospital.

"I heard that you were looking for a young boy. I remembered that boy and the nice American clothing he was wearing. They were nice enough that they stuck out, and I recognized them when I saw the picture.

"Abba, I treated him. I put him in the ambulance and did everything humanly possible to save his life. Then I drove him to Ziv Hospital in Tzefas. The entire way our volunteers tried their hardest to save his life, crying the entire time. I myself was crying so hard I could barely see the road through my tears. When we reached the hospital, the doctors pronounced him dead."

As Eli was having this conversation with his daughter, he saw that Aryeh Morris was calling him once again — and he didn't know what to do or say to Donny's father. The entire time he'd been telling the father that they were trying their best, but now that he knew that Donny had passed away, Eli didn't have the words. The more he thought about it, the more he knew that he would have to delay revealing the truth until he could arrange for someone to go to the Morrises and give them the news in person.

It was the middle of the night in America, and Eli called Simcha Shain in New Jersey and asked him to go and break the news to the Morris family. When they heard the news, the family wanted to fly to Israel immediately but were unable to do so because it was almost Shabbos. They flew in on Motza'ei Shabbos after Eli had succeeded in convincing the government to allow them in despite the confusing Covid-era restrictions against people flying in from other countries. Many of the volunteers attended Donny's funeral, all of them feeling as if it was their own personal tragedy, too. Every one of the volunteers felt as if they had lost family members that night — a feeling that stemmed from the fact that they had been looking at the faces of the people whose lives they were trying so hard to save.

By the time it was all over, United Hatzalah had treated more than a thousand people (many for shock), but the volunteers would always remember those they could not save.

One month after the Meron tragedy, United Hatzalah asked every volunteer who had been in Meron that Lag BaOmer to return to the place where the victims had been brought on that fateful night. There, along with the families of those who had been taken, they reenacted the events of the night, with the entire group making their way down the ramp of death — together.

They were accompanied by Rav Dovid Lau, the chief rabbi of Israel,

Singing and mourning

while chareidi radio host and media personality Menachem Toker described the significance of the bridge on which they were walking.

"All of us," Toker then said, "will now sing '*K'Racheim Av*,' the song composed by Reb Shragee Gestetner, at the very spot where it all took place."

Shragee Gestetner, a singer from Montreal with a warm and beautiful voice, was one of those who lost their lives that night. Toker explained that it was Shragee's song that had turned into the anthem of the night and was being sung all around the world by a nation still trying to make sense of the tragic event from which they had been left reeling.

Then all the volunteers stood in rows and sang Shragee's song, as music played in accompaniment and a conductor led them in their tribute to forty-five wonderful human beings who were taken from this world in the prime of life.

The United Hatzalah volunteers were comprised, as always, of a mixture representing all the citizens of Israel — Sefardim, Ashkenazim, chassidim, *litvaks*, *dati leumi*, *chilonim* (they covered their heads out of respect), and even a few Arab volunteers (who stood and sang the song with everyone else) sprinkled in for good measure.

It was a night of recovery and closure for the members of Hatzalah

Dovie Maisel back in Meron

in the place where they had experienced such incredible trauma just a short while earlier.

One of the members of Hatzalah hadn't left his home from the night of the Meron tragedy. After that night, he crawled into his bed and barely left it. A chassid from Haifa, his Rebbe had tried talking to him, as had his friends. Nothing helped. He was in the grip of a deep depression, and nothing anyone did had any effect.

Eli called him and told him that he was coming to Meron for this event and that he wanted him to come as well.

The man was crying on the phone, crying like his heart was breaking into a million pieces.

"I want you to come," Eli said. "I'm going, and I want you to come with me. More than that. If you don't go, I'm not going either."

He hung up on Eli.

On the night itself, Eli saw the chassidic volunteer from Haifa, who had finally agreed to join the others in Meron. He was lying on the floor and crying — in the exact spot where he had performed CPR on a youngster, trying his utmost to save the child's life. Many people tried to help this man still paralyzed by grief, but no one knew what to do.

Rav Lau speaking at Meron

"In the end," Eli says, "I did the only thing I could think of to do. I lay down beside him on the ground, in my suit and all, and hugged him with all my might. I just lay there and hugged him, both of us crying together. At first, he didn't even look to see who it was who was lying next to him. After about twenty minutes, he became hysterical and he looked at me, realizing who was hugging him for the first time. Then he began hugging me harder than anyone had ever hugged me in my life. He was literally bawling like a baby, the tears spilling out of his red-rimmed eyes and down his sunken cheeks.

"I sat with him and we hugged one another, and I told him how much we loved him and how he was part of the family.

"'You are a soldier,' I said. 'You have the mitzvah of saving lives. You can't let this stop you. You need to remember that for every person who died, there were ten people you saved. You are going to get up today, and you're going to continue saving lives — just as you always have. You are a soldier in our army, and saving lives is your responsibility!' "

Finally, they rose together and the two of them walked down to where all the volunteers were waiting to start the song, along with the families of the victims and other invited guests.

Then the chassid from Haifa took his place among his friends and sang his heart out.

Today he is back to normal — back to saving lives.

When Eli looks back at what happened in Meron, in his mind it was the most challenging time that the members of United Hatzalah experienced. They went through many traumatic events through the years. Terrorist attacks and bus bombings. They had taken part in wars and lost multiple heroes. But what happened in Meron had been harder than all those things. And that was why the healing process took so much longer than it normally did.

But there was never a question of carrying on.

Because the volunteers of United Hatzalah are soldiers, and soldiers don't give up the fight.

# CHAPTER FIFTY-ONE

# A Dog Named Lucy

"Whenever Dovie Maisel calls me," Eli says, "I know that it's bad news. He'll never call to invite me to a birthday party. It's always, 'Earthquake in Haiti — should we send people?' or 'Earthquake in Nepal — send people?'"

United Hatzalah not only has volunteers who save lives in Israel, but they often send their people to countries that have suffered from natural disasters. In addition to all the valuable assistance they can provide, the teams also have the opportunity to learn what to do in case a major natural disaster happens in Israel.

In 2010, a 7.0 magnitude earthquake shattered Haiti, killing more than 220,000. United Hatzalah volunteers were sent there to help and remained there for two weeks as they took part in search-and-rescue efforts. They would return to Haiti when the country was struck by Hurricane Matthew, establishing emergency clinics to help as many people as possible, and they traveled to Nepal when it was hit by an earthquake in 2015. Many young Israelis travel there for long stretches of time after completing their three-year stint in the army. By the time the team was getting ready to land, they already knew that about one hundred and fifty Israelis were missing. They took a flight from Hong Kong to Bangladesh. The plane emptied out — all except for the team from United Hatzalah, two other Israelis who worked for an insurance company, and a businessman from Nepal. No one boarded their jumbo jet, and they took off soon afterward — so few people for such a huge plane.

The businessman was impressed that the United Hatzalah volunteers were traveling all the way from Israel to Nepal to help his people in their hour of need, and he asked Dovie Maisel how he could be of assistance.

"Thank you for asking," Dovie said. "We're going to need jeeps and generators."

On the spot, the man took out a satellite phone and managed to get in touch with United Hatzalah's point man on the ground in Nepal. By the time they landed, there were jeeps waiting for them at the airport, and he continued helping them with whatever they needed during their stay in his country. In addition to the volunteers from United Hatzalah, the Israeli government flew in a field hospital as well. While the hospital was stationary, the volunteers traveled around the area by jeep, going to a different village every day and offering medical assistance to anyone who needed it.

Their mission was divided in two. Part one was devoted to searching for the missing Israelis. Every single Israeli was eventually found, and the one person who had died in a landslide was brought home to receive a Jewish burial. Part two was about providing medical care for as many Nepalese as possible. United Hatzalah ended up giving medical assistance to thousands of people.

All this means that United Hatzalah has extensive experience dealing with disasters of all sorts around the globe. But even after being involved with natural disasters for so many years, the news about the building that collapsed in Surfside, Florida, in June 2021 hit Eli Beer really hard.

Eli spends a lot of time in Miami and has hundreds of friends there. He was reborn in a Florida hospital after almost losing his life to Covid. When he heard the news about the collapse, he couldn't believe it.

"Which building?"

Dovie told him.

The moment the picture was clear in his mind, Eli said, "Dovie, get our best psycho-trauma team together and get over there. We don't need to bring rescue teams there. I'm sure that the Florida police and local Hatzalah are doing a wonderful job, but they're going to need our psycho-trauma team, because that's something they don't have."

The psycho-trauma team had been established a few years ago in response to the trauma that many volunteers experience in the course of their work. Once the team was up and running, they were also employed to help other people in addition to the Hatzalah volunteers.

During the Meron tragedy, one hundred and fifty United Hatzalah volunteers received therapy themselves to help them get over the heartbreaking events that occurred. But the usual reason the unit is called is when a family experiences a tragedy, G-d forbid. The trauma team will arrive soon after the paramedics and will begin working with the rest of the family members to help them get through the loss of a relative, a car accident, or a terrorist attack. On an average day, the trauma team handles three or four such calls. They're very effective and very good at what they do.

"Bring the people who had experience from Meron and other massive tragedies," Eli told Dovie. "There will be plenty of work for everyone."

In Surfside, the psycho-trauma unit had a very important mission to accomplish. They didn't engage in search and rescue because the Americans were handling that. Instead, the psycho-trauma team was there to help families in the community. While only one building collapsed, it was a massive building, and it was situated in the center of the Jewish community, where there were many members who were major supporters of United Hatzalah. Now it was United Hatzalah's turn to give back to them.

During the fifteen-hour flight, there was plenty of time for the volunteers to explain to the members of Israel's Home Front Command, who were also coming, how they could assist them once they were on the ground. Israel's Home Front Command, or Pikud HaOref, as they are called, was responsible for preparing the people of Israel for a disaster or war and assist them during a crisis. They were coming to Surfside to use their expertise to map out for the Americans where to search and find the bodies that were trapped inside the rubble. The Americans had the equipment, the trucks and the cranes, but the Israelis, unfortunately, have the experience in finding missing bodies.

Throughout the flight, the Home Front team used special software to study videos of the collapse and determine through the building's blueprints where each apartment had been before the collapse and where it would be found afterward. When they landed and reached the area, the Home Front officers set up three tables at what was called the Family Reunification Center, with an officer and United Hatzalah volunteer at each one. There they sat with family members who had lost relatives in the collapse and worked with them to map out exactly where their relatives had been situated in the building. All the information they were given — such as which room a relative generally slept in, the floor, where the bed was situated — was fed into the computer and analyzed so that recommendations could be promptly given to the search-and-rescue teams.

At first, the Americans were skeptical, but that quickly changed when they saw that the bodies they were searching for were located exactly where the Israelis said they would be. At that moment, the Americans realized that the Israelis' expertise was the real thing and they asked them to help them find as many bodies as possible.

The United Hatzalah volunteers had a completely different, yet no less vital mission: they sat with every family member and allowed them to get everything they were holding in off their chest, while helping to facilitate the flow of crucial information so that the Home Front Command team could do their job.

Lucy the Hatzalah dog

To help them carry out their work, they had a dog with them whose job was to identify which people needed help, so that the team could pinpoint where they needed to focus their efforts most. Lucy the dog has been well trained to detect sadness and loss and instinctively knows who needs her special warmth and attention.

Some of the people in the reunification center had been sitting there for days without talking to anyone. In came the dog (her name was Lucy, one of the cutest dogs on the planet, who is also outfitted in an adorable United Hatzalah vest), and within seconds she would figure out who needed her most and would begin to zero in on them — without guidance from anyone.

Soon the people would begin to pet the dog. From there it wouldn't take long until they broke down and began to talk about their loss through the tears, while giving valuable information to the Home Front Command so they could conduct the search more effectively.

The United Hatzalah team had another very important job as well, and that was providing support for the American first responders, firefighters, and search-and-rescue workers.

The technique was simple. First responders are more prone to open up to someone who is not on their own team, and most people can't help but respond when they see the United Hatzalah trauma dog. The team just stood nearby with the dog, and first responders would approach them and ask, "Can I pet the dog?"

Over and over they saw massive firemen, as tall as six foot five with huge muscles, get down on the ground and hug the dog, sometimes for four or five minutes, then say, "Thanks, I needed that," and walk away.

But everything that United Hatzalah did in any of their lifesaving operations abroad paled in comparison to the role they would play in the war between Russia and Ukraine. And while no one dreamed that a real war was about to break out between the two neighbors, from virtually the first moments of the war, the United Hatzalah volunteers found themselves saving lives on a whole different level.

# CHAPTER FIFTY-TWO

# The Baby Under Fire

On the day Russia invaded Ukraine, United Hatzalah flew twelve medics to Moldova. Because of the constant flow of Jews to Uman, United Hatzalah had founded an active branch in Ukraine, composed of over a hundred local volunteers. Now those volunteers were calling the home office and urging them to send as much assistance as possible.

At first, Eli Beer didn't think that war was actually going to happen, but the members of his team — Dovie Maisel, Linor Attias (an expert in crisis management), and his son-in-law Aharon Ben Haroush — all felt otherwise, and they were the ones who made the decision to send twelve volunteers to Moldova. The reason they chose Moldova was simple. Many of the countries surrounding Ukraine are part of the EU or have a treaty with NATO. Moldova, on the other hand, is not part of the EU or NATO. It's just a poor European country with very limited resources. It was clear to the team that when the Ukrainian refugees would start streaming across the border into Moldova, they would need assistance, which the Moldavian government would not be equipped to extend.

The volunteers landed in Moldova on the first day of the war and immediately set up headquarters in one of the local Jewish shuls. Then the team headed for the border, where they were in for a shock.

Thousands of women and children were crossing the border, having been forced to leave their husbands and fathers behind. Ukraine was forbidding all men between the ages of eighteen and sixty from leaving the country so that they could stay and fight. It was freezing cold, the ground was covered in snow, and refugees kept amassing at the border. Shock and confusion reigned and the members of United Hatzalah could hardly believe what they were seeing. It was like pictures out of a history book.

They say that history repeats itself. At that moment, the volunteers from Israel comprehended in the most genuine way how true that was. Who would have thought that a war would have broken out between two countries like Russia and Ukraine? Who would have thought that two nations with such close connections would be engaged in such brutal fighting? And who would have thought so many people would be displaced from their homes, tired, hungry, and without shelter? It was reminiscent of the chaos of World War II, when so many people fled from the homes they had known. And yet it was all real, and it was literally happening before their eyes.

With no choice, the team shut down their emotions and got down to the very serious business of saving lives. When you have to choose whom to help — a sick woman, an elderly man, or a busload of children — and you know that you have limited resources and have to make a decision on how to employ those resources, there's no room for emotion. Not when you're talking about life-and-death situations.

When the war broke out, Eli was in Boca Raton as a guest in the home of Murray and Basheva Goldberg. The Goldbergs are generous supporters of United Hatzalah, as well as the parents of Rabbi Efrem Goldberg, *rav* of the Boca Raton Synagogue. Eli had been invited to serve as the scholar in residence at the shul that Shabbos. None of them imagined the drama that was about to unfold.

Eli was still at the Goldberg home a few days into the war when he received a call from Ron Yeffet, a businessman and United Hatzalah supporter who had an emergency on his hands that no one else had been able to solve. Talking to Ron, Eli could hear a woman crying in the background. Ron put the woman on the phone, and her first words were, "Please save my daughter!"

The woman was the mother of a baby who needed Eli's help in the most urgent of ways. She had tracked him down all the way to Florida after calling so many people to beg for help, but no one had been able

Murray and Basheva Goldberg

to do anything for her. When Eli answered her call that day, he could hear the desperation in her voice.

It turned out that the baby had been born in Kiev a short while before and was supposed to be raised by this Israeli woman and her husband. They had been anxiously awaiting their baby's arrival, but now war had broken out and they were afraid that their baby was going to be killed in the bombing.

"I'm begging you to save my baby," she said to Eli over and over. "Please, please, save my baby and bring her to Israel!"

The baby had recently been born in a little medical clinic in Kiev, while she, the mother, was in Israel with no obvious way to get to her baby.

Meanwhile, bombs were falling in Kiev, so all the women and babies in the clinic had been moved to the basement of the building, which was filthy and barely inhabitable, to take shelter.

"Please save my baby!" the woman implored. "I called so many organizations, and everyone told me they couldn't help me. All they could suggest was that I have the baby sent to an orphanage in Ukraine until the situation calms down."

The mother couldn't stop crying, and Eli's soft heart felt like it was being torn in half. How could anyone tell a mother that she should send her newborn baby to some orphanage and forget about seeing her?

"I'll do everything within my power to save your baby," he told the distraught mother. "I don't know whether I'll be successful, but I'll do my best!"

Getting this baby to her mother was no simple matter. At the moment she was a Ukrainian child, and if United Hatzalah stepped in, they could potentially be accused of kidnapping. It was a situation that needed to be handled with the greatest of care.

Once off the phone with the mother, Eli dialed the number of his son-in-law Aharon, who at that moment was in Moldova, cooking for thousands of refugees at the makeshift kosher soup kitchen that United Hatzalah had set up near the border. United Hatzalah had rented an Irish pub that had been closed for two years due to Covid. They kashered the premises and paid all the overdue electric bills. Now the operation was up and running, and they were producing five thousand meals a day for people who hadn't eaten properly in days since they'd had to abandon their homes and run for their lives.

"Aharon," Eli said to his son-in-law, "I need you to have someone take over the cooking."

"What's going on?"

"I have a mission for you. There's a newborn baby stuck in the basement of a medical center in Kiev. We need to get it out of there and then bring the baby to her mother.

"So you mean something small…"

"Exactly. Nothing beyond your capabilities."

"Give me a status report."

"Okay. The baby is a newborn. The mother is in Israel and can't get to her because of the war. The nurses who were taking care of the baby are running for their

Eli's son-in-law Aharon

lives, they're going to transport the babies to who-knows-where, and bombs are falling in the vicinity of the clinic. We need to save this baby out of eighty newborns, before she is put into an orphanage and gets lost in the shuffle."

"Got it," Aharon told his father-in-law. "Let me put together a team and get cracking."

Step number one was finding an ambulance company that was willing to drive to Kiev to collect a newborn baby. They called twenty-nine ambulance companies, and none of them wanted the job. The ambulances in Kiev didn't want to leave Kiev. The ambulances in other cities didn't want to enter Kiev. And besides the danger on the roads, there was also an acute shortage of gasoline. The ambulance drivers weren't interested in finding themselves stranded on some road in the middle of nowhere and unable to get home because they had run out of gas.

But Aharon is a very smart and resourceful young man, who'd spent much time working with United Hatzalah in Uman during Rosh Hashanah. He speaks Russian and has a wide range of friends and acquaintances in Ukraine. He contacted a seventy-five-year-old doctor in Kiev whom he knew.

"I need you to do something for me."

"What kind of thing?"

"I need you to go to a clinic for me and pick up a baby. I'll send you all the documents that I have proving that you have a legitimate right to remove the child from the clinic. The head nurse in the clinic knows the story, and we've already informed her that we are trying to arrange for someone to come get the baby."

"You sound like you're out of your mind."

"Listen, I'm talking about a mother in Israel who is going crazy with fear because she thinks her baby will be killed by a bomb. Can you save this baby's life or not?"

"You're making it sound very simple. But in case you didn't notice, there's a war going on. No one is allowed to leave their homes. There is a curfew. People who leave their homes without permission get shot."

"Yes, but you're a doctor. You're allowed to leave your home, especially for a humanitarian mission."

"I really don't want to leave my house in the middle of a war when trigger-happy soldiers are guarding every street corner — even for a good cause like saving a baby."

"I hear you," Aharon said, "and that's why I'm offering you fifteen hundred dollars to do this job for me. Are you in? Yes or no?"

It was very difficult for the doctor to make up his mind — money or no money. He was frightened, and for good reason. It would be a dangerous mission. In the end, he agreed, leaving his home and heading toward the clinic. On the way, he was stopped several times by soldiers, but he showed them his papers and they let him through each time.

When the staff allowed the doctor to take the baby, he wrapped her up in blankets and placed her in the back seat of his car, disguising the fact that there was a baby there, because he understood that having a baby in the car made him look like a kidnapper. So he hid her, and none of the soldiers noticed the tiny bundle lying in the shadows of the back seat, which was a very fortunate thing — papers or no papers.

The doctor drove the baby home, and the next day United Hatzalah managed to find an ambulance driver in Odessa who was willing to make the drive to Kiev and transport the baby to Moldova. The price for making this journey of about 600 miles was a cool twenty-five thousand dollars, sponsored by Ron Yeffet. But it would take time

Eli and Ron Yeffet

United Hatzalah ambulance in Ukraine

until the funds could be transferred, and in the meantime they had to lay out the money. Aharon called Rabbi Yaakov Bleich, the chief rabbi of Ukraine, and asked if they could borrow the money for a short time after explaining the situation. He immediately agreed, and a messenger was sent to pick up the money so that the doctor and ambulance could be paid.

Now it was just a matter of obtaining sufficient gasoline to make the journey. Eventually they found a gas station in Uman that was willing to sell them gas for eight hundred dollars. When they reached the Moldovan border, Israel's ambassador to Moldova, Joel Lion, was waiting for them, having driven four hours from Kishinev to make sure that everything went smoothly. The ambulance crossed the border into Moldova with its precious cargo. The baby, watched over by United Hatzalah volunteers, spent the night in Moldova, and then headed toward the Romanian border to meet her Mommy.

While all this was going on, Eli asked a friend of his who owns a plane and serves as his own pilot to fly the baby's mother to Romania, where she would meet the baby and his son-in-law for the return trip to Israel. A doctor and nurse would accompany them as well to check the baby and make sure she was healthy and well enough to fly. After all, she had just been through an incredibly difficult journey — a journey that would have been challenging for anyone, let alone a newborn.

And so the mother and her newborn baby daughter were united at last. And it all came about because Eli Beer agreed to accept a mission when no one else felt able to give a helping hand.

This was just the beginning of one of Hatzalah's greatest operations ever. By the time the situation in Ukraine had calmed down a little, the organization had succeeded in doing the kind of things normally done by trained covert operatives, while healing countless people and saving thousands of grownups and children.

It would prove to be one of United Hatzalah's finest hours.

# CHAPTER FIFTY-THREE

# Operation Orange Wings

United Hatzalah ended up establishing two field hospitals on the border of Moldova, as well as an additional field hospital in Kishinev, Moldova's capital city. It was the middle of the winter, snowing and freezing cold, and the volunteers treated the endless stream of refugees that came to them with a wide variety of medical issues. They also treated people of all ages for hypothermia. The worst case of hypothermia was a ninety-seven-year-old woman who was

United Hatzalah volunteers

At the border

treated by a group of doctors from Tel HaShomer Hospital who had been flown in by United Hatzalah, using medical supplies and equipment also donated by the hospital.

To accomplish all this, during his visit to the United States Eli contacted El Al and told them that he needed to rent a plane to fly equipment and supplies to Moldova.

They refused. "It's too dangerous. The closest location we're willing to fly to is Bucharest, Romania."

"That's almost fifteen hours away. That won't work."

The next idea was to land in a city called Iasi, also in Romania, but only three hours away from Moldova. In order for that to happen, members of Israeli security had to fly there first and check out the situation on the ground. Once this was done, the airport was secured, and El Al was given the go-ahead to begin flying medical equipment and tons of kosher chickens and meat into Romania, where they were then loaded onto vehicles and driven to Moldova to feed the thousands of refugees who were massing at the border seeking medical care and shelter.

Of course, all this cost an incredible amount of money. And so, within a short time, Eli was heavily involved in creating what would become known within the walls of United Hatzalah as Operation Orange Wings — the rescue mission in Ukraine 2022.

More doctors were flown in from Israel. Meanwhile, ambulances were being rented in Ukraine for twenty thousand dollars each to transport the wounded and sick to Moldova — and worth every penny.

To pay for all this, Eli began a massive fundraising effort. One family initiated the entire project. While Eli was in Boca Raton, Mrs. Laub, a Holocaust survivor from New York, called, asking to sponsor rescue flights for refugees from Ukraine to Israel. She recalled that when she escaped the Nazis, there was no one waiting to greet her, and she wanted to be involved in this mitzvah. Veteran donor Amy Korenvaes let Eli know that she would sponsor five planes. George Weiss did the same. They were joined by other members from the Boca community and many other incredible supporters throughout the world.

Meanwhile, United Hatzalah established a command center in Kishinev. With the word out that United Hatzalah was there to help, it took thirty people to answer phones and address all the refugees who were trying to get out of Ukraine and reach Eretz Yisrael.

The whole situation had snowballed before anyone was ready for it.

The refugees had traveled from their homes in Ukraine to the border of Moldova. They drove as far as they could by private car or bus and walked for miles in the cold to reach the border. Many had left in such a hurry that they had no travel documents. At first it wasn't a problem: They didn't necessarily need passports in order to cross to Moldova because they were refugees.

Once they crossed the border to Moldova, United Hatzalah volunteers were waiting for them with hot food and a bus to the Agudah shul in Moldova, where they were housed until they could get on a flight to Israel.

The air space in Moldova was closed for fear of Russian fighter planes, so United Hatzalah landed its planes in Iasi, a city in Romania about a three hours' trip from Moldova. The problem was that the Romanian border patrol would not allow them over the border without passports. This was a serious issue for many refugees.

Linor Attias, one of United Hatzalah's top international staff and one of the people on the ground from the beginning of the operation, reached out to the Israeli ambassador to Moldova, Joel Lion, who put them in touch with the commander in charge of Moldovan airspace.

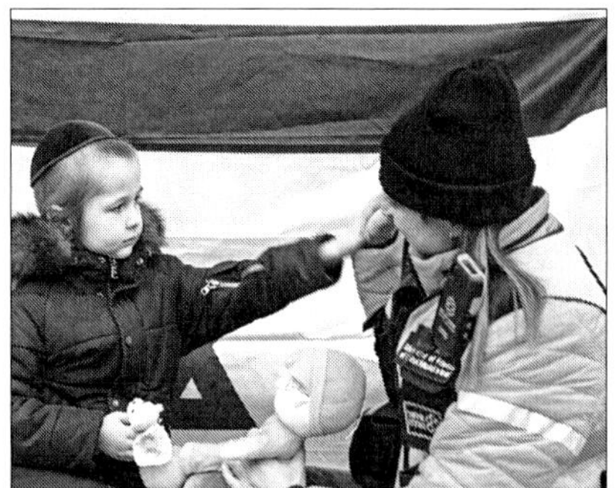

Scenes of kindness:
Linor and her young Ukrainian friend, Linor giving diapers to a Ukrainian mother

"You're allowing planes to land at your airport with all sorts of goods, correct?"

"Yes."

"So why can't we land our planes in your airport as well?"

"The difference is that we are talking about people here, not goods — people who could be killed by a Russian missile."

"Not if we use Air Moldova to get them out. The Russians aren't attacking your planes so there's little risk. This is a great opportunity for you. Your airline was shut down because of Covid. Now it's shut down again because of the war. I'm offering to pay you money — a lot of money — for every flight you allow in and out of your airport."

The commander considered the offer.

In the end, he agreed.

"But my permission is granted only for United Hatzalah flights."

So it was that flights were allowed in — just for them.

By mid-June 2022, about four months after the start of the war, about seven hundred volunteers had come in and out of Moldova. Some were bringing food to refugees; others were handling logistics. There were doctors and psychologists, all of them there to help in the biggest operation the organization had ever initiated outside Israel. They had been in Haiti for close to three weeks. But the Ukraine operation involved months of intense work and lifesaving operations, not to mention extraordinary funding. Millions of dollars were spent bringing in equipment and medicine and flying out refugees from the war zone.

The money was raised through small donations given by many people — eighteen dollars, twenty dollars, and fifty dollars — as well as supporters who gave donations of a million dollars or more.

Throughout it all, the teams from United Hatzalah had to remain up to date on the military situation in whichever territory they were entering. They had to know who was in charge and where they might be stopped by Ukrainian soldiers who would be checking to see if they were smuggling Russian soldiers in an ambulance. Gathering the right intelligence was no simple matter, but it was necessary to ensure that no one would be harmed. It was imperative that whoever was guarding the roads would be informed before the ambulance arrived so they could travel unharmed. And just to be sure, whenever an ambulance came through, the volunteers in the ambulance would give the soldiers medical equipment — bandages, tourniquets, and other essentials for the battlefield — in order to smooth the way.

An ambulance might cross the border into Ukraine for several reasons. It would enter cities and villages to bring back documents people needed, to deliver medical equipment to hospitals and civilians who needed it, or to bring out the sick and wounded — people who were unable to sit on a bus for the forty-eight hours it would take them to reach Moldova from Ukraine. Of course, in order for this to happen, they needed to make sure that they had sufficient fuel. So they brought huge amounts of gasoline into the country, from various European countries, and hid it in several locations, just in case. They even rented storage shelters in the middle of Ukraine and filled them with a very large quantity of gasoline.

At the Moldovan-Ukrainian border, United Hatzalah was a major presence, standing there with Israeli flags and Hatzalah flags. Many of them wore orange jackets or vests over their clothing. Most of the refugees had arrived at the border from cities that had been badly bombed by the Russians. Some of them, even those with children, had little more than a small bag or two to their name. All of their possessions were reduced to a little bag.

There were no fathers in the procession of women and children. The fathers had to stay behind to fight. It was up to the wives and mothers to make their escape on their own with children in tow. And those children were not happy campers. The Hatzalah team could hear them screaming and crying from a mile away, their voices reverberating through the empty, snow-covered terrain that comprised the no-man's-land between Ukraine and Moldova.

It was a hard trek through pouring rain and snow-packed earth. A walk with children clinging to them, terrified by the unceasing sounds of war coming at them from every direction. Then they would arrive at the border, and Hatzalah was there, waiting to greet them.

"You can't imagine how grateful they were for everything we were doing," Eli says. "It was a *kiddush Hashem* of the highest magnitude. I'd recall all the pictures I had seen of refugees walking across borders during World War II, and I knew that if I had been alive then, I would have been doing the exact same thing as I was doing now. This was a case of history repeating itself. This was what my father had been doing back in 1938 and 1939, raising money for the Agudah's rescue efforts, and that's what I was doing, having flown in from Israel after almost dying from Covid, standing at the border in the freezing cold with candy for the children and kosher food to give out to the weary people who had made the trek."

Among the refugees was a ten-year-old boy.

He was all by himself.

His name was Misha.

He didn't know English or Hebrew, so Slava, a Ukrainian Israeli lawyer from Ashkelon who volunteers for United Hatzalah and had been among those who flew to Moldova, spoke to him.

"My father couldn't leave because he's in the army," the boy explained.

"What about your mother?"

"She didn't want to leave my father. My mother packed me a bag and put me on a bus heading for the border. I have an aunt living in Israel. She wants me to go there."

He had a piece of paper with him. On it, his mother had written her sister's phone number and address in Tel Aviv.

This was no simple matter. Misha had crossed the border with a hundred people and gotten lost in the shuffle. And while he did have a passport, it was against the law to put a child on a plane alone and send him to a different country, even if he wanted to go and even if his parents had written a note affirming that they wanted him to go.

Misha was brought to the United Hatzalah base in the nearby Agudas Yisrael shul while the team conferred with the Israeli ambassador to Moldova, Joel Lion, who had come to add his aid in Moldova.

A Jew with a big heart in his chest and a big *kippah* on his head, Joel worked diligently to ensure that everyone who needed papers received them. He reminded Eli of the diplomats back in World War II who used their positions in government to save as many people as they could. Men like Sugihara and Raoul Wallenberg. People whose main concern was saving lives. At the same time, Joel also ensured that the team was doing their best to ascertain that the refugees they were bringing to Israel were actually Jewish.

Misha in Ukraine

"Most of the people arriving at the border are coming without the proper documentation," he told them. "I'm relying on you to make sure that the people we will be sending to Israel are really Jewish, because if they aren't, they can go to England, Germany, or Poland. If I'm giving people papers to travel to Israel, I want to know that they deserve them."

During the first few weeks after the war broke out, United Hatzalah was tasked with the job of trying to figure out who was a Jew and would be able to emigrate to Israel and who was not. This was in addition to the rescue work they were doing.

Now they had to figure out what to do with a ten year old boy who wanted to go to Israel and was all on his own.

"Where did you come from?" they asked him.

It turned out that Misha was from Uman, the famous burial place of Rabbi Nachman of Breslov, and so volunteers from United Hatzalah in Ukraine were dispatched to his home to have the parents sign papers stamped by a notary and a lawyer to prove that they had given permission for their son to leave the country and travel to Israel on his own.

United Hatzalah had thirty people who spoke Hebrew and Russian whose job was to sit with each person claiming to be a Jew and ask them

Jews coming home

an entire list of questions to ascertain if this was true.

"Do you have family in Israel?"

If they said yes, they would ask for the relatives' names and contact information. Those people would then be contacted for confirmation.

"On which holiday do Jewish people eat matzah?" was another question.

Sometimes there were people about whom they weren't sure. In those cases, they would make a point of asking for papers. Often the answer was that they had left the documents at home. In such cases, United Hatzalah sent volunteers who were inside Ukraine to the homes of those refugees to find the papers and bring them to the border. Sometimes they sent volunteers from Moldova, who drove there in the ambulances that United Hatzalah had purchased from local ambulance companies to get them over the border and over to the homes of those begging to come to Israel. In almost every case, the documents were right where they claimed to be, and those documents showed that they were, in fact, Jewish. With the entire Europe suddenly wide open for Ukrainian refugees, they had no reason to choose Israel as a destination — unless they were Jewish and specifically wanted to be there.

In short, it was a madhouse, with throngs clamoring to cross the border and flee the war zone. And among the endless waves of refugees were many Jews and even elderly Holocaust survivors who didn't have any documents at all — forget about an up-to-date passport.

Misha and his sister, ninety-four years old and ninety respectively, were from Kharkov and had somehow managed to make their way to the Ukrainian-Moldovan border. By the time they arrived, they appeared to have aged ten years. This was no exaggeration. They were beyond exhausted, and to have mounted an escape at their age was serious business. But they'd had no choice. They couldn't remain where they were and had to leave.

"This is the second time I'm running away," Misha said to Eli when they met at the border. "I remember being on the run from the Nazis. My mother took stale bread and soaked it in rainwater so that I would be able to eat it. Now, all these years later, I've been walking for three days straight trying to escape the Russians…"

Misha asked for kosher food. They took him to the local shul where United Hatzalah had set up their headquarters and fed him the first hot meal that he'd eaten in days.

"Misha," Eli said, "I will make sure that you get to Eretz Yisrael!"

"I'm afraid of flying," Misha confessed.

Having never flown in his life, it wasn't easy to convince him that getting on a flight wasn't a big deal. But they managed it in the end.

One of the Ukrainian United Hatzalah volunteers was drafted into the Ukrainian army. He had been a volunteer for years and immediately got in touch with Linor and asked her to help him. She wasn't sure if there was anything she could do, but she told him she would try her best. Somehow she managed to reach his commanding officer, and the two of them had a conversation.

"Look," she told the Ukrainian officer, "I've known Mikhail for years. He is a wonderful person and an outstanding human being, but he's not a good fighter."

"So what are you saying?"

"I'm saying that I'm not asking you to release him of his duty altogether, but instead of sending him to the front, when he is so not suitable for that, we will give him an ambulance, and he can drive around treating injured soldiers and civilians."

And so Mikhail the United Hatzalah volunteer was given permission to drive a United Hatzalah ambulance and go around the country saving lives.

Linor met Paulina at the border. Paulina was in her eighties and had arrived with cuts and abrasions all over her face. She had survived the Russian bombs and had somehow, miraculously, made her way to the border. The first thing Linor did was clean and bandage her wounds. Then she took Paulina and another hundred fifty refugees who had arrived around the same time to Kishinev, first stop on their journey to Israel.

"I sat with her for a long time," Linor recounts. "The truth is, I really didn't have time to do this, but there was something about her that spoke to me, and I found myself being drawn to get to know her better."

It turned out that Paulina was a Holocaust survivor. As she ate a bowl of hot soup from the United Hatzalah soup kitchen, she recounted that it had taken her forty-eight hours to reach the border from the city she had lived in for so many years. In the middle of the conversation, Paulina started to cry, finally allowing herself to show signs of mourning for her husband, whom she had lost to a Russian tank only days earlier.

"He went downstairs to wait on line for bread," she told Linor. "None of the stores were open, and people were starving. Bread, vegetables, and water were delivered every three days, and you had to wait on line to receive your share. So he went downstairs to go and wait. And then I heard the sound of rumbling, and I looked out the window as a Russian tank came rolling down the street and crushed many of the people waiting in line. The tank crushed innocent people who had done no wrong. People who were just waiting in line for bread and water. My husband was unable to get out of the way in time, and I saw the tank murder my husband. And it reminded me of how I had to wait on line for bread all those years ago under a different regime with different tanks who also crushed innocent people for no reason."

After hearing her story, Linor decided that she was going to personally make sure that Paulina got out of Eastern Europe. She didn't have any of her documents with her, so a team of United Hatzalah volunteers traveled to the Kharkov region to retrieve them. When they arrived, they made contact with some of the Jewish Ukrainian soldiers in the area and told them what they were looking for — the name of the village where Paulina used to live and the address of her home. They themselves were unable to enter the area — it was too dangerous — but the soldiers managed to retrieve Paulina's passport and any other important papers she would need.

The documents were under the exact piles of clothing that Paulina described, and when the team returned to the border, Linor accompanied her on the flight back to Israel, where she lives right now, finally at peace and able to recover from the rigors of war.

"To think that a Holocaust survivor in her eighties had to live through something like that all over again," Linor says. "But at least we were able to help her get to Israel and start a new life."

During one of the never-ending trips into the cities and villages of Ukraine, a United Hatzalah volunteer named Andre suddenly recognized a playground that sat nestled between a few buildings.

"I remember this playground from when I was a kid," he told the other volunteers who were with him.

Snapping a photo, he sent it to his mother and asked her if they had lived in the vicinity before moving to Israel.

"Yes. You grew up playing at that park," she wrote back.

"My mother moved with us back when we were kids," Andre told the others. "My father didn't come along. My mother told us that he didn't want to have anything to do with us. Every birthday I used to pray to G-d that my father should get in touch, even just to wish me a 'Happy Birthday,' but it never happened. Yet now I am once again standing on the ground of our village. Which means that there's a good chance that my father is still here."

He sent a message to his mother, asking her to describe exactly where they had lived, and she told him where the apartment was located. Andre went over and knocked on the door, excited at the prospect of finally having a reunion with his father, but no one answered the door. Dejected, he left the building. Downstairs on the street, he ran into an elderly woman.

"Do you by any chance know my family?" he asked her, and he told her their name.

"Yes," she replied. "I know them, and they still live here. I even remember you as a child."

"Does my father still live here?"

"Yes. He remarried and has children from his second wife."

"Please give me his phone number."

That night, Andre called his father.

"It's Andre," he told his father. "Can we meet?"

"I would love to meet you," his father told him. "After your mother and I were divorced, she moved away, taking all of you with her. I was never able to track you down, no matter how much I searched."

The reunion was emotional, and Andre got to meet his half-brothers and -sisters. Andre told his father that he had twin grandchildren who had been born two months earlier in Israel. All in all, it was a beautiful moment between father and son, a moment that neither of them had thought possible.

United Hatzalah has brought more than thirty-five planeloads of refugees out of the war zone of Ukraine to the safe shores of Eretz Yisrael, the vast majority of whom they were fairly certain were Jewish. To Eli, it was a matter of *pikuach nefesh* — lifesaving in its purest form — and he related to the whole situation as if it was a continuation of his own father's quest to save his fellow Jews back when he was a kid.

In a show of gratitude to the many donors who helped save lives during this harrowing time, those who helped fund the flights that either flew refugees out of Ukraine or brought equipment into Ukraine were presented with a model of a bright-orange plane, the color of United Hatzalah — the color of rescue. Written on each model plane, in black lettering, were the words: "We cannot do all the good the world needs, but the world needs all the good we can do."

United Hatzalah's good friend and generous donor Bob Kraft, owner

Bob Kraft visiting United Hatzalah

of the New England Patriots football team, sponsored a plane filled with refugees, and Eli presented him with a model of one of the planes at a meeting at United Hatzalah headquarters that was supposed to take forty-five minutes and ended up lasting three hours.

Bob loved the plane that they gave him.

It was majestic, an authentic model of the type of planes that had been used, and best of all, it was a bright-orange color — the color of United Hatzalah — the color of **rescue**.

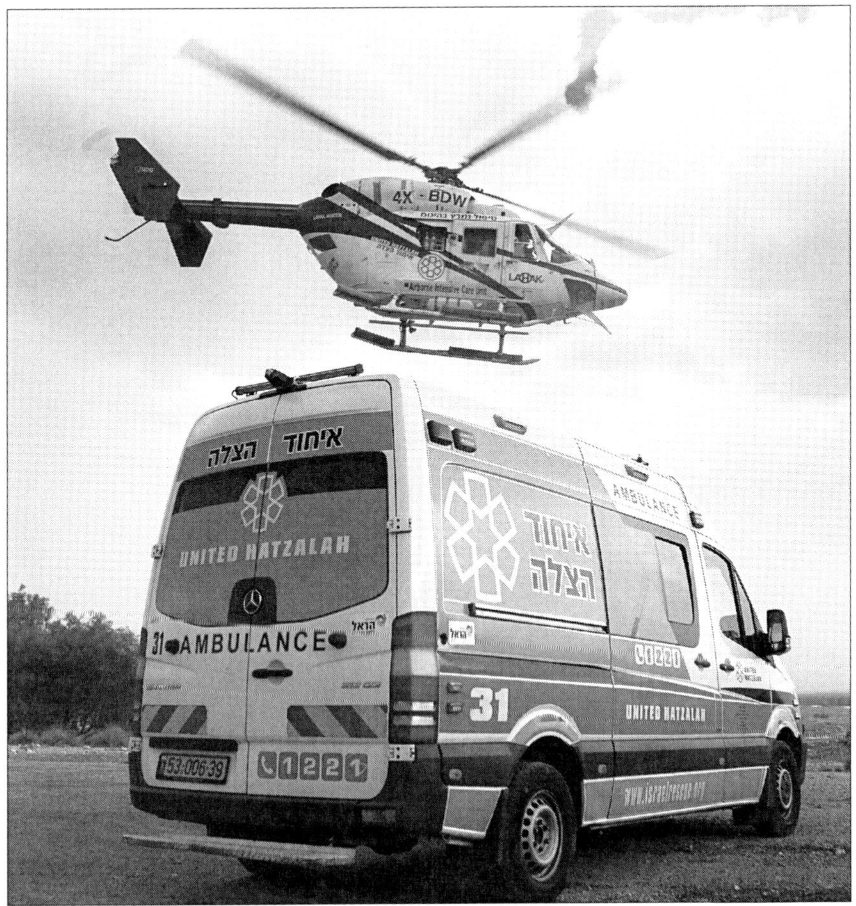

The "color of rescue" takes to the skies, with United Hatzalah's Helicopter Unit, established as the book goes to print.

# Epilogue

$O$nce again, Eli received a call from Dovie Maisel about yet another disaster. A powerful and deadly earthquake had hit Turkey, a 7.8 magnitude killer. Thousands of buildings had collapsed, and it was obvious that the damage and the loss of life would be huge and that a human tragedy was taking place, just a few hours' flight from Israel.

"Eli," Dovie wanted to know, "can we send a team over there?"

"Do it now."

For years, United Hatzalah had sent teams of volunteers to help with disasters in various locations around the globe. Now, they did not have to waste precious time putting teams together — hundreds of volunteers were prepared and trained to drop everything and fly out to help, wherever they were needed.

Eli still remembered the horror — and the lessons he'd learned — at the first disaster he had witnessed, the collapse of the Versailles wedding hall in Jerusalem. That was when he learned firsthand what it means to save people trapped under tons of rubble, victims who cannot communicate their locations. That disaster was small compared to some of the horrific sights and scenes that United Hatzalah teams would witness in the future. But it prepared them and provided knowledge and skills that came in handy in the years to come.

Eli Beer, Eli Pollak, and Dovie Maisel decided to send a team of thirty-five professionals to Turkey. As soon as they informed the volunteers who had been chosen, the team members dropped whatever they were doing and set to work putting together the necessary supplies. The team worked non-stop for twelve hours making sure they had sufficient medical equipment, humanitarian aid, food, tents, batteries, and satellite phones that would work in every location. They also packed special drones used for search and rescue that are designed to find people based on the body heat they give out. (In a unit that is constantly expanding, United Hatzalah has more than ten volunteer medics who are trained and licensed to fly drones.) Meanwhile, Eli Pollak was on the phone with El Al, which graciously agreed to give United Hatzalah a plane to use at cost price.

Twelve hours after they'd heard about the disaster, the volunteers were boarding their plane to Turkey.

Hatzalah joined the Israeli army unit of one hundred and fifty soldiers — many of them search and rescue experts — who were also traveling to bring aid and their rescue know-how. This was not the first time that the IDF had sent such help to Turkey. They did it in 1999 as well, when Turkey had been hit by another deadly earthquake. The fact that United Hatzalah was able to join with them was a huge blessing since that meant top security for the United Hatzalah crew.

When the team landed in Turkey, they knew almost immediately that they weren't going to have much local logistical help. This was not Ukraine, where United Hatzalah had teams of people both there and in neighboring countries. Here the group was landing in the middle of a major disaster area. Thirteen million people had been affected in one way or another; it seemed as though they had landed in the middle of Gehinnom. The electricity grid was down and the gas stations were all shut. Through Eli's connections, United Hatzalah had been in touch with Nissim and Yossi Cohen, local Jewish leaders in Turkey, who connected United Hatzalah with a man named Eddie who arranged for a truck to meet the team at the airport. They loaded ten tons of medical supplies and expensive equipment into the truck.

Another plane had landed right next to the Israeli volunteers. This flight was filled with Iranian rescue personnel, and when the Iranians realized who these volunteers were, they wouldn't look at them. Disregarding their behavior, the team made sure to say hello to them and wish them well — but the Iranians ignored them and their yarmulkas and Israeli flags and pretended the Israelis didn't exist.

In the brief time the United Hatzalah team was there, they succeeded in saving the lives of fifteen people, primarily children, and assisting over three thousand people in countless ways. They had initially planned on remaining in Turkey for two weeks, but ultimately they had to leave after only six days, when their presence there was deemed a security threat.

Ironically, the initial danger wasn't coming from anti-Semitic groups. The first two days the local people walked through the ruins in a state of shock. The next two days the people gratefully accepted any help that came their way — thanking and hugging those who had come to assist them. But then the survivors began to realize that their loved ones were not going to return, and even their bodies might not be found. This was made very clear by the Turkish government's decision to bring in bulldozers to begin clearing the wreckage sites, and bury all the dead in mass graves.

That was when the survivors' frustration began boiling over, and sorrow was replaced by fury. Heartbroken and confused, the locals began to confront the search-and-rescue teams, forcing them to continue searching for survivors at gunpoint. At times the volunteers were only able to escape when the police came to rescue them.

Then came frightening news: Apparently, members of ISIS who had escaped from local prisons were headed in their direction. The United Hatzalah leadership understood that the time had come to get out of Turkey. El Al didn't have any available planes, and Eli turned to Dr. Miriam Adelson, who provided a plane to fly their volunteers out of Turkey that day.

"While we were busy getting our people out of Turkey," Eli Beer remembers, "the volunteers were saving the life of a local sixteen-year-old girl. They worked for twelve hours to pull her out of the rubble, somehow managing to put an IV into her arm to keep her from dehydrating. Hundreds of local Turkish people were watching, and when our team succeeded, the onlookers began to scream 'Allah Akhbar,' in praise to the Creator for having allowed us to save this girl's life.

"Ironically, at about the same time that we were pulling a young Muslim girl out of the wreckage, a terrorist drove his car into a group of Jews standing at a bus stop in Ramot, killing the newlywed Alter Shlomo Lederman and two young brothers, Yaakov Yisrael (Yanky) Paley and Asher Menachem (Ushy) Paley. I arrived at the scene, which is not far from my home, in less than three minutes. When I got there, United Hatzalah volunteers — including our CEO Eli Pollak — were already working on the victims. As the terrorist used his car to try and kill even more Jews, one of our volunteers heard him screaming 'Allah Akhbar' at the top of his lungs, until he was shot by a policeman and killed.

"So while one Arab was screaming 'Allah Akhbar' as he mercilessly murdered Jewish children, hundreds of Muslims were using the same words to praise Israel and the Jews for helping to save their children's lives.

"Hearing a story like that, and knowing that Turkey has not been very friendly to Israel, many people have asked why we sent volunteers to help them.

"First of all, I tell them, the people of Turkey get along with us. It is their leaders who have a problem with Israel.

"Second, on a practical level, though of course we pray we should never have to face such tragedies, the experience we get when dealing with natural disasters is invaluable if *chas v'shalom* we ever do have to deal with them.

"And most of all, we aren't helping them because they are Jewish. We are helping them because we are Jewish — and Jews help others whenever they can. That's a true *kiddush Hashem*. And isn't that what United Hatzalah is all about?"

# Glossary

*Admor (pl. Admorim)* — leader of a chassidic community

*afikoman* — 1. portion of matzah hidden during the Passover Seder and eaten toward its conclusion. 2. the *pesach*-offering

*aliyah* (pl. *aliyos*) — lit., *going up*. 1. spiritual elevation. 2. act of being called to recite a blessing at the public reading of the Torah. 3. immigration to Israel.

*Ashkenazim* — lit., *from Ashkenaz* (Germany); European Jews or their customs.

*bar mitzvah* — 1. 13-year-old boy. 2. ceremony marking the coming of age of a Jewish boy.

*bas mitzvah* — 1. 12-year-old girl. 2. ceremony marking the coming of age of a Jewish girl.

*Belzer* — a follower of the chassidic dynasty of Belz.

*berachah* (pl. *berachos*) — a blessing recited before performing a mitzvah and before and after eating; a formula for acknowledging a gift from Hashem, whether material or spiritual.

*Breslover* — a follower of the chassidic dynasty of Breslov.

*bris* (*bris milah*) — circumcision of male infants, generally performed on the eighth day after birth.

*Chanukah* — Hanukah.

*chareidi* (pl. *chareidim*) — generally used to describe people who are strictly religiously observant.

*charoses* — a mixture of different foods made to resemble bricks, used and eaten as part of the Passover Seder.

*chassid* (pl. *chassidim*) — 1. pious person. 2. the follower of a Rebbe (chassidic leader).

*chassidic* — following the customs of a chassidic leader (Rebbe).

*chavrusa* — a study partner.

*chesed* — acts of kindness; lovingkindness; charitable giving.

*chevrah kaddisha* — burial society.

*chiloni* (pl. *chilonim*) — a secular Jew.

*chizuk* — encouragement; strengthening; corroboration.

*Chol HaMoed* — the intermediate days between the first and last days of Pesach and of Succos.

*chutzpadik* — rude; impudent.

*dati leumi* — generally used to describe people who are Modern Orthodox.

*daven* — (Yiddish) to pray.

*Eretz Yisrael* — the Land of Israel.

*Erev Pesach* — *Passover eve.*

*Erev Shabbos* — the eve of the Sabbath; Friday.

*Erev Yom Kippur* — the eve of Yom Kippur.

*esrog* (pl. *esrogim*) — citron, one of the Four Species taken in hand during the Succos Festival.

*gabbai* — (Yiddish) person responsible for the proper functioning of a synagogue or other communal body.

*gedolim* — lit., great; great Torah scholars; a term used to refer to persons of great stature.

*Gerrer* — a follower of the chassidic dynasty of Ger.

*Haggadah* — liturgy recited at the Pesach Seder.

*halachah* — Torah and Rabbinic law.

*halachic* — pertaining to Jewish law.

*Hashem* — lit., *the Name*; a respectful way to refer to G-d.

*Hesder* — a program in the Israeli army in which soldiers learn Torah for a specified amount of time, and then serve in IDF combat units

*kiddush Hashem* — doing something that brings honor to Hashem; sanctification of Hashem's Name.

*kippah* (pl. *kippot*) — a yarmulke; a skullcap.

*Klal Yisrael* — Jewish people in general; the Jewish nation.

*Kosel* (also pronounced Kotel) — the Western Wall.

*Lag BaOmer* — 18 Iyar, the 33rd day of the *Omer* (the period between Passover and Shavuos; the anniversary of the death of Rabbi Shimon bar Yochai, a day that is often marked by bonfires in Israel and, in chassidic circles, by the first haircut of three-year-old boys.

*Litvak* — of Lithuanian descent; non-chassidic.

*litvish* — lit., *Lithuanian*; adjective describing non-chassidic Jews of Eastern European extraction

*Lubavitcher* — a follower of the chassidic dynasty of Lubavitch.

*lulav* (pl. *lulavim*) — a palm branch, one of the Four Species taken in hand on Succos.

*Maariv* — the evening prayer service.

*maror* — bitter herbs; the bitter herbs used at the Passover Seder.

*Mashiach* — Messiah, the awaited redeemer of Israel, who will usher in an era of universal recognition of the Kingship of Hashem.

*matzah* (pl. *matzos*) — unleavened bread.

*mezuzah* (pl. *mezuzos*) — small parchment scroll in a casing, affixed to a doorpost and containing the first two paragraphs of the *Shema* prayer.

*minyan* (pl. *minyanim*) — quorum of ten men necessary for conducting a prayer service.

*Mishlo'ach manos* — gifts of food mandated to be sent to friends on Purim.

*mitzvah* (pl. *mitzvos)* — a Biblical or Rabbinic commandment; a merit; a good deed.

*nachas* — pleasure, usually from one's children; spiritual or emotional pleasure.

*parnassah* — livelihood.

*Pesach* — Passover.

*peyos* — sideburns or side curls, worn by Orthodox Jewish males.

*pikuach nefesh* — mortal danger; a life-and-death situation.

*Ponevezh* — a leading yeshivah in Bnei Brak, Israel.

*posek* (pl. *poskim*) — halachic authority; authoritative Rabbinic decisor.

*Purim* — holiday established by Queen Esther, commemorating the Jewish survival after a decree that they would be annihilated in Persia in fifth-century BCE (see *Esther* 9:31-32).

*rabbanim* — rabbis.

*rav* (pl. *rabbanim*) — rabbi; a spiritual leader; (u.c.) a title of respect for a rabbinic leader.

*Rebbe* — a chassidic rav; a rabbi or teacher.

*rebbe* (pl. *rebbeim*) — a male teacher.

*rosh yeshivah* — the dean of a yeshivah; senior lecturer in a yeshivah.

*sandak* — person who holds the baby while the *bris* is performed.

*Satmar* — a chassidic group originally founded in Hungary; a follower of the Satmar Rebbe.

*Seder* (pl. *Sedarim*) — Pesach-night ritual during which the Haggadah is recited.

*Sefardim* — Jews of Middle Eastern origin.

*sefarim* — books, specifically books on holy subjects or a learned topic.

*sefer Torah* — a Torah Scroll, written on parchment.

*segulah* — a spiritual remedy.

*semichah* — Rabbinical ordination.

*seudah* — a festive meal, esp. one served on the Sabbath or a holiday

*Shabbos* — the Sabbath.

*Shacharis* — the morning prayer service.

*Shamayim* — Heaven; the Heavens.

*Shema* — short for *"Shema Yisrael, Hashem Elokeinu, Hashem Echad!* — Hear O Israel, Hashem is our God, Hashem is the One and Only"; this prayer, recited twice daily, expresses the essence of the Jewish faith.

*shul* — (Yiddish) synagogue.

*siyatta diShmaya* — Heavenly assistance; help from Hashem.

*Succos* — Festival of Tabernacles; the Festival during which one dwells in a *succah.*

*tallis* (pl. *talleisim*) — four-cornered prayer shawls with fringes at each corner, worn by (married) men during morning prayers.

*talmid* — disciple; student.

*tefillin* — phylacteries, small black leather boxes containing parchment scrolls inscribed with Biblical passages, bound to the arm and forehead of adult Jewish males during the weekday morning prayer service.

*Tehillim* — the Book of Psalms.

*tzaddik* (pl. *tzaddikim*) — a righteous person.

*tzedakah* — charity.

*Vizhnitz* — a chassidic group originally founded in Austria-Bukovina (now Ukraine)

*yahrtzeit* — (Yiddish) the anniversary of a person's passing.

*Yerushalayim* — Jerusalem.

*yeshivah* — a school of Jewish studies; a Torah academy.

*yeshivish* — of or pertaining to a yeshivah; typical of a yeshivah student.

*Yom Kippur* — the Day of Atonement.

*Yom Tov* — a Jewish holiday.